Leadership for Social Justice

Making Revolutions in Education

Catherine Marshall

University of North Carolina

Maricela Oliva

University of Texas at San Antonio

Boston • New York • San Francisco
Mexico City • Montreal • Toronto • London • Madrid • Munich
Paris • Hong Kong • Singapore • Tokyo • Cape Town • Sydney

Senior Editor: *Arnis E. Burvikovs*
Series Editorial Assistant: *Kelly Hopkins*
Marketing Manager: *Tara Kelly*
Prepress and Manufacturing Buyer: *Andrew Turso*
Editorial-Production Coordinator: *Mary Beth Finch*
Editorial-Production Service: *Modern Graphics, Inc.*
Electronic Composition: *Modern Graphics, Inc.*

For related titles and support materials, visit our online catalog at
www.ablongman.com

Between the time Website information is gathered and then published, it is not unusual for some sites to have closed. Also the transcription of URLs can result in unintended typographical errors. The publisher would appreciate notification where these errors occur so that they may be corrected in subsequent editions.

Library of Congress Cataloging-in-Publication Data
Leadership for social justice : making revolutions in education / [edited by] Catherine Marshall, Maricela Oliva.
    p. cm.
  Includes bibliographical references and index.
ISBN 0-205-41209-2
  1. Educational leadership—Social aspects—United States. 2. Educational equalization—United States. 3. Social justice—United States. I. Marshall, Catherine. II. Oliva, Maricela.

LB2805.L3352 2006
370.11'5—dc22

                                                        2005048100

Printed in the United States of America
10   9   8   7   6   5   4   3   2   1   10   09   08   07   06   05

We dedicate this book to those who most inspired our belief in making a better world, our parents, Constancia and José Oliva and Grace and Nelson Marshall, and to our Leadership for Social Justice colleagues who support and sustain us in that effort.

Contents

4 *Educational Leadership Along the U.S.–México Border: Crossing Borders/Embracing Hybridity/Building Bridges* **64**

Gerardo R. López
Maria Luisa González
Elsy Fierro

5 *Bridge People: Civic and Educational Leaders for Social Justice* **85**

Betty M. Merchant
Alan R. Shoho

8 *Meeting* **All** *Students' Needs: Transforming the Unjust Normativity of Heterosexism*   *145*

James W. Koschoreck
Patrick Slattery

9 *Teaching Strategies for Developing Leaders for Social Justice*   *167*

Madeline M. Hafner

12   *Releasing Emotion: Artmaking and Leadership for Social Justice*   233

Preface

We know that you have heard the terms equity, diversity, transformational leadership, and the achievement gap. We have all heard these phrases used with a focus on better management of schools. But to get to the heart and spirit of the matter, we need to move beyond the technical. We must engage with new terminology and concepts such as border culture, heterosexism, wholistic visioning, bridge people, equity audits, hybridity, and others that go beyond the technical aspects of school leadership. This book engages school leaders with chapters that connect these ideas to the contemporary challenges they face. These terms are about what is happening in today's schools. The new terminology usefully moves us to think in new ways.

The authors of this book are a diverse group of today's educational leadership scholars. What is special about this group emanates from their shared determination to challenge themselves and their own field to "get real" about equity and social justice. Recognizing the need to do more than just tear down school people, they are constructing new thinking, new methods, and new tools for teaching and doing social justice. We are all indebted to the willingness of this large group of scholars who gave their all for this book, in the spirit of spreading the wealth of social justice thinking, terminology, and tools. Revolutions need such efforts and willing spirits!

Leadership for Social Justice: Making Revolutions in Education begins with two chapters that introduce the issues and define leadership that encompasses social justice. Chapters 3, 4, 5, and 6 display the efforts of leaders and policy-makers' to find ways to make social justice real in their work lives. The next several chapters go into detailed discussions illustrating specific marginalizing practices in schools, such as heterosexism and religious intolerance. So given these dilemmas, are there actually any tools available for being or becoming social justice leaders? Yes! Five chapters provide teaching strategies and social justice tools to help make the conceptual goal a reality. Even after reconceptualizing and connecting with reality and providing the teaching strategies and tools, are there not remaining dilemmas? Yes! The last two chapters address the need to stay the course despite the temptation to regress into more comfortable, old traditions of leadership. Finally, the book recognizes that school leaders cannot do this alone. To be successful, school leaders must engage with school board members who need re-educating, they must recognize larger societal resistance to equity and social justice, and they must recognize that they are carving out new territory when they assertively use schools as tools to eliminate economic, social, and political injustice.

What is juicy about the content is the stories of real leaders successfully addressing the problems they face. What is useful are the tools for leadership and for learning about social justice. In this book you will find fantastic annotated references and bibliographies from leading scholars. You will also find provocative discussion questions and engaging class and individual activities for learning. Chapters in this book contain what is needed for the field, for professors, for students, and for school leaders to feel comfortable in knowing the terminology and tools and then to embrace the spirit of social justice, with confidence and commitment to revolutionize their practices.

We know the temptation to be comfortable with traditional practice. We also know the challenges inherent in taking a more critical, creative, social justice stance. But more importantly, as women and scholars of color, we know what it feels like to be marginalized and left behind. So we are committed to seeing that this does not happen to today's students. We began this book project knowing that educational administrators desire conceptualizations and tools that bring about the revolutionary changes that eliminate marginalizing practices in schools. We offer this book to invite others to join us in this noble and necessarily collaborative venture.

We are grateful to the following individuals who reviewed our manuscript: Margaret Grogan and Michelle Young, University of Missouri.

CM
MO

About the Authors

Gary L. Anderson is a professor in the Steinhardt School of Education, New York University. He is a former middle and high school teacher and principal. His two most recent books are *Performance Theories in Education: Power, Pedagogy, and the Politics of Identity* (co-edited with Bryant Alexander and Bernardo Gallegos) and *The Action Research Dissertation* (co-authored with Kathryn Herr). He is currently co-editing the three-volume *Encyclopedia of Activism and Social Justice* for Sage.

Maenette K. P. Benham, a Native Hawaiian scholar and teacher, is a professor in the Educational Administration department at Michigan State University. As a scholar, mentor, and teacher for the past 12 years, she has built a strong base of inquiry that centers on (a) the nature of engaged educational leadership, particularly in native/indigenous communities; (b) the wisdom of knowing and praxis of social justice envisioned and enacted by educational leaders; and (c) the effects of educational policy on native/indigenous people.

C. Cryss Brunner is an associate professor in the Department of Educational Policy and Administration at the University of Minnesota–Twin Cities. Previously, she was on faculty at the University of Wisconsin at Madison. Before that she had served as a teacher and an administrator in elementary and high schools for 27 years. Two previous publications include an article in the *Journal of School Leadership*, "Invisible, limited, and emerging discourse: Research practices that restrict and/or increase access for women and people of color to the superintendency," and a book, *Principals of Power: Women Superintendents and the Riddle of the Heart*.

Nelda H. Cambron-McCabe is professor and former chair of the Educational Leadership department at Miami University of Ohio. She is co-author of *The Superintendent's Fieldbook: A Guide for Leaders of Learning* (Corwin, 2005); *Public School Law: Teachers' and Students' Rights* (Allyn and Bacon, 5th ed., 2004), and *Schools That Learn: A Fifth Discipline Fieldbook* (Doubleday, 2000). She has served as president of both the Education Law Association and the American Education Finance Association and as editor of the *Journal of Education Finance.*

Michael Dantley is the interim associate dean and an associate professor in Educational Leadership at Miami University of Ohio. He has served as an urban elementary principal and administered certified personnel in Cincinnati. He is president-elect of the University Council for Educational Administration and the editor of the *Journal of Cases in Educational Leadership*. His research in leadership, spirituality, and social justice has appeared in the *Journal of School Leadership*, the *Educational Administration Quarterly*, *Education and Urban Society*, the *International Journal of Qualitative Studies in Education*, and the *International Journal of School Leadership*.

Elsy Fierro is project director of a school leadership grant at New Mexico State University entitled, Leadership in Border Rural Areas. She has over 20 years of experience working with public schools as a teacher and district-level administrator. In addition to her work on the teaching and learning of English-language learners, Dr. Fierro's research interests include career paths of Latina administrators, the role of critical race theory in the preparation of school administrators, and the effects of cultural and social capital in creating parent–community engagement in schools.

Juanita Garcia is an assistant professor in the Public School Executive Leadership program and director of the Principalship program at the University of Texas at Austin. Her research focus most recently has been on school transformation leading to high achievement with all students, innovative practices in school leadership program redesign, and the creation of settings for multilevel leadership development (principals, teachers, parents, and students).

María Luisa González is a regents professor and department head of Educational Administration at New Mexico State University. Her research has focused on the education of marginalized groups, including homeless children, children of undocumented workers, children for whom English is a second language, and on administrators working with bilingual education and minority populations. She has published in English and Spanish and her 1997 book, *Educating Latino Students: A Guide to Successful Practice*, was on leaders' roles in addressing the needs of the growing numbers of Latino students and their families.

Madeline M. Hafner is an assistant professor in the Educational Leadership & Policy department at the University of Utah. Her K–12 school district teaching and leadership experiences have been in the area of special education. Dr. Hafner's research and teaching interests focus on teaching for social justice in leadership preparation programs and effective leadership practices for students receiving special education services. She studies postmodern notions of leadership as well as spirituality and leadership.

James W. Koschoreck is an assistant professor in the Educational Administration program at the University of Cincinnati. He has co-edited a special issue of the *Journal of School Leadership* with Catherine Lugg on LGBTQ issues in educational administration. His research, which focuses on heteronormativity in education, has recently been published in *Leading and Managing: Journal of the Australian Council for Educational Leaders*.

Gerardo R. López is an assistant professor in the Educational Leadership and Policy Studies department at Indiana University. His areas of interests are parent involvement, school–community relations, critical race theory, and migrant education. He has published in a variety of journals, including the *American Educational Research Journal*, the *Harvard Educational Review*, and *Educational Administration Quarterly*. He also co-edited a book with Larry Parker entitled *Interrogating Racism in Qualitative Research Methodology* (Peter Lang, 2003).

Catherine A. Lugg is an associate professor in the Education department at Rutgers University. She serves as associate director for publishing, University Council for Educational Administration, and is associate editor for the *Journal of Gay and Lesbian Issues in Education*. Recent publications include the book chapter "Social justice: Seeking a common language," with Alan Shoho and Betty Merchant, in the *Handbook on Educational Leadership* and the article "One nation under God? Religion and the politics of education in a post 9/11 America" in *Educational Policy*.

Catherine Marshall is a professor of Educational Leadership and Policy at the University of North Carolina at Chapel Hill. Her career began as a junior high teacher, when Title IX had just passed, and a woman thinking of school administration was an anomaly. Since then, for the past twenty-five years she has pursued scholarly agendas combining gender issues and politics, dating back to a time when those agendas were career risks. Her eight books include *Reframing Educational Politics for Social Justice* (Allyn and Bacon), *Feminist Critical Policy Analysis* (Falmer), *The Assistant Principal* (Corwin), and *Designing Qualitative Research* (Sage). Catherine was vice president of Division L, Politics and Policy, of the American Educational Research Association (AERA), was the 2003 recipient of AERA's award for activism and research on women and girls in education, and also of a Ford Foundation grant to support Leadership for Social Justice (LSJ), thus supporting many of the projects that have maintained LSJ's momentum. Current projects include: research on "activist educators," on politicking social justice, and international perspectives on social justice leadership.

Betty M. Merchant is interim dean of the College of Education and Human Development at the University of Texas at San Antonio. Before going to Texas, she taught at the University of Illinois Urbana–Champaign and in public schools, preschool through high school, and in tribally controlled Native American schools in the southwest. Her research interests focus on educational policy, equity, student diversity, and school leadership.

Glenn L. Nolly is director of the Leadership Academy for Austin (Texas) Independent School District. A former area superintendent, high school principal, and teacher, his research interests include preparation of urban school administrators and mathematics achievement among African American students.

Maricela Oliva is an assistant professor of Higher Education at the University of Texas at San Antonio. The oldest of nine children, she grew up in South Texas along the Texas/Mexico border and was the first in her family to attend college. Oliva has 20 years of experience in higher education, including administration and policy work with the Texas Higher Education Coordinating Board. She serves on the editorial boards of the *Review of Higher Education, International Journal of Qualitative Studies in Education,* and the *Journal of Hispanic Higher Education (JHHE).* Research interests include higher education policy, access to college for underrepresented students, and school–university collaboration. Recent publications include a 2004 special issue in the *JHHE,* "College access and the K–16 pipeline: Connecting policy and practice for Latino student success."

Christen Opsal is a graduate student in the Educational Policy and Administration department at the University of Minnesota–Twin Cities. In addition, she is a staff member at the Institute of Community Integration, a university center for excellence in developmental disabilities education research and service. She has presented papers at the annual meetings of the University Council for Educational Administration and the American Educational Research Association.

Laurence Parker is a professor in the Educational Policy Studies department at the University of Illinois at Urbana–Champaign. His research centers on critical race theory and educational policy issues. His most relevant social justice publication appeared in the April 2000 issue of the *Journal of Special Education Leadership* on African American student perspectives on school discipline and Black students. He has participated in some of the efforts to promote equity for low-income and minority students in his home area of Urbana, Illinois.

E. Renée Sanders-Lawson is the director of the Office of Supportive Services at Michigan State University. Prior to this position, she served as a school counselor, assistant principal, middle school principal, and human resources director for Johnston County Schools and Hickory City Schools in North Carolina. She is the co-author of "Violent crime, race, and black children: Parenting and the social contract," a chapter in *Black Children* (McAdoo).

James Joseph Scheurich is professor and department head in the Educational Administration and Human Resource Development department at Texas A&M University; previously, he was an associate professor at The University of Texas at Austin. Recent publications include *Leadership for Equity and Excellence* (with Linda Skrla, 2003, Corwin Press) and "Equity Traps: A Useful Construct for Preparing Principals To Lead Schools That Are Successful with Diverse Students" (with Kathryn Bell McKenzie, *Educational Administration Quarterly*).

Laura Shapiro serves on the faculties of Goddard College and Lesley University, Creative Arts in Learning Division. She is the director of Art Works (*www.artworksgroup.com*), an arts-based professional development, consulting and research organization devoted to working with schools, colleges, nonprofit organizations and businesses to create democratic, socially just communities. Shapiro is a former elementary school principal and administrator for curriculum and instruction programs. She is an active member of GLSEN and serves on her local school district's Health Advisory Committee.

Alan R. Shoho is an associate professor in the Educational Leadership and Policy Studies department at the University of Texas at San Antonio. He recently published a book chapter in the *Handbook of Educational Leadership* entitled, "Seeking a Common Language," which addresses the multiple meanings of social justice and how this creates difficulties for discourse among theorists and practitioners.

Linda Skrla is an associate professor and Public School Administration program chair in the Educational Administration and Human Resource Development department at Texas A&M University. She was formerly a middle school and high school teacher, assistant principal, and district curriculum director in Texas public schools. She is the author of numerous journal articles and four books, the most recent of which is *Educational Equity and Accountability: Policies, Paradigms, and Politics* (with Jim Scheurich, 2003, Routledge-Falmer).

Patrick Slattery is a professor of Teaching, Learning, and Culture at Texas A&M University. Previous positions include teaching at Ashland University in Ohio and elementary and secondary school principal positions in Louisiana. He is co-author with Dana Rapp of *Ethics and the Foundations of Education: Teaching Convictions in a Postmodern World*, which focuses on aesthetics and social justice in education. Also, he is author of *Curriculum Development in the Postmodern Era* (Garland, 1995).

Sabrina I. Smith-Campbell is the curriculum coordinator for Detroit Public Schools and an adjunct professor of Wayne State University in the Teacher Education department. She has presented at several national meetings and conferences, including the American Educational Research Association and the Patterson Research conference on social justice issues concerning African American women school leaders in urban school settings.

Zeena Tabbaa-Rida is a recent graduate of Rutgers University. As an independent researcher, her research interests include religion and education, women's educational experience, sociological studies in education, ethnographic studies on student life in schools, and international/comparative education. She is writing "Muslim Women Reflecting on American Education: A Question of Educational Identity" and presenting at conferences such as the Association of Muslim Social Scientists and The Middle East Studies Association.

Linda C. Tillman is associate professor in the Educational Leadership Program at the University of North Carolina at Chapel Hill. Recent publications include "Leadership for social justice: Identifying the terrain, crafting a mission and purpose" in *Shaping the Future: Policy, Partnerships, and Emerging*

Perspectives (2003). She is the co-editor of a forthcoming special issue of the *Journal of School Leadership* on teaching for social justice and is a member of the AERA Social Justice Action Committee.

Michelle D. Young is the executive director of the University Council for Educational Administration and a faculty member in the Educational Leadership and Policy Analysis department at the University of Missouri, Columbia. Her scholarship focuses on how leaders and policies can ensure equitable and quality experiences for all students and adults in schooling. She has published widely and received the William J. Davis award for the most outstanding article in a volume of the *Educational Administration Quarterly*.

1

Building the Capacities of Social Justice Leaders

Catherine Marshall
Maricela Oliva

The Challenge

A realized ideal of schooling as a vehicle for social mobility, for ridding society of inequities, and for embedding democratic principles among citizens
has been elusive, appearing more in rhetoric, less in reality. This book appears at a new moment in time when policymakers' rhetoric and policies and
scholars' promotion of ways to achieve equity through schooling are aligning.
Policymakers and scholars talk about what can or should be done, but educational leaders are the people who must *deliver* some version of social justice and equity.

The purpose of this book is to conceptualize and explore a social justice framework for educational leadership, both theoretically and practically.
Doing so can kick efforts forward—in leadership preparation, in staff development in educational administration, and in practice—to build the capacity
and will to transform leaders. Closer to a realized ideal of leadership, leaders
would not be disinterested managers of their environments and contexts, but
astute activists, ready with strategies and the sense of responsibility to intervene to make schools equitable.

Leadership for Social Justice: Making Revolutions in Education makes theory and research and models of practice more accessible to university faculty
and school practitioners. For example, a university professor might think, "I
understand the need to prepare my students for the reality of schools today,
and for making sure that their practices are focused on providing equitable

1

access to learning. But I do not have the time to learn the new theory and research before developing social-justice-oriented materials for my educational leader preparation program." By the same token, a school administrator, staff development director, or instructional leader might say, "I have students in my school and classrooms who are more diverse and less familiar to my teachers than students they have had in the past. The new students don't seem to be having the kind of success that other students are having, and I just don't understand what to do." The leader-in-training may say, "I wish my doctoral classes provided me with knowledge and practice that would give me the courage and skills to take strong stands for equity." The goal of this book is to help the professor, administrator, and student by providing theory upon which to base arguments for activist stances and tools to diagnose where positive policy and other interventions can be made for groups of disenfranchised and underserved students or stakeholders.

Although we have come a long way from the ingenuous and naïve blindness to racism and inequity that is highlighted by Cervantes' poem of over 20 years ago, there is still a lot to accomplish for the achievement of real social justice with regards to racism, sexism, homophobia, and other such issues. Furthermore, despite our desire that things be where they should be for all children, the stories, data, and experiences described in the following chapters belie this fact. Metaphorically, if not literally, we are still at war against the inequities that remain, even if, as some argue, those inequities are no longer callously overt and intentional. They may now be covert, subconscious, or even unintentional. However, the latter kind of war against the marginalized is the most insidious and damaging because it persists in questioning or disregarding the view of the very groups that continue to be hurt by institutional practices.

For us, as for many committed educators, it is difficult to acknowledge that our society and our institutions (such as schools) are still marginalizing and oppressing some individuals and communities. Much of what we are told and asked to know (and perhaps what we prefer to believe from the comfort of our privileged social location) is that the race/culture/inequity and oppression battles are over, and that we no longer have those "wars" to fight. However, evidence, such as the persistently poor and inequitable outcomes for the student and educator communities discussed here, and our experiences, as well as those of the chapter authors, reflect that we still have much to do to achieve the equitable and socially just education for all that is our democratic birthright. The things we do in our institutions are arguably still metaphorically targeting people of color, the poor, women, gay/lesbian/transgendered individuals, those with unfamiliar backgrounds or in unfamiliar territories, and others. It is, ironically, only the most successfully schooled of those persons (like Cervantes) who have the legitimacy and voice to speak this "fact." Others, such as school dropouts, become silenced by the limited life opportunities that reproduce a subordinate social position for their children and communities. Although educators over the years have done much to improve education for some children, that success is uneven. We, the editors, call on

Poem for the young white man who asked me
How I, an intelligent, well-read person could
Believe in the war between races

In my land there are no distinctions.
The barbed wire politics of oppression
have been torn down long ago. The only reminder
of past battles, lost or won, is a slight
rutting in the fertile fields.

In my land
people write poems about love,
full of nothing but contented childlike syllables.
Everyone reads Russian short stories and weeps.
There are no boundaries.
There is no hunger, no
complicated famine or greed.

I am not a revolutionary.
I don't even like political poems.
Do you think I can believe in a war between races?
I can deny it. I can forget about it
when I'm safe
living in my own continent of harmony
and home, but I am not
there.

I believe in revolution
because everywhere the crosses are turning,
sharp-shooting goose-steppers round every corner,
there are snipers in the school . . .
(I know you don't believe this.
You think this is nothing
but faddish exaggeration. But they are
not shooting at you.)

I'm marked by the color of my skin.
The bullets are discrete and designed to kill slowly.
They are aiming at my children.
These are facts.
Let me show you my wounds: my stumbling mind, my
"excuse me" tongue, and this
nagging preoccupation
with the feeling of not being good enough.

These bullets bury deeper than logic
Racism is not intellectual.
I can not reason these scars away.

(continued)

Outside my door
there is a real enemy
who hates me.

I am a poet
who yearns to dance on rooftops,
to whisper delicate lines about joy
and the blessings of human understanding.
I try. I go to my land, my tower of words and
bolt the door, but the typewriter doesn't fade out
the sounds of blasting and muffled outrage.
My own days bring me slaps on the face.
Everyday I am deluged with reminders
that this is not
my land
and this is my land.

I do not believe in the war between the races

but in this country
there is war.

From *Emplumada*, by Lorna Dee Cervantes, 1981, Pittsburgh, PA, University of Pittsburgh Press.

us all to passionately commit to the moral transformative goal of more systemic and creative change and social justice to benefit all of our children and communities.

To move forward for social justice, educators need the strategies, *revolutionary* ones in some contexts, for rethinking school practices to better meet diverse students' needs and the language to translate intellectual concepts into practice and experiential understandings. They need guidance, encouragement, examples, and support to practice leading discussions with community groups and politicians. This book provides all of this in order to move social-justice-oriented work on theory development, discussion, and agenda setting to the implementation phase. It not only helps typical educators to better understand inequity and the lack of social justice for certain students in our schools at the intellectual level, but also to more fully understand it the way such students do—at the experiential level. The chapters of this book engage educators' emotions, their yearning for caring, just, and empowering schooling processes, and the challenges and frustrations stemming from resistors of change. Educators need to know that these issues run deep for students.

In the section that follows, we introduce the book, prefacing with a few words on the challenge of defining *social justice*, on the real social justice challenges in schools, and on the need for leaders' preparation and professional cultures to provide space and support for the emerging leader whose courageous interventions and articulate stances will redefine school leadership.

Students Know the Shame of Not Belonging

I am not a revolutionary/I don't even like political poems./Do you think I can believe in a war between races?/I can deny it. I can forget about it/When I'm safe/Living in my own continent of harmony/and home, but I am not there. . . .

Let me show you my wounds: my stumbling mind, my/"excuse me" tongue, and this/nagging preoccupation/with the feeling of not being good enough.

From *Emplumada*, by Lorna Dee Cervantes, 1981, Pittsburgh, PA, University of Pittsburgh Press.

Evolving Definitions and Challenges to Capacity Building

What is the social justice challenge? To answer this question, we sometimes simply speak of equity or cultural diversity. Sometimes our conversations expand to the need for tolerance and respect for human rights and identity. Sometimes our answer is that it is the achievement gap, or democracy and a sense of community and belongingness (or our nostalgia for that), or inclusion of groups that do not immediately come to mind in our planning, such as the "differently abled," girls and women, or those American families with different cultures, languages, or religions. Often it goes beyond even inclusion, to actually valuing the differences that have been identified above. Sometimes we say that it means reaching to the deep roots of injustice emanating from competitive market forces, economic policies, political practices, and traditions that maintain elite privilege.

The Very Real Challenges from Demographics and Cultural Diversity

Policymakers in demographically diverse states, such as Texas, Georgia, and others, publicly acknowledge that communities, and, consequently, student populations in their schools, are changing. The fact that policymakers report that minority students are already the majority in elementary grades (Oliva & Menchaca, 2001) poses a problem for educators and policymakers in that such students have higher dropout rates than Anglo students and do not perform as well on standardized tests scheduled throughout K–12. In Georgia, the Atlanta area experienced 800% growth in the Latino student population during the 1990s; consequently, educators there are now working feverishly to increase practitioner knowledge and capacity about how to work with recent immigrant, language minority, and culturally diverse students (Gerstl-Pepin, 2001).

Similar changes are occurring in North Carolina, Florida, California, and other states. Demographic data in these states highlight a dramatic growth in minority, second-language learner, and economically disadvantaged student populations that traditionally have not fared as well as traditional students in the public schools (Anderson & Herr, 1993; Cambron-McCabe, 2000; Larson & Ovando, 2001; Maxcy, 1998; Parker & Shapiro, 1992). It also points to a related need to develop tools for K–16 educators that allow them to more adequately address such diverse students' needs. Although Hispanics are now the largest minority group in the United States, they are only one part of the school population that suffers from educational underachievement. Hispanics and African Americans together will soon make up the majority minority population of several states (Murdoch, White, Hoque, Pecotte, You, & Balkan, 2002), meaning that over half of the population will be minority. Despite this demographic reality, racial and ethnic minority students continue to suffer educational disenfranchisements, such as disproportional high dropout rates, educational underachievement in K–12, and inequitable access to and retention in college (Rendón, Jalomo, & Nora, 2000; Texas Higher Education Coordinating Board, 2000; Timar, Ogawa, & Orillion, 2003). These are the statistics, but the real stories lie with those living in those borderlands.

Unaccomplished Equity

In the educational administration discipline, professors and researchers alike increasingly recognize and acknowledge the need to improve practice and student outcomes for minority, economically disadvantaged, female, gay/lesbian, and other students who have not traditionally been served well in schools (Brunner, 2000; Cambron-McCabe & Harvey, 1997; Cordeiro, 1999; Furman-Brown & Merz, 1996; Grogan, 1999; Koschorek, 1999; Larson & Ovando, 2001; Marshall, 1997; 1999, Parker & Shapiro, 1992; Skrla, Reyes, & Scheurich, 2000). Through a concerted effort, education and education administration scholars recently have developed critical, evidence-based understandings of why such students do not perform as well as their mainstream peers (Anderson, Bentley, Gallegos, Herr, & Saavedra, 1997; Foster, 1999; Gay, 1997; Maxcy, 1998; McDonnell & Elmore, 1991; Miller, 1995).

One of the important contributions of this work is the understanding that inequitable outcomes are not merely the result of deficiencies in the students, nor of the communities from which they come, as was often assumed to be the case. Instead, inequitable outcomes often result from systemic organizational practices and policies (McNeil, 2000; Poland & Carlson, 1993; Sewell, DuCette, & Shapiro, 1998) endemic to schools and administrator practice (Kozol, 1991; Scheurich & Laible, 1995) that have not been analyzed or acted on with respect to their impact on nonmainstream students (Cochran-

Painful Borderlands, Dividing Lines, States of Transition

The U.S.–Mexican border *es una herida abierta* where the Third World grates against the first and bleeds. And before a scab forms it hemorrhages again, the lifeblood of two worlds merging to form a third country—a border culture. Borders are set up to define the places that are safe and unsafe, to distinguish *us* from *them*. A border is a dividing line, a narrow strip along a steep edge. A borderland is a vague and undetermined place created by the emotional residue of an unnatural boundary. It is in a constant state of transition. The prohibited and forbidden are its inhabitants.

From *Borderlands/La Frontera: The New Mestiza*, by Gloria Anzaldua, 1987, San Francisco, Aunte Lute Books, p. 3.

Smith et al., 1999; Foster, 1999; Larson & Ovando, 2001; Lomotey, 1995; Marshall, 1993). Fortunately, these research- and theory-grounded realizations provide clear evidence that ongoing inequities in the schools can be remedied through sustained, systemic, and evidence-based intervention (Cambron-McCabe, 2000; Contreras, 2000; Erlandson, Skrla, Westbrook, Hornback, & Mindiz-Melton, 1999; McDonnell & Elmore, 1991; Scheurich, 1998; Shapiro, Sewell, & DuCette, 1995). Still, not enough has changed in training, credentialing, recruiting, and promoting school leaders or in national education policies (such as No Child Left Behind) for new leaders to believe that their instinct to enact social justice leadership will be understood and supported by district school boards.

Searching in Schools for Democracy, Community, Emotion, and Relationship

School leaders sometimes do equity work when they implement equity-related policies. That is called "doing my job." Some go further, demanding better than the letter of the law, for example, by joining in political coalitions or in legal actions for school finance equity, for the preservation of bilingual programs, and the like. However, the activist, interventionist stance of social justice leadership goes even further, inspired not just by an intellectual ideal, but also by moral outrage at the unmet needs of students and a desire for a caring community where relationships matter. Further, bureaucratic structures and leadership deny or sanitize passion and outrage and prohibit loving, nurturing relationships in schooling. But many educators' career inspirations came from just such a caring perspective.

Social justice leadership reconnects with emotional and idealistic stances. It supports leaders' impulses to transgress, to throw aside the traditional bureaucratic rationality and the limiting conceptualizations of leadership. For example, social justice leaders are outraged when funding formulas leave rural districts floundering. Social justice leadership supports their search in their work lives for joy and a sense of community and the pursuit of democratic ideals when their relationship-building activities create bridges (Venezia, Kirst, & Antonio, 2003; see especially Chapter 5 in this text) for marginalized families and their children. It supports educational leaders seeking strategies for developing and implementing antiracist curricula, for preventing homophobic and sexist bullying, for intervening when tensions over religion or immigrant status heat up. It supports their search for ways to critique leadership styles and schooling structures that prevent women and minority participation. It supports their efforts to conceptualize and articulate models of leadership that incorporate democratic community engagement, spirituality and emotion, and caring and connection. In this way, social justice leaders build their capacities to walk the talk in order to move beyond that which is just philosophical, just rhetoric, and just short-sighted, quick-fix policy.

The Challenges in Policy and Preparation for Social Justice in School Leadership

The challenges of demographics and of inequities are chronic and remain unresolved by the piled-on years of traditional practice, scholarship, theory, and professional training in educational administration. Recent attempts in policies (e.g., No Child Left Behind) and licensure (e.g., Interstate School Leaders Licensure Consortium) for educational administrators set an expectation for equitable outcomes. They do not connect the dots, however, to integrate social-justice-oriented methods, strategies, and training, never mind theory and research into educational leadership preparation programs that train future educational leaders (Chase, 1995; Cordeiro, 1999; Donmoyer, Imber, & Scheurich, 1995; Parker & Shapiro, 1992). As a consequence, they are not well incorporated into educational practice (Anderson, Bentley, Gallegos, Herr, & Saavedra, 1997; Marshall, 1993; Skrla, Reyes, & Scheurich, 2000).

Some policymakers and professors of educational administration assert the need to orient leadership training toward social justice and equity; many see it as somebody else's job (often a token or underpowered and overburdened woman or person of color), as an add-on that impinges on the "real" training, or as something to be managed in a rather surface manner, such as with a workshop. Delving deeply into social justice issues requires challenging the status quo, traditional patterns of privilege, and deep assumptions about what is real and good. It requires a surfacing of biases and a releasing of emotions that many find to be very uncomfortable. Furthermore, no staff development director, professor, student, or administrator can take on these challenges alone. Social justice leaders need space and sustenance for their efforts within the universities, districts, communities, and professional associations that encompass their careers and work.

Thus, among the remaining challenges for equity-oriented faculty and practitioners—indeed, for all educators—is the creation of classes, workshops, and seminars to translate research and theory into tools that can readily be used by faculty and by practitioners who are interested in fostering more equitable student performance.

Making Revolutions in Education: An Overview of the Chapters

Capacity building for social justice leaders requires a blending of theory, research, reflections on practice, tools for teaching and other interventions, strategies for engaging passion and emotion, and, finally, realistic engagement with the challenges in real-world policy and practice. In this book, each chapter provides this blending. After our introductory chapter, each chapter ends with Assignments and Activities as well as Annotated Readings to guide readers to sources for deeper exploration.

Chapters 2 through 5, taken together, provide a range of ways to view social justice leadership and praxis. Chapter 2 describes what we mean by *social justice* and why we need a social justice framework. The authors describe how social justice is connected to democracy and moral/transformative leadership. They illustrate how this kind of orientation obligates leaders to intervene as activists to transform schooling, professional and disciplinary associations, and society, building upon long-standing moral traditions in education and American society. Chapter 3, "Wholistic Visioning for Social Justice," presents a leadership perspective at the intersection of African American and female worldviews. Discussing leadership from a racialized gender perspective, the chapter confronts the chronic gender equity and racial bias challenges in school leadership while blending theory with the words and career experiences of administrators.

The particular leadership dilemmas that arise when working in predominately Mexican American communities along the U.S.–Mexico border are explored in Chapter 4. Exemplary leaders for such contexts illustrate how their boundary-crossing and culture-sensitive skills, insights, and understandings lead to better policy and practice. This chapter incorporates recent theoretical insights regarding minority students socialized and located at the bicultural rather than monocultural Texas–Mexico border.

Eight high-profile individuals in an urban area were interviewed for Chapter 5. Reading about their actualized orientations to social justice as reflected in their educational and civic leadership, one can see the personal and experiential characteristics that shape leaders toward the often-difficult work of equity-oriented leadership. The rich personal and narrative description of life events can stimulate self-reflection and visceral reactions for readers coming to grips with marginalization and discriminatory, exclusionary practices as the eight urban leaders did.

A mix of research and practical strategies are included in Chapters 6 through 13. Chapter 6 gets political as it explores a specific policy issue—educator licensure—using long-term discussions among social-justice-oriented scholars, policymakers, and school practitioners from various states. It also explores ways to create much needed policy and training. In this way, it serves as an introduction and preliminary response to the questions, "Whose interests do the licensure policies reflect?" "What leverage points exist for shifting current licensure policies and practices to include a meaningful focus on social justice?"

Chapter 7 broaches the sensitive topic of religion in schools and the ways in which the privileging of particular orthodoxies and practices negatively affect students of different religious beliefs and practices. When school leaders and cultures conceive of religion in normatively particular ways, they can create, unintentionally as well as intentionally, uncomfortable and even hostile environments for students who do not share the same religious beliefs.

In the succeeding chapters, we move on to more practical tools. Chapter 8 describes the exclusionary practices and harm to which gay, lesbian, and transgendered students are subject in heterosexist schools. Readers of the chapter learn about this often-invisible student population and about things that can be done to promote their educational success. Teaching strategies for social justice, detailed in Chapter 9, are presented to help university and school personnel think and act concretely about instructional issues and anticipate dilemmas and contested terrain that may arise from social-justice-oriented instruction. Chapter 10 presents and illustrates case studies as an instructional strategy for embedding social justice in educational leadership preparation. The dilemmas in the case studies provoke debate and support practitioners' planning for engaging in ways that challenge dominant practices. They allow students to experience the difficult challenge of conducting equity-oriented and informed decision making. Thus, various interventions can be explored collectively, and alternative intervention strategies can be weighed for degrees of appropriateness and moral utility.

Changes at the personal level are required if educational leaders are to work toward socially just outcomes for their students. Chapter 11 presents methods for experiential learning in educational leadership preparation, showing how simulations provide students with experience as the "other." In this way, no one can avoid and evade the (simulated) experience of exclusion and discrimination, and social justice is felt on a personal level, not just a cognitive or intellectual one. On a related note, Chapter 12 describes an arts-based professional development strategy that engages emotions, from joy to rage. Art-making, poetry, and other artistic media help educational leaders articulate dilemmas and affective responses as they seek to do social-justice-oriented work, unpacking emotions around issues such as the impact of high-stakes testing in schools with high ELL populations, the ousting of a woman African American principal without notice, and working poor parents. Chapter 13 presents equity auditing, a new tool for education leaders who want to create more equitable outcomes for their students. School leaders can readily utilize this tool with existing data in exploring the extent to which school practices are equitable. Audits unearth inequitable practice and also set up a collaborative stance in districts to bring along resistant stakeholders who prefer to close their eyes to what is happening in local schools and maintain the status quo.

As both a conclusion and a presentation of the challenges ahead, Chapter 14 and the Afterword lay out the remaining challenges and tasks. Chapter 14, the closing chapter, first evaluates a preparation program that focuses on equity. By showing how difficult it can be to sustain commitment to social justice in practice, the chapter powerfully illustrates that social justice leadership is a long-term commitment rather than a periodic curriculum revision or program-reform event. We see that although a preparation program may be social justice oriented, practices in the local field are slow to change. The chapter forces us to confront the reality of our need for broader societal engagement and for continued vigilance and K–16 collaboration to ensure that new leaders can get and keep jobs while they confront privilege and disrupt inequitable practices. Finally, the Afterword presents a challenge for educators and policymakers to support each other as they demand political change—to engage with and convince power brokers to get on board with social justice school leaders and support their efforts to make schools the well-supported instruments for instilling principles for a democratic and a just and caring society.

A Call for Action

Leaders cannot make social justice happen by their passion and will alone. The huge shifts in cultural understandings and societal and school expectations will happen only with the shared values, coalitions, networking, and mutual support that comes with the power of enlarging groups of people in social movements, which results in the building of social capital and, eventually, political power. This truly can happen! For example, beginning in late 1990s, a grassroots effort was organized in an effort to reorient policy and practice in educational administration that was deemed overly focused on technical aspects of educational management at the expense of the moral, social-justice objective of preparing citizens for equitable participation in democratic society. Imagine! This effort has grown from a conversational group of 4 to an active participation group of over 150 scholar practitioners from around the country and beyond. Known as the Leadership for Social Justice (LSJ) group, the participating members now have a Web site and listserv through which they communicate routinely. Teaching materials and strategies are posted to the Web site, as are faculty and administrator job announcements from across the country (see *www.leadershipforsocialjustice.org* for more details). We, the editors, and many of the authors of chapters in this book, are founding members of LSJ. We truly do find sustenance for social justice work from our shared network.

Similarly, readers inspired and guided by the chapters in this book and by the authors' passions for using education to promote social justice can create networks of organizations and associations that focus on educational reform. It is important that we collectively reframe assumptions about leadership, so that we act to meet the needs of minority and disenfranchised families and students along the K–16 continuum. In the state of Texas, potential partner organizations and partner network members at the state level include the Texas Education Agency, the Texas Association of School Administrators, the Texas Association of Chicanos in Higher Education, and the Texas Higher Education Coordinating Board. Regional and national networks include the Hispanic Border Leadership Institute and Rethinking Schools. Similar actual and potential partners and partner networks exist in other states, provinces, and regions or could easily be created. At a national level, coalitions for action can call upon the executive directors (and their membership) of powerful associations such as National School Boards Association, the American Association of School Administrators, the National Association of Secondary School Principals, the National Association for Bilingual Education, the University Council for Educational Administration, the Council of Chief State School Officers, and more.

The authors, Maricela Oliva and Catherine Marshall, discussing this book after the LSJ meeting in Montreal, Canada, in 2005.

Throughout the book, the theories, research, practical strategies, and models should inspire and support action for social justice stances and interventions. Readers are encouraged to take advantage of and choose among the discussion questions, the suggestions for further reading, and the exercises at the end of each chapter that provide opportunities to practice applications and to plan training and interventions in the more sheltered venue of a university classroom or staff development workshop. Then, when confronted by the need to act in real-life social justice challenges—often the very next day—educational leaders will have the will, the words, the facts, and the guts to make a difference. From such courage and passion and from such models of social justice leadership, schools can more honestly assert their status as institutions of empowerment, democracy, and equity.

References

Anderson, G. L., Bentley, M., Gallegos, B., Herr, K., Saavedra, E. (1997). Teaching within/against the backlash: A dialogue about power and pedagogy in the 1990s. In R. Chavez & J. O'Donnell (Eds.), *Speaking the unpleasant: The politics of nonengagement in multicultural education.* (pp. 274–295). Albany, NY: SUNY Press.

Anderson, G. L , & Herr, K. (1993). The micropolitics of silence: Moving from diversity of bodies to diversity of voices in schools. In C. Marshall (Ed.), *The 1993 Yearbook of the Politics of Education Association: The new politics of race and gender.* (pp. 58–68). London: Falmer Press.

Anzaldua. G. (1987). *Borderlands/La Frontera: The new mestiza.* San Francisco: Aunte Lute Press.

Brunner, C. C. (Ed.). (1999). *Sacred dreams: Women and the superintendency.* Albany, NY: SUNY Press.

Brunner, C. C. (2000). Unsettled moments in settled discourse: Women superintendents' experiences of inequality. *Educational Administration Quarterly, 36*(1), 76–116.

Cambron-McCabe, N. H.. & Harvey, J. (1997). *Supporting learning for all children.* St. Louis, MO: Danforth Foundation Monograph.

Cambron-McCabe. N. (2000). School as an ethical endeavor. In P. Senge, N. Cambron-McCabe, T. Lucas, B. Smith, & J. Dutton (Eds.), *Schools that Learn: A Fifth Discipline fieldbook for educators. parents, and everyone who cares about education.* (pp. 276–287). New York: Doubleday.

Cervantes, L. D. (1981). *Emplumada.* Pittsburgh, PA: University of Pittsburgh Press.

Chase, S. (1995). *Ambiguous Empowerment: The Work Narratives of Women School Superintendents.* Amherst: University of Massachusetts Press.

Cochran-Smith, M., Albert, L., Dimattia, P., Freedman, S., Jackson, R., Mooney, J., Neisler, O., Peck, A.. & Zollers, N. (1999). Seeking social justice: A teacher education faculty's self-study. *Leadership in Education, 2*(3), 229–253.

Contreras. A. R. (2000). *Hispanic values and viewpoints about centers: Don't homogenize us in!* Paper presented at the American Educational Research Association, New Orleans, LA.

Cordeiro, P. (1999). A balcony view: UCEA membership and the preparation of educational leaders presidential address, 1998. *UCEA Review, 39*(3), 3, 7, 11–13.

Donmoyer, R., Imber, M., & Scheurich, J. J. (Eds.). (1995). *The Knowledge Base in Educational Administration.* Albany, NY: SUNY Press.

English, F. W. (2000). Commentary: Pssssst! What does one call a set of non-empirical beliefs required to be accepted on faith and enforced by authority? [Answer: a religion, aka the ISLLC standards]. *International Journal of Leadership in Education, 3*(2), 159–167.

Erlandson, D. A., Skrla, L., Westbrook, D., Hornback, S., & Mindiz-Melton, A. (1999). Reshaping urban education: A school–community–university collaborative initiative. *Journal of School Leadership, 9*(6), 552–573.

Foster, W. (1986). *Paradigms and promises: New approaches to educational administration.* Buffalo, NY: Prometheus Books.

Foster, W. (1999). *Toward a critical practice of leadership.* Paper presented at the University Council on Educational Administration, Minneapolis, MN.

Furman-Brown, G. (Ed.) (in press). *School as community: From promise to practice.* Albany, NY: SUNY Press.

Furman-Brown, G., & Merz, C. (1996). Schools and community connections: Applying a sociological framework. In J. G. Cibulka & W. J. Kritek (Eds.), *Coordination among schools, families, and communities: Prospects for educational reform* (pp. 323–347). Albany, NY: SUNY Press.

Gay, G. (1997). Multicultural infusion in teacher education: Foundations and applications. *Peabody Journal of Education, 72*(1), 150–177.

Gerstl-Pepin, C. (2001, April). Administrative licensure and social justice in Georgia. Paper presented at the American Educational Research Association annual meeting, Seattle, WA.

Giroux, H. A., Lomotey, K., McJamerson, E. M., & Perry, T. (1994). *Domain I: Societal and cultural influences on schooling; domain overview.* New York: McGraw-Hill.

Grogan, M. (1999). Equity/equality issues of gender, race and class. *Educational Administration Quarterly, 35*(4), 518–536.

Hall, V. (1999). Skating not dancing? The author's response. *Educational Management & Administration, 27*(1), 99–103.

Koschoreck, J. J. W. (1999). Resistance and complicity, personal sacrifice, and image management: A life narrative exploration of gender and sexuality. *Journal of Curriculum Theorizing, 15*(2), 41–56.

Kozol, J. (1991). *Savage inequalities: Children in America's schools.* New York: Harper.

Larson, C. (1997). Is the Land of Oz an alien nation? A sociopolitical study of school community conflict. *Educational Administration Quarterly, 33*(3), 312–350.

Larson, C., & Ovando, C. (2001). *The color of bureaucracy: The politics of equity in multicultural school communities.* Atlanta: Wadsworth.

Lomotey, K. (1995). Social and cultural influences on schooling: A commentary on the UCEA Knowledge Base Project, Domain I. *Educational Administration Quarterly, 31*(2), 294–303.

Marshall, C. (1993). The politics of denial: Gender and race issues in administration. In C. Marshall (Ed.), *The new politics of race and gender* (pp. 168–175). London: Falmer Press.

Marshall, C. (1997). *Feminist critical policy analysis I: Perspectives from K–12.* London: Falmer Press.

Marshall, C. (1999). *Missing in action: Equity and ethics in educational leadership.* Paper presented at the Keynote speech at the Center for Ethics and Leadership, Charlottesville, VA.

Maxcy, S. J. (1995). Beyond leadership frameworks. *Educational Administration Quarterly, 31*(3), 473–483.

Maxcy, S. J. (1998). Preparing school principals for ethno-democratic leadership. *The International Journal of Leadership in Education, 1*(3), 217–235.

McCarthy, M. (1998). Inclusion of children with disabilities: Seeking the appropriate balance. *Educational Horizons, 76,* 116–119, reprinted in *Educating Exceptional Children* (Spring 1999). Guilford, CT: Dushkin/McGraw-Hill.

McDonnell, L. M., & Elmore, R. F. (1991). Getting the job done: Alternative policy instruments. In A. R. Odden (Ed.), *Education Policy Implementation* (pp. 157–183). Albany, NY: SUNY Press.

McNeil, L. M. (2000). Creating new inequalities: Contradictions of reform. *Phi Delta Kappan, 81*(10), 728–734.

Miller, S. (1995). *An American Imperative: Accelerating Minority Educational Advancement*. New Haven, CT: Yale University Press.

Miron, L. (2000). *Free jazz, Dario Fo and dynamic texts: Using the ISLLC standards in the practice of educational judgment*. Paper presented at the American Educational Research Association, New Orleans, LA.

Murdoch, S., White, S., Hoque, M. N., Pecotte, B., You, X., & Balkan, J. (2002). *A summary of the Texas challenge in the twenty-first century: Implications of population change for the future of Texas*. College Station, TX: TAMU Center for Demographic and Socioeconomic Research and Education.

NASSP. (1998). *Is there a shortage of qualified candidates for openings in the principalship? An exploratory study*. Alexandria, VA: National Association of Secondary School Principals. Retrieved July 20, 2000, from www.naesp.org/misc/shortage.htm.

NCEEA. (1987). *Leaders for America's Schools*. Tempe, AZ: National Commission on Excellence in Educational Administration, University Council for Educational Administration.

Oliva, M., & Menchaca, V. (2001). Social justice and Texas educator certification. Paper presented at the American Educational Research Association annual meeting, Seattle, WA.

Parker, L., & Shapiro, J. P. (1992). Where is the discussion of diversity in educational administration programs? Graduate students' voices addressing an omission in their preparation. *Journal of School Leadership, 2*(1), 7–33.

Poland, P., & Carlson, L. (1993). Program reform in educational administration. *UCEA Review, 32*(1), 4–7, 12.

Rendón, L., Jalomo, R. E., & Nora, A. (2000). Theoretical considerations in the study of minority student retention in higher education. In J. M. Braxton (Ed.), *Reworking the student departure puzzle* (pp. 127–156). Nashville: Vanderbilt University Press.

Reyes, A. (1999). *The need for school leaders in Texas: A position paper for the University of Houston College of Education*. Houston, TX: University of Houston.

Scheurich, J. J. (1998). Highly successful and loving, public elementary schools, populated mainly by low-SES children of color: Core beliefs and cultural characteristics. *Urban Education, 33*(4), 451–491.

Scheurich, J. J., & Laible, J. (1995). The buck stops here—in our preparation programs: Educative leadership for all children (No exceptions allowed). *Educational Administration Quarterly, 31*(2), 313–322.

Sewell, T. E., DuCette, J. P., & Shapiro, J. P. (1998). Educational assessment and diversity. In N. Lambert & B. L. McCombs (Eds.), *How students learn: Reforming schools through learner-centered education* (pp. 311–338). Washington, DC: APA Publications.

Shapiro, J. P., Sewell, T. E., & DuCette, J. P. (1995). *Reframing diversity in education*. Lancaster, PA: Technomic Publishing Company.

Shipman, N., & Murphy, J. (1999). ISLLC Update. *UCEA Review, 40*(2), 13, 18.

Skrla, L., Reyes, P., & Scheurich, J. J. (2000). Sexism, silence, and solutions: Women superintendents speak up and speak out. *Educational Administration Quarterly, 36*(1), 44–75.

Texas Higher Education Coordinating Board. (2000). *Closing the gaps: The Texas higher education plan*. Austin: THECB.

Timar, T. B., Ogawa, R., & Orillion, M. (2003). Expanding the university of California's outreach mission. *The Review of Higher Education, 27*(2), 187–209.

Venezia, V., Kirst, M. W., & Antonio, A. L. (2003). *Betraying the dream: How disconnected K–12 and postsecondary education systems undermine student aspirations*. Palo Alto: Stanford Institute for Higher Education Research.

2

Social Justice and Moral Transformative Leadership

Michael E. Dantley
Linda C. Tillman

Introduction

Our task in this chapter is to articulate definitions of the term *social justice*. We also will discuss the imperative for continued and expanding discussions about the various perspectives of leadership for social justice. Linked closely with perspectives on leadership for social justice is the concept of moral transformative leadership and how leaders as transformative or public intellectuals serve as social activists who are committed to seeing a greater degree of democracy practiced in schools as well as in the larger society. The terms *social justice* and *leadership for social justice* are used interchangeably in this chapter. Additionally, our definition of social justice amplifies three essential components: leadership for social justice, moral transformative leadership, and the praxis of social justice.

This chapter will focus on the three components of social justice. First, we provide an overview of the definitions and the scholarship in the areas of social justice and moral transformative leadership. Next, we consider in what ways school leaders as public intellectuals can draw on the principles of social justice and moral transformative leadership in their daily practice. Finally, we discuss several forms of social justice praxis: research and scholarship, conference presentations, and teaching.

Defining Social Justice

Recent commemorations of the 50th anniversary of the *Brown v. Board of Education* decision, the 40th anniversary of the Civil Rights Act, and the 30th

This chapter defines leadership for social justice and its link with moral transformative leadership. The chapter frames notions of social justice through the work of scholars who have provided the groundwork and some of the principles of social justice and educational leadership. It then articulates definitions of moral transformative leaders who implement a social justice agenda as public intellectuals. The chapter concludes with how the social justice agenda is being moved forward through current research, national conference presentations, and pedagogical practices of professors of educational leadership.

anniversary of the *Lau v. Nichols* decision have emphasized how movements for social justice have helped to define American history. Additionally, these commemorations have served as an impetus to refocus our thinking on how school leaders can become social justice advocates and activists. Discussions about social justice in the field of education generally, and in educational leadership more specifically, have typically framed the concept of social justice around several issues (e.g., race, diversity, marginalization, gender, spirituality). Although these areas are vitally important to any discussion of social justice, we add the formidable issues of age, ability, and sexual orientation to this discourse.

Leadership for social justice investigates and poses solutions for issues that generate and reproduce societal inequities. Generally, social justice theorists and activists focus their inquiry on how institutionalized theories, norms, and practices in schools and society lead to social, political, economic, and educational inequities (Tillman, 2002). Numerous scholars have offered conceptualizations and frameworks for the application of social justice to educational leadership. A brief discussion of several scholars' work that has a social-justice orientation follows. Although all of these scholars do not specifically use the term *social justice*, principles of social justice can, nevertheless, be found in their work.

Foster (1986) did not specifically use the term *social justice*; however, it is clear that the theoretical underpinnings of his seminal work, *Paradigms and Promises: New Approaches to Educational Administration*, focus on the application of moral, transformative, and socially just leadership conceptualizations and practices. Foster's perspective is informed by critical theory—a view of school leadership and education that interrogates the uses as well as the abuses of power in social, economic, and political structures. According to Foster, "... leadership must be critically educative; it can not only look at the conditions in which we live, but it also must decide how to change them" (p. 185). Thus, Foster's work illuminates one of the premises of critical theory; that is, that institutions such as schools regularly generate and reproduce power inequities.

Another influential concept linking the work of school leaders with a social justice agenda is the multidimensional ethical framework proposed by

Staratt (1994). This intriguing concept is based on the ethics of care, justice, and critique. In Staratt's framework for school leadership, care, justice, and critique combine to form a human, ethical response to unethical and challenging environments and situations that many school leaders face. Positing justice as one of the ethics, Staratt suggests that school leaders give serious consideration to the ways in which students, particularly those from marginalized groups (i.e., African Americans and other racial/ethnic minorities and gay, lesbian, bisexual, poor, and female students), are socialized in the school setting. For example, the multidimensional ethical framework would assist leaders in exploring how they could use a socially just perspective or mindset to address discipline and due process for all students.

Kumashiro (2000) presents a framework for anti-oppressive education that is intended to bring about socially equitable change in schools. Kumashiro uses the term *other* to,

> . . . refer to those groups that are traditionally marginalized in society, i.e., that are *other than* the norm, such as students of color, students from under- or unemployed families, students who are female, or male, but not stereotypically "masculine," and students who are, or are perceived to be, queer. (p. 26)

Kumashiro's anti-oppressive framework includes (a) education of the other (focus on improving the experiences of students who are othered); (b) education about the other (focus on what all students—privileged and marginalized—know and should know about the other); (c) education that is critical of privileging and othering (focus on examining not only how some groups and identities are othered, but also how some groups are favored); and, (d) education that changes students and society (focus on how oppression begins in discourses that frame how people think, feel and interact). According to Kumashiro, each of the components of the framework has strengths and weaknesses that must be considered when attempting to affect change in educational structures. Kumashiro's work can serve as a foundation for a leadership practice that recognizes and addresses, in a socially just manner, the various ways that students can be systemically oppressed in schools.

Diversity and inclusiveness are critical aspects of social justice (Riehl, 2000). In her review of the literature on the principal's role in creating inclusive schools, Riehl notes that several leadership tasks directly respond to diversity: fostering new meanings about diversity, promoting inclusive practices within schools, promoting inclusive teaching and learning, molding inclusive school cultures, and building connections between schools and communities. According to Riehl,

> When wedded to a relentless commitment to equity, voice, and social justice, administrators' efforts in the tasks of sensemaking, promoting inclusive cultures and practices in schools, and building positive relationships outside of the school may indeed foster a new form of practice. (p. 71)

Implicit in Riehl's discussion is the imperative for leadership practices that include the principles of social justice.

Larson and Murtadha (2002) offer a theoretical perspective for the definition, application, and requirements of leadership for social justice. They note that recent shifts in the nature of inquiry regarding just and equitable education have focused on three strands: (1) deconstructing existing logics of leadership (issues that are prominent in this strand include critical race theory, gender representation, modernist critiques, multiculturalism, and leadership theories for women and people of color); (2) portraying alternative perspectives of leadership (issues that are prominent in this strand are the ethics of care, spirituality, love, and leadership); and (3) constructing theories, systems, and processes for social justice (it is in this strand that researchers will have to go beyond theorizing about social justice leadership to making recommendations for practice; in constructing theories, systems, and processes, researchers must do more than articulate theories that can contribute to change in schools). According to Larson and Murtadha, it is the third strand that is the least developed but that holds the greatest possibility for impacting positive change in educational administration.

The conceptualizations and definitions discussed here have similar themes. These perspectives emphasize moral values, justice, equity, care, and respect and the imperative for investigating the impact of race, ethnicity, class, gender, sexual orientation, and disability on the educational outcomes of students. Clearly, the concept of social justice focuses on marginalized groups—those groups that are most often underserved and underrepresented and who face various forms of oppression in schools.

As we have noted, the essential components of a definition of social justice include leadership for social justice, moral transformative leadership, and social justice praxis. Leadership for social justice interrogates the policies and procedures that shape schools and at the same time perpetuate social inequalities and marginalization due to race, class, gender, and other markers of otherness.

The next component, moral transformative leadership, has three distinct characteristics. First, moral transformative leadership views education and educational leadership from a progressive or critical theoretical perspective. That is, moral transformative leadership focuses on the use as well as the abuse of power in institutional settings. Second, moral transformative leadership deconstructs the work of school administration in order to unearth how leadership practices generate and perpetuate inequities and the marginalization of members of the learning community who are outside the dominant culture. Finally, moral transformative leadership sees schools as sites that not only engage in academic pursuits, but also as locations that help to create activists to bring about the democratic reconstruction of society.

The third component of our definition, social justice praxis, is defined as activities such as research and scholarship, conference presentations, and

Components of Social Justice

"These three essential components—leadership for social justice, moral transformative leadership, and social justice praxis—link the principles of democracy and equity in proactive ways so that the social justice agenda becomes a vibrant part of the everyday work of school leaders. Leaders for social justice represent what some critical theorists call *transformative*, or *public, intellectuals*."

---

pedagogical methods that can be used to articulate a broader discourse on leadership for social justice and moral transformative leadership. These three essential components—social justice, leadership for social justice, and social justice praxis—link the principles of democracy and equity in proactive ways so that the social justice agenda becomes a vibrant part of the everyday work of school leaders. Leaders for social justice represent what some critical theorists call *transformative*, or *public, intellectuals*. In the next section, we discuss the notion of transformative leaders as public intellectuals who implement a social justice agenda in schools.

Transformative Leaders as Public Intellectuals

Critical interrogation is a moral endeavor that is linked with social justice. Through this process, current, as well as prospective, school leaders personally grapple with issues of race, class, and gender; signifiers of difference; and the marginalizing strategies of institutions perpetuating elitist notions of the dominant culture. Public intellectuals recognize the demanding labor of examining the ways in which schools and other systems help to maintain the social, political, and economic status quo. The public intellectual scrutinizes social and cultural realities using the tenets of democracy as guiding principles. A public intellectual also questions these cultural realities motivated by a need to understand the underlying presuppositions and values that provide an explanation as to why these cultural realities exist.

Public intellectuals are those who are steeped in the politics of education (Giroux, 1997). This perspective broadens the dimensions of the educational discourse, because such a perspective includes the social and cultural dynamics that intersect and so deeply influence what takes place in America's schoolhouses. School leaders who also are public intellectuals view school leadership/administration as more than management and work to impact the shape and contour of future democratically grounded societies.

Public intellectuals believe that the pedagogy in schools must be focused on morally impacting ends. According to Giroux (1997),

> Whether in schools or in other spheres, public intellectuals must struggle to create the conditions that enable students and others to become cultural producers who can rewrite their own experiences and perceptions by engaging with various texts, ideological positions and theories. (p. 263)

Schools, according to Giroux's perspective, are sites where the intellectual activity taking place in them is inextricably linked to broader social and cultural concerns. For example, curriculum content, special education, and other class placement based on race, class, gender, and disability may reflect society's discriminatory perceptions and practices. The moral nature of transformative leadership, unlike traditional notions of school administration, not only locates the work of schools in a broader social context, but argues that students should become accountable as well as responsible for their own education. Rather than subscribing to the ideals of banking education (Freire, 1970; hooks, 1994), where students are perceived to be empty containers passively awaiting intellectual deposits from the omniscient teacher, educational leaders who base their work in moral transformative leadership facilitate an environment where students learn from one another and express their own ideas. Students, according to the ideals of public intellectuals, function in schools where they are

> . . . given the opportunity to challenge disciplinary borders, create pluralized spaces from which hybridized identities might emerge, take up critically the relationship between language and experience and appropriate knowledge as part of a broader effort at self-definition and ethical responsibility. (Giroux, 1997, p. 263)

Leaders who have adopted a moral position as public intellectuals recognize the formidable task of education in freeing students to inquire and interrogate the traditionally accepted purposes of schools and the curriculum that supports them.

Cornel West (1999) augments these ideas regarding public intellectuals and the moral posture they assume. He argues that an intellectual actually articulates a truth that frees suffering to speak. By this he means, "it creates a vision of the world that puts into the limelight the social misery that is usually hidden or concealed by the dominant viewpoints of a society" (p. 551). School leaders who are public intellectuals are willing to engage in critical self-reflection as well as to critically interrogate institutions, such as schools, in order to uncover as well as construct strategies to combat the rituals and forms of institutionalized oppression these organizations perpetuate. Michael Dyson's (2003) definition of *public intellectuals* contextualizes the work of these transformative intellectuals in higher education, calling them "paid pests." These are the scholars "whose function is to disrupt and intervene in conversations in ways that are disturbing and that force people to ask why they frame the questions in the way that they do or why they make the analysis they do" (p. 24). Transformative leadership "not only assumes a different position to the conventional forms of school leadership but also promises a reformed, if indeed not a totally reconstructed definition of this social construction" (Dantley, 2003, p. 3).

Implied in the idea of transformative leadership is the exchange of new ideological and theoretical frames and practices for the more celebrated profession-forming ones that have traditionally informed the field of educational leadership. Inherent also in notions of transformative leadership are the exigencies of individual and institutional change. These ideas of change, however, are based on a critical theoretical and moral frame that dares to interrogate the rituals as well as the underlying presuppositions and assumptions that craft administrative practices in schools.

David Purpel (1989) and Herbert Marcuse (1969) provide useful definitions of morality that can ground a discussion of transformative and moral educational leadership for social justice. Leadership practice considered to be moral is couched in the supreme necessity of liberation for all. This includes liberation from "hunger, disease, fear, bigotry, war, ignorance and all other barriers to a life of joy, abundance, and meaning for every single person in the world" (Purpel, 1989, p. 30). Another perspective of moral leadership argues that morality is a product that has resulted from political radicalism (Marcuse, 1969). From the perspective of political radicalism, the work of moral transformative leadership is not moral because it honors a conservative religious perspective. The work of leadership is moral and transformative because it is committed to a pedagogy of freedom (Freire, 1998) that labors to see democratic practice and equitable treatment of all members of the learning community, regardless of race, gender, class, ability, age, or sexual orientation.

We have developed the conceptual framework for social justice and moral transformative leadership. But it is vitally important to demonstrate how this conceptual work has been implemented through actual practice. The next section of this chapter describes the ways in which the theoretical foundation for leadership for social justice serves to propel the agenda for social justice through research and scholarship, conference presentations, and teaching.

The Praxis of Leadership for Social Justice

The praxis or reflective action of leadership for social justice can be found in three areas of educational leadership: research and scholarship, conference presentations, and teaching. Each of these areas will be discussed briefly in this section.

Research and Scholarship

One form of social justice praxis can be found in the various forms of research and scholarship in educational leadership. In 2001, members of the organization Leadership for Social Justice (LSJ) were awarded funds from the Ford Foundation to conduct research in the area of social justice. The various types of research exhibited in this investigation represented groundbreaking avenues in bridging theory and practice. Real-life examples of school leaders who have implemented policies and procedures from a social justice perspective that were intended to improve the educational outcomes for all students, particularly marginalized students, were included in this significant research. For example, James Scheurich, Linda Skrla, and Juanita Garcia, who are university professors, and Glen Nolly, who is an associate superintendent in a major urban school district, received a grant to develop a leadership tool called an *equity audit*. An equity audit can be used to examine school or district data such as assignment to special education, disciplinary actions, or assignment to advanced placement courses in order to ascertain the number of students of color, poor students, and female students who are disciplined or enrolled in these classes. The researchers used the equity audit in school districts in the Austin, Texas, area and found that those who use equity audits need to be prepared to address and work through issues of race and ethnicity, because the presentation of the data can move teachers, principals, and parents in either a positive or a negative direction. The researchers believed there was a need for social justice theorists, social justice faculty, and social justice educators in schools to develop practical tools that faculty, educators, and parents can use to move schools and districts toward equity in schooling. The researchers were interested in grounded social justice practice rather than simply social justice critique.

The topic of social justice has generated a great deal of scholarship over the last decade. Some of this work has been noted in this chapter, and other rich descriptions of the applications of social justice to schooling and leadership can be found in other chapters of this book. As we previously noted, it is significant that this book captures a variety of rich perspectives and examples/vignettes that bridge theory and practice and also produces significant research and scholarship for the field.

Several educational leadership/administration journals have published special issues devoted to the topic of leadership for social justice, including the *Journal of School Leadership* (2002) and the *Educational Administration Quarterly* (2004). The September 2004 issue of the *Journal of School Leadership* included an article by Catherine Marshall and Michael Ward that investigated what powerful educational leaders think about training practitioners for social justice. Included in that issue were four responses to the Marshall/Ward article from leaders representing the American Association of School Administration, the National Association of Secondary School Principals, the National Association of Elementary School Principals, the National Council for Accreditation of Teacher Education, and the National Association of State Boards of Education. Finally, the Fall 2003 issue of the *University Council for Educational Administration Review* was a special theme issue focused on diversity and social justice in the field of educational leadership. Among other articles, this issue also featured an interview with distinguished scholar Dr. Barbara Jackson from Fordham University, who reflected on diversity in UCEA, past, present, and future (Lopez, 2003).

Conference Presentations

Conference presentations represent a second form of social justice praxis. The importance and prominence of leadership in the social justice movement can be seen in conference presentations at the annual meetings of the American Educational Research Association (AERA), the University Council for Educational Administration (UCEA), and the National Council for Professors of Educational Administration (NCPEA). These presentations help to advance the field toward a more socially just agenda and provide students, faculty, and school leaders with opportunities to seriously engage and reflect on these issues.

Michelle Young, Executive Director of UCEA, shared in a 2004 interview that the LSJ group was formed at the 1999 UCEA convention in Minneapolis and that the development of such a group was not entirely welcomed by the total membership of UCEA at that time. Young offered, "It now appears to be either embraced, accepted, or at least tolerated by all faculty involved in the organization. More importantly, it has enhanced the organization and its annual meeting in numerous important ways." (M. Young, personal communication, June 22, 2004). She shared that one of those important ways involved the UCEA mission. This organization has always supported excellence in research and the preparation of school leaders. However, according to Young, with LSJ members and other like-minded faculty and practitioners, UCEA has broadened its commitment to the children who are ultimately impacted by the research and professional preparation for school leaders. For example, Gerardo López organized panel discussions for two consecutive years (2002, 2003) at UCEA conferences on the topic of social justice leadership. Additionally, at the UCEA 2002 Annual Meeting, UCEA and the American Educational Studies Association (AESA) co-sponsored a general session titled "Building Support for Diverse Communities: Perils and Possibilities." According to the panel's organizers, Catherine Lugg of Rutgers University and Frances Kochan of Auburn University, the invited panel "focused their remarks on issues of leadership related to building community while honoring diversity" and "the purpose of the session was to engage conference participants in a dialogue about issues of community and diversity" (Lugg & Kochan, 2003, p. 7). The session also included small group discussions and data collection through surveys. Results indicated that "There appears to be a strong realization within the UCEA community that much more needs to be done in these areas by professors, educational leaders working in public schools, our respective institutions, and our organizations" (p. 8).

Conferences and related presentations are valuable. They are excellent venues to teach, inform, dialogue, and bring together diverse viewpoints that can lead to moral transformative leadership in schools.

Teaching

A third form of social justice praxis is teaching. Our teaching can and should have a significant impact on the leadership for social justice movement. It is in our university and K–12 classrooms that we ensure that the principles of social justice and moral transformative leadership are studied, adopted, and practiced. It is imperative that we use our influence as professors, teachers, and school leaders to promote leadership for social justice in education broadly and educational leadership more specifically. It is imperative that we put our beliefs into practice as one way to work toward a more equitable and just society and educational system.

Numerous scholars bring their research, scholarship, and advocacy into their classrooms. For example, Colleen Capper of the University of Wisconsin-Madison infuses a social justice framework into each of her classes (Tillman, López, Larson, Capper, Scheurich, and Marshall, 2003). Capper assigns students research projects that require them to investigate, interrogate, and think critically about social justice as it relates to K–12 schooling. According to Capper (Tillman et al., 2003), when students collect data on race, ethnicity, and other issues, such as the percentage of students in gifted and special education classes by race and gender, there is always evidence that

> . . . inequalities and injustice are happening in a school district no matter where it is located in our state or in our area. And that brings students to a point of crisis saying that "we talk about the theories and the big ideas, but this is happening in my school, this is happening in my classroom," and they felt compelled to do something about it. (p. 90)

Edith Rusch (2003) of the University of Nevada, Las Vegas notes that social justice work can be difficult for both students and faculty. According to Rusch, "Discourse about diversity and equity is intertwined with emotional and value-laden positions on privilege, meritocracy, affirmative action, gender, race, class, ethnicity, sexuality, and disability" (p. 12). While on the faculty of Rowan University, Rusch attempted to "weave diversity and equity issues into all coursework" (p. 12) in a doctoral cohort. She notes that students were expected to become "generative listeners, skillful discussers, and reflective thinkers about issues of equity, diversity, and social justice" (p. 12). As the first course progressed, students became uncomfortable with honest reflection and encountered awkward experiences when discussing diversity and social justice. Rusch notes that "I realized how easy it was to be passionate about social justice and how quickly passion dissipates in the face of emotionally volatile work" (p. 12).

While her early experiences were disappointing, she continued to explore ways to advance a social justice oriented curriculum and discourse in the doctoral cohort. Rusch also noted that "Faculty charged with developing leaders who can navigate equity and diversity in school communities need a learning space that supports increasing capacity for discomfort" (p. 14).

Both of the authors of this chapter use socially just leadership frameworks in their teaching. Linda Tillman uses Staratt's (1994) multidimensional ethical framework to prepare administrators to work with schools, parents, and communities in the greater metropolitan Detroit area. Masters-level students are introduced to the framework and given a series of assignments that require them to use the ethics of care, justice, and critique to analyze situations and to develop leadership plans. Students are expected to reflect on how the framework can be used in their particular educational contexts. The purpose of these assignments is to train future leaders not only to be administrators and managers, but also to become leaders who have dispositions toward and proactively practice the ethics of care, justice, and critique. It is hoped that students will think critically about the work that awaits them as future leaders and begin to pose solutions from a socially just perspective.

Michael Dantley uses the tenets of moral leadership, transformational leadership, and critical spirituality in his classes at Miami University of Ohio. Every seventh session of the semester Dantley holds a Sabbath Session. Each Sabbath Session provides an opportunity for students to engage in critical self-reflection about the course and specifically their own issues of race, class, gender, and otherness. Students work individually and in small groups to discuss issues such as how the organizations they are a part of perpetuate marginalization of persons due to race, class, and culture. Students reflect on and discuss questions that include: How do they themselves perpetuate these practices? How have they lodged opposition against such practices? What does it take to lodge such opposition? What is the source of their sensitivity to issues of race, class, and gender? What readings and class discussions have assisted them in thinking about social justice issues and doing something with their reflections and thinking?

For all of these instructors, the issues of social justice are not "add ons" to their classes. Rather, these issues are intricately interwoven into the very fabric of their classes and what they do. These forms of social justice praxis must continue to grow and expand within the field of educational leadership. If social justice is to become a vital part of the language of school leadership, then preparation programs must be willing to embrace the hard work that is required to move notions of social justice from rhetoric to effective action.

Conclusion

In this chapter, we have posited a definition of *leadership for social justice*: Leadership for social justice interrogates the policies and procedures that shape schools and at the same time perpetuate social inequalities and marginalization due to race, class, gender, and other markers of otherness. As advocates for social justice, it is imperative that we continually strive for a more equitable and socially just society. This work begins with the educational leaders in our schools. Our collective and individual roles as professors and practitioners is to work through our research, scholarship, and teaching to keep leadership for social justice and moral transformative leadership in the forefront of the movement to equitably educate all children. We must put into practice our socially just ideologies. We must move from passive discourse and involvement to conscious, deliberate, and proactive practice in educational leadership that will produce socially just outcomes for all children. As scholars and leaders, we must be committed to participating in the *generation and production* of a socially just society, rather than the generation and reproduction of an unjust society that blames children and their families for situations that place them at risk and that is unaccepting of differences.

Further, this chapter has explored how various forms of social justice praxis are operationalized in professional practice. The praxis of the social justice agenda has been demonstrated in research and scholarship in educational leadership, national conference presentations, and teaching. Leaders for social justice take the moral position to critically deconstruct as well as to reconstruct schools in a fashion that demands that schools be sites for the equitable treatment of all students. These leaders also work to create schools where quality educational practices in a democratic, socially just environment take place.

Discussion Questions and Activities

1. Think carefully about your educational leadership preparation program. In what ways were issues of race, class, gender, and sexual orientation and other markers of difference topics of focus? What readings or class assignments examined these issues? How do you think you have been prepared to deal with the matters of race, class, gender, and sexual orientation in a morally just way? How could your preparation have been enhanced?

2. Using Riehl's notions of diversity/inclusiveness, create a chart that highlights the inclusive practices you have observed in your school. What was the motivation for the initiation of these inclusive practices? Discuss with faculty members, students, and parents their perceptions of the effectiveness of these inclusive practices. What were some of the leadership behaviors that were essential foundations for this inclusion to take place?

3. If schools are to be democratic sites, what can school principals do to encourage and facilitate democracy in schools? What are some indicators or characteristics in schools that you know that demonstrate that a democratic atmosphere is pervasive in the school? What specific behaviors and attitudes of the administration, faculty, students, and parents lead you to believe that the school is a democratic site?

4. In what ways (e.g., teaching methods, curriculum development, and administrative practices) are racism, class marginalization, sexism, and homophobia perpetuated in the schools that you are familiar with? Select one of the areas mentioned above and devise a comprehensive plan to address how that area may be transformed in order to perpetuate equitable and democratic practices in the school that may even transcend into the community.

Annotated Readings

William Foster's (1986) *Paradigms and Promises: New Approaches to Educational Administration* is the classic text in educational leadership that grounds school administration in a critical theoretical context. The text brings the work of the Frankfurt School to the schoolhouse and requires practicing and prospective school leaders to deal with the inequities that schools and their leadership systemically create. It dares to ask very difficult questions regarding school administrators' roles in generating, as well as perpetuating, societal power inequities based on race, class, and gender. Foster further offers school leaders who are thinking about a whole new paradigm of educational leadership what he calls a radical reconstruction of schooling that couches the work of schools in a broader social, economic, and political context. This is a valuable text to serve as a foundation for discussion of school leadership for social justice. Although Foster uses the word *administration* in the title of the text, this book transcends traditional ideas of management and administration and places this work in the proper context of leadership.

Henry Giroux's (1997) *Pedagogy and the Politics of Hope* places the work of education in a highly politicized venue. Giroux's text critically deconstructs what takes place in schools that minimizes the creation of a more radically democratic society. In fact, Giroux's argument is that much of what happens in the greater society that marginalizes people of difference is taught through the curriculum that serves to ground much of the teaching and learning taking place in schools. Giroux's notions of educators as public intellectuals frame much of the discourse in this text. He calls for educators to become political activists who not only articulate the systemic ways institutions, such as schools, continue the oppression of people outside the dominant culture but also offer in their places more democratic and equitable ways to include people of difference into the very fabric of the American society. Giroux's ideas are radical and can overwhelm a reader who does not see education as having serious political implications on the greater American society.

David Purpel's (1989) *The Moral and Spiritual Crisis in Education: A Curriculum for Justice and Compassion in Education* contextualizes education and the curriculum that serves as its foundation in a political and moral space. Purpel contends that school leaders have spent much of their time majoring on minor issues, leaving the weightier matters of the residuals of education untouched. Purpel maintains that educators must not only deal with academic issues, but also must see those issues in a context where more and more Americans are living in poverty and without adequate health care, many are homeless, and the political apparatus is consistently denying the realities of these inhuman conditions. Purpel calls for an educational leadership of compassion. The text does a fine job in disconnecting morality from a specific religious discourse. It defines moral behavior as the act of working to rid our nation of the blatant inequities and undemocratic practices that seem to oppress many and plague us all. This book is a foundational text for those who are interested in crafting a more compassionate perspective of education and of the role that the curriculum can have in meeting that goal. It is a must-read for scholars, students, and practitioners who are interested in forwarding an agenda for social justice in education.

Cornel West's (1999) *Cornel West Reader* is a compilation of portions of many of the texts this prolific scholar has written. West's text helps school leaders to see their work from the perspective of a prophetic pragmatist. That is, West contours the work of educators in a frame that boldly declares a future that is consistently working toward the eradication of the social, economic, and political inequities in our society. West spends some time in the reader outlining the responsibilities of, as well as the barriers to, socially conscious intellectuals and calls for them to become politically active through their research and grassroots efforts to bring about radically new social constructions. This book is not ordinarily read in educational administration classes. Its focus is not specifically on education, but it provides educators with substantive philosophical underpinnings that can appropriately serve in their pursuit of more democratic practices in educational leadership. West's writing is scholarly and at times complex, but because it covers the kinds of philosophical and intellectual arguments that can ultimately positively affect one's thinking, it is worth the struggle.

References

Dantley, M. E. (2003). Critical spirituality: enhancing transformative leadership through critical theory and African American prophetic spirituality. *International Journal of Leadership in Education: Theory and Practice, 6,* 3–17.

Dyson, M. E. (2003). *Open mike: Reflections on philosophy, race, sex, culture and religion.* New York: Civitas Books.

Foster, W. (1986). *Paradigms and promises: New approaches to educational administration.* Buffalo, NY: Prometheus Books.

Freire, P. (1970). *Pedagogy of the oppressed.* New York: Continuum.

Freire, P. (1998). *Pedagogy of freedom, ethics, democracy and civic courage.* Boulder, CO: Roman and Littlefield.

Gadotti, M. (1996). *Pedagogy of praxis: A dialectical philosophy of education.* Albany, NY: SUNY Press.

Giroux, H. A. (1997). *Pedagogy and the politics of hope: Theory, culture and schooling.* Boulder, CO: Westview Press.

Grogan, M. (Ed.). (2002). Leadership for social justice. A special issue of *Journal of School Leadership, 12*(2).

Grogan, M. (Ed.). (2002). Leadership for social justice. A special issue of the *Journal of School Leadership, 12*(3).

hooks, b. (1994). *Teaching to transgress: Education as the practice of freedom.* New York: Routledge.

Joiner, L. J. (2003). State of Black children. *The Crisis, 110,* 24–29.

Kumashiro, K. (2000). Toward a theory of anti-oppressive education. *Review of Educational Research, 70*(1), 25–53.

Larson, C., & Murtadha, K. (2003). Leadership for social justice. In J. Murphy (Ed.), *The educational leadership challenge: Redefining leadership for the 21st century* (pp. 134–161). Chicago: University of Chicago Press.

López, G. (2003). Justice or just us: A critical conversation with scholars of color surrounding leadership for social justice. Proposal submitted to the University Council for Educational Administration.

Lugg, C., & Kochan, F. (2003). Building Support for Diverse Communities: A Brief Report. *University Council for Educational Administration Review, 45*(3), 7–8.

Marcuse, H. (1969). *An essay on liberation.* Boston: Beacon Press.

Marshall, C. (Ed.). (2004). Social justice challenges to educational administration. A special issue of *Educational Administration Quarterly, 40*(1).

Marshall, C., & Ward, M. (2004). "Yes, but . . .": Education leaders discuss social justice. *Journal of School Leadership, 14*(5), 530–563.

Purpel, D. (1989). *The moral and spiritual crisis in education: A curriculum for justice and compassion in education.* New York: Bergin and Garvey.

Riehl, C. (2000). The principal's role in creating inclusive schools for diverse students: A review of normative, empirical, and critical literature on the practice of educational administration. *Review of Educational Research, 70*(1), 55–81.

Rusch, E. (2003). Social justice work: From intellectualizing to practice. *University Council for Educational Administration Review, 45*(3), 12–14.

Skrla, L., Scheurich, J., Garcia, J., & Nolly, G. (in press). Equity audits: A practical leadership tool for developing equitable and excellent schools. In C. Marshall and M. Oliva (Eds.), *Leadership for social justice: Making revolutions in education.* Boston: Allyn and Bacon.

Staratt, R. J. (1994). *Building an ethical school: A practical response to the moral crisis in schools.* Washington, DC: Falmer Press.

Tillman, L. (2002). The impact of diversity in educational administration. In G. Perreault & F. Lunenburg (Eds.), *The changing world of school administration* (pp. 144–156). Lanham, MD: Scarecrow Press.

Tillman, L. C., Lopez, G., Larson, C., Capper, C., Scheurich, J. J., & Marshall, C. (2003). Leadership for social justice: Identifying the terrain, crafting a mission and purpose. In F. C. Lunenburg & C. S. Carr (Eds.), *Shaping the future: Policy, partnerships, and emerging perspectives* (pp. 60–75). Lanham, MD: Scarecrow Press.

West, C. (1999). *The Cornel West Reader.* New York: Civitas.

3

Wholistic Visioning for Social Justice: Black Women Theorizing Practice

Renée Sanders-Lawson
Sabrina Smith-Campbell
Maenette K. P. Benham[1]

Background Information on Our Dialogue (by Maenette Benham)

I was sitting in my office with three Black women, all school professionals and doctoral candidates, talking about the lessons I had learned through a study I had recently completed that had resulted in the book *Let My Spirit Soar! Narratives of Diverse Women in School Leadership* (1998). This led to an engaging and humbling conversation that reminded us of the important work that women of color do in schools. We were enlightened by each others' experiences, and our understanding and appreciation for one another deepened as we shared the struggles that both admonished and uplifted us. As the dissertation adviser to all three women, I was excited that each wanted to pursue a deeper understanding of what it meant to Black women to place social justice in the forefront of one's leadership practices. Because we believed that there was a wealth of knowledge in the lives of Black women school leaders, the three women decided to work together to develop three dissertations on a common theme: Black women creating socially just learning environments.[2]

Shaping their doctoral journeys required that I set up frequent group meetings to discuss and scrutinize big ideas, to push them to liberate their minds in order to view old problems through new lenses, and to guide them in the construction of vibrant texts (in this case dissertation text) that captured the courage and truth of the lives of their interviewees. Throughout these conversations I kept detailed meeting notes, we each wrote and shared our deeply honest journal reflections, and we communicated in lengthy e-mails. We also presented our works-in-progress at numerous research conferences, engaging in multiple conversations with other scholars who helped us to better learn from the powerful stories we were collecting. What is presented in this chapter is some of our dialogue and thinking and the stories that illuminate what we have learned. We began with wonderment, we were sustained by the energy of thought, and in the end we came to know the importance of and responsibility of social justice.

Introduction to Our Thinking

There has been an explosion of conceptual and empirical work that acknowledges the power of cultural wisdom, which may lead to effective educational leadership. As scholars of color, we have benefited from this inclusive invitation to explore alternative views of knowing and doing leadership, and yet we marvel at the power and peril of this vibrant dialogue. We say *power*, because new ways of viewing leadership can effectively dismantle rigid typologies that narrowly define the roles, responsibilities, and interrelations of school leadership and have served to disenfranchise and alienate groups of people (in particular, Black women). In effect, these traditional perspectives of schools and school leadership have determined who participates (and to what extent), who

Here, the three authors converse over definitions and deeper meanings.

receives what resources, what knowledge will be represented (or not), and where particular groups and individuals belong (a particular bin or category), as well as defining how to "deal with them." We know that these views are based on stereotypes and misinformation that define both the secular and the spiritual in our schools and that have become an obligatory construct of many school communities (see also Banks, 1995; Benham & Cooper, 1998; Collins, 1998, 2000; hooks, 1994; Lomotey, 1989, 1993; Tatum, 1997).[3]

The power of current dialogue and debate to explore issues of social justice in our school setting is that it has the potential to contest the binary views of the dominant and the other. This conversation embraces the promise that we can create learning environments that nurture, reconcile, and establish common ground. Yet, although there is power in this movement, there also is peril. We need to acknowledge the muddy terrain that we have entered. It is fashionable today to join the social justice bandwagon and to use our cultural lenses to impart profound platitudes that justify our advocacy. Therefore, the honest part of our journey as authors of this chapter (i.e., to avoid the peril) is to think through how our philosophical beliefs are communicated so that it helps to move both explicit and implicit action for socially just learning communities.

We acknowledge that as scholars and practitioners we risk this peril in our chapter; however, it is a gift to be included in this volume of work that explores ideas and presents diverse theories and experiences to explain what socially just leadership is and what it looks like. The purpose of our focus is to engage the reader through our dialogic writing style to think about what leadership looks like when it comes from the spirit and embraces everyone involved in the learning process. The conceptual lens we propose, which we have named *wholistic visioning*, is grounded on the practice and theorizing of Black women school leaders (four African American urban school superintendents, three African American urban secondary school principals, and six African American urban middle school principals). In this chapter, we present the narrative stories of these leaders told in their own words (voices). (See the endnotes for an overview of our narrative method.)

Building a Conceptual Model: Literature on Feminist Thought, Leadership, and Social Justice

As multiple views of women-womanism, feminism, and social justice journey into the twenty-first century, there is a need to locate women of courage who have been working in visible ways to achieve equity in their school communities. Simultaneously, there are loud calls for women to return to "modesty" (Shalit, 1999), which is reminiscent of the nineteenth-century doctrine of domesticity. In light of this puzzling polarity facing women in the workplace, gaining clarity on the work of women, in particular women of color, in today's society can be a challenging pursuit. In particular, gaining access to and permission to share the stories of women school administrators of color who are leading for social justice requires a great deal of trust between researcher and participant, because the process of sharing is a political action.

To ensure that we honored the courage of our participants, we listened closely to their stories in order to demystify the work of social justice and move it to a more empowered stance. As we listened to the unique stories of pain, love, hardship, and celebration, we found common ground—common themes that captured the essence of their work. We began to realize that a conceptual model of leading for social justice was emerging from the stories.

How did we arrive at this conceptual lens? Our conversations began with intense theoretical discussions of "meaning." That is, we would ask such questions as: "What does it mean that she builds her relations on her spirituality?" "What does it mean that shades of color both hinder and assist action?" "What does it mean to mother?" "What is the meaning of her struggle within the intersections of race, gender, and class?" We began to engage these questions by employing Black feminist theories, school leadership theories, and social justice theories. What we ended up with was a model we call *wholistic visioning*. To help the reader understand how we collectively framed the wholistic visioning model, we bring together pieces of our conversations (conducted over a year and a half) to reveal a snapshot of how we came to understand a body of work and then employed our growing understanding to locate meaning in the stories of the women we interviewed.

Beginning with a Discussion of Feminist and Black Feminist Theories

Maenette: Why examine feminisms? Historically, contemporary feminists (Grumet, 1988; Martin, 1992; Noddings, 1992; Ruddick, 1989) have viewed feminism in education as caring, concern, and connection (Martin, 1992). In practice, however, the "3 C's" have been the burden of women in the schools; indeed, to a great extent these good values have fallen into the laps of women of color (Benham, 1997; Benham & Cooper, 1998), thereby falling short of an empowering perspective (Hartsock, 1983). In fact, one can argue that these feminisms have served only to marginalize women economically, socially, and politically. It is essential, then, that researchers who employ feminist lenses to create theories of practice must also critique feminist theories. This approach to generating new understanding represents a fruitful way for researchers to create an opportunity to examine more deeply the particularities of the structure of power in the lives of women school leaders and to move beyond valorizing the niceties of feminine values to a deeper embrace of feminism that attends to the issues of social relations and social justice.

So, let's begin by thinking and talking about the absence of Black voices during the early years of the feminist movement, which has been attributed to the lack of privilege women of color had within feminist circles. According to bell hooks (1994),

> In the beginning of the feminist movement, Black feminists were afraid to speak out, out of fear of isolation. Yet, Black feminists understood the need to study feminist work and to see gender from a Black standpoint in order to help understand the Black experience. This in turn helped Black feminists to develop a Black consciousness for the future of the Black liberation struggle. During the initial stages of this feminist movement, feminist scholarship and writing were groundbreaking. The works sought to articulate, define and speak to and against the glaring omissions in feminist work the erasure of Black female presence. (p. 117)

Black feminists criticized the white liberal and radical feminist movements for articulating an overarching message of the female experience that did not recognize the differences among women due to color and class.

Sabrina: Because Black women were excluded from the women's movement and feminist thought, for the most part they resisted mainstream feminists' ideas. Nevertheless, Black feminists have acknowledged that race, gender, and class inequalities are significantly related to their plight. For instance, King (1988) contended that race, gender, and class have independent effects on the status of Black women. In her eyes, the effects of these types of discrimination are not equivalent. Instead, she argued, "Each discrimination has a single, direct, and independent effect on status, wherein the relative contribution of each is readily apparent" (p. 297). As a result, Black women have found themselves "marginal to both the movements for women's liberation and black liberation irrespective of our victimization under the dual discrimination of racism and sexism" (p. 299).

Renée: Black feminist theory emphasizes race, class, and gender as categories of connection. Spelman (1982) stated:

> It would be quite misleading to say simply that black women and white women both are oppressed as women and that a black woman's oppression as a black is separable from her oppression as a woman because she shares the latter but not the former with the white woman. An additive analysis treats the oppression of a black woman in a sexist and racist society as if it were a further burden than her oppression in a sexist and non-racist society, when, in fact, it is a different burden. (p. 42)

In addition, Collins (1989) stated that we need to move toward race, class, and gender as categories of connections. We need to step out of the box of dichotomous thinking and move away from the *either/or* and toward the *both/and*. According to Collins, we can do this by building relationships and coalitions that will bring about social change. Furthermore, she said that each of us is responsible for making individual choices about which elements of race, class, and gender we will accept and which we will work to change.

Sabrina: That marginalization is evident in the commonalities that Black women are supposed to share with White women and Black men. For instance, Black women are supposed to share a commonality with White women because of their gender. Furthermore, Black women are supposed to identify with Black men because they both share race and class issues. Hence, Black women have been asked to decide what cause they are fighting for or what interests they are advancing. As Renée began to allude to, Collins (1991) argued that Black women must address race, gender, and class issues. Collins wrote that suppression by White women and by men is a way of "maintaining the invisibility of Black women and our ideas [and] is critical in structuring patterned relations of race, gender, and class inequality that pervade the entire social structure" (p. 5). Furthermore, despite Black women's experiences of oppression, each woman's experiences may vary. Such factors as ethnicity, region of the country, urbanization, and age combine to produce a web of experiences shaping diversity among Black women.

I think it also is important to add that the theme of silenced voices is prevalent in the work of Black feminists. The lack of voice and exclusion of the Black woman are essential components of Black feminist theory. Sojourner Truth, one of the first Black feminists, strove for her voice to be heard. During the nineteenth century, she was one of the Black women most responsible for voicing critical issues of Black women's gender and racial identities. White women in particular objected to Truth's speaking publicly, because they believed their cause would be damaged as a result, but she continued to use her voice.

Maenette: And yet, the concept of empowerment was not new to Black women, because for centuries they had organized collectively to develop strategies for empowering their families and communities (Davis, 1989). The message of Black feminism led to the epistemological concept of "power with." This idea offers an opportunity for the creation of collective power through which social injustices can be addressed. The struggle, however, of the Black feminist movement is determining how to "lift" both Black men and women of all social classes, while addressing the remnants of oppression, subordination, and iconic worship of individuals (Davis, 1989).

Renée: Our conceptualization of Black feminist theory is based on themes of racial differences, gender differences, and differences in power and privilege. Collins (1989) and hooks (1990) are among those scholars who have advocated keeping race and gender at the center of examinations of policy and practice in leadership. In addition, the scholars we have studied maintained the importance of acknowledging that social systems, of which schools are a part, award varying degrees of power and privilege (i.e., social capital) to different groups of people. Clearly, the differences in power and privilege affect the ability of Black women school superintendents and principals to create change and act for social justice.

Adding Sabrina's and Renée's Discussion of School Leadership Theories

Sabrina: As we shift our focus to school leadership theories and how they explain or fail to explain what Black women school leaders do, I am reminded of Lomotey and Swanson's (1989) work on urban schools. They wrote that leadership in the urban school is in turmoil, "partly due to the fact that principals have little control over the curriculum, the hiring of staff, and fiscal matters" (p. 442). A key factor in this tension, they wrote, is that "most critical decisions are made at the district level, with limited input from the schools. The structure is highly bureaucratic, contributing to many of the problems that arise in these schools" (p. 442). However, the authors found urban schools that had been able to go beyond these structural limitations: "Effective urban schools operate within the same bureaucratic structure as do other urban schools; nevertheless, the principals and teachers, through creative insubordination, have been able to achieve meaningful changes and meet the specific needs of their students" (p. 443). Lomotey and Swanson observed:

> Principals of effective urban schools are confident in the ability of their children to learn are committed to seeing that all of their students receive the necessary tools for success, and have compassion for and understanding of their students and the communities from which they come. The principals of effective schools make an effort to participate in neighborhood affairs and encourage parents to become involved in the education of their children. (p. 443)

Renée: I go back to a more historical view of school leadership literature. Historically, all literature about women in educational leadership was derived from studies of males and from a traditional scientific management perspective. Furthermore, much of the literature on school leadership has ignored women and often has implied that managers are males or has assumed a gender-free position (McGregor, 1960). This stance also has ignored the important element of race and has disregarded the experiences of Black women school leaders in particular. A close examination of the literature will reveal that women and people of color were absent from the study of leadership until the late 1970s.

Only recently have women begun to study other women in leadership and specifically in the superintendency (Schmuck, 1999). Astin and Leland (1991) studied "women leaders and the social movement—the modern women's movement" (p. xvii) over a period of 30 years. Three major themes emerged from their study: (1) the women viewed leadership as a process of working with and through people, thus using power in a collective manner; (2) they all shared a strong, passionate commitment to social justice and change; and (3) the women's performance as leaders consistently demonstrated a thoughtful approach that included clear values, listening to and empowering others, and always doing their homework. Astin and Leland concluded that the women leaders worked through collective and nonhierarchical action with other like-minded people to accomplish the social reform they desired.

Sabrina: Relating more specifically to women school leaders, Dorn, O'Rourke, and Papalewis (1997) argued that "women involve themselves with staff and students, ask for and get participation, and maintain more closely knit organizations" (pp. 18–19). Further, Carr (1995) wrote:

> Research is clear that communication behaviors described traditionally as "female" are most effective for working with groups and work teams. Participative leadership is being described as the most effective leadership style in schools, and the vehicle of site-based decision-making is pointing toward the necessity for principals and superintendents to model this style. (p. 195)

Lyman et al. (1993) studied 10 women's approaches to change during their first years in administration and found that these women used shared decision making in their schools. They discovered that "the changes made by these women varied from school to school, but the approaches used to bring about these changes were similar. Of the women interviewed, eight said they used shared decision making to bring about change in their schools" (p. 33). Lyman et al. also reported that "all eight of the principals who used shared decision making agreed that two-way communication was critical to the effectiveness of shared decision making as a leadership technique" (p. 34).

Renée: Yes, Sabrina, this research provides a nice springboard. However, inquiry on and conducted by women and people of color will add depth and dimension to our current discussion and study of school leadership. Even with more research being conducted, there is still a paucity of research on both women and people of color, and considerably more research is being done on women than people of color (Banks, 1995). How can we account for this negligible amount of research? What can we do as Black women scholars?

Adding Social Justice Theories to Our Knowledge of Feminist Thinking and School Leadership

Sabrina: Theorists have attempted to dispel the myth of social justice, but they have confronted a challenge when examining social justice because it does not have one particular meaning. According to Rizvi (1998), "Social justice is embedded within discourses that are historically constituted and that are sites of conflicting and divergent political endeavors. Thus, social justice does not refer to a single set of primary or basic goods, conceivable across all moral and material domains" (p. 47). As Rizvi explained, social justice needs to be articulated in terms of particular values, which, although not fixed across time and space, nevertheless have to be given specific content in particular struggles for reform. Therefore, social justice has been interpreted in various ways to reflect changing social and economic conditions. Although Rizvi articulated social justice to reflect inequities in social and economic conditions, he did not acknowledge the long-standing hierarchical power relations of race, economic class, gender, and education that are still prevalent today, making Black women and children lower-class citizens.

Renée: Yes, Sabrina, one confronts immediate difficulties when examining social justice because it does not have one particular meaning. Numerous theorists have defined social justice in a variety of ways. For example, Sadurski (1985) said that *legal justice* is about conforming to the rules, whereas *social justice* is about the distributive qualities of those rules. Judgments about social justice confirm that the rule distributes burdens and benefits justly among members of a community. Several other authors have expanded this basic premise. For example, Rawls (1972) said that the principles of social justice provide a way of assigning rights and duties and distributing the benefits and burdens of social cooperation. Griffiths (1998) agreed, describing social justice as a movement to a fairer and less oppressive society. She went on to say that education is central to this movement and shared a working definition of social justice that emerged from her discussion. She stated:

1. It is good for the common interest where that is taken to include the good for each and also the good for all, in an acknowledgment that one depends on the other.
2. The good depends on there being a right distribution of benefits and responsibilities. (p. 4)

Organizational justice theory helps us understand how these Black women school leaders work to create socially just schools. Equity theory, one of the earliest approaches to understanding organizational justice theory, presents three lenses through which to define social justice. First, *distributive justice* is the criterion that determines the distribution of resources. Second, *procedural justice* includes the process that determines whose voices are heard and whose voices are silenced. Third, *interactional justice* includes relationships with subordinates, specifically the communication between supervisors and subordinates. Adams, Bell, and Griffin (1997) argued that social justice is about full and equal participation of all groups in a society that is mutually shaped to meet their needs. In a socially just society, the distribution of resources is equitable and all members are physically and psychologically safe and secure.

Sabrina: Collins (1989) acknowledged that many people feel compelled to take action against injustice when they care deeply about searching for justice. In particular, she wrote that some Black women experience "social mobility into the middle class by gaining formal entry into historically segregated residential, educational, and employment spaces [which] represents bona fide change" (p. 13). However, as some Black women gain access, many others "remain disproportionately glued to the bottom of the bag" (p. 13). I think it also is important to point out Collins's argument that "even though Black women's concern for justice is shared with many others, African-American women have a group history in relation to justice" (p. 244). It is because of this unifying theme that Black women school leaders will often reject individual strategies and instead work to build collective capacity to create change. As Collins wrote, Black women believe "fighting on behalf of freedom and social justice for the entire community [is], in effect, fighting for one's own personal freedom . . . Therefore, Black women are taught to see their own needs as secondary to those of a collectivity of some sort, whether it be the family, church, neighborhood, race, or Black nation" (p. 27).

Renée: The metaphor that I chose to explain my initial conceptual model on social justice is "Double Dutch." Many women, specifically Black women, jumped rope as little girls. Those who were skilled would advance to the "Double Dutch" style, which is the addition of a second rope that is turned simultaneously with but in the opposite direction from the first. This feat requires numerous skills, which can be likened to the skills that Black women school superintendents must possess or acquire in order to create socially just schools. She must jump to a rhythm that allows her to stay on her feet while jumping through, across, over, and sometimes between the ropes of race, gender, class, slavery, oppression, isolation, segregation, and glass ceilings. The Black woman superintendent is indeed the "outsider within." She is in the club, but never a part of the club, jumping and dodging all the ropes, but never once having the chance to "turn the ropes."

Sabrina: In my study, I did not want to stereotype Black people by reinforcing the image of the Black as having "natural rhythm." Rather, my purpose in using the dancing (or dance) metaphor was to provide the reader with a visual image of how these Black women middle school principals used multiple complex movements or practices in their work to create socially just and equitable urban middle schools. The image of these Black women that I wanted to portray was that of successful women who challenged prevailing stereotypes as they contributed to their communities. Similarly, these school leaders performed various complex choreographed dances in their tireless efforts to achieve leadership for justice. It was through their personal and professional experiences, likened to their styles of dance, that they have been able to create socially just learning environments. Therefore, in my study, I viewed dancing as more than just a series of movements performed in patterns and set to an accompaniment (Grau, 2000). I perceived dancing as a form of artistic expression that is characterized by movements with a particular goal in mind. Therefore, dancing in my study symbolized the variety of movements and maneuvers the principals used in order to create socially just and equitable urban middle school settings.

Renée: In my critical analysis of why Black women are compelled to struggle for justice, I must repeat what Collins (1998) asserted: that Black women believe that it is the right thing to do.

Defining Our Conceptual Model: Wholistic Visioning

Our conversations helped us to better understand feminist philosophy through the work of several Black feminist thinkers (Collins, 1989, 1990; Henry, 1993; hooks, 1989, 1994) and other feminists of color (Allen, 1986; Anzaldua, 1987; Benham & Cooper, 1998; Trinh, 1989). In addition, exploring numerous conceptual and empirical works on school leadership and social justice helped us to better understand the intersection of power, pedagogy, and school leadership and led us to ask the question: What drives our leadership and pedagogical practices to create socially just learning environments? It is important to note that this idea of wholistic visioning emerged after all three dissertations were completed (and defended). The process included numerous conversations among the four women and additional conversations with the interviewees and other scholars.

In essence, the complex lives and work of Black women to create spaces for communal knowledge, learning, and teaching requires a seeing and doing that goes beyond the daily tasks of educational leadership and management. Wholistic visioning describes how Black women link mind, body, and spirit to see and to know, a conscious seeing, the human potential in their school communities. This way of being is subtle and complex, intuitive and logical, and is based on five key principles: (1) strength of womanhood, (2) a core of spirituality, (3) foundation of home, (4) living and leading within and beyond your skin, and (5) paying it forward.

Strength of Womanhood

The first principle of the model—strength of womanhood—is illuminated in each of the narratives we present in this chapter. The women's strength is evidenced in their compassionate demeanor and professional dress. It also is revealed in their "can do" attitude, commitment to helping and mentoring others, determination to work with teachers to create challenging learning activities, and tireless efforts to mother and nurture their students. Strength and resilience are fundamental constructs of Black feminist theories. In our study of the four narratives, we found three interlocking constructs that best define this principle of strength of womanhood. The first is disposition. We viewed this as a combination of emotional, intellectual, and moral qualities focused on creating socially just and culturally appropriate learning environments. What distinguishes these particular Black women school leaders from other school leaders is that they explicitly, through their communications with others, command respect for this mission. Collins (2000) supported our finding, stating. "The emphasis that Black feminist thinkers have placed on respect illustrates the significance of self-valuation. In a society in which one is obligated to respect African-American women, we have long admonished one another to have self-respect and to demand the respect of others" (p. 115).

The second construct defines the Black women school leaders as nurturing *and* professional. In particular, it explains their effort to dress professionally, to develop and maintain a physical aura of confidence, and to work hard to listen and respond to others in both appropriate and helpful ways. The stories we share indicate how these women often had to appear decisive and "in control" during times of turmoil when even they felt weary and confused. In addition, the women shared their ongoing efforts to rewrite the ways in which Black women have been stereotyped. hooks's (1981) examination of Black women in the workforce revealed the stereotypical images of these women: "The stereotypical image of the black woman as strong and powerful so dominates the consciousness of most Americans that even if a black woman is clearly conforming to sexist notions of femininity and passivity she may be characterized as tough, domineering, and strong" (p. 83).

The third construct of this principle is hard work. In each of the stories, we marvel at the 110% effort the school leaders gave to the form, meaning, and culture of their schools. The women talked about this giving as a natural part of who they are and what they share with generations of Black women. All called this their mothering nature. Collins (1991) asserted, "Within African-American communities, women's innovative and practical approaches to mothering under oppressive conditions often bring power and recognition" (p. 133).

A Core of Spirituality

There has been much thought and writing to the effect that, until the end of slavery, many Blacks clung to religion because they had no other means of normal outward expression (Pipes, 1997). Therefore, the church and church community remain an important construct in the anchor of this principle of wholistic visioning. Spirituality is the appeal to a higher power, the reverence and respect for a higher being, by whatever name. According to Hill (1971), spirituality is one of the most distinctive features of African American culture. Among African Americans, after the family, the church has been the strongest institution and continues to be one of the anchors of the Black community today (Sudarkasa, 1997). What we found across all four of the narratives was that it was a spiritual core, which many linked to a church community, that helped to sustain these school leaders. Including the spiritual as a construct was inevitable, because the church, the family, and the school are the three most critical institutions whose interactions have been responsible for the viability of the African American community (Roberts, 1980).

Anchoring spirituality are the feelings of peace, care, and commitment that arise from one's belief in a higher being. This was revealed when the women talked about their religious upbringing as well as their ongoing search to get in touch with their own spirit and soul and to be at peace. The theme also was evident when they talked about the children and families whom they served. For example, Sally Walker (one woman's narrative presented in this chapter) shared her search to get in touch with her own spirit or soul:

> I've learned to become a leader through reflective thought and thinking, spending time alone, retreating, and spending lots of time on the inside. Knowing who you are, what you stand for, how you're wired, and what you're all about and then celebrating it. (Interview, Sally Walker)

The women clearly related that their efforts to sustain a grounding source of inner strength was not easy in light of their highly stressful jobs, but that it was essential to gaining a solid sense of peace. Sally Walker shared:

> With those high and enhanced standards, then we've got to be mindful of taking good care of ourselves. The care-taking piece is a formidable challenge. I put in long hours. I think that some time should be private time, time for doing what's necessary so that when you return you're going to be in the best form. So taking care of us, eating right, proper diet, getting the exercise that you need and doing everything that you need to do [is imperative]. (Interview, Sally Walker)

Whereas each of the women found a different degree of peace or centeredness, the importance of spirituality as a means to attain this balance was clearly present.

The Foundation of Home

The Black women administrators we interviewed had a strong sense of commitment and dedication to both their biological/extended and school–community families. Again, they defined their dedication and connection as a form of mothering. Collins (2000) defined a Black woman's perspective on mothering as follows: "The institution of Black motherhood consists of a series of constantly renegotiated relationships that African-American women experience with one another, with Black children, with the larger African-American community, and with self" (p. 176). Furthermore, she wrote: "Even when relationships were not between kin or fictive kin, African-American community norms traditionally were such that neighbors cared for one another's children" (p. 179). This support was evident in the numerous activities in which each of the women engaged that embraced and included many participants in the work of the school, the school community, and community school services.

Lomotey (1993) identified three qualities shared by some Black principals in predominantly Black schools. These qualities included commitment to the education of all students, confidence in the ability of all students to learn, and compassion for and understanding of all students and the communities in which they live. Lomotey (1989) also claimed that principals "are responsible for all functions that take place in and around the school. . . . Principals are the main link between the school and the community" (p. 145). The women in our study took this to heart and made the school a significant part of home by working hard to create a safe and mutually respectful environment that included the students, families, staff/teachers, and community partners in the real work of learning and teaching.

Living and Leading Within and Beyond Your Skin

Some of the women we interviewed experienced complex and difficult challenges due to their skin shade/color or personal appearance. According to Tatum (1997), "The concept of identity is a complex one, shaped by individual characteristics, family dynamics, historical factors, and social and political contexts" (p. 18). After asking "Who am I?" Tatum declared, "The answer depends in large part on who the world around me says I am. Who do my parents say I am? Who do my peers say I am? What message is reflected back to me in the faces and voices of my teachers, my neighbors, store clerks?" (p. 18). Similarly, the Black women we worked with were concerned with maintaining as well as transforming and recreating their images of color and appearance.

In the book *The Color Complex*, Russell, Wilson, and Hall (1992) wrote:

> Intraracial color discrimination is an embarrassing and controversial subject for African Americans. While many prefer not to discuss it, especially in the company of Whites, others contend that skin color bias no longer exists—that it's history, water over the dam. Yet beneath a surface appearance of Black solidarity lies a matrix of attitudes about skin color and features in which color, not character, establishes friendships; degree of lightness, not expertise, influences hiring; and complexion, not talent, dictates casting for television and film. (p. 1)

Russell et al. invited readers to "delve a little deeper, and you will find a reservoir of guilt and anger that threatens to overflow, exposing the African-American truth—that skin color still matters" (p. 1). They contended:

> Being Black affects the way a person walks and talks, his or her values, culture, and history, how that person relates to others and how they relate to him or her. It is governed by one's early social experience, and history and politics, conscious input and labeling and the genetic accident that dictates external appearance. Skin color appears to affect identity, but in complex and seemingly unpredictable ways. (p. 62)

We grappled with this theme as researchers, practitioners, and women of color over several months. Sabrina explained her view of this theme:

> As a woman of color, I must live and lead within my own skin. The color of my skin brings experiences that have shaped my life. Some of the injustices that I

have experienced are a result of the skin I am in, and have caused my brown skin to illuminate strength, courage, endurance, and perseverance. Although my skin is a magnificent shade of brown that illuminates femininity, it is also able to withstand the struggles that go along with it. Therefore, I use those experiences to assist me in this battle for justice/equity. I am constantly forced to prove myself professionally and socially. In order to do that, I must be the best, do my best, and exceed the expectations of others to be acknowledged and respected.

Our discussion of this theme was further deepened with Renée's perspective:

I grew up in the mid-sixties as a member of a family that was well known throughout the surrounding communities as activists for social justice. I remember marching in protest of inhuman treatment of Native Americans, American Indians, as a youngster. I remember participating in a rally organized by my brother denouncing police brutality against minorities. I remember the worried look on my mom's face as she waited to hear word about my brother and my cousin as they attempted to integrate a local eating establishment or later as two cousins integrated the public library. I carry those memories with me.

I live and lead within my skin because I have no choice. As a professional and like many other women of color, I'm often "the first" and often still "the only" one at the table in many settings. Living and leading in my own skin means I must be as comfortable as one can be in those situations. Living and leading within my own skin means I remember that the struggle for social justice is not about me as an individual but about all women and people of color as a collective group. I'm simply one member that has a part to play.

Paying It Forward

The concept of "paying it forward" is not a new one, especially in the African American community. Sabrina shared:

My mother, Mary Bowden Smith, and father, Saborn Isadore Smith, instilled in me the importance of helping others. I remember my mother often saying to me, "Sabrina, don't forget where you came from. Don't forget to look back and pull someone else up with you." I know that my accomplishments are a result of someone looking back and pulling me up with them, and I must continue this tradition. Therefore, I vowed to instill this sense of urgency to "pay it forward" in both of my sons, Jon Maurice Campbell, Jr. and Saborn Isadore Campbell. It is essential that African Americans, regardless of gender, continue this legacy of commitment. Although this is my responsibility, it also is rewarding to "pay it forward."

The Black women school leaders we interviewed received motivation and encouragement from their nuclear families, extended families, and the communities their schools served. As a result of receiving encouragement from a large community of people, they worked diligently to give back to others. They felt compelled to reciprocate. According to Black feminist literature, women helping other women encourages sisterhood. For instance, Collins (1990) explained, "Black women's centrality in families, churches, and other community organizations allows us to share our concrete knowledge of what it takes to be self-defined Black women with younger, less experienced sisters" (p. 211). Therefore, this sense of paying it forward was constantly in motion among their families, colleagues, staff, students, and school communities. As a result, reciprocity had become a standard and expectation. What we heard from students and teachers was that they, too, were being challenged to "pay it forward."

Renée shared her views on this theme:

> Countless persons have had an impact either overtly or covertly on my educational and professional development. There were persons along this journey who saw potential and strengths in me that I was not yet able to see. As a woman of color, I have a moral obligation to "give back" or "pay it forward." Just as I stand on the shoulders of many other persons, I have an obligation to provide a platform on which other women and persons of color can stand. As a college administrator who received her Ph.D. fairly recently, I've made it a personal mission of mine to help at least 10 other women receive their Ph.D. My support of these women comes in different forms, serving as cheerleader, linking them with appropriate resources, or helping them determine how to best navigate the system based on their particular circumstances.

Four Narratives That Illuminate Wholistic Visioning

To better understand the model of wholistic visioning, we share the leadership vignettes of Ballet, Religious, Mary Mack, and Sally Walker (pseudonyms) in both the voice of the interviewer as well as the voice of the interviewee. The interviewer begins, sharing with the reader some contextual information about her interview, the interviewee, and why a particular pseudonym was used. So as not to mediate the power of each individual's spoken word, the remainder of the narrative that focuses on leadership and social justice is presented in the actual words (voice) of the women interviewed. (See endnote for information regarding our methodological approach.[4])

The Story of Ballet

> "As public educators we need to find out who we are and where we want to go. School systems have got to do this, or we are going to lose this battle." *(Ballet)*

When I think of ballet, I envision a graceful woman dressed in a pastel-pink leotard accented by an ornate wrap skirt and wearing satin pointed shoes with satin ribbons that encircle her feet and ankles. This dancer has an erect posture and holds her head high with confidence. Her movements convey the illusion of weightlessness as she performs. The ballerina's technique has been refined over decades to create an ideal of beauty. As I think of this form of dance, I immediately picture the soft-spoken, graceful principal I interviewed over several months. I gave her the pseudonym Ballet because, "respectful of tradition, ballet is also daring, ambitious, as restless as the culture from which it springs" (Jonas, 1992, p. 134). In addition, in the most challenging of times she continued to find beauty in the struggle and found creative ways to overcome limitations. Indeed, as Jonas (1992) wrote in his description of the art of ballet, this principal's personal and professional stories revealed how she rose above constraints, leaving a "clear imprint of . . . improbable triumphs in the mind of the beholder" (p. 134).

Ballet, like the form of dance, began to refine her leadership skills and work for social justice through youth leadership and advocacy opportunities. She explained that she believed she was a "born leader" and had always been that "leader child." The youngest of seven children of Tennessee farmers, she grew up valuing education and hard work. Ballet told several stories of how she championed various student causes, ranging from what they read in classes to choices of extracurricular activities. She said she had realized early in her life that it was important to speak out for equity. After college, she took a teaching position in her hometown. She also worked as a student service assistant and an assistant principal while she raised her two children. Ballet later moved to her current school district and took the position of middle school principal there. She said of her middle school experience:

> I would say middle school is more demanding than elementary and high school because a middle school child has to have good knowledge and a physiological base. [Middle school] is a very difficult area to put together. I have worked at the elementary, high school, and college levels. It is more difficult to work at this level, but it is what I want to do. My brother tells me that I am crazy, but I think it takes a special person to be in the middle school. You have to have the right skill to get the right staff to work with the middle school kids and to be patient. This is the age when they are really developing emotionally and physically. I don't think we helped ourselves when we moved ninth graders and put them into high school. I think we lose more kids than what people think. They are not ready for a high school mind-set. The adults want them to come already mature and independent, but they are not ready. That's why we lose them. (Interview, Ballet)

Leadership: Ballet in "Her Own Voice". My role models have always been people who I thought were concerned about children and who were focused on what schools should be about. I remember my high school principal being about business. I also remember receiving advice from other role models while I was in college. They encouraged me to take on various leadership roles. As I took on those leadership positions, I enjoyed them more and more. As a result of those leadership experiences, I knew that being an educational leader was my calling.

I would say the person who helped me the most in becoming an educational leader was a principal I worked with for a long time. I first worked with him as a student services coordinator. I think he did more to help me firm up how to be effective than anyone else did. We really did wonders together because he was an excellent principal and I had the other side of it, which was the people side. We balanced each other. That helped me find exactly where I felt I needed to be. He would always tell me I spent too much time with one child. He would tell me that I had to process them and get them out. But that wasn't me. I wanted to work the problems through. I wanted the change to occur within the child. After working with student services, I became his assistant principal for 12 years. That experience helped me know what I wanted to do and how to do it effectively.

There are things that impede but don't stop me. I'll find a way to get done what I know needs to be done for the children. Certainly there is the need to get it done faster and quicker. Sometimes you have to take a step back and say, "Okay, how do I get this done? A roadblock has been thrown. This needs to be done." So you work it through. I don't care where you are, something or someone will try to get in the way of progress, but you can't let it.

I studied school law because, as a principal, I wanted to be knowledgeable about educational laws. You'd better know the law because, if you don't, you can make a major mistake that you could regret or end up taking up all of your time trying to work your way out of it. In fact, I know all of the laws that are coming from the state. I don't like them, but I know them. For instance, I had to know the recent school code because I have to stay abreast in order to work with the mind-set of the law and yet realize that I am dealing with children. The one piece of the middle school program that bothers me is expulsion. Schools are expelling kids for normal situations, so I read the law and look at the situation. I assess how I can help the child or the parents and still uphold the law. It is a fine line. It is easy to kick a kid out of school, but I can't always do that.

We operate as a full staff. Topics are brainstormed by the staff. For instance, the school improvement team makes recommendations on different issues and then it goes to the staff for their stamp of approval. From there, change begins to happen with those people who want to move it. They want their students to be great, so they get the movement going. I don't mind sharing my power; I don't have to be a part of everything. I give them the power to take something and run with it. I think that is why I am successful—because I can trust people to do a job and get it done. I am a monitor; I know how to do that and not be dictatorial.

Social Justice: Ballet in "Her Own Voice". An example of my work is when I developed a student-involvement program for White and Black students to become more involved so they wouldn't be at each other's throats. I got federal funding to continue that program and chose to work with the most difficult school. The school was dealing with racial issues because it had been an all-White school and then they started busing Blacks into that school. So I went into that school along with my colleagues and put the school together so that [White and Black kids] could learn together. I got kids involved and had them make decisions about different issues in their school. I did that until they merged two middle schools and the funding ran out.

Another example of how I deal with a roadblock is a situation that occurred recently when I was trying to keep our library clerk. Some schools decided to cut their libraries and library clerks out of their site base. The contract with the library clerks says the person who is cut can bump somebody else. So, my excellent librarian was about to be bumped out by a person that was pretty incompetent [and whose] technology skills were not good. The library is going high tech this year! I have been fighting this roadblock to our students' learning because the [district] administration is going to let it happen. I had to leap some hurdles and say, "No, I am not going to accept this person." I even called this person and said, "I don't know you and you don't know me, but I have this person that I want in my building." It is something that shouldn't happen. If I see the need to keep a staff member who can move my school forward, there shouldn't be a way that somebody else can just bump them. The one thing middle schools need is stability.

I have noticed, since I've been in education (33 years), that the White schools always get much more, but this hasn't stopped us from doing all that we can for the kids. Learning and teaching don't always take money. I can teach math with or without a computer. You do with what you have and you work at getting those things you want to have for your children.

The Story of Religious

> "Dear Lord, I know that you are anointing me. Through Your presence I can do Your work with Your arms around me." *(Religious)*

I immediately knew that the metaphor of a religious movement best fit this particular school principal. Our initial meeting consisted of quoting the Bible, giving praise to God, and praying together. I was touched by her compassion when I told her we would have to reschedule our next interview because my uncle had died. She immediately clasped my hands and asked if we could pray for my family. As we held hands and prayed, a warm feeling of comfort came to rest in my heart. With tears in my eyes, I thanked Religious for her compassion. I gave the pseudonym of Religious to this particular principal because, as Jonas (1992) described, with this form of dance, "the initiate (who has undergone a long period of instruction and training) dances to invite a particular god to visit the world of the living" (p. 37). It was clear to me that spirituality guided her work to achieve justice.

Religious grew up in the Midwest, the middle child in a single-parent, working-class family. Her mother exemplified qualities of perseverance, strength of womanhood, and hard work. Religious explained that her mother had worked two jobs to support their family and at the same time attended college courses. Education and hard work were priorities in her home. These lessons had been important in Religious' life, especially over the course of her 20 years in K–12 schools. She had been a classroom teacher, a social services liaison/worker, and both an assistant and a deputy principal. The stories Religious shared about her professional life always began with gratitude for her family and her spiritual foundation. In fact, she shared that it was her strong family roots, her passion for learning, and her belief in God that had helped her through her husband's passing and her acceptance of a school principal's position only a week after his death.

Leadership: Religious in "Her Own Voice".   I am so tired of hearing people blame the children for their lack of success when we, as adults, are in total control of the situation. Kids react to their circumstances. They react to the way they are treated. I know that the "kid" teachers are talking about is the one from a single-parent home, the kid whose father is not in his [her] life. I was that kid teachers talk about, and I am offended by that. Although they may not be talking about my mother specifically, they are talking about mothers who are in a similar situation, that is, on welfare. That is why I always look out for the kid teachers talk about. I say, "Don't talk about my kids. You don't know which one will be the next Dr. Martin Luther King, Jr., the next Bill Clinton, the next Carl Sagan, or the one who will discover a cure for cancer. If you don't know who these kids are, you have no right to talk about them or not teach them. You have no right to keep them from fulfilling their potential."

The principal of the high school where I taught became my mentor for administration. I had no idea or desire to be a principal, but she had approached me and asked whether I was interested in administration. I told her I was, but I knew how it worked—it's who you know and not what you know. She didn't say anything to me for about a month, and then she came back again. This time, instead of asking me if I wanted to be an administrator, she said she had noticed some things about me that would make me a good leader. She explained that she had watched teachers, students, and parents come to me, and she'd observed my involvement and that I should think about administration. However, although she encouraged my pursuit, she said, "I must tell you that if you do pursue administration, you're going to have to take out those braids [in your hair]." When I asked why, she explained that the administrators in that district were quite conservative and that "braids are considered militant." I said, "Well, I am militant!"

When I discussed my concerns with my husband, he didn't understand what the fuss was about. I explained that I just wanted to be me, and by telling me that I must wear my hair a certain way, she was telling me that I must look like a White woman to do my job. My hair is not naturally straight, and an Afro is not militant, nor are braids. But then I realized that it was about getting in, getting that first job. So three weeks after I got my first administrative position, I had my braids back. The next time the principal saw me, she just looked at me in disbelief. As a matter of fact, after I got the braids, I started seeing more and more Black women throughout the district wearing braids. I think it was just a matter of somebody taking the first step.

I think that all leaders must have their own vision and must observe what other middle schools are doing. It's not all about the test; it's about other measures that I am interested in. I want to be able to network with people to get more resources to bring something to the kids. One of my bosses who called just a moment ago said, "It's all about her babies. She's always looking out for her babies." And I said, "I sure am. It's all about these babies."

Social Justice: Religious in "Her Own Voice".   When I think of what social justice in an organization looks like, I think of equal opportunity. It means that everyone has an equal opportunity. So the more talent you have, the more you can use. If I had to envision something, I would envision the United Nations as an example of social justice. In the United Nations, diversity is there first. Not just racial diversity, but economic diversity, educational diversity, diverse ways of thinking, and even the way people were educated—whether it is public, private, parochial, or boarding school. I see a welcoming environment for people who are different, including people who are handicapped. It is a utopian world that I see, but I know that can happen.

In terms of equal opportunity, I talk to my staff about equity and equal opportunity, and I tell them not to do anything to or for "these kids" [primarily African American] that they would not do to or for their own kids. I had one teacher who told the students to memorize the presidents for their final exam. He thought he would give them a "break" because they had been working hard all year. I said, "Excuse me! List the presidents?" I asked him, "If your child came home and said, 'Look, Dad, I only have to know the presidents of the United States for my final exam.' What would your reaction be?" The teacher said he would want his son to be challenged. So I told him that his "easy" exam wouldn't happen anymore. I think children should be challenged and should not be treated differently.

I had another instance with three counselors, two Black and one White, who doubted whether my children could succeed. So, I asked them, "Do you believe these children can learn?" One started to say, "Well. . . ." I said, "No, no, no. All I want is a yes or no." One counselor said, "I have to qualify something first." I immediately said, "No, you don't have to qualify anything. Yes or no?" One of the counselors said, "No." I told her, "I don't need you to work for me because if you don't believe these children can learn, considering the many variables and circumstances in their home lives, then you don't need to be working with my children. We may not be able to change their home lives, but what we can deal with for the eight hours that we have the kids is where we can move them both academically and emotionally." Now that just about knocked them out of their chairs.

This is my whole message: You have to believe in each child. It does not make sense to just talk about "those children." We must make things happen. I need teachers to go outside of the classroom and connect to the students' world. Students are so much more sophisticated than adults realize. Those are some of the things that I have to help my teachers see and do with our kids.

The Story of Mary Mack

"We can't continue to limit ourselves to trying to serve only majority/minority publics. Every kid in America needs to see us." (*Mary Mack*)

Mary Mack, a 59-year-old Black woman, was born the second child of three in Los Angeles, California. Both her parents died when she was young, her dad when she was three and her mom when she was five; subsequently, her grandparents raised her and her brother (family friends raised their sister). This meant a move from California to Little Rock, Arkansas. To Mary Mack, the two places were worlds apart. Her grandparents constantly reminded her and her brother of the importance of education, as did an uncle and aunt who took a special interest in the informal education that she and her brother received. They constantly exposed her to varied activities and provided experiences (i.e., plays, theater, sports, and so on) that would broaden her cultural horizons.

Mary Mack was raised in an environment with many extended family members. She described her close-knit family as working class with middle-class attitudes and values. Her father had been an automobile mechanic and her mother a homemaker. Her grandfather was a custodian and her grandmother did other people's laundry. She described her grandfather as a very proud person who always dressed immaculately. Mary Mack shared with pride that he would leave home every morning wearing a three-piece suit, white shirt, and tie. He would change into his work clothes to clean the building, and when he was finished he would change back into his suit, white shirt, and tie.

Leadership: Mary Mack in "Her Own Voice".   I see myself as a collaborative, engaged leader, one who rolls up her sleeves and doesn't mind getting dirty. There are no tasks that I wouldn't do. I've gone into situations and people have said, "What are you doing? You don't need to do that." I would say that it has to be done, so let's do it. I will do anything from moving chairs to stuffing envelopes. I can't separate the real work from what some people view as what I do.

I believe that we as educational leaders must ensure that all of our students are educated, self-directed, and productive members of society. To accomplish this, educational leaders must garner support for the mission of schooling. Educational leaders are in the classroom and in the community, as well as in central office and on school boards. I believe that youngsters should come out of school able to go into some field of work or to enter college. It's their decision, but they're prepared for either one. And it's not done just when they're in eighth grade, ninth grade, or tenth grade. It's just done throughout. They must leave school knowing that they have a choice, that they have all the necessary prerequisites. I always tell my students that I want an "A" student to be my plumber or the contractor who's going to build my house. I don't want a person who was a "D" student, who was just put over there to learn monotonous tasks, but one who has a broader knowledge. I don't think we do right by kids to "pigeonhole" them so early.

I think that Black women educational leaders' major challenge is to be heard and respected for what we know and our ability to handle tough situations. School boards want to know whether I'll be able to relate to the non-Black population. I'm sure this board [a predominantly White board] sat there and asked, "Can she relate to us?" "Can she relate to other Whites in this community?" Those are appropriate questions for them to ask themselves. Those are clearly fair questions, but they shouldn't be disqualifiers.

Social Justice: Mary Mack in "Her Own Voice". As I think of my life experiences that have fueled my passion to work for fairness and equity, a lot of instances or experiences that I've encountered come to mind. When I was in third grade, I realized I had read everything that was appropriate for me to read at the "Colored branch" of the public library. There were no more books for me to read. The librarian constantly made lists [of books] for me to go to pick up at the "main library." I couldn't go in and browse and "pick out books." I could just "pick them up." I thought that this was just the worst thing that could happen to me.

Another experience I recall is when I came home one day to find Daisy Bates in my kitchen asking my grandmother whether I could participate with a group of students trying to integrate Central High School. At a time when other parents or grandparents may have quickly said, "No, it's too risky, it's too dangerous," my grandmother said that it was up to me. At age 17, I chose to become a part of a delegation of students who attempted to integrate Central High School and was featured in the January 23, 1956, edition of *Life* magazine with Daisy Bates and the other students. We paved the way for "The Little Rock Nine," who integrated during the very next school year.

And then there was the time I was teaching first grade and the social studies lesson was about community helpers. . . . Every picture in the text was of Whites, while my classroom was full of Hispanic, Asian, and Black students. I went out, found a Black fireman, a Black policeman, a Black airline pilot, and Black flight attendants, took my own pictures of them, and used those pictures to supplement the text. Using the textbook as it was written would be "following the rules." Taking my own pictures, well, that's not following the rules. I don't believe I broke the rules, but I bent them.

The Story of Sally Walker

"I know that each and every person has greatness in them." (Sally Walker)

Sally Walker was 53 years old and in her first year of her second superintendency. She was born the second of five siblings and was raised on a farm in Smyrna, Delaware. Sally described her mother as a homemaker who was "a wonderful seamstress and splendid cook. She made a lot out of just a little, and she knew how to stretch a dollar." Sally's father, 21 years older than her mother, was a laborer and also worked their family farm. Life, she said, revolved around school and church. Sally was raised in the Pentecostal Holiness Church, and religious life was very much a component of who they were as a family. Sally stated that if they had a family crest it would comprise three parts: (1) a farm, exemplifying a strong work ethic; (2) books, expressing the family's emphasis on scholarship and learning; and (3) a cross, signifying the importance of religion in their lives. Sally left home to attend Delaware State College on a full academic scholarship.

I remember my first contact with Sally Walker because I was so impressed with her. I received a response from her on the very day that I faxed my initial letter of introduction. What was even more impressive was that the phone call was from Sally Walker herself and not her secretary. Her voice was so soft and easygoing. She said she had received my letter and wanted to respond. She shared, too, that her dissertation also was about African American superintendents. We decided during that phone call to meet for lunch to talk further about my study.

The day of our first meeting, I arrived at the district office. I had to ring a buzzer to be admitted to the building. I waited in the reception area and was surprised when Sally Walker greeted and escorted me to her office. From her soft-spoken voice, I was expecting a petite woman, but Sally Walker is tall and statuesque. I was impressed by her brightly decorated office. She asked me if I would care for anything to drink. It was as if I were visiting her in her home. Her sense of hospitality was extended to my husband as well. When she found out that he had driven me to the interview, she made arrangements for him to work in her office while she and I went to lunch at a nearby restaurant. I learned many things about leadership and social justice from Sally, as her 22-year career has included work as a teacher, a supervisor, a vice principal, a director, an assistant superintendent, and a superintendent.

Leadership: Sally Walker in "Her Own Voice". I am much more prone to embrace diversity. I am a collaborator. I like to hear many, many voices concerning any and all issues. I think it is important to be an active listener, and I am not threatened by hearing the different voices. I am very democratic in terms of decision making and like participatory leadership. I empower people who are close to the source to make wise judgments. I see my role really as a facilitator to make good things happen for children on behalf of all of our children. I see myself as a servant leader. I am here with that sincere, solid, service orientation. What is it that I can do as an extra set of hands and eyes to make your job a bit easier, not losing sight, of course, of the vision and the overarching aim that we have for this district? So, there is a combination of vision and a good overarching view of where we are headed. At the same time, I have a goodly number of management skills and an orientation that is task oriented, and I have to attribute that to my early background and training. I believe you need to get your work done before you play.

Leadership is the ability to inspire, help others, catch a glimpse of a vision in a place where we are able to collectively be that's greater than where we are. That's my goal for Highland Park, and it's working. People are catching sight and a glimpse in their mind's eye of that future that is greater than where we are right now, and conceptually they have begun to make the shift to higher ground. It is not there for the most part right now, but we are putting the infrastructure pieces in place bit by bit to support us as we make the conceptual journey. They are excited. There is a wonderful sense of intolerance of the status quo.

I believe in children. That's my collective bottom line, and I believe that we're going to be successful in reaching each and every child we have in this district or any district that I lead. As educational leaders we want to empower people so that they can be solid contributors to our society. And how do we do that? First of all, by developing those people and helping them reach a certain level of potential. We know that humankind, even those high achievers, just happen to use such a small percentage of what they're capable of achieving so we use terms like *maximize potential*. We don't ever come near that, even with the superstars of this world. The whole idea is to have that citizenship and economic infusion perspective. Let's make certain that we shatter any chains that are holding us back from achieving the kind of victory that we know people are capable of accomplishing in all aspects of their lives.

Educational leadership is the ability to inspire, to galvanize, to mobilize, and to help bring a critical mass of people together and then the ability to sustain that level of energy and commitment toward a common and well-defined goal. I think that that's pretty much the essence of leadership. A companion piece would indeed be modeling what it is that you're preaching and being a lead learner. You can't lead anybody if you're not sure where it is that you're going. You can't be hazy. You've got to have clear, clear parameters by which folk realize the path, the course that you'll take to get from where you are to where a group of people would be capable of going.

Social Justice: Sally Walker in "Her Own Voice".   When I was in college, the civil rights movement gave the perspective that Black is beautiful, and I was very much involved in a number of speakers coming to our campus. I participated in a number of demonstrations, and one of the demonstrations led to the closing of school early one year. No one could believe that someone as responsible and serious as I would participate in student demonstrations, but I was always of the opinion that if you had firm and definite convictions about something, it was important to step forward and take that stand for what you believe in, and I guess I have always been that way.

Living in this world, each individual needs to have an opportunity to experience a level of success that is not constrained by forces that would be counter to having them realize the success that they are destined for and capable of achieving. The success would be multifaceted in all aspects of one's life. People should achieve the attainables. Students should be able to achieve those things that they very much want to attain in life.

I think for this community, shattering the chains of poverty and somehow attacking the culture of poverty head on can bring about social change. There are some wonderful works that I read in the seventies [that] dealt with culture and poverty and how you can shatter and break through. I think my life is a testament to how powerful that breakthrough can be for people who, for whatever reason, are born into circumstances that were far less than ideal. The educational piece is key. In terms of mobilizing people, I think you are able to do that by your sheer presence, role modeling, and example of professionalism. I have been speaking with a new and added dimension of conviction. I think of it as that force that is beyond me. I have been able to tap into it, and it has been just marvelous for me to witness that unveiling.

Social justice is fairness, fair play, everyone operating on a certain code of ethical conduct and standards and actually following up and being consistent in terms of candor, frankness, and treating the other person as you'd like to be treated. Social justice would indicate many of the principles under which our country was founded. It would echo the Constitution and the Bill of Rights. It would echo so many of those things that are just a little elusive. Yes, we've made wonderful strides and tremendous inroads and we need to celebrate our quantum leaps, but some of the shortfalls have been well written and documented. We know that we have no ideal world, but we're all very much focused and striving to take the next step, and the next step.

What We Learned from the Narratives

We wrestled with the meaning of these stories and how they illuminated the key concepts of our wholistic visioning model. As we unpacked each narrative, we noted five key elements: (1) skin color, gender, and class do make a difference; (2) privilege through affiliation with a particular group is rarely a commodity of Black women school leaders; (3) spirituality illuminates the core of a Black woman's work for social justice; (4) creativity, courage, and compassion appear to be the "3 C's" (instead of caring, concern, connection) for Black women constructing socially just learning environments; and (5) the power of articulating a vision for learning and teaching, one that is socially just, in a dominant culture engages and empowers "other" voices that are not often heard. The women, however, taught us much more about the essence, the soul, of social justice. A brief synopsis of our discussion provides the best illumination of how we each individually and collectively made sense of what we had learned:

Maenette: Beyond and perhaps much deeper than these universal conclusions, we have learned much more about ourselves—that is, who we are as women of color, scholars, teachers, and educational leaders. When I work with passionate women like Renée and Sabrina, I feel connected to the soul, the spirit of what we do as scholars and educators. Their stories of resiliency are powerful reminders of the work that still needs to be done to create just and engaged communities of learning. The momentum is palpable. I know that I have learned to be a better mentor, scholar, and friend.

Sabrina: I have learned through my experiences as a doctoral student, a practitioner, and a researcher/author that I do not walk alone in my experiences. Although the path I have chosen may be different from that of people around me, my journey is similar to others' who have traveled before me. I am faced with challenges that have made me better able to overcome obstacles of oppression. Yet, I am charged with finding solutions to make the journey easier for those who come after me. As I look at this charge, this is what my colleagues have been doing, but in diverse ways. And yet, we continue to strive to create a sense of hope for the future.

"Paying it forward" is not merely an option. It is my responsibility as a Christian, as a woman, and as a Christian African American woman. All of these characteristics make it impossible for me to forget my responsibilities to help others who are experiencing the injustices of race, class, and/or gender. Every African American woman has experienced these injustices at several points along her journey and has persevered because of the help she received along the way. Regardless of the ethnicity or gender of the persons from whom they received assistance, it must be reciprocated and paid forward. In fact, the only way to be successful is to "pay it forward." You can't forget from whence you came and who helped you along the way.

Renée: As a Black woman with several years of administrative experience, I came to this research with the perspective of a Black woman school leader. My professional, personal, and academic experiences have shaped my perspective, and thus determine how I view the world. I have learned how much my own earlier interactions with and impressions of Black women leaders in my life influenced my own leadership style. I think back to that first Black teacher, Mrs. Smith, that I had in first grade and Mrs. Ann Sanders, my second grade teacher. In addition, within my church were many other respected Black women school leaders. Forty years later I remember and can vividly reflect on their expressions of leadership and their gentle yet forceful struggle for social justice.

Having grown up surrounded by these women, as well as the influence of my mom, who was also a community leader, I realize how much these earlier experiences influence how I lead and fight for social justice. I realize how my observations of their navigation of the educational landscape during the aftermath of segregation still influence the leader I am becoming. I have the responsibility to remember the struggles and successes of those Black women leaders who blazed the trail for me, but equally important, I must keep in the forefront that I'm responsible for keeping the path clear for those women leaders who follow me.

Conclusion

In our minds and in our hearts, we understand that the philosophy of our knowledge about leadership for social justice is deeply affected by the culture, context, and content of our lives. We began to understand that working for social justice means that one needs to have the courage to step out of a system that contributes to inequality and to chart a new course. In addition, for us as cultural people, because we have distinct ideas on learning, it is important for us to think and talk about what this means, and what's worth knowing and doing. Although this appears, on its face, to be a difficult step, we learned that it is really the easiest. Because for us as author/researchers and for the women we interviewed, telling the truth about justice is the most pure action in our professional and scholarly work.

Discussion Questions and Activities

1. **Seeing Beyond the Story**. You will need a sheet of notepaper. Divide the paper in half. On one side of the paper write "cognitive" and on the other "affective." As you read the narratives presented in this chapter, jot down words and/or draw pictures that describe how you "feel" or are "moved" by the story on the affective side of the paper. On the cognitive side of the paper, jot down words and/or pictures that might explain how the women lead. This activity is best done within the context of leadership study or after students have read a cluster of books presented in the list of annotated readings or the references. Students should be invited to share their affective notes with others; this may lead to more stories. Discussion that emerges from the cognitive notes could lead to deeper discussion of philosophical concepts presented by the chapter or by other authors. Students should be encouraged to define exploratory questions focused on leadership for social justice that might lead to further study.

2. **Know Thyself.** One of the lessons we learned from the women we interviewed is that in order to do this work for social justice one has to "know thyself." There are numerous leadership inventories and self-actualization activities and simulations that an educator can draw on. We take this activity from our interviewing process. In a class or group situation, each person should bring three items that best exemplify who they are as an educational leader working for social justice. *Note:* This activity is best done in a group where initial trust and care has been established and after the group has read several of the texts in our annotated readings list or the references as well as texts on social justice theory (see the references). Several individuals are invited to share how their items define their practice(s) for social justice. The class is then invited to engage the presenters in conversation that seeks to further unpack the individual's meaning of social justice and how that meaning is in fact translated (or not) in their practice. In light of this discussion, presenters are asked to reflect (either orally/publicly or in a written document) on what they are learning about their work for social justice.

3. **Critical Incident.** Again, this suggested activity emerged from our interview process. In the case of our work, a *critical incident* is a description of a situation that has defined or helped a person to define who they are and what they do as an educational leader. Again, this exercise is best done within a larger process that includes readings, discussions, and other experiential activities. First, the participant(s) is asked to identify a critical incident that defines action or advocacy for social justice in which she (or he) has played an intimate role. The participant is then invited to share the critical incident. Discussion of the critical incident can be guided by the following probes: (1) What did you learn from the incident, about yourself, about the school organization, and about issues of difference? (2) What were the tension points in this situation (e.g., structural, policy oriented, authority or power) and how did you handle them or how might they have been handled differently? (3) How did difference (cultural, gender, economic, language, so on) affect the process? (4) In light of this discussion, how might you describe your action and what words of wisdom might you pass on to your peers?

4. **Feminism from Different Vantage Points.** We presented a thumbnail sketch of feminist perspectives. Although we did not include, due to space and the focus of this paper, either Chicana/Mexicana- or Asian American/Asian-derived feminist pedagogies or Native/Indigenous epistemologies, it is clear that there are both differences and similarities across these views. Because we believe that feminist thought provides scholars and practitioners an opportunity to challenge practices that sustain inequities, construct exclusive governing hierarchies, and restrict the inclusion of diverse world views, students should investigate these philosophies further and employ them to explore their own work. To begin your study of these different perspectives, please see the annotated reading list and the references.

5. **Walking in My Shoes.** Students should shadow an administrator of color in an effort to observe and learn about the diverse challenges of race, class, and

gender she or he faces. Students should reflect on their experiences in a journal, synthesize what they are learning, and report to the class. As students share their experiences, they can record similarities and differences on the board, which could then be linked to both conceptual and empirical study. Several texts are available that can help you to better frame this activity, including Benham & Cooper (1998), Casey (1993), and Clandinin & Connelly (1994).

6. **Learning While I Lead**. This activity is not meant to be a "stand-alone" exercise, but should be integrated in an overall process of learning about oneself and educational leadership. This exercise grew out of Renée and Sabrina's own personal learning activities. Both kept a learning journal throughout their dissertation process. Much of our discussions in preparation for this chapter drew from their journals. Students are required to keep a learning journal, a vehicle that provides them with an opportunity to reflect on their own leadership experiences related to social justice issues. Journal entries should have at least two major emphases: (1) They should be oriented toward the development of self as a professional and (2) they should be oriented toward improving practice by forming a link between theory and practice.

Annotated Readings

While we acknowledge the important contributions White feminists have made to gender issues, we maintain that teachers and leaders of social justice must take into account the intersection of race, gender, and social class as a feminist issue. Black feminists have called our attention to these tensions, beginning with bell hooks' many writings, in particular *Teaching to Transgress: Education as the Practice of Freedom* (1994). Concurrently with hooks, Patricia Hill Collins challenges us to rethink the educational experience through a Black feminist lens in *Black Feminist Thought: Knowledge, Consciousness, and the Politics of Empowerment* (1991). What both hooks and Hill-Collins bring to the conversation is the important exploration of the politics of Black feminist thought and its potential impact on creating loving and optimal learning environments.

Annette Henry's (1998) *Taking Back Control: African Canadian Women Teachers' Lives and Practice*, Sara Lawrence-Lightfoot's (1994) *I've Known Rivers: Lives of Loss and Liberation*, Maenette Benham and Joanne Cooper's (1998) *Let My Spirit Soar! Narratives of Diverse Women in School Leadership*, and Kathleen Casey's (1993) *I Answer with My Life: Life Histories of Women Teachers Working for Social Change* are important contributions to the critical stories/narratives of women doing the work of social justice in school. The narratives present portraits of men and women, exploring the contradictions of their perspectives with that of the mainstream. Each story illustrates the hurt and anger, as well as hope and passion, that leads each person to "act" on what is just and fair. Indeed, the need for alternative standpoints and for transformative educational strategies is clearly made.

Knowing the lessons of other's lives can teach us much about doing the work of teaching and leading for social justice. Maurianne Adams, Lee Anne Bell, and Pat Griffin, editors of *Teaching for Diversity and Social Justice: A Sourcebook* (1997), provide a much needed resource. The text provides the practitioner–scholar with thought-provoking and interactive learning experiences grounded on solid pedagogical principles. The text should be read alongside the aforementioned books, which will engage the reader to better understand the meaning of social difference, oppression, and justice in their personal lives and in the social and educational systems.

This is a short list of readings we would offer; however, we strongly recommend that you also review the works we cite in the references.

References

Adams, M., Bell, L., & Griffin, P. (Eds.). (1997). *Teaching for diversity and social justice: A sourcebook*. New York: Routledge.

Allen, P. G. (1986). *The sacred hoop: Recovering the feminine in American Indian tradition*. Boston: Beacon Press.

Anzaldua, G. (1987). *Borderlands, la frontera: The new Mestiza*. San Francisco: Aunt Lute Books.

Astin, H. S., & Leland, C. (1991). *Women of influence, women of vision: A cross-generational study of leaders and social change*. San Francisco: Jossey-Bass.

Banks, C. A. M. (1995). Gender and race as factors in educational leadership. In J. A. Banks & C. A. M. Banks (Eds.), *Handbook of research on multicultural education* (pp. 65–80). New York: Macmillan.

Benham, M. (1997). Silences and serenades: The journey of three ethnic minority women school leaders. *Anthropology and Education Quarterly, 28*(2), 280–307.

Benham, M., & Cooper, J. (1998). *Let my spirit soar! Narratives of diverse women in school leadership*. Thousand Oaks, CA: Corwin Press.

Carr, C. S. (1995). Women as administrators: No longer tokens. *The Delta Kappa Gamma Bulletin, 61*(4), 39–42.

Clandinin, D. J., & Connelly, F. M. (1994). Personal experience methods. In N. K. Denzin & Y. S. Lincoln (Eds.), *Handbook of qualitative research* (pp. 413–427). Thousand Oaks, CA: Sage.

Collins, P. (1989). Towards a new vision: Race, class and gender as categories of analysis and connections (A publication for the *Research Clearinghouse and Curriculum Integration Project Center for Research on Women*.) Memphis, TN: Memphis State University.

Collins, P. (1990). *Black feminist thought: Knowledge, consciousness, and the politics of empowerment*. New York: Routledge.

Collins, P. (1991). *Black feminist thought: Knowledge, consciousness, and the politics of empowerment*. London: HarperCollins Academic.

Collins, P. (1998). *Fighting words: Black women and the search for justice*. Minneapolis: University of Minnesota Press.

Collins, P. (2000). *Black feminist thought: Knowledge, consciousness, and the politics of empowerment* (2nd ed.). New York: Routledge.

Davis, A. (1989). *Women, culture and politics*. New York: Random House.

Dorn, S. M., O'Rourke, C. L., & Papalewis, R. (1997–1998). Women in education: Nine case studies. *National Forum of Educational Administration and Supervision Journal, 14*(2), 13–22.

Grau, A. (2000). *Dance*. New York: Dorling Kindersley.

Griffiths, M. (1998). *Educational research for social justice: Getting off the fence*. Philadelphia: Open University Press.

Grumet, M. (1988). *Bitter milk*. Amherst: University of Massachusetts Press.

Hartsock, C. M. (1983). The feminist standpoint: Developing the ground for a specifically feminist historical materialism. In S. Harding & M. S. Hintikka (Eds.), *Discovering reality: Feminist perspectives on epistemology, metaphysics, methodology, and philosophy of Science* (pp. 283–310). Boston: D. Reidel Publishing.

Henry, A. (1993). There are no safe places: Pedagogy as powerful and dangerous terrain. *Action in Teacher Education, 15*(4), 1–4.

Hill, R. (1971). *The strengths of Black families*. New York: Emerson.

hooks, b. (1981). *Ain't I a woman: Black women and feminism*. Boston: South End Press.

hooks, b. (1989). *Talking back: Thinking feminist, thinking Black*. Boston: South End Press.

hooks, b. (1990). *Yearning: Race, gender, and cultural politics*. Boston: South End Press.

hooks, b. (1994). *Teaching to transgress: Education as the practice of freedom.* New York: Routledge.

Jonas, G. (1992). *Dancing: The pleasure, power, and art of movement.* New York: Henry Abrams.

King, D. K. (1988). Multiple jeopardy, multiple consciousness: The context of a Black feminist ideology. In N. Malson, E. Mudimbe-Boyd, J. O'Barr, & M. Wyer (Eds.), *Black women in America* (pp. 265–296). Chicago: University of Chicago Press.

Lawrence-Lightfoot, S. (1994). *I've known rivers: Lives of loss and liberation.* Reading, MA: Addison-Wesley.

Lomotey, K. (1989). *African-American principals: School leadership and success.* Westport, CT: Greenwood Press.

Lomotey, K. (1993). African-American principals, bureaucrat/administrators and ethnohumanists. *Urban Education, 27*(4), 395–412.

Lomotey, K., & Swanson, A. D. (1989). Urban and rural schools research: Implications for school governance. *Education and Urban Society, 21*(4), 436–454.

Lyman, L. L., Eskildsen, L., Frank, T., Nunn, C., & O'Day, O. (1993). Female principals: Change, credibility, and gender. *Planning and Changing, 24*(1/2), 30–40.

Martin, J. R. (1992). *The schoolhome: Rethinking schools for changing families.* Cambridge, MA: Harvard University Press.

McGregor, D. (1960). *The human side of enterprise.* New York: McGraw-Hill.

Noddings, N. (1992). *The challenge to care in schools.* New York: Teachers College Press.

Pipes, W. H. (1997). Conceptualizations of African American families. In H. P. McAdoo (Ed.), *Black families* (pp. 41–46). Thousand Oaks, CA: Sage Publications.

Rawls, J. (1972). *A theory of justice.* Cambridge, MA: Belknap Press of Harvard University Press.

Rizvi, F. (1998). Some thoughts on contemporary theories of social justice. In B. Atwel, S. Kemmis, & P. Weeks (Eds.), *Partnerships for social justice in education* (pp. 47–56). New York: Routledge.

Roberts, J. D. (1980). *Roots of a Black future: Family and church.* Philadelphia: The Westminster Press.

Ruddick, S. (1989). *Maternal thinking: Toward a politics of peace.* New York: Random House.

Russell, K., Wilson, M., & Hall, R. (1992). *Color complex: The politics of skin color among African-Americans.* New York: Doubleday.

Sadurski, W. (1985). *Giving desert (dessert?) its due: Social justice and legal theory.* Hingham, MA: Kluwer Academic Publishers.

Schmuck, P. (1999). Foreword. In C. C. Brunner (Ed.), *Sacred dreams: Women and the superintendency* (ix–xiii). Albany: SUNY Press.

Shalit, W. (1999). *A return to modesty: Discovering the cost virtue.* New York: The Free Press.

Spelman, E. V. (1982). Theories of race and gender: The erasure of black women. *Quest: A Feminist Quarterly, 5*(4), 36–61.

Sudarkasa, N. (1997). African American families and family values. In H. P. McAdoo (Ed.), *Black families* (3rd ed.). Thousand Oaks, CA: Sage.

Tatum, B. D. (1997). *Why are all the Black kids sitting together in the cafeteria? And other conversations about race.* New York: Basic Books.

Trinh, T. M. (1989). *Woman, Native, other: Writing postcoloniality and feminism.* Bloomington: Indiana University Press.

Endnotes

[1]This chapter is a collaboration that drew from the dissertation work of two students, Renée and Sabrina, and the conceptual guidance of their dissertation chair, Maenette. Renée interviewed six African American women school superintendents. Two are presented in this chapter. Sabrina interviewed six African American women school principals. Two are presented in this chapter.

[2]Thidziambi S. Phendla. 2000. *Musadzi U Fara Lufhanga Ngu Hu Fhiraho: Black Women Elementary School Leaders Creating Socially Just and Equitable Environments in South Africa*. Renee Sanders-Lawson. 2001. *Black Women School Superintendents Leading for Social Justice*. Sabrina Smith-Campbell. 2001. *Exploring the Work of Black Women Middle School Principals*.

[3]For those unfamiliar with the concepts of *typology* and *other*, we briefly explain our use of these ideas in this chapter. *Typology* can be defined as the organization of shared character-istics within a group. An illustration of typology for the purposes of this chapter is women of color tackling the social justice question through their voices and actions. As women of color, many will share common experiences of race, class, gender, stereotypes, and so on. Our use of the "other" describes nondominant individuals and/or groups that have been historically powerless or that have had less power and influence than a dominant group.

[4]*On our narrative approach*: Narrative inquiry focuses on an individual's life story. The researcher explores a story told by the participant and records that story through the con-struction of narrative. This method assumes that people's lives are stories, and the researcher seeks to collect data to describe those lives. Clandinin and Connelly (1994) wrote, "The main claim for the use of narrative in educational research is that humans are storytelling organ-isms who, individually and socially, lead storied lives. The study of narrative, therefore, is the study of the ways humans experience the world" (p. 2). Benham and Cooper (1998) grounded their study of nine diverse women school leaders in narrative inquiry. These scholars consider narratives to be a valuable tool because "They allow us to understand the world in new ways and to help us communicate new ideas of others" (p. 10). Their rationale for using narrative is that "Narrative methods might very well be more responsive to the researcher's and practi-tioner's intent to bring to the surface those experiences that go beyond superficial masks and stereotypes" (p. 7).

Lawrence-Lightfoot's (1994) use of narrative in her research and writing confirms its suitability for this type of study. She argues, "The African-American legacy of story telling in-fuses these narratives and serves as a source of deep resonance between us" (p. 606). She sup-ported her contention that the Black culture is rooted in stories by stating, "A strong and persistent African-American tradition links the process of narrative to discovering and attain-ing identity" (p. 606). It is through narrative that Lawrence-Lightfoot's Black storytellers could reveal their life's journey. She allowed her participants to be active storytellers and considered them "modern day griots, perceptive and courageous narrators of personal and cultural expe-rience" (p. 606) who found storytelling to be a creative process.

4

Educational Leadership Along the U.S.–México Border: Crossing Borders/ Embracing Hybridity/ Building Bridges

Gerardo R. López

Maria Luisa González

Elsy Fierro

"Along this border, there is no fence long enough, wide enough, or high enough to contain the will of the people who reside there.... They are an amalgam of two cultures that interact daily, seemingly unperturbed by a border or its fences. They, and it, are evolving as a culture onto itself with its own sense of place, its own language, and its own vision of the future." (Quiocho et al., 2003, p. 1)

This chapter aims to describe effective school leadership practices in Latina/o-impacted schools and districts along the U.S.–México border. We contend the beliefs and practices we describe herein—socially conscious, politically informed, and change-driven leadership—provide an ontological space for a new politics of educational leadership to emerge. In this discussion, we refer to the border as both a physical location as well as a liminal[1] space where cultures, traditions, and worlds merge, overlap, and intersect to create a new identity and distinct worldview. We utilize both of these meanings to illustrate how effective educational leaders in these contexts transgress and/or cross cultural borders in order to effectively engage the diverse students, parents, teachers, and larger communities who study, live, and work in this region.

As Gloria Anzaldúa (1987) attests, the U.S.–México border is *"una herida abierta,* where the Third World grates against the first and bleeds" (p. 3). What emerges from this "open wound" is a unique creation—a border culture—that divides and demarcates two territories and yet unites and connects these disparate worlds. Vacillation between these entities results in a meztiza/o epistemology[2] and mind-set—an identity formed within and between the interstices of two distinct worlds (see also Bhabha, 1994). In effect, the border is a deterritorialized space: "a rhizome with no beginning or end . . . always in the middle, between things, interbeing, *intermezzo*" (Deleuze & Guattari, 1980/1987, p. 25, emphasis in original). As a metaphor, the border embraces the *intermezzo* as a fluid space where nations, cultures, traditions, and identities clash, collapse, and are born anew. As such, the border embodies epistemological, ontological,[3] and spiritual meaning.

To reside and/or inhabit the borderlands is to be in a constant state of flux and transition. One's identity is *ni de aquí, ni de allá* ("neither from here nor there")—a cultural exile (Said, 1993) who simultaneously resides in two worlds, yet does not exclusively belong to either (see also Delgado Bernal, 1998; Wortham, Murillo, & Hamann, 2002). In effect, individuals who seamlessly cross borders—both real and imagined—embody a borderless or "trans-*frontera*" (Saldivar, 1997) orientation and reside in two worlds at once. This position eludes the politics of polarity and homogeneity, while embracing hybridity, paradox, difference, and interbeing (Johnson & Michaelson, 1997).

From our collective research and experience, we believe effective school leaders who cross cultural borders embody a hybrid leadership style and epistemology that allows them to work across national contexts, as well as a host of other cultural frontiers. To be certain, the borders they navigate on a daily basis engender linguistic, social, economic, generational, political, historical, psychological, physical, and other logistical and/or positional spaces. In the words of Patti Lather (2001), these principals, superintendents, and educational leaders demonstrate they can effectively "work the ruins" of the border, utilizing it as a unique vantage point from which to engage their work. In effect, they do not recognize cultural borders as barriers or limitations, but as sites of possibility, new openings, and unique opportunity; places where new and different leadership styles, cultural forms, organizational values, academic expectations, school traditions, and worldviews live and thrive.

In our opinion, the U.S.–México border provides a unique location for the study of school leadership. Not only do educational leaders in these contexts work with populations that constantly navigate within two or more worlds, but they also work to provide an organizational climate and context where educational success for all students is not only viable, but attainable. In an environment where populations and identities are constantly "in flux," the

Border Leadership Characteristics

"We believe educational leaders who cross cultural borders, engage their work in fundamentally different ways. They are not only socially conscious but politically conscious as well: using their positions and influence to create caring and/or emancipatory spaces for students, parents, teachers, and other constituents in the school organization (Eaker-Rich & Van Galen, 1996; Henry, 1996; Scheurich & Skrla, 2003). Their leadership is progressive, distributive, and change driven (Spillane, Halverson & Diamond, 2001). . . . "

border leader must adapt to new challenges, demands, and sociopolitical realities on both sides of the border.

Indeed, as immigration, family, and economic patterns continue to challenge our cultural topography and national identity (Suarez-Orozco, 1998; Suarez-Orozco & Suarez-Orozco, 2001)—in effect, as the border becomes more commonplace *within* the physical boundaries of the United States—such realities are rapidly becoming the norm rather than the exception. In fact, recent U.S. Census figures demonstrate that cities and states across the nation have witnessed a dramatic shift in their racial, ethnic, and socioeconomic compositions, particularly in recent years (Aponte & Siles, 1994; U.S. Bureau of the Census, 1992, 1996, 2001). The large increase in the Latina/o population alone has prompted social service providers, researchers, and policy makers to rethink traditional approaches to identification, outreach, and delivery of goods and services to this population (Hayes-Bautista, Hurtado, Burciaga Valdez, & Hernández, 1992; Hurtado & García, 1994; Sosa, 1993; Suarez-Orozco & Suarez-Orozco, 2001; Valencia, 1991, 2002). Clearly, what we teach in educational leadership programs is insufficient to adequately prepare leaders to work in this multicultural and politically complex schooling environment (López, 2003; Parker & Shapiro, 1992; Young & Liable, 2000; Young & López, forthcoming).

To be certain, today's educational leaders must interact with a diverse array of constituents—many of whom are from different cultural backgrounds/experiences/traditions and speak languages other than English. In fact, today's school leaders must be able to effectively navigate schools toward increased success and accountability—in addition to having a thorough understanding of race, gender, sexual orientation, disability, class, and other areas of difference and how such factors impact the schooling process for everyone within the organization. In effect, they must have a keen awareness of school–community relations, group dynamics, intercultural tolerance, politics and power, team building, and community engagement and how to effectively bridge these "borders" in order to collectively work toward success. This is why we believe educational leadership can learn a great deal from the actual border and from the border metaphor and/or trope.

FIGURE 4.1 The cheerleaders and audience at a Gear-Up Pep Rally at the University of Texas-Pan American display the rising presence of Hispanics in student populations.

Photo by Maricela Oliva

We believe that educational leaders who cross cultural borders engage their work in fundamentally different ways. They are not only socially conscious, but politically conscious as well, using their positions and influence to create caring and/or emancipatory spaces for students, parents, teachers, and other constituents in the school organization (Eaker-Rich & Van Galen, 1996; Henry, 1996; Scheurich & Skrla, 2003). Their leadership is progressive, distributive, and change driven (Spillane, Halverson, & Diamond, 2001) and is used as a conduit for social justice and school change (Scheurich & Skrla, 2003). They have a heightened sense of political responsibility and constantly engage the broader school community in dialogue about the social, political, and economic systems that surround them (Skrla, Scheurich, García, & Nolly, 2002). In a nutshell, they are social activists as well as educators who seek to challenge and change the world through their praxis.

Therefore, school leaders who cross cultural borders use their leadership for social justice ends, that is, for the good of the school as well as the various communities it serves (Scheurich & Skrla, 2001). Although most educational leaders inherently believe in the value of collaborating with parents and the broader community, those who are particularly effective in their practice firmly believe that the fundamental purpose for engaging the community is not to educate parents, improve test scores, or meet specific accountability criteria, but to mobilize the community—both socially and politically—toward self-empowerment and self-reliance (Hargreaves, 1999). They believe in student, parent, and teacher voice (Mediratta & Fruchter, 2001; Riester, Pursch, & Skrla, 2002), in community engagement and self-sufficiency (Dantley, 1990, 2003), and in the power of naming and addressing difficult issues such as poverty, racism, and discrimination (Hargreaves & Fullan, 1998). In effect, they cross the border between being a leader for the school and being a leader for the community as a whole. In the process, they disrupt the organizational, structural, and social relationships inherent therein.

In this discussion, we will provide a glimpse into the world of a school principal[4] who we think is particularly effective in crossing cultural borders. Not only does this principal (who is a White male) live and work with a low-SES Mexican population along the U.S.–México border, but his actions, grassroots-style organizing, and political involvement also challenge many of the taken-for-granted norms and behaviors of typical school administrators (i.e., detached, bureaucratic, conventional). He has grown to become an advocate for children, as well as a change agent and ally for the community at large. He has taken both personal and professional risks for his border-crossing behavior—transgressing the social norms and expectations for a school leader—and has developed deep, loving and caring relationships with parents, students, and teachers in the process. In short, he has become a symbol of hope and possibility in a sociopolitical climate where hope is often lost and possibility often abandoned (see also Capper, Hafner, & Keyes, 2002; Dantley, 2003; Quantz, Rogers, & Dantley, 1991; Scheurich & Skrla, 2003, for other examples).

Effective Leadership at the Border: An Example

"Schools ... don't know, the big problems that parents are having: how many people are unemployed, how many people are working for poverty wages, how many people have two or three jobs and don't have time to spend with their kids. . . . [I]t seems to me like we need to go into the communities and address some of those issues. Even though our expertise and our major efforts are in the schools, we can't ignore what's going on [in the community] because those are big issues. . . . The children are going to do better if the parents are doing better. But we put blinders on. We don't look at all the issues and we limit ourselves to what's in front of us." *(Phil Jones, telephone interview)*

Phil Jones (a pseudonym) is an extraordinary principal who is deeply committed to changing the lives of students—not only educationally, but in every aspect that impacts their educational success. For Jones, being an educator is more than working with "what's in front of us" (i.e., children devoid of a historical, economic, linguistic, and social context), it also engenders a conscious commitment to recognizing and changing the oppressive living conditions of our most marginalized communities. In other words, rather than taking a passive approach to education and administration, Jones has adopted a more proactive leadership stance: consciously choosing to remove his "blinders" and recognize the multiple needs of the children and families he serves. In the process, he has redefined his own role as a professional educator, as well as the school's role within the larger community.

This process of challenging himself and others to constantly think about issues of social justice has been both spiritually uplifting and professionally taxing. To be certain, it has not been an easy road to tread. In fact, his values, beliefs, and actions (both pedagogical and political) often have been highly unpopular with his colleagues—especially those in positions of power—who are reluctant or unwilling to take on a more advocacy-oriented role within the school. Yet, his determination to bring about school–social change is, in his own words, "well worth the risks."

Jones is the new school principal of East Lake Elementary School. He has worked in multiple schools along the U.S.–México border. When he was assistant principal at Ricardo Elementary, he was the first administrator in his district to seriously consider implementing a two-way bilingual education program at his school. He learned about the program and the innovative approaches to language learning when his district hired a nationally recognized scholar to discuss the program's philosophy and its various benefits.

After meeting with the language and literacy consultant, Jones became deeply interested in issues of bilingual education and sought research articles and other periodicals that specifically focused on the two-way bilingual approach. He quickly learned about the various academic, pedagogical, and interpersonal benefits of this specific instructional strategy. With this strategy, English speakers and non-English speakers are placed in the same classroom, provided with instruction in both languages, and encouraged to reach greater levels of proficiency in both (Christian, Montone, Lindholm, & Carranza, 1997; Lindholm, 1992). Because of the linguistic barriers facing many students in his district, Jones deeply wanted to implement the two-way bilingual program at his school, but his administrative position did not provide him with the flexibility or leverage to do so.

Notwithstanding, when Jones was offered the position as lead principal of the school, he quickly seized the opportunity to implement this approach. Soon after assuming the position, he traveled to California with several of his teachers to visit schools that had successfully implemented the two-way bilingual program. During his visit, he observed the pedagogical practices of effective bilingual teachers, talked with the school leadership and broader community about the program, and interviewed children about their classroom experiences. He returned with a renewed sense of commitment and eagerly shared his "findings" with his staff at Ricardo Elementary. Although Jones had a small cadre of equally committed and enthusiastic teachers, he was not very successful in convincing others about the utility of this approach. In a hopeful attempt to convince his staff, he resorted to a rather savvy influence technique—hiring individuals with similar values and dispositions as his own and letting parents and the larger community view the efficacy of this approach. He states:

> [T]he first year I could not convince the teachers. So [the following year], when I was hiring a kindergarten teacher, I hired a teacher that was willing to begin the two-way bilingual education program. . . . The second year, I was able to hire another teacher for first grade. Once the model was set in place, parents [began to see] the benefits for their children and were asking us to expand [the program]. (Phil Jones, personal interview)

In effect, it was the parents who recognized the value of the bilingual program and began to insist that their children continue at successive grade levels. Interestingly, parents of the *English*-speaking students were the most enthusiastic supporters of the bilingual approach. Not only were they quite vocal in expressing their desire to recruit and hire teachers who were bilingual, but they insisted that the school hire teachers who were specifically trained in the two-way bilingual method. Jones quickly capitalized on these parental demands and used them as a justification for increased professional development for his teachers and staff. Within a short period of time, Jones managed to nurture parental passion into a schoolwide movement in support of bilingual education; parents, students, and teachers from all walks of life recognized and celebrated the multiple benefits of speaking two languages.

In 1995, Jones was ready for a new challenge and accepted the principal's position at Cesar Chavez Language Academy—an elementary school that specifically focused on language development and maintenance. Naturally, parents and teachers at Ricardo Elementary were quite upset that Jones would be leaving and were openly worried that the new leadership would not embrace the culture and climate of bilingualism at the school. In response, Jones insisted that the program was not of his own creation, but was a collective effort to educate all children. He once proclaimed, "I am not the program, you are the program!"—reminding everyone at the school that the success of the bilingual program was not his own, but was a collective result of parents and teachers working together for a common goal. Consequently, Jones worked

"Jones believes that because most schools along the US/México border ignore critical issues of language, they exclude a large number of parents from their school. As a result, many Spanish speaking parents, who live in the community and want to be involved in their children's educational lives, may find that schools are not making a genuine effort to address their needs and concerns."

closely with a transition team of parents and teachers to help mentor and educate the new principal about the importance and centrality of the language program at Ricardo Elementary.

At his new school, Jones continued the tradition of dual-language education, but added a new dimension to his vision: He now wanted all children to develop literacy skills in a third language. His rationale for this decision was that language is, by its very nature, both inclusive and exclusive. The dual-language approach he helped implement at Ricardo Elementary, while certainly important and pedagogically sound, often reproduced social inequities in the classroom. Not only did the English-dominant children have an advantage when instruction was in English, but the Spanish-dominant children were equally privileged when the classroom dynamics were reversed. Phil Jones wanted to create a space where *both* Spanish- and English-dominant children were on an equal footing. With the full support of the district, he and his staff worked vigorously to redesign the language program at Cesar Chavez. Under his new plan, students would receive instruction in the two core languages (English and Spanish), but would also study a third language of their choosing (German, Chinese, Japanese, French, or Russian). For Jones, this third language would serve as a clearing space where power dynamics and social relationships were more equal. Moreover, he worked vigorously in other significant ways to minimize similar social disparities:

> [L]ike most schools, we had a uniform policy . . . If there were kids who couldn't afford clothes, we bought them uniforms, and we would purchase what an average family would have. We wouldn't just give them two shirts we would give them five shirts. And we also had a parent's payment plan [for the uniforms]. Sometimes that only meant five bucks, or it might be that they paid five bucks a month, but they paid off the whole thing. . . . [In other words,] everybody was in the same boat. The kids were on equal status with each other. And the language issue really helped kids not have barriers between them. If you think about it, the English speakers could help the Spanish speakers at times, and the Spanish speakers could help the English speakers at times. And then, they were all in the same boat when it came to Chinese [because neither of them] knew what was going on! (Phil Jones, personal interview)

Not only was language used to leverage power dynamics in the classroom, but Jones also realized the entire school also needed to address and leverage the

language needs of parents and the broader community and take active steps
to remedy this disparity:

> You know, [as educators,] we set up schools with good intentions, especially
> around language. And [yet] we set up programs where English is the only lan-
> guage. There are two languages in border communities on the Mexico–U.S. bor-
> der, there are two cultures and two languages, [but] we ignore the predominant
> language of the community. We exclude these people, and we keep repeating it.
> And we're the "experts" and yet, we keep doing it . . . . I think a pattern in [our
> district] is that the English speaking parents are more confident in school. Of
> course everything [they do in the district] is in English, so the Spanish speak-
> ing parents aren't going to feel as welcome . . . So I tell the teachers: you need
> to value both [languages], so people don't feel like they are in any kind of sys-
> tem that doesn't recognize their language and culture. . . . (Phil Jones, telephone
> interview)

Jones believes that because most schools along the U.S.–México border
ignore critical issues of language, they exclude a large number of parents from
their school. As a result, many Spanish-speaking parents who live in the community and want to be involved in their children's educational lives may find
that schools are not making a genuine effort to address their needs and concerns.

In his quest to search for involvement that is more meaningful to parents, Jones became a member of the Frontera Community Group (pseudonym)—an organization rooted in the philosophy and activism of Saul Alinsky
that is committed to grassroots-level organizing and community empowerment. Deeply moved by the vision and ideals of the Frontera Group, Jones
started to organize the parents and broader community at the Cesar Chavez
Language Academy—including churches and community groups—in an attempt to reconnect schools to their communities and engage them in critical
dialogue about the root causes of student failure and success.

For example, with the guidance of the Frontera Group, parents learned
about issues of power and the importance of institutional relationships to bring
about social change. Through community meetings and school-supported activities, parents at Cesar Chavez began to understand the benefits of collaborative action as well as the importance of confronting and challenging
government and school district officials who represent them in the political
process:

> I have learned many things from being politically involved with [the Frontera
> Group]. The[ir] training changed the way I live and view the inequities so many
> of us accept as a way of life. We all live in the same community. I know that I
> have to change things and I use their training [to help me mobilize others]. I
> can't let things happen anymore . . . I have to challenge the status quo and stir
> things up . . . . [For example], parents have learned how to lobby for after-school
> money. With the help of [the Frontera Group], we prepared them to travel to

[the state capital], to lobby at the state level ... [O]ur parents would get together, get on a plane, go to [the state capital] and actually meet with the legislators, and chase them down the hall and ask them how they were going to vote, and telling them why it was important to have the funding and explain what we were doing at our schools. (Phil Jones, personal interview)

Empowering parents to become politically involved, however, certainly comes with risks. One of those risks is that it upsets and challenges those who are in positions of power—especially those with legislative and/or decision-making power. It is exactly this challenge that once put Jones in direct conflict with his superiors:

That's one of the reasons why I had problems with the past superintendent. ... You see parents from the [Frontera Group] organized and wanted him to make some decisions and he totally disregarded them. So the parents and staff worked on "get out the vote" walks and the board election [results] were affected. The board members supporting the superintendent were replaced. This really upset the superintendent and he asked me to "control" the parents. When I refused, he tried to find ways to get me out of the school. (Phil Jones, personal interview)

Because Jones refused to genuflect to the demands of the superintendent, and because he was now seen as a potential threat to the existing power structure, he was accused of administrative noncompliance and was subsequently reprimanded for general misconduct and professional wrongdoing. This was not only a blatant attempt by the district to defame Jones' character, but was also intended to signal to other building administrators the possible ramifications/consequences of "political" involvement and activity of any kind.

Parents at Cesar Chavez were overwhelmingly supportive of Jones and publicly refuted the district's allegations. Nevertheless, he was voluntarily transferred to East Lake Elementary School. Despite the fact that Jones was initially reluctant to accept the terms of the transfer, he conceded to the move because he was both "physically and emotionally exhausted" (Phil Jones, telephone interview) from having to defend both his political activism as well as his professional reputation. Prior to his transfer, however, Jones spoke with the parents of Cesar Chavez, asking them to stay focused on the real issues in the community and not to be sidetracked with the political maneuverings of the district administration.

Although Jones has politically and professionally recovered from the controversy since his transfer, he still continues to organize parents at his new school and still pushes his faculty/staff to better understand the context and lived reality of their students. He also continues to advocate aggressively for the efficacy of the dual-language program, firmly believing that it is a critical component of intercultural learning and educational success:

I continue to challenge the system. Like the other day at the principals' meeting, we were given test scores and the tendency [of the other principals] was to blame the students who speak Spanish! These schools continue to segregate students in the bilingual education programs. They don't understand the benefits of two-way dual language programs. Everyone should learn about second-language acquisition. Two-way dual language programs benefit all children. (Phil Jones, personal interview)

At East Lake Elementary, Jones is actively implementing a foundation for a two-way dual language program across all grade levels. He also continues his work with the Frontera Group and his search for better ways to engage parents—specifically low-income Spanish-speaking parents—in the political and decision-making process of both the school and the community. As he had done at previous schools, he also continues to open his school's doors to the community, holding meetings at his school and in community centers, as well as hosting "house meetings" in the homes of families and other community leaders:

Instead of just meeting with [parents] and giving out information . . . [we] sit with them and have them share stories around their own education. And then, eventually, we get into the hopes and dreams for their children. That way the classroom teacher is a critical connection to the community's [hopes and dreams]. . . . [O]nce they have these kind of meetings and people open up to each other, and talk to each other, and help each other, they [realize] there are a lot of resources there that can help a teacher. (Phil Jones, telephone interview)

Clearly, Jones' vision of removing his blinders and recognizing the needs of the broader community has not waned despite his political conflicts with the district administration. He firmly believes that when educators build genuine connections between the home and the school and validate the "funds of knowledge" in the larger community—described by Moll (1992) as "cultural practices, bodies of knowledge and information [in] households" (p. 21)—they build true connections and relationships with families; connections that are mutually rewarding and satisfying (see also, González et al., 1995; Moll, Amanti, Neff, & González, 1992; Moll, Vélez-Ibáñez, & Rivera, 1990).

In short, Jones believes that the foundation of a democratic community *begins* with school-driven efforts to authentically engage the community with sensitivity and without prejudgment. By planning effectively and maintaining an ongoing dialogue with his different constituencies, Jones has not only managed to increase the awareness of school staff, but also to connect families with social service providers in the community. Through this relationship-building strategy, families are better supported and empowered with the tools to make a real difference in their own lives. Teachers also are more aware of the needs of the community and are armed with the wisdom that they *can* make a difference in their student's lives:

It is through these types of meetings that we get to know ourselves and the school community which we serve. We hear people's stories and we understand the things people need. . . . I want teachers at my school to help build a sense of community. I believe that . . . through this sense of community, the teachers move away from just teaching the minimum and [begin to] challenge the students, because they have taken the time to get to know the students and their parents and recognize the strengths in the families and out in the community . . . I also explain to teachers that we also have to go out and . . . start talking to [the parents] about the dream of their children attending college. . . . The building of hope and possibility for their child's education is just as important as understanding their needs. Many times we tend to focus on just their needs and never discuss the possibilities for their children's future . . . When you are committed to not only your school, but to your community and improving life in your community, you are asking people to come up and tell their stories and to talk about real life, hard issues, and to get emotional about it. (Phil Jones, telephone interview)

In effect, educators need to remove their proverbial blinders but also be prepared—both emotionally and psychologically—to listen to painful stories of families as well as the "real issues" impacting the community. Although this process certainly is eye-opening, it does place enhanced demands on educators in that it makes them confront and reflect on their own emotions, vulnerabilties, assumptions, and prejudices:

The emotion is what drives a lot of people to want to change things, because they see the parents suffer themselves. [Parents] have a lot of stories to tell, and a lot of hardship. Poverty is hardship. [But] you don't avoid it . . . you don't become detached, and you don't put your blinders on and pretend like you don't see them. You have to learn to listen and ask the probing questions in order to understand the issues . . . And [you need to listen to] their stories, and what their history has been, what their experience has been [in schools], so that we as educators don't just keep repeating it. (Phil Jones, telephone interview)

In this regard, schools need to listen to—and reflect/learn from—community narratives and make changes to their practice so as not to continue reproducing social inequities. In fact, schools need to hold themselves accountable, not to state education agencies or accrediting institutions, but to parents and the larger community of the school. They need to listen and reflect on community stories and educate themselves about how to meet the multiple needs of the community on a daily and ongoing basis (see also López, Scribner, & Mahitivanichcha, 2001; Dryfoos, 1994).

Jones firmly believes that schools are primarily responsible for ensuring parental well-being and self-sufficiency and fully recognizes that unless parental needs are met, any effort to collaborate with the community will reap less-fruitful results. He also believes that schools need to engage parents in dialogue about larger social issues and provide them with the tools, resources, and education necessary for self-empowerment and self-determination. The extensive focus on families suggests that school staffs need to operate from a unique epistemological framework that is deeply rooted in accountability and commitment fueled by a common vision of promoting the educational success of students through a concerted effort of recognizing, validating, and meeting the multiple needs of families.

Toward a Border Epistemology of School Leadership

> "As border citizens, this is our greatest challenge: to invent new languages capable of articulating our incredible circumstances." (Gomez-Pena, 1986, p. 1)

The story of Phil Jones provides an interesting glimpse into the world of a school principal who crosses cultural, personal, and professional borders in order to effectively engage the Mexican-origin community with whom he works. His vision of equitable outcomes for all students, along with his understanding of community engagement and empowerment, has forged an unlikely partnership with the grassroots-based Frontera Group. Together, they have organized parents and the larger community to advocate for social change and to utilize the political system to exercise their collective voices and concerns. At the same time, they have opened the school to the community—oftentimes taking the school *to* the community—in order to engage parents on their own terms and educate school personnel about the social conditions and needs of the broader community.

Indeed, Jones has crossed the border between being a "school leader" and being a "leader for the school." In the process, he has reinvented and/or rearticulated the role of the educational leader: no longer is the building-level administrator strictly concerned with the administrative and organizational tasks of the school building, but shoulders a much broader responsibility. While building-level responsibilities should never be minimized, today's educational leaders must also work with the broader community in addressing their needs, provide them with the tools for self-sufficiency, and mobilize them politically for self-determination.

Such a vision, however, requires principals to "remove their blinders" and be particularly reflective in their practice—engaging their own emotions and negative attitudes about the community while critically examining their pedagogical and curricular practices. Finally, it asks educators to take both personal and professional risks—challenging existing power structures and mindsets and using their positions to advocate for others who are less powerful and/or disenfranchised. It is an epistemology that urges leaders to step outside their comfort zone, embrace social justice, cross rigid distinctions/borders, and blur traditionalist assumptions of their practice. The end result, although professionally risky, is—according to Jones—well worth those risks:

> [W]hen you challenge the existing power structure, there is always going to be a fight. . . . [A]nd there were a lot of fights that I saw, and I came out on top for the most part, but there were a lot of blows being thrown that hurt forever—and they were dirty. But . . . I wouldn't take back [what I did], because it was worth it. [The Cesar Chavez Academy] was worth it by itself. And [East Lake], in a few years will all be worth it. . . . It's worth it. It's an investment. And whenever you get into a fight, it takes a lot out of you. But it *is* worth it. I wouldn't give it back, I wouldn't take it back, and I wouldn't want to do it again. I mean I *am* doing it again, but I am trying to be smarter about it. And if a fight comes, I'll be ready for the fight. I'm more experienced with it, I've had a lot of dealings with it. Practically nothing scares me anymore. (Phil Jones, telephone interview)

Conclusion: Border Leadership for All Schools

"Never do for others what they can do for themselves." (Cortés, 1996)

In summary, Jones has consciously chosen to situate his praxis in the border between "school leader" and "community activist." In the process, he has *worked the ruins* of the leadership borderlands: redefining, transgressing, and challenging traditional roles of building level leaders. For example, he has adopted a hybrid leadership style that blurs the rigidity between the school and the community, the professional and the political, the personal and the social, the leader and the supporter, and the self and the other. Moreover, he also challenges traditional assumptions of what it means to be a school principal and professional educator by removing one's blinders, engaging one's emotions, mobilizing and empowering parents, and taking political risks.

Indeed, for Jones, leadership is neither exclusively procedural nor positional (Yukl, 2000), but primarily attitudinal in nature: It is a way of thinking and working with others, a motivation to challenge oppressive systems, a desire to work toward social justice ends, and a willingness to take personal as well as professional risks to ensure that justice is being served. This mind-set requires leaders to step outside their proverbial comfort zones and examine the possibilities that become available when one crosses cultural and social borders and engages the community in such a critical fashion.

Clearly, the need for this type of leader cuts across *all* schools and is not solely for schools along the U.S.–México border and/or schools with large concentrations of marginalized youth. In this rapidly changing social context, schools need leaders who recognize the powerful role of the principalship in shaping institutional, organizational, and social relationships. Schools need leaders who are willing to think differently about their role and their practice and are willing to work in fundamentally different ways than others have in the past. Schools need leaders who are willing to take risks and cross cultural borders, leaders who are willing to work both in the school and the community it serves, and leaders who are willing to challenge themselves and others toward social justice ends. Indeed, schools need leaders who are willing to stand in the interstices of two worlds (the school and the community) and who can function seamlessly in both for the collective benefit of everyone.

Implications for Practice

When viewed holistically, we argue that school leaders need to embrace a new politics of educational leadership, adopting a "trans-frontera" (Saldivar, 1997) orientation, attitude, leadership style, and epistemology that confronts the status quo, embraces difference, and challenges traditional leadership roles and stances. Through the example of Phil Jones, coupled with our collective experience in working with similar leaders, we believe that five characteristics typify such leaders:

1. They are instructional leaders above anything else. They know which instructional policies and practices are good for children and constantly challenge educational methods, content, and mind-sets that are not conducive to effective learning.
2. They are introspective. They constantly challenge themselves (and others) to remove their blinders to the broader social and economic issues that impact the community around them.
3. They engage parents and community members in critical dialogue about their needs, desires, and expectations. Their overarching goal is to mobilize parents in significant ways (politically or educationally) to ensure that those dreams become more of a reality.
4. They are not afraid to engage their own emotions. They constantly seek parent stories and concerns—not in a voyeuristic way, but simply to learn about community needs and concerns in more detail. They respond to criticism by reflecting and changing their own biases and unexamined practices.
5. They make a personal investment in families and communities. They take both personal and professional risks by advocating for families and challenging the assumptions, expectations, beliefs, and practices of others.

These leadership characteristics—many of which are highly gendered and/or regulated by sociocultural scripts (Belenky et al., 1986; Blount, 1999; Brunner, 1999, 2000; Grogan, 1996; Young & Skrla, 2003)—not only chal-

"... whenever you get into a fight, it takes a lot out of you. But it *is* worth it. I wouldn't give it back, I wouldn't take it back, and I wouldn't want to do it again. I mean I *am* doing it again, but I am trying to be smarter about it. And if a fight comes, I'll be ready for the fight. I'm more experienced with it, I've had a lot of dealings with it. Practically nothing scares me anymore." (Phil Jones, telephone interview)

lenge the field to rethink traditional leadership responsibilities and duties, but also encourage us to confront our most fundamental assumptions surrounding the daily role and function of school administrators. To be certain, Phil Jones not only crossed multiple borders, but deliberately *transgressed* those borders in order to do an effective job as a school administrator. We believe this leadership style directly emerged from the unique geographic and geopolitical space of the U.S.–México border region. In effect, the region itself provided a liminal space for his praxis. As educational leaders, we, too, must embody this liminal space and metaphorically adopt the U.S.–México border as a way of seeing and being in the world.

In other words, if school leaders are to break the mold of their practice, they must first be provided with opportunities that allow them to reflect on their current practice and identify the different kinds of borders (geographic, cultural, epistemological, classed, gendered, other) that operate in their schools. They must also be provided with opportunities for professional development and personal growth and be allowed the time and/or resources to collaborate with community-based organizations and other community leaders to collectively identify community needs and concerns. Finally, both administrators and teachers need to be afforded opportunities to examine current trends in home/school/community partnerships, community building, education organizing, and "full-service" schools and search for ways to work with families in more meaningful ways.

Moreover, what we teach in administrator preparation programs must also be critically reevaluated. School leaders must be prepared to work with individuals who are not only culturally different, but who face a variety of social and economic challenges. Consequently, we need to prepare leaders who recognize the reproductive functions of schooling and have the courage to envision different possibilities for schools and school leadership. We need to prepare leaders who can take the school to the community, listen to its concerns, mobilize parents to challenge and change current power dynamics and to raise their voices and be heard. In sum, we need to prepare leaders who will transgress social and cultural borders in order to become true leaders—not only for the school, but for the community as a whole.

Assignments and Activities

1. Reflect on your own leadership preparation experience. Create a list of ways in which you were taught to collaborate with the community. Include the knowledge gained in your leadership preparation program as well as the "best practices" work that has become widely popular in schools. After doing this, create a separate list of the ways in which Phil Jones worked and collaborated with the community surrounding his school. In what ways are the two lists similar? In what ways do they differ? How do you envision working with the community as the principal of your school? Why do you have this particular vision?

   a. Use your lists to share and discuss Phil Jones's vision of community engagement/collaboration with teachers and administrators at your school. What is their general reaction to the leadership style and practices of Phil Jones? How do they see their own involvement in the community? Are their "espoused beliefs" consistent with their "beliefs in action"? How do people's beliefs, values, and dispositions structure and shape their relationships with families?

   b. Do this same activity with community activists, church-based organizations, and other community groups. What is their general reaction to the leadership style and practices of Phil Jones? Compare their reaction with those of teachers and practicing administrators. In what ways are the reactions similar? In what ways are they different? How can you, as a principal, bridge the divide/border between these two worlds?

2. Identify the different kinds of borders (geographic, cultural, epistemological, class, gender, other) operating in your school or other educational unit that shape the educational experience and achievement of students. Consider the extent to which school practices position students on one or another side of metaphoric or actual dividing lines. How can such borders be transgressed or transformed into liminal spaces to more justly and equitably serve students and communities?

Annotated Readings

Gloria Anzaldúa's (1987) *Borderlands/La frontera: The New Mestiza* provides a cogent theoretical overview of the border in all its manifestations—utilizing poetry, prose, and other nontraditional forms of representation to understand Chicana/o epistemology and consciousness. Her work provides a solid background for understanding the work of educational scholars such as González's (2001) *I Am My Language: Discourses of Women and Children in the Borderlands*, Valdés' (1996) *Con Respeto: Bridging the Distances between Culturally Diverse Families and Schools*, González, Huerta-Macías, and Villamil Tinajero's (1998) *Educating Latino Students: A Guide to Successful Practice*, and Reyes, Scribner, and Paredes Scribner's (1999) *Lessons from High-Performing Hispanic Schools: Creating Learning Communities*. These latter texts are valuable resources for understanding the lived realities of children and families along the U.S.–Mexico border and what schools need to do to better address their diverse needs.

James Scheurich and Linda Skrla's (2003) *Leadership for Equity and Excellence* provides a powerful examination of how the vision and deeply-held beliefs of school leaders can create positive environments that are conducive to learning for our most marginalized students. This text should be read concurrently with Paulo Freire's (1970) classic text,

Pedagogy of the Oppressed, which forces us to examine new possibilities for critical education and how we can work with our most marginalized communities toward liberation and dialogic action.

References

Anzaldua, G. (1987). *Borderlands/La frontera: The new mestiza*. San Francisco: Aunt Lute Books.

Aponte, R., & Siles, M. (1994). *Latinos in the heartland: The browning of the Midwest* (JSRI Research Report #5). Lansing, MI: Julian Samora Research Institute, Michigan State University.

Auerbach, C., & Silverstein, L. (2003). *Qualitative data: An introduction to coding and analysis*. New York: New York University Press.

Belenky, M., Clinchy, B., Goldberger, N., & Tarule, J. (1986). *Women's ways of knowing: The development of self, voice, and mind*. New York: Basic Books.

Bhabha, H. K. (1994). *The location of culture*. New York: Routledge.

Blount, J. M. (1999). Manliness and the construction of men's and women's work in schools, 1865–1941. *International Journal of Leadership in Education, 2*(2), 55–68.

Brunner, C. (1999). *Sacred dreams: Women in the superintendency*. Albany, NY: SUNY Press.

Brunner, C. (2000). *Principles of power: Women superintendents and the riddle of the heart*. Albany, NY: SUNY Press.

Capper, C. A., Hafner, M. M., & Keyes, M. W. (2002). The role of community in spirituality centered leadership for justice. In G. Furman (Ed.), *School as community: From promise to practice* (pp. 77–94). Albany, NY: SUNY Press.

Christian, D., Montone, C., Lindholm, K., & Carranza, I. (1997). *Two-way bilingual education: Students learning through two languages*. Washington, DC: ERIC Clearinghouse.

Cortés, E., Jr. (1996). *Reweaving the social fabric*. Retrieved July 1, 2004 from www.tresser.com/ernesto.htm

Dantley, M. (1990). The ineffectiveness of effective schools leadership: An analysis of the effective schools movement from a critical perspective. *The Journal of Negro Education, 59*(4), 585–598.

Dantley, M. (2003). Critical spirituality: Enhancing transformative leadership through critical theory and African American prophetic spirituality. *International Journal of Leadership in Education, 6*, 1–15.

Deleuze, F., & Guattari, G. (1987). *A thousand plateaus. Capitalism and schizophrenia* (Trans., Brian Massumi). Minneapolis, MN: University of Minnesota Press [Originally published 1980].

Delgado Bernal, D. (1998). Using a Chicana feminist epistemology in educational research. *Harvard Educational Review, 68*(4), 555–579.

Dryfoos, J. G. (1994). *Full service schools: A revolution in health and social services for children, youth, and families*. San Francisco: Jossey-Bass.

Eaker-Rich, D., & Van Galen, J. (1996). *Caring in an unjust world: Negotiating borders and barriers in schools*. Albany, NY: SUNY Press.

Freire, P. (1970). *Pedagogy of the oppressed*. New York: Continuum Publishing Company.

Gómez-Peña, G. (1986). *Border culture: A process of negotiation toward utopia/La linea quebrada = The broken line*. Tijuana, BC, Mexico: Centro Cultural de la Raza.

González, M. L. Huerta-Macías, A., & Villamil Tinajero, J. (1998). *Educating Latino students: A guide to successful practice*. Lancaster, PA: Technomic Publishing Co.

González, N. (2001). *I am my language: Discourses of women and children in the borderlands*. Tucson, AZ: University of Arizona Press.

González N., Moll, L. C., Tenery, M. F., Rivera, A., Rendón, P., Gonzales, R., & Amanti, C. (1995). Funds of knowledge for teaching in Latino households. *Urban Education, 29*, 443–470.

Grogan, M. (1996). *Voices of women aspiring to the superintendency.* Albany, NY: SUNY Press.

Hargreaves, A. (1999, April). *Professionals and parents: A social movement for educational change.* Invited address to the Times Educational Supplement Leadership Seminar, University of Keele, Keele, England, UK. Retrieved July 1, 2004 from www.keele.ac.uk/depts/ed/kisnet/interviews/hargreaves.htm

Hargreaves, A., & Fullan, M. (1998). *What's worth fighting for out there?* Toronto: Ontario Public School Teacher's Federation.

Hayes-Bautista, D., Hurtado, A., Burciaga Valdez, R., & Hernández, A. (1992). *No longer a minority: Latinos and social policy in California.* Los Angeles: UCLA Chicano Studies Research Center.

Henry, M. (1996). *Parent–school collaboration: Feminist organizational structures and school leadership.* Albany, NY: SUNY Press.

Hurtado, A., & García, E. E. (Eds.). (1994). *The educational achievement of Latinos: Barriers and successes.* Santa Cruz: University of California at Santa Cruz.

Johnson, D. E., & Michaelson, S. (Eds.). (1997). *Border theory.* Minneapolis: University of Minnesota Press.

Kaplan, C. (1996). *Questions of travel: Postmodern discourses of displacement.* Durham, NC: Duke University Press.

Lather, P. (2001). Postbook: Working the ruins of feminist ethnography. *Signs: A Journal of Women in Culture and Society, 27*(1), 199–227.

Lindholm, K. J. (1992). Two-way bilingual/immersion education: Theory, conceptual issues, and pedagogical implications. In R. V. Padilla & A. Benavides (Eds.), *Critical perspectives on bilingual education research* (pp. 195–220), Tucson, AZ: Bilingual Review/Press.

López, G. R. (2003). The (racially-neutral) politics of education: A critical race theory perspective. *Educational Administration Quarterly, 39*(1), 68–94.

López, G. R., Scribner, J. D., & Mahitivanichcha, K. (2001). Redefining parental involvement: Lessons from high-performing migrant-impacted schools. *American Educational Research Journal, 38*(2), 253–288.

McCracken, G. (1988). *The long interview, qualitative research methods.* Newbury Park, CA: Sage.

Mediratta, K., & Fruchter, N. (2001). *Mapping the field of organizing for school improvement.* New York: Institute for Education and Social Policy, New York University. Retrieved July 9, 2004 from www.nyu.edu/iesp/publications/cip/mapping/mapping_final_report.pdf

Merriam, S. (1988). *Case study research in education: A qualitative approach.* San Francisco: Jossey-Bass.

Merriam, S. (1998). *Qualitative research and case study applications in education.* San Francisco: Jossey-Bass.

Merriam, S. (2002). *Qualitative research in practice: Examples for discussion and analysis.* San Francisco: Jossey-Bass.

Moll, L. C. (1992). Bilingual classroom studies and community analysis: Some recent trends. *Educational Researcher, 20*(2), 20–24.

Moll, L. C., Amanti, C., Neff, D., & González, N. (1992). Funds of knowledge for teaching: Using a qualitative approach to connect homes and classrooms. *Theory Into Practice, 31,* 132–141.

Moll, L. C., Vélez-Ibáñez, C., & Rivera, C. (1990). *Community knowledge and classroom practice: Combining resources for literacy instruction.* (ERIC Document Reproduction Service No. ED341968).

Parker, L., & Shapiro, J. P. (1992). Where is the discussion of diversity in educational administration programs?: Graduate student's voices addressing an omission in their preparation. *Journal of School Leadership, 2*(1), 7–33.

Quantz, R. A., Rogers, J., & Dantley, M. (1991). Rethinking transformative leadership: Toward democratic reform for schools. *Journal of Education, 173*(3), 96–118.

Quiocho, A., Dantas, M. L., Masur, D., Halcón, L. J., & von Son, C. (2003). Education on the border: The myths and realities of teaching on "la nueva frontera." *El Bordo: Revista sem-*

anal de investigación artículos y análisis, 11(1). Retrieved July 6, 2004 from www.tij.uia.mx/elbordo/vol11/education7.html.

Reyes, P., Scribner, J. D., & Paredes Scribner, A. (1999). *Lessons from high-performing Hispanic schools: Creating learning communities.* New York: Teachers College Press.

Riester, A. F., Pursch, W., & Skrla, L. (2002). Principals for social justice: Leaders of school success for children from low-income homes. *Journal of School Leadership, 12*(3), 281–304.

Said, E. W. (1993). *Culture and imperialism.* New York: Alfred A. Knopf.

Saldivar, J. D. (1997). *Border matters: Remapping American cultural studies.* Berkeley: University of California Press.

Scheurich, J. J., & Skrla, L. (2001). Continuing the conversation on equity and accountability: Listening appreciatively, responding responsibly. *Phi Delta Kappan, 83*(4), 322–326.

Scheurich, J. J., & Skrla, L. (2003). *Leadership for equity and excellence: Creating high-achievement classrooms, schools, and districts.* Thousand Oaks, CA: Corwin Press.

Skrla, L., Scheurich, J. J., García, J., & Nolly, G. (2002, April). *Educational equity profiles: Practical leadership tools for equitable and excellent schools.* Paper presented at the annual meeting of the American Educational Research Association, New Orleans, LA.

Sosa, A. (1993). *Thorough and fair: Creating routes to success for Mexican-American students.* Charleston, WV: ERIC Clearinghouse on Rural Education and Small Schools.

Spillane, J. P., Halverson, R., & Diamond, J. B. (2001). Investigating school leadership practice: A distributed perspective. *Educational Researcher, 30*(3), 23–28.

Suarez-Orozco, M. M. (1998). *Crossings: Mexican immigration in interdisciplinary perspectives.* Cambridge, MA: Harvard University Press.

Suarez-Orozco, C., & Suarez-Orozco, M. M. (2001). *Children of immigration.* Cambridge, MA: Harvard University Press.

U.S. Bureau of the Census. (1992). *Statistical abstract of the United States, 1992.* Washington, DC: U.S. Government Printing Office.

U.S. Bureau of the Census. (1996). *Current population report.* Washington, DC: U.S. Department of Commerce, Economics, and Statistical Administration.

U.S. Bureau of the Census. (2001). *Profiles of general demographic characteristics, 2000.* Washington, DC: U.S. Department of Commerce, Economics, and Statistical Administration.

Valdés, G. (1996). *Con respeto: Bridging the distances between culturally diverse families and schools.* New York: Teachers College Press.

Valencia, R. R. (1991). *Chicano school failure and success: Research and policy agendas for the 1990s.* London: Falmer Press.

Valencia, R. R. (2002). *Chicano school failure and success: Past, present, and future.* London and New York: Falmer Press.

Wortham, S. E., Murillo, E. G., & Hamann, E. T. (2002). *Education in the new Latino diaspora: Policy and the politics of identity.* Westport, CT: Ablex.

Young, M. D., & Laible, J. (2000). White racism, antiracism, and school leadership preparation. *Journal of School Leadership, 10*(5), 374–415.

Young, M. D., & López, G. R. (forthcoming). The nature of inquiry in educational leadership. In F. English (Ed.), *Handbook of educational leadership.* Thousand Oaks, CA: Sage.

Young, M. D., & Skrla, L. (Eds.). (2003). *Reconsidering feminist research in educational leadership.* Albany, NY: SUNY Press.

Yukl, G. (2000). *Leadership in organizations* (5th ed). Upper Saddle River, NJ: Prentice Hall.

Endnotes

[1]Throughout this article, we use the term *liminal* to mean a threshold-like space where identities and perspectives are defined in multiple and overlapping ways (see also Anzaldúa, 1987; Bhabha, 1994; Deleuze & Guattari, 1980/1987; Kaplan, 1996).

[2]*Epistemology* is the branch of philosophy that deals with the nature, scope, origin, and limits of knowledge. In this discussion, we use the term broadly to describe "ways of knowing" or fundamental beliefs and suppositions about the world.

[3]*Ontology* is the science of being and existence. Ontology provides the vocabulary for representing the world and communicating knowledge about the world, including (but not limited to) the essence and attributes of the world itself as well as the interrelationships of those things within the world.

[4]A total of four interviews were conducted with the principal using an unstructured interview format (see McCraken, 1988; Merriam, 1988, 1998, 2002). Three of the interviews were face to face; one interview was done over the phone to confirm information on selected quotes. Interview data were transcribed by the researchers. Each researcher independently read the transcripts and coded key themes. The researchers then met to agree on the key themes found in the transcriptions and selected quotes (see also Auerbach & Silverstein, 2003; Merriam, 2002). Key themes and analysis data were shared with Phil Jones to create the "funnel-like design" process of qualitative data analysis as described by Merriam (1998).

5

Bridge People: Civic and Educational Leaders for Social Justice

Betty M. Merchant
Alan R. Shoho

Introduction

In this chapter, Alan Shoho and I discuss research we conducted to better understand the formation and practice of social justice from the perspectives of eight individuals who were nominated for participation in our study because of their reputation as stewards of social justice in the communities in which they live. We specifically were interested in identifying leaders whose professional and personal lives reflect a lifelong commitment to issues of equity and fairness and whose actions are guided by well-defined notions of social justice. Our decision to focus on such individuals emanates from our concern about the extent to which school administrators have become preoccupied with responding to current public school accountability policies and practices rather than critiquing those policies and practices from a social justice perspective. We believe that too narrow a focus on compliance with federal, state, and district mandates distracts administrators from raising important questions about the consequences of implementing such mandates, which is likely to perpetuate serious inequities in student learning opportunities and outcomes. As members of a department of educational leadership and policy studies, we are concerned about the preparation of educational leaders in general and in the development of administrators who are knowledgeable about and committed to critiquing educational policies and practices for the purposes of understanding how these policies and practices support or inhibit the provision of just and equitable educational experiences for all students. Our research was supported by funds awarded from the Leadership for Social Justice, led by Catherine Marshall, and provided by the Ford Foundation.

In this chapter, we discuss our interviews with eight individuals who are recognized as leaders for social justice and equity in San Antonio, Texas, and the surrounding area. We examine how these individuals have internalized and sustained a lifelong commitment to these values as well as the ways in which their personal and professional actions have embodied this commitment. We also discuss the extent to which they feel that school leadership preparation programs can increase students' awareness of the struggles faced by individuals whose experiences and opportunities are unfairly mediated by their race, ethnicity, income level, extent of English language fluency, and any other characteristics that place them at the margins of mainstream society.

Although they were not all educators, each has played a significant role in improving access and opportunity for children historically marginalized by mainstream public schooling. Five of these individuals have achieved national distinction for their roles in shaping the agenda for educational reform. Our research participants consisted of four public school administrators (three principals and a retired superintendent), three university-level administrators (a university president, a college of education dean, and a director of a university policy research center), and one lawyer in a firm defined by its strong social justice advocacy. Two of the participants, the college dean and one of the principals, were female. Two of the individuals we interviewed were white; the other six were Hispanic. The interviews were between 45 and 90 minutes in length and each was audio and videotaped; all of these tapes were transcribed and reviewed for emergent themes.

As we conducted our interviews and transcribed the tapes, we became increasingly convinced that the most powerful revelations about the formation and practice of social justice were to be found in the words of the participants themselves. Despite their many painful encounters with discrimination, none of these individuals were bitter or isolated. Rather, they were committed to creating a bridge between themselves and others for the purposes of improving the lives of all those with whom they worked. As such, they functioned as "Bridge People" in the fullest sense. In recognition of this, we decided to em-

Bridge People

"... they were committed to creating a bridge between themselves and others, for the purposes of improving the lives of all those with whom they worked. As such, they functioned as 'Bridge People' in the fullest sense."

phasize their words at length in the quotes that we used to illustrate the themes that emerged from our interviews with them.

In reviewing our interview data, we found that the research participants shared a number of characteristics, including:

- A strong orientation toward social justice and equity issues that was instilled early in their lives by parents/significant adults whose actions regarding these issues were unequivocal, consistent, and passionate.
- A strong sense of purpose and belief in their ability to succeed from as far back as they could remember that was communicated and reinforced by their parents/significant adults (including teachers and administrators, many of whom were white).
- Powerful experiences of marginalization that shaped their determination to succeed and to improve things for others in similar situations. All but one described a lack of bitterness over these events/interactions, acknowledging the social/political realities of the contexts within which they experience(d) these things and articulating a generous sense of compassion that characterizes their lives and relationships.
- A lifelong commitment to social justice and equity issues that permeates their personal and professional lives.
- A deep appreciation for the value of creating community and high expectations among those with whom they work.
- A humility about their visibility in the community and an appreciation for the role of luck in shaping their professional and personal lives.
- An awareness of the influence of the social/political movements of the 1950s and 1960s and the ways in which their involvement in these movements strengthened their commitment to social justice and equity issues.

The participants in this study reflected a profound knowledge of self, a strong connection to their parents, and an intimate understanding of the political, social, economic, and educational inequities in their communities and in the nation as a whole. They function at the intersection of numerous and conflicting forces with an unshakeable confidence in themselves and a deep sense of social purpose. Although they share a passion for action, they also are patient and recognize the fact that change is often slow and painful. Although these individuals have either experienced or witnessed deeply hurtful acts of discrimination and other forms of social injustice, they persist in their efforts to eradicate inequities. In taking this position, the individuals whom we interviewed maintain their viability as persons who communicate effectively between and among groups for the purpose of improving the lives of the people for whom they advocate. To borrow a phrase from our interview with the college dean, all of these individuals are "Bridge

People" and, in a very real sense, this accounts for their success in creating more just and equitable conditions for children and families who enjoy few, if any, of the benefits of mainstream society.

Early Orientation to Social Justice

All of the individuals we interviewed made explicit links between their commitment to social justice and the modeling provided to them by their parents as they were growing up:

> I consider myself a tremendously privileged human being because I was raised in a family that apparently must have been motivated by a strong concern for social justice. I don't have histories, but I have a fairly strong sense that it is multigenerational. My dad's large extended family were community leaders in the sense that they were always seen as the people who would come up with the intelligent response and they were also pretty good orators across the board. (College dean)

> There's a very strong relationship between my childhood and my interest in social justice, and that is, when I was growing up, my father was involved with the Civil Rights Movement in the early 1950s. Dr. Hector Garcia from Corpus Christi established a veterans' organization of Mexican Americans, and it was called the American GI Forum, and my dad was one of the first to enlist in this new movement in 1948.
> [Referring to the story of Felix Longoria, a Mexican American soldier whose body was refused by the funeral home in Three Rivers, Texas, and ultimately buried in Arlington Cemetery as a response to the scandal by then-Senator Lyndon Johnson]: There's something wrong for a community that tells a veteran's widow something, that tells a veteran—my dad was a veteran—they say, basically, "You fought for your country and you risked your life, but when you come back to Texas, when you come back to San Antonio, you will be a second-class citizen." There's something wrong with that. I think my dad un-

Confronting Discrimination

> "My dad knew of places that discriminated against Mexican Americans. He wanted to challenge it, so he . . . had five kids and my mom and every once in awhile, they'd say, 'OK, it's time to go confront.' And he would take us to places and they would turn us away and tell us, basically, 'We don't allow Mexicans—we don't serve Mexicans here. You'll have to go elsewhere. This is not a place for Mexicans.' But you know, he was gonna confront . . ." (University president)

derstood and before you knew it, we understood it, and social justice became something for us. And truly, I credit my parents for instilling that in us and being sure that we understood what our position in society was and to always vow to struggle. (University president)

I was influenced, first of all, by my own family—by my father who died when I was five, but whose legacy I heard, and my mother. (Female principal)

The passion [for social justice] is very personal—nothing to do with professional preparation. A lot was expectation from my parents—not that they had much education. (Male principal #1)

It's interesting that people make distinctions and put labels on people. It plagued me quite a bit while growing up inadequate, not feeling "as good as." My parents didn't play into this. My father was extremely strong in this—not educated but well read—could read Thoreau. I can remember him reading some of what Thoreau wrote about social justice. I guess it got embedded in me in some place. All those feelings, all those questions, all that introspection ... especially at a young age, make me extremely sensitive to all people. (Retired superintendent)

Looking back, my mother was an educator, a former principal, school board member. It stems back to her. My father always pushed education on my brothers and sisters and me ... the way this would most help us succeed in life. (Male principal #2)

[My] family was moderate politically, but both my parents were interested in helping the little guy. (Lawyer)

We were dirt poor, and we were the only family that we knew that were on public assistance ... my mom was sort of a Union organizer. ... So I learned a lot of community organizing probably from watching my mother. It's one thing to demolish an idea; it's another thing to actually help somebody succeed, and I had from my mother the importance of doing both of these, and build my whole campaign around her and then once you do one thing and get known for it, you have carte blanche to do almost anything you want. (Policy center director)

The individuals we interviewed were in their 40s and 50s, and as such, their notions of social justice were affected by the events of their time, as illustrated by the following quote:

I grew up in the '60s and went to high school and college in the '60s—the growth of the Civil Rights Movement, the [Vietnam] war. I went from a small town in Texas to Boston for college—the center of activity. In terms of going to college in the '60s, I was impressed by many of the faculty who were antiwar and I saw the effect of student protests and faculty on the war. (Lawyer)

And at particular points, important points, in the struggle for desarrollo of the Mexican American community in Texas and the Latino community nationally, I think that I found my voice. (College dean)

In many of these cases, as evidenced above, one or both of the parents of the individuals we interviewed were known in their communities for their activism and respected by the people for whom they advocated. The university president provided a rich description of this kind of activism:

> My dad knew of places that discriminated against Mexican Americans. He wanted to challenge it, so he . . . had five kids and my mom and every once in awhile, they'd say, "OK, it's time to go confront." And he would take us to places and they would turn us away and tell us, basically, "We don't allow Mexicans—we don't serve Mexicans here. You'll have to go elsewhere. This is not a place for Mexicans." . . . But you know, he was gonna confront—he was confronting that segregation, period. This is 1955, and you know, those things are instilled in you. (University president)

> My mom was sort of a Union organizer. Even though we had nothing, seeing us as responsible for the welfare of the people around us, I mean it was a very powerful experience. (Policy center director)

The two quotes that follow illustrate how the activities of the interviewee's parents were consistent with the notion of "Bridge People" who build connections between and among communities:

> My mother took me to high school with her to do literacy training in Tijuana twice a week for about two years to a little barn out in the outskirts of Tijuana where we would work with adults who didn't know how to read. My big sister volunteered for two years as a teacher in a migrant camp in Texas. (Female principal)

> Several of the members of my family, my father in particular, were what I call "Bridge People." In a completely racially divided environment of the 1950s, they were the Mexicans who would serve on a jury, or they were the Mexicans who might occasionally be invited to a meeting of the hospital board, or something on this order. My dad only went to the third grade and my mother went to the eighth grade, but nonetheless he and about five or six other gentlemen in the community served this role and what was interesting was how they served it. Because my dad and two of his cousins always went in and gave them hell! Some of the other individuals really were more accommodating and as a result, they made a lot of money, but we felt really good about what we were doing! So that kind of model was there. (College dean)

> I remember daddy being called at the last minute to a state district judge, a wonderful man who had experienced discrimination himself because even though he was Anglo, he was very dark-skinned. So he had been asked to, you know, go around the back of a restaurant and he had this great friendship with my

Discovering Marginal Identity

"I discovered I was a Mexican when I was about 8 years old....I was out there playing with a bunch of white kids, and at a certain point ... we heard the parents of some of the kids say, 'We better watch it, we heard our son is playing with some Mexicans.' We went outside and asked, 'Who's a Mexican?' Our idea was, 'Let's go look for them.' Later that day, I realized I was Mexican." (Retired superintendent)

dad. So he always said, "When I have a tough case, I call Rudy." And he called my daddy and it was a police brutality case, the sheriff of the county had really brutalized a young Hispanic boy, and so Judge ___ called daddy in for the grand jury. And this wasn't a very fair practice, but the judge chose his jurors and of course, at the time, there were about five Mexican men who served on juries, and nobody else did. Dad was the only Hispanic on the jury, but when the judge gave the instructions, dad caught on to some instructions that would make indictment inevitable, and so when they went into the jury room, the jury was going to no-bill the sheriff, and dad said, "Before we take a vote, I want a clarification on some of the instructions from the judge." So that was the kind of environment in which I grew up, in which examining, understanding, and finding solutions to the blatant discrimination that Mexican Americans experienced as I was growing up was a very big part of my life. (College dean)

Vivid Personal Experiences of Marginalization

The people with whom we spoke recounted vivid experiences of marginalization and/or boundary-crossing efforts that played a key role in motivating them to devote themselves to improving the lives of others. Some of these experiences were relatively positive:

When I was about seven or nine years old, we integrated the swimming pool, and then that same summer, we integrated basically, the library services, and my parents prepared me for that; they were without incident. So then, I just never felt that there was any need to hesitate to advance rationality because I think social injustice is irrational. (College dean)

I never felt discrimination during high school. My first taste of prejudice was when I went to college—a predominately Lutheran college. That was my first taste of that. But I think I had been prepared by my teachers [most of whom were Caucasian] to deal with this, so that never really bothered me. (Male principal #2)

Other experiences were extremely hurtful:

I remember clearly one day when he [my father] took all the kids and we went out to Lake McQueeney, and we got there and we were kinda—we were hungry. So we got there and we said, "Hey, Dad, when can we eat?" and so he said, "Well, let's see what's going to happen here" so he went over there and said, "We'd like a table." It's a big picnic ground—a public park—and they said, "Well, we don't serve Mexicans here. You have to go elsewhere." And we just thought, "Oh my god . . . OK." So we just tried to just tell him, "Oh, we're not that hungry dad—that's OK—don't worry." But, you know, he was gonna confront. . . . (University president)

Most of my passion comes from my negative experiences. I was born in Texas and segregated because I couldn't speak English. . . . I was a migrant worker [earning] $60 a month. (Principal #1)

I discovered I was a Mexican when I was about 8 years old. One summer, my family and I took off for the coast to Corpus Christi. There were courts, or summer cottages, and I was out there playing with a bunch of white kids, and at a certain point we wanted to drink some water so we snuck into the kitchen to get some water and we heard the parents of some of the kids say, "We better watch it, we heard our son is playing with some Mexicans." We went outside and asked, "Who's a Mexican?" Our idea was, "Let's go look for them." Later that day, I realized I was Mexican. (Retired superintendent)

My mom was raised in an orphanage, so we were very poor, and my dad was schizophrenic, so he was hospitalized in a state institution. . . . So I remember I had to go—I was the oldest son—to go pick up the eggs and the cheese from the welfare. I remember people just spitting at me and treating me like garbage and it's—it was a very profound experience to see people see you as garbage and then to be at home and it was the complete opposite. (Policy center director)

Although the lawyer we interviewed did not refer to any specific instances of marginalization, the retired superintendent who had worked alongside him in the legal battle over inadequate school funding, noted:

By discipline, he has an engineering degree from MIT and a 5,000-year history [as a Jewish person]—a wonderful combination—brings heart and mind to the critical issues. The social justice concept has so many layers, to be able to go through them all and line them up properly. He is the engineer, the one who lays it open completely and who has that keen insight into the heart. That amazed me to watch him work, because I'm not that smart, and I could see the gears working. He's one of the people of whom I've got lots of memories. (Retired superintendent)

Often, schools provided the context for this marginalization:

I think some had to do with the fact that, initially, I was viewed as a tough case. I mean, we integrated—and we were the first group of kids that integrated a junior high school after the *Brown* decision, and they were certain that we would be troublemakers. They were convinced, I mean that's one part of the initial confrontations and when we ... [Authors' note: recollecting these events was very painful for the college president, and necessitated a few minute's pause in the interview, as we respectfully waited for him to gather his thoughts.] Well, you know, it was right after the *Brown* decision and districts were changed and about 12 of us or 15 of us—I don't remember any more—ended up at this all-white school. And it was all white, and they had not ever had but a very token representation of Hispanic kids there—maybe one or two, because it was an all-white neighborhood, but the districts had changed. So there was a real struggle, there was a real struggle for several years. And I think that they discovered in us—and I was with my brother—I don't know if I could have made it by myself. And my brother is a very bright kid—I think they discovered in us some talent, and they realized that we were just normal kids. So they began to work with us. (University president)

Early Recognition and Support

Two of the individuals we interviewed spoke about the role of their communities in their development of a sense of purpose, negative as well as positive:

> There was discrimination from the majority as well as within our own race. Anyone who wanted to go above and beyond was criticized for being Anglo. ... Some people in the community recognized something in me and started supporting me ... took me to a college homecoming game—set up expectations for me. (Principal #1)

> I was raised in a community where people came together to, I think they were pursuing the dignity of the individual and the dignity of the group. And then they acted upon it. They were—I grew up with a strong locus of control—the notion that I could act upon the world. I never felt like a victim. (College dean)

Athletic ability also attracted recognition and support, as was the case for the university president:

> And I think from then on, when I went on to high school, it was a kind of different setting—within a year, people started, because of my track specialization and abilities, again, people started to come to me and say, "Wow! You know, you're really good and you're gonna go to college. You're gonna get a track scholarship, so you've gotta get ready. You gotta get ready for college."
>
> . . . .
>
> I remember an occasion when I was a senior and I had about 60 scholarships. I had the best time in America—the best time in a mile in America. I had about 60 scholarships, and one of them was to the University of Texas. And one of the counselors had said, "Well I don't know—this is a big, big jump for this kid, from a vocational school to the University of Texas," but my coach thought, "Well, I think that's where he should go." Apparently they were having some

discussion about this. So one day my coach said, "Well, you got to come in the morning to take a test. So tomorrow morning, come at seven, to take the test." It's fine—I used to get to school early, and I got there at seven in the morning and dropped in and they said, "Sit down," and I took a test and walked out of that and by the afternoon they had the results back. I had taken an IQ test and my coach said, "Well, you passed the test." And I said, "Really?" He said, "Yes." I said, "What kind of test was this?" "It was an IQ test." And I said, "Well, how do you know I passed?" And he said, "Well, you have a higher IQ than I did when I went to college."

And it was one of those things, you know, again it was all these sort of like different tests, and there was this sort of low expectations by some, high expectations by others, no expectations by others, so it was a struggle for a lot of the kids from my generation, no question about it. I happened to be lucky, I happened to have a skill and a talent . . . I was state champion. . . . I had the best time in America, and so I knew I was going—I knew I was going off to college, but that mentoring and people sort of. . . . it was a very important question for me, and I needed for somebody to answer that question, but I also needed somebody to defend me. I needed somebody to say, "See, I told you so. This kid is capable." I didn't need for them to say, "This kid's brilliant or this kid was . . . " I didn't need that—I just needed somebody to say, "You can do it." "You oughta go to college." That's all you need and you're ready to go, and I think there were so many of those kids there who just needed one little pat, one little assurance, somebody to just say, "You can do it," and they would have taken off. (University president)

Lifelong Commitment to Social Justice and Equity

All of the research participants articulated a lifelong commitment to social justice and equity issues that permeates their personal and professional lives. They described the formative events that occurred relatively early in their lives, many of which were credited to luck or destiny:

> By eighth grade, I was the only one left [of the Mexicans]. Some were still behind, others left and married. Only two Hispanics graduated from my class. I was one of the only Hispanics to go to college, despite seeing talents in other Hispanics, including cousins. I promised to improve this situation—I'm not going to be the hinge to the gate—I'm going to open it up. (Male principal #1)

> As the oldest son in a Hispanic family, I was ready to drop out. We didn't have any food, so after I put my books away, I went to the [school janitor's] closet and got a broom and started cleaning closets. I thought this was a great job, working indoors. I wanted to drop out and went to my mom to tell her this. The most significant time came when I was a sophomore. We were on welfare—my dad was in the hospital from loading martini onions. The coach [of our school] got fired and this SMU cheerleader came and taught history. I was in

love with this lady—got extra credits. I had two pants and two shirts for the school year. She said, "I need to see you out in the hall." In my school this was nothing good; I was shaking and in fear—I didn't want trouble or to disappoint her. She said, "What college are you going to?" I didn't know what to say—[I was] dumbfounded! She said, "If you haven't thought about it, you should." With all the hormones I was feeling, I was going to do it. When I was a senior, I weighed 99 pounds and was about 4'2". I didn't get hired as a laborer . . . It was destiny—mystical . . . things happened to prevent me from making a wrong choice. In fact, I got a scholarship—people pushed me in that direction. . . . (Male principal #1)

I came from the Edgewood District, but while there I had some excellent teachers who repeatedly told us we were as good as anyone. The idea of college was planted in our minds early on. They worked well beyond the school day . . . they and our parents made us believe we could do this. My own wife is a product of that same school and is now a principal in ____. She would say one of the reasons that we succeeded is that we had teachers, counselors, and principals who believed in us. I don't remember them saying, "If you go to college" but "When you go to college," not "If you take these tests" but "When you take your tests." As far as becoming an educator, I can very quickly look back at my former high school band director and he's the reason why. (Male principal #2)

My fourth grade teacher, who was Mexican American, came from Del Rio, Texas. He was a gifted artist and an athlete and decided to teach elementary school. Everyone looked at him as a rebel—a troublemaker. He was very Indian looking—some kind of agnostic—like Indigenous people—that god was out there—the sun, the moon. He would teach fourth grade by building paper maché horses and so on as the medium of how one learns certain things. He was the one that also really inculcated in your mind, "You don't have to take this. You don't have to put up with this. You don't have to agree." For a fourth grader, this was pretty powerful stuff. I can see him and hear him clearly now. This was 1943—a long time ago—and I'm getting older and losing it, but I remember him. He was very critical in my life. You don't pull yourself up by your bootstraps if you don't have the boots. (Retired superintendent)

The second thing that is extremely important to me was the experience with teachers that I've had on schooling, both positive and negative. My dad went into the hospital for the last time the day before they gave the IQ test in the sixth grade, and in New York City they gave all sixth graders an IQ test, and you had to get 130 cutoff. If you got 130, you went into something called "Rapid advance" or "SP," which you skipped the eighth grade, so I was the only child except for the one girl who didn't get 130. We had to go into the dummy classes, and all my friends—my whole peer group—went into algebra in the seventh/eighth grade combined, so it wasn't a big deal in the seventh, but when I was in the eighth, they were taking algebra and I wasn't and they would tease me mercilessly—just "XX, what's X?" you know, cruelty of adolescence. So, I went to the library and I started reading math books secretly at night and started learning . . . When I had got to the ninth grade, all my friends were gone and

I had this young wonderful teacher, and she—Day 1 of algebra—and I couldn't believe the book. I had done four years or five years of math and instead of—because I was a tough kid—instead of singling me out, she gave me her college books and I just sat in the back of the room and read math books. So I had this extraordinary piece of luck, but nothing compared to the next year.

I went to high school and I wasn't allowed to take regular geometry or honors Geometry because I had a substandard IQ for my peer group and I acted out and called the teacher a name, and I was sent to the math chair—there were 8,000 kids in the ____high school—a big school—so the math chair was the senior administrator and he told me—instead of beating me up—he said, "Tell me what you know." And I laid out all the stuff I had done and he had retired from Columbia, and he was teaching as public service, and then he called me in with another kid and said, "You have won a scholarship. I've shown your work to my friends, and you've won a scholarship, and every week, you come to me and I will give you tokens and lunch money and you go up and take classes at Columbia and CCNY." And I did this—I didn't even know what a scholarship was. Ten years later when he died, we went to his funeral and there were about 25 kids, all of whom got this same made-up story. He paid for us and our tuition out of his own pocket! (Policy center director)

And I had the kindest homeroom teacher who, when I got to her class, I could tell she was, like, "Un oh, they've given me another problem kid." And my great joy was that, after three years in her class, she was really seeing me develop, and she said, "We have to elect a classroom president, because we're going to go to the awards ceremony and we need a classroom president—somebody that represents us." And she said, "So you all have to elect, but I'm gonna make a recommendation." Before they could pop up in class, she said "I'm going to nominate Ricardo." And there was a sort of silence. "I think all of you know him—I think you have seen him come from way back." The kids [were going] "you know . . ." and so somebody said, "Well that's a good nomination" and so I won! And so that day, at the honors presentations, they were calling out all the classroom groups and it was all these white kids when their names would be called out and saying, "And representing the eighth grade is the president of the eighth grade so and so." And there were all these rooms—I mean there must have been about 15 different classrooms. "And so, representing the ninth grade class" [announced] Mrs. Randolph, who was this wonderful teacher, "[my name]" so I walked down the aisle, and it was like, "Oh Yes! I've arrived!" you know, and I walked down that aisle—it seemed like five miles of walking, just like every step, and I thought, you know, "It's gonna be fine. People believe in me and I believe in myself and I've surprised people, which is fine. I like kinda surprising people!"

One of the real major accountability factors here is whether or not we care about the success of our students. And if the answer is yes, then we gotta take some steps and we have to get to know our students, we have to interact with them, we have to be ready to mentor them, we have to be ready to say to them, "I can write that letter for you because I know who you are" rather than to say, "Gee, I wish I knew a little bit about you—I'm sorry you've been in my classes for two years now but I don't know who you are and I can't help you. If you want to go to law school or medical school, I just can't help you." I think that would be such a devastating remark to a young person. . . . That is part of our responsibility, and I think it really speaks well to leadership. What kind of leader are you if no one respects you? What kind of leader are you if nobody comes to seek your guidance or advice? You just might as well live out in a cave somewhere. (University president)

I've always felt that I needed to provide some kind of leadership somewhere. I became a principal when I was 25. I was one of those Teachers of America—nominated two years in a row, and I got selected. After my third year of teaching, I became a principal of a junior high. I just get a real charge out of working with the parents and working with the teachers. I get a lot of satisfaction from a child bringing me a little piece of paper, saying "You really helped me out." [shows us a photograph of a boy in a football uniform with the inscription, "Thank you for being there. I will do my best."] (Male principal #1)

The people we interviewed also identified observations and insights gained while in college that further strengthened their resolve with respect to addressing social justice issues:

Universities were also a negative—the extent to which universities were dedicated to making money. I don't think the professors [in law school] did much regarding social reform. They were not particularly interested in the area. . . . None were dedicated to changing the world through law—they were dedicated to changing their clients. (Lawyer)

The university constructed this marketing campaign and recruitment campaign that drew out from all these inner-city schools, extraordinary people, and then routinely failed them. And it was clear to me that the university didn't have any understanding of who these people were and that I would have an opportunity to directly challenge the system. And I went out and I found, in fact, that much of what the university was doing in "good faith" was, in fact, harmful to the people they were trying to serve. (Policy center director)

Creating Community and Maintaining High Expectations

When the people we interviewed talked about their commitment to creating a sense of community and high expectations among those with whom they worked, it was clear that educators had a powerful effect in this regard, both positive and negative:

Aside from my family, the other people who have affected me were other educators. In Las Cruces, I had a principal who said he'd take the children home after school. I was floored by this! How relaxed and comfortable he felt in the community and how comfortable the parents felt when they came to the school—a warm, supportive school environment. When I first started teaching as a bilingual teacher, I asked a teacher how many children would learn to read; the teacher said, with no hesitation, "All of them." (Female principal)

Each of the individuals we interviewed defined social justice in a manner that reflected the knowledge and sensitivities they had acquired within their family, community, school, and national contexts. These definitions guided their actions and sustained them in times of difficulty and hardship:

> In terms of where you get that "fire in the belly," I think that "fire in the belly" comes from the capacity to recognize the injustice but also having cultivated a kind of basic self-confidence and a basic self-assurance. We don't develop a fire in the belly about social injustice in the absence of the cultivation of a strong philosophical base, a sense of competence, and a sense of security in the individual. It involves self-examination, it involves teaching—not just to skills or to knowledge—but to the development of the total human being. And I can't imagine that you can educate leaders without attending to that. (College dean)

> Now I understand [that] because of accident and because of my commitments to things even on the worst days I have the power to do things that matter and almost no one has the right to do that. So you have this special burden and . . . the understanding of how many other people weren't helped just fires me up. (Policy center director)

Striving for Social Justice Without Bitterness

The individuals whom we interviewed experienced painful forms of exclusion at several points in their lives and in some cases were not aware of the full impact of these experiences until they had reached adulthood. What makes them Bridge People, in part, is their conscious decision to resist becoming bitter and isolated, to use their experiences to create a bridge between themselves and others, and to assist them in obtaining access to the opportunities and resources they need to improve the quality of their lives, as reflected in the following quotes:

> No one who looks at schools in Texas can not notice the changes in schools over the last ten years. It was a blessing for me personally to work on this case . . . because of the Edgewood case, changes in funding resulted from this case, [and] lots more money went to where it was deserved. There are still differences between the very wealthiest schools and the others . . . any time you're starting to make progress, anyone who's lost benefits will try to get them back. I truly believe in these things and I know that they all take time. I'm aware of the inequities in the system . . . the new schools with every possible advantage—so that's frustrating. I'm optimistic—I know these things take time. I've seen real

progress. I've been doing this a long time. [It's] what I know how to do best. I enjoy it and have stayed in. (Lawyer)

As a high school principal, I kept saying, "What can I do to really change things?" After a football game and losing by 25 points [to a school that had a] budget for sports that was greater than my academic budget—[I thought about] the difference between the "haves" and the "have-nots." Athletics is a good analogy—we've never had a level playing field—we're always running up hill. Those experiences [can] lead to [a sense of] frustration and anger, when you know it's purposeful—not by accident, but by design. Nobody notices it, especially when you're on the "have" side. All these things welled up to create a sense of anger, which over time, I got smart enough to turn this anger into a more proactive set of activities that have contributed to changing the map not only here but in the state of Texas. (Retired superintendent)

It is difficult to maintain a positive focus on things, as illustrated in the comments of this superintendent a little later in our interview:

Getting to this point in my life, no one specific thing—so many things in my life. The fire in the belly is still there. I still get angry about things. It's something that has to be done as a piece of what we do for children. (Retired superintendent)

This same superintendent went on to say, however

I went to the little town of _____ on the Oklahoma border because we were still out there to get people to jump on the bandwagon to write to their senators [about the school finance suit]. I walk in and all these big, white burly farmers walk in, wearing coveralls and blue jeans. And they said, "you boys here to talk with us?" You know, "boys" has a very negative connotation, so I said, "It's good to be called a boy, given my age." He said, "We call each other boys—no offense taken." They had all the students in their schools write handwritten petitions. With humor, we got white rural area kids to write letters in behalf of a suit that people were still trying to depict as a minority suit. Humor's always played a big part in my life. When you are in situations of high tension, high emotions, it's a wonderful release. You have to laugh at yourself—you can't laugh at other people.

The university president described his efforts to avoid bitterness while engaging in the struggle for social justice:

One thing I learned from my parents, really, was that it sort of was—we had to struggle, we had obstacles, we had challenges, and we would rise up to it. But they never hated anybody. And they taught me, they taught me to love and they taught me not to hate. So there wasn't any bitterness. I mean my dad didn't drive away from that restaurant, saying, you know, "That rude woman who [refused to serve us]." He knew that she was given instructions, and I think he knew that she was pained by it, that it wasn't something she wanted to do—to tell this family, "You're not good enough to be in this restaurant." You know, "Your brown skin means you can't be here." It wasn't her—she knew she had her instructions and so you would never question whether it was hate in that. It was kinda like, you know, every day we're taught that there's a long journey here and we're taking steps every day to correct these injustices and we didn't worry about hating. And so I don't really have any bitterness—I dread the thought of having any vengeance or revenge in my heart. You know, I don't have that, and I hope I never do. (College president)

Conclusion

The individuals we interviewed for this study stressed the role of family members and specific critical incidents in their youth as powerful factors in developing a commitment to social justice. To borrow the expression of the college dean, their passion for equity grew from "a spark in the belly" to a "fire in the belly." This fire was not one of bitterness or hate, but one of compassion and warmth, which allowed them to reach out to others as Bridge People for the purposes of improving the lives of all those with whom they worked.

Each of the Hispanic interviewees conveyed in one way or another the sentiments of male principal #1: "When I look at these faces, I look at me." This raises some difficult questions about whether direct personal experiences are a prerequisite to developing a commitment to social justice and whether we, as university faculty, can develop a sensitivity in students who have not yet had the kinds of marginalizing experiences described by the individuals who participated in our study. This is further complicated by the extent to which faculty members themselves understand the experience of marginalization.

All of the people we interviewed felt that school leadership preparation programs could increase students' awareness of the struggles faced by individuals whose experiences and opportunities are unfairly mediated by their race, ethnicity, income level, extent of English language fluency, and any other characteristics that place them at the margins of mainstream society. They suggested a number of ways in which this could be accomplished, all of which are feasible within a fairly traditional framework of professional preparation programs. For example, several interviewees suggested that we design field experiences for students that would take them out of their comfort zones and into neighborhoods in the community that they knew little or nothing about; experiences that would challenge their taken-for-granted notions of how the world works. The lawyer took this a step further by challenging us to incorporate political activism into the preparation of educational leaders. He and others in the study reminded us of the link between social justice and political action that is virtually absent in professional preparation programs. Others stressed that the students in our programs need to develop a sense of shared responsibility for the learning of all children as well as a confidence in their ability to address the needs of these children. The people we interviewed re-

Incorporating Experience

> "We must move beyond classroom discussions that treat these issues in a theoretical and abstract manner, to providing experiences that will enable students to recognize and combat the inequities that permeate the very systems and institutions in which they work."

minded us that it is important that we and our students realize that social justice is not solely the concern of marginalized groups, but an issue that concerns all of us, and that without our combined efforts, social injustices will continue to occur.

The participants in our study felt that, in order to move from an intellectual appreciation of social justice to the development of a genuine commitment to social justice and equity, university faculty will have to aggressively integrate these concepts and practices into all aspects of their preparation programs. We must move beyond classroom discussions that treat these issues in a theoretical and abstract manner to providing experiences that will enable students to recognize and combat the inequities that permeate the very systems and institutions in which they work. An important component in this process is the development of good communication skills and the ability to interact effectively with a broad range of people. This skill, in particular, is critical to the development of "Bridge People" who, as so powerfully evidenced by the individuals in this study, play a crucial role in addressing the inequities of the communities in which they work.

Out of the deepest respect for the individuals who participated in this research, we end this section with a quote from the retired superintendent that conveys the power of education as a mechanism of social justice:

> A friend of mine was sharing with us that there was a debate between him and a medical doctor about which doctorate was more important [the M.D. or the Ph.D.]. And he said that the medical doctor told him it was the medical doctorate. And my friend said, "You know, you can only fix people to live—we give people [a] reason to live." (Retired superintendent)

Implications for Practice

While our interviews provided important insights into the ways in which the eight research participants had developed, sustained, and enacted their personal commitment to social justice, these interviews also provided us with useful suggestions about the ways in which professional preparation programs might infuse prospective administrators with a strong sense of social justice. Many of the individuals we interviewed spoke about the importance of developing a passion for social justice, although they were often unable to articulate the specifics of how this could be accomplished, as illustrated in the remarks of the college dean:

> For me, social justice is about "desarrollo". . . . And to me, "desarrollo" is the ultimate goal—that is, the development of the full measure of human capacity. And the object of social justice is to break down the barriers to that "desarrollo" in human beings as individuals, as members of groups, as members of community, as citizens of nations, as citizens of the world. And I will tell you, I've spent a lot of time over the last ten days asking myself, "how do we prepare teachers and other educational professionals and leaders who will fight for kids? Who will just damn well fight for kids?!" Because the reality is that once you understand that, for the human being upon whom we are acting as educators in whatever role, we have only two choices. We either fight for their success or we accept their failure. And if we accept their failure, then *they accept their failure.* They think their failure is inevitable. But as long as an educator, we are still fighting for the success of that one individual, then they can't accept failure. (College dean)

In contrast, the policy center director and the lawyer advocated strongly for administrators assuming a more political role in advancing social justice:

> I think that it is a very hard task for school administration programs to produce advocates for social change because schools are principally socializing instruments. It's how we prepare people to live in our world and there are almost no cultures that have the confidence and security to prepare people for change, so one of the jobs of school administrators is not to produce people who will push the system too far. But there have to be people who understand what the driving engines are that move us toward justice. That's the most you can expect. In order to make progress, you need stability, but you also need catalysts for change. So I think it's complicated. (Policy center director)

> I do think that a lot of times people in the school are not sufficiently educated as to being leaders, although they are seen as such. [They are] not encouraged to use their expertise to change communities. In rural Texas, teachers are the largest core of college graduates in their communities. If they get involved, this adds a lot. In urban areas, often teachers and administrators are too focused on local school district policies and raising test scores and forget they are a large core of professionals. Administrators, principals, counselors, most are focused on their particular membership and don't use their membership for social change. I think sometimes they lose their opportunity to use their expertise to change things. (Lawyer)

The retired superintendent criticized the absence of a social justice focus in professional preparation programs for school administrators and he warned against the consequences of continuing to ignore this issue:

> I never had any methods courses that focused on social justice—never did. I remember some professors who used to speak in jest about social justice . . .

What we are doing to prepare our kids for what is happening now is the result of a lot of effort over time, and if you don't continue to struggle, we're going to fall behind. We have to look at children—not deny their distinctions. How do we get administrators to understand that they are not just dealing with the children in front of them, but to the generations that come after them? One of the biggest disappointments I have is when I come across Hispanic administrators who turn their back on these issues because they were socialized into a white model ... you're always Mexican—sorry! If you're an Anglo living in Texas and have been told, "You know, those people are not very good," how do you change this? And make sure that you're not treating them as "less than"? (Retired superintendent)

The college dean argued that a personal, internal locus of control was a necessary attribute of a social justice advocate:

I think it has everything to do with cultivating that locus of control. If a person has locus of control, if they believe that they can change the world, or they believe that they can impact the world to whatever degree, then the fire in the belly begins to ask—let me put it this way—the "spark" in the belly begins to ask for the oxygen that turns it into a "fire" in the belly. And so, yes, I certainly believe that we can create experiences, both in the classroom and outside the classroom that cultivate that in leaders. And I think one of the important ways in which we who prepare educational leaders can cultivate that fire in the belly is by modeling. We have to have that same view about our students. I mean, some people call it "passion," but I think passion can be learned, and I think we do far too little of it in the preparation of our current educational personnel. (College dean)

The policy center director suggested that university faculty have far greater power to change things than they might allow themselves to think. As a consequence, they are largely responsible for the absence of a social justice focus in the courses they offer:

I think that very few people get to have the privilege of working on things they really care about; very few people get to choose what they actually do and whether their work is connected to their values. One group of people who have that privilege are faculty. Faculty have the enormous privilege of working on problems that they alone feel are important. And second, they get to work with the most likely leaders of the next generation; these are extraordinary privileges. Very few faculty take advantage of the privilege or understand these responsibilities. So faculty speak in the language of myth and privilege but don't in fact work on things that are easy to work on from where they are situated. And this I find infuriating and related to administration programs. So individual faculty are blessed with the possibilities of being activists and getting paid for it. That's such a sweet thing. Universities have been constructive players in moving society forward; that is not true today and departments need to think about that. (Policy center director)

Two of the principals talked about the importance of well-planned internships for integrating social justice concepts into the preparation of school administrators:

> Social justice was never addressed [in my preparation program]. Equity was somewhat, but on the whole, the courses were discipline focused—school finance, school law, school improvement were focused on the academics. What is really valuable is example. If they [students] have an opportunity to do internships, [to] shadow different principals who are models, that would be great. Maybe coursework itself could have an equity or social justice component. For example, in school finance, don't just get into balancing books, but look at how finances are distributed . . . it would almost have to be infused into all of the classes. . . . (Female principal)

> When we look at professional standards for administrators, if social justice isn't part of the curriculum, it's kind of outside of the curriculum. Their handle on being able to address social justice issues—[it's] not there. It could be assessed according to a person's ability to work out possible solutions to hypothetical situations. For example, as an administrator, you're going to hire a school nurse. Who would you look for? In this community, we need a nurse who's bilingual, but that's not enough. We also need someone familiar with the community who can refer parents to needed resources. (Female principal)

> Each administrator needs to develop a profile of who they are and why they're doing this and then try to match that profile with what they want out of a school. I wouldn't match with an upper-middle-class school. The other thing is, we'll never reach an understanding without experiencing something. These candidates need to experience a one-year internship working with different personality traits. Whenever you sit in this chair, the whole building develops this personality. I've visited schools all over the country . . . whoever the leader of the school was, it mirrored their personality. With a one-year internship, you can figure out who you are, find out where you are strong, and so on.
>
> If I were looking for an answer, I'd look to the military, because they look for officers based on EQ [Emotional Quotient]. If you look at how they assign their pilots, and so on, they have a big EQ; logistical officers get different assignments. Family, law, judge, medical triage guy—I've got all these roles and I have to be able to handle them and keep my equilibrium. A lot of people can't do this—they have their flow chart. . . . We need someone who can bounce from issue to issue, be empathetic and a risk taker all at the same time. (Male principal #1)

Finally, the retired superintendent stressed the need for university faculty and K–12 educators to collaborate on matters of equity and social justice:

> Without a common dialogue between the university and the schools, [there is] open war. I put together a task force between ____ university and ____ public schools to address the low math achievement of students. We've yet to have one

meeting—they fail to understand the opportunity. I approached another university with the idea of a laboratory in _____. The response was, "We're a university, that is not our issue—what happens in _____ is your issue." I've never heard from them again. That attitude prevails and the talking heads don't talk to each other, and you've got this split that doesn't have to be and we've got one side of the boat paddling one way and the other side paddling the other way and the boat isn't going anywhere. Universities and school districts need to do some introspection. (Retired superintendent)

In reflecting on the issues associated with orienting the preparation of school administrators to issues of social justice, the individuals with whom we spoke presented a strong case for the importance of internalized qualities and dispositions that are deeply rooted in personal experiences that occur outside of professional preparation programs. A few of these individuals offered suggestions for deliberately planning and integrating activities into the educational administration program that might serve as a catalyst for developing these traits. The majority of the suggestions, however, focused on ways in which individuals might be formally socialized to beliefs about the change process and their role as a change agent and political actor that could provide the basis for a strong commitment to improving the education of all children. Taken together, these suggestions serve as a useful starting point for reorienting the role of professional preparation programs toward producing administrators whose beliefs and actions are guided by a strong commitment to issues of social justice.

Discussion Questions and Activities _____

Issues involving social justice are inherently controversial. Despite their controversial nature, they should not be dismissed or ignored. It takes a skilled communicator to negotiate a bridge between people of opposing viewpoints. As Shoho, Merchant, and Lugg (in press) note, "social justice involves an inclusive process whereby all stakeholders must come together" (p. 16). The members of disenfranchised groups should not be the only ones who are concerned about social justice. If issues involving social justice are going to be resolved, then all groups must come to the table and develop a mutual understanding and respect for each other.

1. Reread the section *Implications for Practice* and select a quote from one of the research participants. Use this quote to develop points to one or more of the following questions for group discussion.

   a. What does social justice mean?
   b. What are defining characteristics of social justice?
   c. Who should be involved in social justice issues?
   d. How should social justice advocates avoid the trap of viewing issues from a mutually exclusive perspective that excludes other voices?
   e. What constructive means can social justice advocates develop to reach out to others without the metaphor of a "big stick" or "guilt" trip?

f. How can principals and other school leaders address social justice issues in a system reluctant to change?

2. School leaders are often viewed as stewards of the status quo. What specific structures and behaviors should be instituted in educational leadership preparation programs to prepare future school leaders as social justice advocates? Understanding that it is difficult, at best, to change a school system, what skill-building activities can prepare leaders to have the fire in the belly to overcome school system and societal resistance to social justice initiatives?

3. Social justice issues are inherently framed in a win-lose perspective. How can professors and school practitioners reframe social justice issues into win-win situations? Is it possible? What would it take?

4. In a high-stakes accountability era, how can educational leadership preparation programs inculcate their students on the importance of addressing social justice issues? In addition, why does social justice take a back seat to accountability issues for principals and other school leaders? In theory, resolving social justice issues are complementary to addressing accountability issues, yet the two issues often are decoupled, when, in reality, they are highly integrated and mutually interdependent. What rhetoric, coalition-building, and persuasive strategies can you devise to make this point to resistant educators, parents, and power brokers?

5. Beyond coursework and rhetoric, what are some effective means for preparing future school leaders to be "Bridge People" and to address social justice issues? How can these leaders learn to internalize and *act on*, rather than simply vocalize, social justice concepts?

6. Select two individuals from your community who have distinguished themselves as advocates of social justice. Identify a core set of questions that will guide interviews with these individuals (e.g., How did you become identified as a strong advocate of social justice? What issues are of most concern to you, and how have you attempted to address these issues? What challenges have you faced in pursuing these issues, and how have you dealt with these challenges? How have you been supported in your efforts? What kinds of barriers have you faced? How have you managed to sustain your commitment to issues of fairness and equity? What advice would you give to teachers and administrators who are interested in becoming advocates of social justice?).

Audiotape the interviews. In addition, videotape the interviews, if possible; videotapes can serve as powerful mechanisms for stimulating discussions in your university classes as well as in your district and schoolwide faculty development meetings. Such videotapes can be used as follows:

a. The videotapes can be used as the opening activity in a university class or staff development workshop that is focused on specific national or state educational policy reports, such as *No Child Left Behind*.

b. They can be used as an intermediate activity, after university students or district staff members have engaged in a preliminary discussion about issues associated with educating all children—"no excuses," "no exceptions."

c. They can serve as a catalyst for a discussion about the role of educators in facilitating or constraining children's educational opportunities.

7. The Subjective I exercise (adopted from the work of Alan Peshkin—see, for example, Jansen & Peshkin, 1992) has proven to be a powerful tool for sensitizing school leaders to issues of social justice and equity and to the ways in which their unexamined beliefs and assumptions may further, rather than eliminate, the very inequities that they seek to eradicate. Each of us has many Subjective Is that reflect such things as our age, gender, race/ethnicity, religious traditions, and professional socialization.

   The exercise provides participants with a lens through which to view their interactions with others and to reflect on the ways in which their various subjectivities act as filters through which they conduct and interpret these interactions.

   Directions to Students:

   Divide your paper into three columns. In the first column, describe a recent social interaction in which you were involved. Break this description into segments that reflect the nature and flow of the interaction. In the middle column, next to each segment, identify the Subjective I that was operating at the time. In the third column, comment on the ways in which each Subjective I influenced the interaction. There is no pre-determined length for this paper—write as little or as much as necessary to fully describe the interaction. At the end, provide a paragraph or two in which you reflect upon the experience of doing this exercise and the insights you obtained in the process. This exercise is most useful when it is repeated several times during a semester, with each exercise focused on a different interaction.

   Note to Instructor:

   The instructor is only a facilitator in these exercises; there is no need to comment on the student's Subjective I papers or to be directive in any manner. It is in the act of writing these papers that students begin to understand the ways in which their various Subjective Is filter their interactions with others and reflect biases and assumptions that they may not have realized prior to the exercise. The Subjective I papers testify to the ways in which students unconsciously subvert the very values they purport to demonstrate as educators concerned about issues of social justice and equity.

8. Select a title from the annotated reading list. Present its main points to your class or work group and create discussion questions or an activity based on the ideas presented.

Annotated Readings

In 1932, George Counts, in his speech before the Progressive Education Association and later in his book, *Dare the School Build a New Social Order?* challenged educators to become leaders for social justice. His call was largely unheeded during the 1930s. However, over the past decade, the essence of Counts' dare to create an educational system in which all students can benefit and be successful has reemerged as a driving force in educational discourse and research. Social justice has once again risen to the forefront. What is missing is the articulation of a comprehensive model of inclusiveness where social justice theories are put forth and subjected to empirical investigation. For social justice scholars, Counts' work from the 1930s provides a historical context for theory development.

Although theory development in social justice research has lagged, scholarly interest has not. To date, several studies, such as Reyes, Scribner, and Scribner (1999) and Skrla and Scheurich (2001), have documented evidence that all students can be successful. What is missing is the connection of theory to practice as expounded by Bogotch (2002) in *Educational Leadership and Social Justice: Practice into Theory*. Rawls (1973) put forth one of the early theories for social justice. His model was based primarily on an economic perspective. Despite this effort, theory building involving social justice in education has been scant. One of the problems in developing theories of social justice has been the lack of consensus on a definition of what social justice means. It was noted by Novak (2000) in *Defining Social Justice: First Things* and by Shoho, Merchant, and Lugg (in press) in *Social Justice: Finding a Common Language*. Without a common language, theory development is difficult at best and unlikely in the worst case. As noted by Lange (1998), despite the best intentions and efforts of social justice advocates, unless a coherent body of scholarly work can produce an empirically validated model for social justice, the likely outcome is fragmentation where the lowest common denominator wins out. The challenge for scholars and social justice proponents is to create an organizational culture where social justice advocates can rock the boat knowing they have the support to change the system without fear of reprisal. With education being relatively resistant to change, only time will tell if social justice as a theoretical construct will have the type of impact during the twenty-first century that Counts envisioned in 1932.

Related Readings

Anderson, G. L. (2002). *Can we effectively build credential programs for educational administrators on principles of social justice?: A case study*. Paper presented at the meeting of the University Council for Educational Administration, Pittsburgh, PA.
Brown, K. M. (2002). *Leadership for social justice and equity: Weaving a transformative framework and pedagogy*. Paper presented at the meeting of the University Council for Educational Administration, Pittsburgh, PA.
Johnson, B. C., & Shoho, A. R. (2002). *Social justice in educational administration preparation programs*. Paper presented at the meeting of the University Council for Educational Administration, Pittsburgh, PA.
Merchant, B. M. (2004). Roadblocks to effective K–16 reform in Illinois. In M. W. Kirst and A. Venezia (Eds.), *From high school to college: Improving opportunities for success in postsecondary education* (pp. 115–182). San Francisco: Jossey-Bass.

References

Bogotch, I. (2002). Education leadership and social justice: Practice into theory. *Journal of School Leadership, 12*(March).
Counts, G. S. (1978). *Dare the school build a new social order?* Carbondale, IL: Southern Illinois Press. [Original work published 1932.]

Jansen, G., & Peshkin, A. (2002). Subjectivity in qualitative research. In M. LeCompte, W. Millroy, & J. Goetz (Eds.), *The handbook of qualitative research in education*. San Diego: CA: Academic Press.

Lange, E. (1998). Fragmented ethics of justice: Freire, liberation theology, and pedagogies for the non-poor. *Convergence, 31*(1/2), 81–93.

Novak, M. (2000). Defining social justice: First things. *A Monthly Journal of Religion & Public Life, 108*, 11–13.

Rawls, J. (1973). *A theory of justice*. Oxford, UK: Oxford University Press.

Reyes, P., Scribner, J., & Paredes Scribner, A. (1999). *Lessons from high performing Hispanic schools: Creating learning communities*. New York: Teachers College Press.

Shoho, A. R., Merchant, B. M., & Lugg, C. A. (in press). Social justice: Finding a common language. In F. English (Ed.), *Handbook of educational leadership*. Thousand Oaks, CA: Corwin Press.

Skrla, L., & Scheurich, J. (2001). Displacing deficit thinking in school district leadership. *Education and Urban Society, 33*(3), 235–259.

6

Preparation and Development of School Leaders: Implications for Social Justice Policies

Nelda Cambron-McCabe

Abundant evidence exists that high-quality school leaders make a difference in student learning. However, students and schools are failing at an unprecedented rate and data show widening achievement gap scores and higher dropout rates for minority and low-income students (see, e.g., Huggins & Celio, 2002). Consequently, we find ourselves in a period in which all sectors of the schooling enterprise—states, institutions of higher education, and professional organizations—are questioning aspects of the licensure and development of leaders.

Against this backdrop of national concern, in 1996 the Council of Chief State School Officers advanced a set of standards through the Interstate School Leaders Licensure Consortium (ISLLC), a group representing the major players involved in the licensing and preparation of school leaders. These standards have become a framework for administrator preparation in about 40 states. In 2002, the National Council for Accreditation of Teacher Education (NCATE) adopted the standards for accrediting school administration programs. Although the ISLLC standards have been lauded for focusing attention on leadership and student learning (Hale & Moorman, 2003), critics contend that they are inadequate for addressing social justice concerns or bringing about significant shifts in current practice (Achilles & Price, 2001; Anderson, 2001; English, 2000).

This chapter explores the intersection of leadership, social justice, and equity concerns in the licensure and preparation of school administrators. First, research studies on licensure and preparation programs across seven states are analyzed to identify ways that social justice concepts have been integrated into state policies to reform the education of school leaders. Second, to stimulate thinking about possible policy initiatives and preparation options, several efforts focused on the development of leaders and social justice concerns are highlighted. In the concluding section, implications for policy are explored.

Questions to consider as you read the chapter include the following: What issues do policymakers raise as they examine their licensure policies? What social justice issues are included in the licensure standards? Whose interests do the licensure policies reflect? What leverage points exist for shifting current licensure policies and practices to include a meaningful focus on social justice? What are the next steps in your state, university, or school system?

Administrative Licensure and Social Justice Concerns

Some are concerned that reforms of administrator licensure and preparation programs across states may fail to give adequate attention to pressing social justice concerns. This section contains an analysis of studies by researchers in seven states who investigated licensure policy assumptions and strategies and the extent to which social justice concerns were embedded in the licensure policies (Dantley & Cambron-McCabe, 2001; Gerstl-Pepin, 2001; Larson, 2001; Marshall, 2001; McCarthy & Murtahda, 2001; Oliva, 2001; Rusch, 2001). Data included interviews and document analysis in Georgia, Indiana, New Jersey, New York, North Carolina, Ohio, and Texas. A common protocol was used to interview five or more prominent "informed insiders," such as state superintendents, state board members, association directors, professors, and school superintendents. Some of the primary questions asked were:

1. What do key people think about the strategies for improving the preparation and licensure of principals and superintendents? How has the ISLLC standards affected developments in your state?
2. What do the state and ISLLC standards have to say about social justice concerns? Will strategies to improve administrative licensure do much to increase the number of women and minorities? Will they make administrators more democratic and inclusive of marginalized community groups? Will they create leadership for facilitating caring relationships and empowerment of staff and children? Will they produce leaders who will end school practices that re-create societal inequities?
3. What is your perception of policymakers' interest in social justice? (Marshall & McCarthy, 2002)

Licensure Standards and Assessment

Almost all states require school administrators to possess a license for appointment to an administrative position. Typically, licensure requirements are met through the completion of an approved number of credit hours in a university-based program. The licensure standards delineate broad principles that shape the curriculum and the requirements of these preparation programs. The researchers in the seven state studies examined the status of state licensure standards and the extent to which they embodied concerns, skills, and knowledge about social justice.

Except for one of the seven states, the ISLLC standards were prominent in the state standards, whether based explicitly on ISLLC (Georgia, Ohio, and Texas) or merely informing an individual state's own standards (Indiana, New York, and North Carolina). The ISLLC standards direct attention to the centrality of student learning; each point begins with the phrase "an administrator is an educational leader who promotes the success of all students" (Council of Chief State School Officers, 1996). The standards address the school leader's role in developing a shared vision of learning; sustaining a school culture conducive to learning; ensuring appropriate management of school operations and resources; facilitating collaboration with families to respond to diverse needs; acting with integrity and fairness; and responding to the schools' political, social, economic, legal, and cultural context.

McCarthy and Murtadha (2001) reported that Indiana's standards closely mirror those of the ISLLC. Larson (2001) noted that ISLLC standards can be identified in New York's standards, but that the state's requirements contain far greater specificity to meet its own unique needs. Similarly, Marshall (2001) reported that North Carolina aligned its 10 domains with the ISLLC's 6. Although Rusch (2001) found that ISLLC standards were not used in state licensure, the New Jersey Principals and Supervisors Association used them for professional development.

ISLLC, or ISLLC-influenced, licensure standards were viewed as pivotal across six of the states in shaping leadership preparation and professional development. One respondent commented that the significant accomplishment of the ISLLC standards was "to anchor the principal's management around the theme of academic achievement" (Dantley & Cambron-McCabe, 2001, p. 4). This perspective dominates the states' licensure standards, raising expectations for student performance and redefining principals' primary role as *leaders of student learning*. In Texas, for example, the standards are built around "learner-centered proficiencies" to create a vision for "a 'new' kind of educator"—one who is technically skillful and also cognizant of learners' needs in their school and community (Oliva, 2001, p. 8).

For the most part, the seven states gave considerable attention to formulating detailed, comprehensive standards for administrative licensure. When asked whether the standards included social justice elements, most respondents confirmed the inclusion of a social justice thrust in their state policies. In following up on this response, however, most individuals could not identify specific social justice aspects. Oliva (2001) noted that there was clearly "a preference for dealing with social justice issues implicitly rather than explicitly" (p. 16). This tendency to "read" a concern for social justice into the standards was a common theme among the studies. Respondents felt that shifting greater responsibility and accountability to administrators for student learning would advance social justice in the schools.

Like the testing requirements for K–12 students, most of the states studied require prospective administrators to take a written performance assessment. The School Leaders Licensure Assessment (SLLA), developed by the Education Testing Service to meet the ISLLC standards, is used in Indiana and North Carolina. Individuals respond to a series of vignettes, and a national group of trained assessors evaluates the responses. Georgia adopted PRAXIS II for its assessment, and Texas uses its own examination (ExCET). Not only must applicants for licensure in these states pass an examination, but the states also are tying approval of leadership preparation programs to the performance of their graduate students on the tests (Gerstl-Pepin, 2001; McCarthy & Murtadha, 2001; Oliva, 2001).

Assessment practices raise concerns about how licensure standards ultimately are interpreted. Most respondents believed that high-stakes testing for administrators will prescribe what happens in preparation programs. Undoubtedly, this will be influential if tests are used for licensure as well as for university-program accreditation. Assessment processes can be positive if measures address what is believed to be the essential aspects of democratic, moral leadership. Yet some are concerned about the ability of current instruments to assess the broad range of characteristics important to transformative, democratic leadership—commitment to social justice, community building, risk-taking behaviors, and concern for diversity.

Accountability and Student Learning

State accountability measures have squarely focused everyone's attention on student learning and on the development of curriculum and pedagogy to ensure that all students meet high standards. Some urban superintendents argue that these standards have provided critical leverage for administrators to confront intractable disparities in their schools (Cambron-McCabe, Cunningham, Harvey, & Koff, 2005). However, the same superintendents express concerns about the disparate impact of testing requirements on low-income and minority students. Certainly, accountability standards and assessment place student achievement at the center of the debate over administrators' performance and licensure requirements. In fact, Marshall (2001) commented that accountability, rather than licensure, may be the more powerful policy consideration that affects principals. In McCarthy and Murtadha's (2001) study, one respondent said that for the first time Indiana principals are accountable for the improvement of student achievement at the school level. Arguably, accountability laws directed at increasing student achievement provide important resources and leverage to support students with the greatest needs, but the limited scope of these laws may only implicitly encompass the more acute social justice concerns schools and communities confront.

In the interviews, accountability for student learning primarily revolved around one factor—test scores. This is consistent with the national picture. Almost all states produce district report cards; over one-half of these are based on test scores. McCarthy and Murtadha (2001) described Indiana's policy focus as "clearly on student outcomes, particularly increasing student achievement as measured by the ISTEP-Plus [the statewide test]" (p. 6). Oliva (2001) noted that the Texas assessment system is similarly driven by test performance. To receive the highest ratings, Texas school districts must show that high percentages of all student subgroups (ethnicity, gender, etc.) are passing the test.

When respondents were asked directly about their state's attempts to address social justice concerns, elimination of the student achievement gap was the most frequently mentioned way to address social justice. Respondents readily pointed to state laws establishing high standards, continuous school improvement plans, and stringent assessment processes. Nevertheless, social justice as a by-product of standards and assessment may be problematic. A 50-state survey conducted by *Education Week* of a representative group of teachers indicated that standards and assessment had made their way down to the classroom, but, for the most part, the classrooms still look the same (Olsen, 2001). Others have argued that standards and assessment have exacerbated the situation for poor children in public schools, often unacceptably narrowing the curricular and pedagogical approaches in the classroom (McNeil, 2000; McNeil & Alenzuela, 1998; Kohn, 1999). When accountability is framed narrowly as testing, the policy debate does not challenge the injustices faced by poor students enduring low expectations, crowded classrooms, inexperienced teachers, antiquated buildings, and historical racism (Dantley & Cambron-McCabe, 2001; McCarthy & Murtadha, 2001; Oliva, 2001).

Data show that low-income and minority students experience greater difficulty in passing the state tests and are more likely to live in school districts with fewer resources (Haycock, 2001). Similar to many other states, Ohio's urban schools are experiencing the highest failure rates on the state tests and subsequently the lowest school district ratings. They find themselves disproportionately represented in the "academic watch" and "academic emergency" categories (Dantley & Cambron-McCabe, 2001). Serious equity questions are being raised in the state about the opportunities available to urban youth as they drop out of school in unprecedented numbers. Gerstl-Pepin (2001) pointed out that most "low performing schools" in Georgia have high populations of minority and low-income students, but this fact is not part of the larger policy discourse.

Haycock (2001) documented that "we take the students who have less to begin with and then systematically give them less in school. In fact, we give these students less of everything that we believe makes a difference. We do this in hundreds of different ways" (p. 8). Her data showed that students at risk for school failure are more likely to have insufficient resources, fewer experienced teachers, unprepared teachers, a low-level curriculum, and low expectations for student achievement. Such data raise serious questions about the implicit expectation that the new state standards and assessment will achieve equity for all students.

Social Justice and State Policies

For the researchers of the seven state studies, social justice was constructed broadly to include inequities related to race, gender, class, sexual orientation, and disability. The researchers purposefully did not define social justice in the interviews. A central aspect of the investigation was to gain an understanding of policymakers' and practitioners' assumptions about social justice and how they perceived it in the development of leaders in their states.

Across the seven studies, no one reported that interviewees were comfortable with the term *social justice* or used it without prompting. When asked about their perception of policymakers' interest in social justice and their own concerns, the respondents generally identified one or two major issues they felt raised social justice concerns in their state. Oliva (2001) reported that individuals readily pointed to the pressure of changing state demographics in Texas and educational access at all levels of schooling for students who typically have not been served well by the system. Facing a minority student population that will soon be the majority in schools, respondents felt that policy actions were too limited. A particular concern that surfaced in the Texas study was the "miniscule numbers of Hispanic teachers or administrators in the schools" (p. 12).

McCarthy and Murtadha (2001) noted a high level of consistency about the definition of social justice in Indiana. Most respondents discussed social justice in terms of women and minorities gaining access to administrative positions. Sentiments revolved around creating a level playing field in hiring and personnel decisions. In this context, almost all interviewees felt that the Indiana licensure standards, which are modeled on the ISLLC standards, will have "a positive impact on social justice and on changing the culture of schools and university preparation program to make them more accountable" (p. 6). Although Indiana's performance-based licensure may introduce more objectivity into employment decisions, McCarthy and Murtadha concluded that it appears to be "a vehicle to make administrative preparation more rigorous rather than as a strategy to nurture a commitment to social justice in a broad sense of that term" (p. 7).

Similar to Indiana, New York's Blue Ribbon Panel on School Leadership formally highlighted the low number of women and minorities in school district leadership roles. Along with this concern, Larson (2001) found that the Panel's list of needed traits and skills expands the "conventional" list for effective leadership. She noted that it is too early to determine if these skills and traits (such as concern for moral leadership, willingness to reach out to communities, and capacity to promote student learning) will be deepened in meaningful ways when implemented in preparation programs. Without clear delineation, she fears that "traditional notions of interpersonal skills, community, and student learning will prevail" (p. 17).

With over 30 years of litigation to bring about equity for poor children, New Jersey could be expected to be a model for other states. In fact, Rusch (2001) commented that New Jersey's court-ordered equity has led to new standards for schools that "read like a social justice manual" (p. 5). Notwithstanding state policies, she concluded that reform is taking place in a highly bureaucratic and hierarchical culture focused more on promulgation of regulations than on the achievement of equity. According to Rusch, the paramount issue is not so much a need to address licensure standards for administrators, but "a statewide effort to engage in behaviors that model social justice in action" (p. 11).

Ohio's experience, although shorter in duration, echoes New Jersey's attempts at court-ordered social justice (Dantley & Cambron-McCabe, 2001). Even though litigation provides a means to confront a system that does not work for all children, repeated attempts to devise an equitable funding approach have failed.

With few exceptions, Marshall (2001) found that North Carolina policymakers saw social justice as involving Black–White issues and the achievement gap. Accordingly, words such as *accountability, control, standards*, and *quality* dominated the policy discourse. Underpinning this perspective was the belief that tightening control and raising standards would advance social justice. One respondent's comment exemplified the prevailing viewpoint, "If you define social justice as making sure all students are going to have equal access to education, I don't think North Carolina has ever been more attuned" (p. 9).

In Georgia, Gerstl-Pepin (2001) found that social justice concerns were conflated with economic development discourses. Policymakers reasoned that improving Georgia's image nationally would enable the state to attract more jobs and thus provide more employment opportunities for low-income families. Despite this optimism, respondents agreed that economic development would not necessarily help the families of students in low-performing schools. Gerstl-Pepin noted that Georgia's economic policies have ignored the historical context of racism that produced the current disparities in public schools and their communities.

The seven state studies revealed policymakers' strong interest in reshaping administrator licensure requirements. In pursuing this priority, these states have overwhelmingly turned to the ISLLC standards as their model. Although attention to licensure standards is encouraging as the states focus on improving learning outcomes for all students, significant shortcomings were evident with current approaches that fail to explicitly identify social justice issues. Respondents, for the most part, pointed to rigorous student accountability standards to eliminate the student achievement gap as evidence that social justice was being addressed. Some respondents commented on the centrality of student learning in defining administrators' jobs, greater access for women and minorities to administrative positions, and an emphasis on quality and standards as proxies for social justice. These efforts are important, but they do not directly confront what school leaders must know and be able to do to challenge systemic inequities that deny large numbers of students equal educational opportunities. Policymakers view student achievement, standards, and quality schools as safe topics, as opposed to more controversial concerns regarding race, gender, and gays, lesbians, and bisexuals. With an abundance of concerns that can be taken up in the political arena, policymakers seldom raise troublesome issues that may balkanize voters.

Strategies to Promote Social Justice in Leadership Development

As we attempt to integrate social justice concerns into leadership licensure and preparation, we must be able to draw upon a theory of action (Fullan, 1999). That is, what strategies are available to us to make changes at the state and local levels? Who should be involved? What are the barriers? Several policy and programmatic efforts model possible approaches. Three efforts are highlighted in this section.

Being Strategic in Developing Leaders

Even if state licensure policies and higher education programs incorporate a stronger social justice emphasis, Marshall and Ward (2004) contend that such action alone will not be enough to change the culture within a profession that has not prioritized social justice issues. As they note, few opportunities exist to "practice effective leadership intervention for equity" (p. 533). Furthermore, preparation programs only reach the individuals *aspiring* to administrative positions, not the vast numbers of administrators in practice. Given the complexity of this dilemma, Marshall, an education scholar, and Ward, a state superintendent, joined forces to develop recommendations for strengthening social justice training for *all* administrators in North Carolina. They began their work by interviewing 10 prominent individuals with national perspectives, as well as national influence, to seek their advice about possible options for training of administrators. Their collaborative effort offers a model for others to consider.[1]

In the Marshall and Ward (2004) interviews, respondents agreed that administrators need to know how to address inequities in schooling. At the same time, respondents also acknowledged the difficult barriers confronting administrators who attempt this work. These barriers touched on time, resources, skills, community values, school board sentiments, certain policies, and lack of political will. According to some of the respondents, the most significant barrier may be a reluctance of individual leaders to take on a controversy with inherent risks—"little political will to go after these issues" (p. 539). One respondent succinctly pointed out that administrators are not trained for activism and further commented that "school boards and realtors don't like to have this conversation" (p. 543).

Based on their study, Marshall and Ward (2004) offered the following recommendations:

- *The case must be made for social justice.* Unless administrators are motivated to seek more knowledge and skills to address social justice concerns, it is unlikely that social justice will be a priority. This means raising the visibility of the issues through wide-ranging mediums (e.g., conference topics, professional magazines, recognition for accomplishments) and reinforcing it as part of effective leadership, as part of the job.
- *Use policy as a lever to address social justice.* Policies focus attention. As one of the study respondents noted, "What gets measured gets done" (p. 546). Policies encompassing accountability for student performance, administrator preparation, and professional development can provide significant leverage.
- *Education of administrators for social justice must occur in multiple arenas with collaborative partners.* Universities may still provide "the best opportunity of seriously addressing social justice issues" (p. 548), with reinforcement in ongoing professional development through national and state associations' conventions and seminars. Formation of an institute for social justice could provide a structure to promote state, regional, or national training; partnerships could be formed with other organizations for delivery. Regardless of the training venue, success will depend on multiple approaches and collaboration among many partners—agencies, professional associations, higher education, policymakers, and coalitions of various interest groups.

Marshall and Ward emphasized that collaboration is the lynchpin in their framework—"alone, no group can do this" (p. 557). Table 6.1 shows possible ways to conceptualize the multiple players and responsibilities across five arenas: challenging the culture; credibility and access; social justice standards and policies; delivering training; and funding training. The framework provides a powerful way to initiate collaboration and influence policy and its ultimate im-

TABLE 6.1 *Strengths and Targets for Social Justice Training*

Strengths	Challenging the Culture	Credibility and Access	Social Justice Standards and Policies	Deliver Training	Fund Training
Educational administration professors	X			X	
School boards			X		X
Practicing principals		X			
Central office administrators		X		X	
Professional associations		X		X	X
State and national boards			X		
Foundations	X				X

Source: Marshall & Ward (2004), p. 558.

plementation. It vividly illustrates the challenge confronting the field and the complexity of the task.

Becoming a Policy Actor

Scholars' critiques of the educational administration field readily identify problems and deficiencies that need attention, but few have been involved or consulted in the policy arena (Young, Petersen, & Short, 2002). What has happened to the scholar's role as leader within the profession? Why are scholars not moving their research and writing into political action for reinventing preparation programs to promote social justice for children (Cambron-McCabe & Cunningham, 2002)? Although the profession is faced with a lack of activism in modeling leadership to affect schools and society, a few scholars are taking up the task, and we can learn from their work. Grogan's (2003) concern over preparing school administrators to assume an active role in remedying inequities in schools led her to investigate what an individual could do at the state level to strengthen social justice requirements for licensed administrators.

Grogan's (2003) project was conducted in a southeastern state and involved interviews and conversations with three state policymakers and three superintendents of large school districts. Like other states, this southeastern state had focused attention and resources on accountability to increase student achievement. The state superintendent expressed hope that illuminating the achievement gap would result in administrators taking action to eliminate the gap. Grogan, however, felt the climate in the state was not conducive to administrators questioning their own practices or examining sources of inequities, such as racism. She noted, "In this environment, not only is it difficult to have a conversation about race, but there is still a prevailing belief that student success in school is solely within the grasp of the student. The effect of social structures of race, class and gender are not acknowledged" (p. 11). The state superintendent's reluctance to identify race as a factor in student achievement, preferring to blame socioeconomic status, reflected this climate.

The state policymakers and superintendents, however, were in agreement that principal preparation lacked substance and quality in the state. Furthermore, they also agreed that school leaders were not addressing equity, equality, and diversity issues. Through conversations, Grogan explored possible initiatives that could be implemented in the state to develop leaders with a social justice concern. A number of possibilities emerged (see Grogan, 2003), but the one that seemed most viable to the group was university based. This option involved the creation of an Executive Leadership Certificate, an endorsement beyond the initial license, that would "focus specifically on knowledge and research from a critical perspective to help develop a social conscience in future and current leaders" (p. 20). Operationally, this may involve an official endorsement universities could seek through the state or the higher education institutions could simply offer their own certificates. The critical factor would be the superintendents' "stamp of approval"; that is, giving preference to certificated applicants in the hiring process.

Grogan (2003) described what this educational process might encompass:

> Informed by wide reading and relevant research, participants would be encouraged to analyze data from their own districts; to gather data not previously regarded as important; to disaggregate all data; and to imagine policies and practices that would move marginalized students to the center. Innovative delivery methods could be used to engage students in this work. Participants could draw upon action research to apply new learning to their own settings. Weekend modules could be offered by collaborative teams of professors and practitioners to break away from the traditional somewhat stagnant approach to preparation. (p. 21)

Although Grogan believed that the Executive Leadership Certificate held significant promise, she was not able to follow the idea through to implementation because of relocation to another state. Her failure to build institutional support among colleagues left the idea without a champion in the southeastern state. Building on this lesson and others she learned, Grogan plans to pursue her activism for social justice in another state. Her strategy also can serve as a model for other faculty who may want to take on a more activist role in their state's policy arena.

Refocusing Preparation Programs

Even if state administrator licensure standards do not "explicitly" establish social justice expectations, preparation programs and professional development efforts can prepare leaders to probe existing structures and policies to gain an understanding of how they contribute to injustices. In fact, a number of preparation programs are recruiting diverse faculty members and revising their mission statements to encompass social justice. Like licensure standards, these programs must move beyond vague statement to specific actions to embody social justice. Miami University of Ohio's Educational Leadership Program, with its focus on school leadership as an intellectual, moral, and craft practice, has attempted to take this next step. A central premise of the program is that administrative practice must be informed by critical reflection that is situated in the cultural, political, and moral context of schooling. The implications of this undertaking for school leadership and social justice concerns are enormous:

> School administrators must not only acquire an understanding of schools as sites of cultural conflict but also understand how they in their official roles legitimate specific perspectives and practices. They must be able to assess schooling critically to illuminate the structures and practices that disempower. They must see leadership, not as management, but as a means for working toward the transformation of the school to advance social justice and a democratic school culture. From the role of administrator, they can make visible the tensions between the realities of schools and the promise they hold for transformation. (Cambron-McCabe, 1993, p. 162)

Future school leaders in the preparation program are continually confronted with views, or ways of seeing, that challenge their long-held beliefs about schooling, culture, power, and social justice. Through this critical reflection and questioning, leaders come to understand their role in shaping the nature and purposes of schooling. Educators too often see current practices as neutral and do not examine the appropriateness of the practices or the assumptions that drive them and, accordingly, direct attention to improving the existing practices rather than changing them. Argyris and Schon (1974) described this type of reflection and action as *single-loop learning*, which may bring about some changes but fails to reach the difficult consideration of the structures and norms in place. For example, the pervasive emphasis on measuring principals' effectiveness against the improvement of student learning may simply reinforce bureaucratic control and monitoring rather than redress embedded injustices. Argyris and Shon argued that individuals must engage in double-loop learning to surface and question deeply held beliefs and assumptions. This type of reflection is an integral aspect of the Miami University of Ohio coursework and holds the potential for school leaders to transform not only unjust practices, but also the systemic structures that perpetuate social inequities.

In Chapter 2, Dantley and Tillman urge transformative school leaders to critically deconstruct schools and their contexts. They state that transformative leaders do this by asking poignant, penetrating questions about their schools and by reflecting on their own personal actions that allow undemocratic marginalizing practices. The Miami University of Ohio leadership program creates opportunities throughout its coursework for educators to go beyond neutral rhetoric to engage in the critical deliberations that these authors advocate. An attempt is made to ground classroom learning in terms of the present concrete lives of everyday schools. Cases, problems, and narratives are drawn from school settings to engage moral, ethical, and social justice issues (see Discussion Questions and Activities #5 for an example of a narrative and reflective questions). Students examine equal educational opportunity in poor and urban schools; investigate school reform measures and their impact on school quality and diversity; analyze the affect of discipline practices on diverse student groups; and scrutinize attendance and drop-out data for patterns that may implicate systemic injustices. Learning the skills for this kind of engagement in a leadership preparation program can be a first step in creating a more active democracy for both educators and children and can be applied at all levels of the schooling enterprise.

Implications for Policy Development

Taking up the challenge of social justice is not for the faint of heart. It means leaders must hold difficult conversations in their schools and in the communities in which they live. A beginning point for this work is a state-level policy encompassing social justice standards for preparing school administrators to confront and address inequities. Fullan (1999) proclaimed that "you can't mandate what matters" regarding individuals' commitment to a particular reform but asserted that mandates are important. Mandates often provide the pressure or springboard needed to take up a particular effort as well as provide legitimacy for those who undertake it (Dantley & Cambron-McCabe, 2001). This was clearly demonstrated in the seven state studies; state-level policies drove the reform of higher education preparation programs. For social justice concerns, the critical questions become: (1) What is included in the state standards? (2) Who is involved in the deliberations?

First, what is included in state standards must go beyond the subtle, implied commitment to social justice that was found in the state policies in the seven state studies. As Dantley and Tillman note in Chapter 2, situating school administration positions as realizing democratic imperatives in the everyday life of schools requires an educational leader "to link critical thought to collective action" (p. 17). This poses a substantially different undertaking for preparing school leaders than the historical notions embedded in school administration. Making social justice concerns a priority in schools requires leaders not only to understand and name unjust practices that deprive individuals of their rights and dignity, but also necessitates that they take action to change the structures that perpetuate the injustices. Noguera (2003) said it means debunking racial stereotypes, breaking down racial separations, and confronting the hidden curriculum. Gerstl-Pepin (2001) advised that we must "go beyond discussions of how the system works and what is wrong with it, to encompass discussions of how programs can give [leaders] the skills to be advocates for disadvantaged children, parents, teachers, and communities" (p. 20). Systemic structures that caused and now sustain those injustices must be confronted.[2] Not only must leaders pose difficult questions for others, but, ultimately they must also face their own assumptions—What about their own thinking allows these conditions to exist?

The second question, who is involved in the deliberations, requires all groups connected to school administration to rethink their roles and connections. Activism for social justice on the part of the groups identified by Marshall and Ward (2004) (see Table 6.1) can create pressure to shift policies, but only if activism is collaborative. Young, Petersen, and Short (2002) call for such collaboration among all stakeholders to define expectations for licensure and preparation programs. Formation of the National Commission for the Advancement of Educational Leadership Preparation in 2001 was an attempt to bring diverse interests together to facilitate collaborative design of new plans for educational leadership development. At the center of the Commission's work is the proposed formation of a league involving practitioners, university faculty, community organizations, school boards, professional associations, and government agencies. If this proposed league were to make social justice central to its work, collective action could lead to a powerful reconceptualization of what it means to lead schools.

Clearly, we cannot talk about policies without recognizing that accountability demands will continue to shape school administrators' work. The No Child Left Behind Act (2002), with its spotlight on the student achievement gap, has given us not only ample evidence that extreme inequities exist in many school districts, but it also has placed national pressure on the system to respond to those needs. Consequently, federal and state policies have initiated a proliferation of "technical" fixes, but, for the most part, they fail to take up the deeply rooted issues that led us into this crisis. Heifetz (1994) distinguishes between *technical problems* where workable solutions already exist and *adaptive problems* where a shift in people's values, attitudes, and beliefs is required. The latter problems, often those involving social justice concerns, are the most obstinate and can be resolved only with learning and engagement within a school and community.

Linking accountability with social justice requires such adaptive work—to hold difficult conversations to probe deeper when students fail. Who is ultimately accountable when high numbers of children fail? For what are they held accountable? Is there really flexibility to create local curricula and develop alternative instructional approaches when state tests drive what is taught? What is the risk when local schools decide what will be taught based on students' needs in their community rather than state accountability measures? Who is winning in our schools and who is losing? Can we live with that knowledge (Cambron-McCabe, 2002)? Although Heifetz's framework provides leaders' guidance, he cautions that they still may not survive when they take up these difficult questions. Certainly, leaders need an understanding of the social justice challenges, but equally important, they must possess the skills to do the work. Few risk takers will survive without profoundly different preparation.

Marshall and Ward (2003) encountered a lack of commitment or interest in schools and communities to focus on social justice concerns. That point, maybe more than any other, frames the challenge for school leaders. How do you create a space to surface and engage beliefs that restrict options for pursuing equity? What does this mean for state policy and leadership preparation? What experiences must be provided to enable school leaders to raise questions about their own assumptions, to engage in double-loop learning? Then, what practical knowledge and skills are required to lead in this environment? These are the questions that must guide policy deliberations about the preparation of school leaders.

A consistent sterility characterizes the burgeoning reports on school leadership. One cannot argue with their calls for rigorous preparation and refocusing administrators' work on instructional leadership, high expectations, continuous improvement planning, diversity, and community engagement. However, noticeably absent from these reports is the stark reality troubling too many schoolchildren today. Without situating leadership preparation within this reality, these reports only skim the surface of the challenge ahead. As Marshall and Ward (2004) proposed, what we need is a "fundamental leap" into a new paradigm of leadership for social justice—one that places students' interests first, that works toward democratic imperatives, and that promotes moral reflection and action.

Discussion Questions and Activities _____

1. Identify aspects of your administrative preparation program that prepare (or prepared) you to engage social justice issues. Include topics, readings, videos, internships, observations/activities, and pedagogical approaches. What else is needed to strengthen your capacity to do this work?

2. How do accountability laws, such as No Child Left Behind and state proficiency tests, support or hinder your efforts to achieve equity in your school?

3. Several chapters in this text (see Chapters 2 and 3) propose new paradigms for leadership that encompass spirituality and feminism. What political contexts prevent serious engagement of these alternatives in licensure standards and preparation programs?

4. Examine the administrative preparation licensure standards in your state by reviewing published documents and interviewing selected educators and state officials.

   a. What strategies have been implemented to improve the preparation and licensure of school administrators?
   b. Have the ISLLC standards been adopted for administrator development? If so, how are they reflected in preparation programs and licensure requirements?
   c. Identify social justice components in the licensure standards.
   d. How are the licensure standards assessed (i.e., performance measures, paper and pencil test, other measures)?
   e. What other state policies address social justice concerns and schools?
   f. From your review of administrator licensure, what is your assessment of the commitment to social justice by policymakers? Educators? Citizens in general?

5. Use the narrative of Frantz, an African American male, to engage in double-loop reflection to examine what equal educational opportunity means in today's schools.[3] Analysis of narratives, such as this one or others created from your experiences, can be used to illustrate the moral and ethical deliberation required of today's leaders to confront inequitable practices (see Chapter 11 for additional cases).

During the early elementary school years, Frantz, an African American male, socialized with most of his peers in school. Living in a small community allowed him the opportunity to know his classmates quite well from an early age. In the early years, he had many friends, but he found that when it was time to work in "teams" for class assignments, he repeatedly worked with the same group of friends.

As he moved through the elementary grades, the first day of school was always bittersweet, because with each passing year, some of his friends from previous years were assigned to other classes. By the time he reached the fifth grade, he noticed that most of his classmates had been with him since the third grade.

Frantz was sure as he moved into middle school that he would reconnect with some of his friends from the early elementary grades. He was amazed, however, to see that the majority of his classmates were still his old friends from the fourth and fifth grades.

As Frantz entered his second year of middle school, he ran into Paul, a familiar face from his elementary school who had not been in any of his classes over the past few years. After engaging Paul in the usual middle-school talk, Frantz began talking about his schedule.

Frantz shared, "I'm really excited about my classes this year. My counselor, Mr. Smith (Caucasian) helped me to sign up for a good schedule. He's so cool because he wanted to make sure that I didn't sign up for anything that would be too hard for me. He even warned me that one of the toughest classes I will take this year is Foundations of Mathematics. He told me that he wanted to make sure that the rest of my classes would not be too hard so I can concentrate on getting through this one. So what about you? What classes are you taking this semester?"

"Foundations of Mathematics? I'm taking pre-algebra," responded Paul. "Mr. Smith told me that this class as well as other classes I'm taking would be a challenge, but if I stuck with it, after this year, I can take Algebra I and Physical Science in eighth grade for high school credit."

Frantz, puzzled, remarked, "I never knew that you could get high school credit in middle school. I wonder why Mr. Smith never told me about it. I'll ask him if I can take those classes that offer high school credit."

Frantz's story is played out each year in schools as "neutral" assignment practices result in a disparate impact on various groups of students. Using the questions below as a guide, discuss the narrative and its implications for your leadership role.

a. Are all students provided opportunities to achieve at high levels in your school? Who enrolls in college prep, vocational, or general programs? Who has access to honors and advanced placement classes? Have you carefully examined students' assignments and the work expected and produced in courses? Is your school a sorting machine?
b. What is the impact of exclusionary practices on marginalized students?
c. When issues of race and class arise in your school, do people fall silent? Or, are they able to discuss these challenges openly? Is there a different answer to these questions in your community and in your school?
d. Is the category of African American males recognized as one meriting special attention? Have you analyzed the data regarding African American males (placement, attendance, discipline, etc.)?
e. Have you provided a space to hear the voices of African American students? If so, what have you learned? If not, where do you start?
f. Whose interests are being served in this narrative?
g. Are teachers and administrators willing to discuss the challenges presented by the narrative? Is the community willing?

Annotated Readings

Cambron-McCabe, Cunningham, Harvey, and Koff's *The Superintendent's Fieldbook: A Guide for Leaders of Learning* (2005) is a valuable resource. Specifically, the sections "Leading Your Schools" and "Addressing Race and Class" reframe how leaders take up difficult conversations in their schools and communities based on the experiences of a group of school superintendents and their principals. This book can be used as a resource in creating suggested licensure standards for social justice. Does your current state licensure standards incorporate these understandings? What recommendations would you make to your state based on these findings?

Larson and Ovando's *The Color of Bureaucracy* (2001) contains an in-depth case study of a school ripped apart by racial conflict (see Chapter 3). Use this case to critique and engage in conversations about the bureaucratic logic that underpins most administrator licensure, preparation, and professional development programs. What are the implications for licensure and preparation standards?

Volume 9 of the North Central Regional Educational Laboratory's *Bridging the Great Divide: Broadening Perspectives on Closing the Achievement Gap* (2002), which is part of NCREL's *Viewpoints* series, contains information about the achievement gap, examples of innovative programs targeted toward closing the gap, and voices from the field discussing the perspectives surrounding this issue. The multimedia resources create a context for you to critique the challenges confronting the development of school leaders committed to achieving equity in schools. What are the implications for preparing school administrators? What are the implications for state licensure standards? See also NCREL's Closing the Achievement Gap Web site at www.ncrel.org/gap/.

As students examine state administrator licensure standards, questions arise about how ethics and moral issues can be reflected. Shapiro and Stefkovich's short book (122 pages), *Ethical Leadership and Decision Making in Education: Applying Theoretical Perspectives to Complex Dilemmas* (2001), shows the application of multiple ethical paradigms (justice, care, critique, and profession) to moral dilemmas school leaders confront in their schools. How can these perspectives be incorporated into licensure standards? Is the requirement a separate standard or embedded throughout? Draft suggested wording for your state administrator standards to strengthen social justice.

References

Achilles, C. M., & Price, W. J. (2001). What is missing in the current debate about education administration standards. *AASA Professor, 24*(2), 8–13.

Anderson, G. (2001). Disciplining leaders: A critical discourse analysis of the ISLLC national examination and performance standards in educational administration. *International Journal of Leadership in Education, 4*(3), 199–216.

Argyris, C., & Schon, D. (1974). *Theory in practice: Increasing professional effectiveness.* San Francisco: Jossey-Bass.

Cambron-McCabe, N. (1993). Leadership for democratic authority. In J. Murphy (Ed.), *Preparing tomorrow's school leaders: Alternative designs.* University Park, PA: UCEA.

Cambron-McCabe, N. (2002). Educational accountability in the USA: Focus on state testing. *Education and the Law, 14*(1), 117–126.

Cambron-McCabe, N., & Cunningham, L. (2002). National Commission for the Advancement of Educational Leadership: Opportunity for transformation. *Educational Administration Quarterly, 38*(2), 289–299.

Cambron-McCabe, N., Cunningham, L., Harvey, J., & Koff, R. (2005). *The superintendent's fieldbook: A guide for leaders of learning.* Thousand Oaks, CA: Corwin Press.

Council of Chief State School Officers (CCSSO). (1996). *Interstate school leaders licensure consortium: Standards for school leaders.* Washington, DC: CCSSO.

Dantley, M., & Cambron-McCabe, N. (2001, April). *Administrative preparation and social justice concerns in Ohio.* Paper presented at the annual meeting of the American Educational Research Association, Seattle, WA.

English, F. (2000, April). *The ghostbusters search for Frederick Taylor in the ISLLC standards.* Paper presented at the annual meeting of the American Educational Research Association, New Orleans, LA.

Fullan, M. (1999). *Change forces: The sequel.* Philadelphia, PA: Falmer Press.

Gerstl-Pepin, C. (2001, April). *Social justice and administrative licensure in Georgia.* Paper presented at the American Educational Research Association, Seattle, Washington.

Grogan, M. (2003, April). *A university executive leadership certificate aimed at building a social justice conscience.* Paper presented at the annual meeting of the American Educational Research Association, Chicago, IL.

Hale, E. L., & Moorman, H. N. (2003). *Preparing school principals: A national perspective on policy and program innovations.* Washington, DC: Institute for Educational Leadership.

Haycock, K. (2001). Closing the achievement gap. *Educational Leadership, 58*(6), 6–11.

Heifetz, R. (1994). *Leadership without easy answers.* Cambridge: Belkap Press.

Huggins, E. M., with Celio, M. B. (2002). *Closing the achievement gap in Washington State.* Seattle: Center on Reinventing Public Education, University of Washington and Washington State Academic Achievement and Accountability Commission.

Kohn, A. (1999). *The schools our children deserve: Moving beyond traditional classrooms and "tougher standards."* Boston: Houghton Mifflin.

Larson, C. (2001, April). *Rethinking leadership: New York's efforts to create skilled and knowledgeable leaders for our schools.* Paper presented at the annual meeting of the American Educational Research Association, Seattle, WA.

Larson, C., & Ovando, C. (2001). *The color of bureaucracy.* Belmont, CA: Wadsworth.

Marshall, C. (2001, April). *School administration licensure policy in North Carolina.* Paper presented at the annual meeting of the American Educational Research Association, Seattle, WA.

Marshall, C., & McCarthy, M. (2002). School leadership reforms: Filtering social justice through dominant discourses. *Journal of School Leadership, 12,* 480–502.

Marshall, C., & Ward, M. (2004). Strategic policy for social justice training for leadership. *Journal of School Leadership, 14*(5), 530–563.

McCarthy, M., & Murtadha, K. (2001, April). *Standards-based certification for Indiana school leaders and social justice concerns.* Paper presented at the annual meeting of the American Educational Research Association, Seattle, WA.

McNeil, L. (2000). *Contradictions of school reform: The educational costs of standardized testing.* New York: Routledge.

McNeil, L., & Alenzuela, A. (1998). *The harmful impact of the TAAS system of testing in Texas: Beneath the accountability rhetoric.* Boston: The Civil Rights Project, Harvard University.

No Child Left Behind, 20 U.S.C. 6301 et seq. (2002).

Noguera, P. A. (2003). Joaquin's dilemma: Understanding the link between racial identity and school-related behaviors. In M. Sadowski (Ed.), *Adolescents at school: Perspectives on youth, identity, and education* (pp. 19–30). Cambridge: Harvard Education Press.

North Central Regional Educational Laboratory (2002). *Bridging the great divide: Broadening perspectives on closing the achievement gap,* vol. 9. Naperville, IL: NCREL.

Oliva, M. (2001, April). *Texas educator certification and social justice.* Paper presented at the annual meeting of the American Educational Research Association, Seattle, WA.

Olsen, L. (2001). Quality counts 2001: Finding the right mix. *Education Week, 20*(17), 12–20.

Rusch, E. (2001, April). *Preparing leaders for social justice in New Jersey.* Paper presented at the annual meeting of the American Educational Research Association, Seattle, WA.

Shapiro, J. P., & Stefkovich, J. A. (2001). *Ethical leadership and decision making in education: Applying theoretical perspectives to complex dilemmas.* Mahwah, NJ: Lawrence Erlbaum.

Young, M. D., Petersen, G. J., & Short, P. M. (2002). The complexity of substantive reform: A call for interdependence among key stakeholders. *Educational Administration Quarterly, 38*(2), 137–175.

Endnotes

[1]For too long, scholars and policymakers have worked in isolation of each other. Marshall and Ward (2004) demonstrated that collaboration can be done across institutional boundaries to create viable options. Such collaboration not only enhances the likelihood that all perspectives are considered, but that new approaches will be implemented and supported across institutions.

[2]Even with explicit social justice licensure standards and preparation programs, school leaders' work will be undermined if school structures and communities do not support the same values (see Anderson & Oliva, Chapter 14).

[3]Narrative written by Craig A. Saddler, Doctoral Student, Miami University, Oxford, Ohio.

7

Social Justice, Religion, and Public School Leaders

Catherine A. Lugg
Zeena Tabbaa-Rida

Over the last decade, educational leaders working within public schools have begun to pay attention to issues of social justice. In part, this attention has been stimulated by the growing mismatch between the demography of the profession and the demography of their clientele (Marshall, 2004). Although much of the current research focuses on issues of race, ethnicity, gender, orientation, ability, and social class, far less attention has been paid to issues of social justice and religion and their intersection at the public school. Yet, religion plays a profound role in the lives of many U.S. public school students. Educational leaders who are sensitive to these needs can make a positive influence in the lives of their students, particularly those who are religious minorities. For example, Amal, a young Muslim woman, fondly recalled her public high school principal:

> We had Mr. Assad. He was Arab—Arab Christian. He was Egyptian. But not everybody knew that. And for us, even though he was not Muslim, just the fact that he was Arab in Arcadia, which is like all white school . . . I guess we just felt comfort in that. That he was from a similar background. Even though I am not Arab . . . I asked him permission to pray in high school, so I went to him . . . and he gave me the keys to a room to pray. (Tabbaa-Rida, 2004, p. 123)

However, educational leaders, although officially secular regarding religion and religious practices, in many parts of the United States have historically been more or less Protestant (Fraser, 1999). Consequently, tensions between long-established local practices and the rights of students (religious majority, religious minority, and those who follow no religious doctrine) can arise. This chapter explores the shifting terrain of religion and religious expression within the United States and places it within the context of social justice, educational leadership, and public schools. We conclude by drawing some implications for practice, as well as offering some short, provocative case studies and activities for aspiring administrators.

Religion, Secularism, and U.S. Public Schools

Although officially secular since their inception in the nineteenth century, historically, the U.S. public school system has embraced a loose Protestant ethos reflecting more a majoritarian ethic than one of social justice (Fraser, 1999). Throughout the nineteenth century and most of the twentieth, the majority of public schools required students to recite a collective prayer as well as read verses from the Bible, typically the King James Version (Fraser, 1999). These Protestant practices were considered to be "secular"; that is, not tied to a specific doctrinal sect, such as Methodism or Presbyterianism. The religious exercises were typically justified under the rubric of cultivating a common morality in a pluralistic society (Button & Provenzo, 1983; Nasaw, 1979; Tyack & Hansot, 1982).

In many areas, these religious practices were used to impose a common religious faith on students, regardless of their own religious backgrounds. In particular, public schools could be fiercely anti-Catholic and anti-Semitic, depending on the political tenor of a given era (Ahlstrom, 1972; Bennett, 1995;

The attire and the religious freedoms of the Muslim girls create complex challenges for school leaders.
Laurent Rebours/AP Wide World Photos

Fraser, 1999). Even if the schools were not overly hostile, they could remind religious minority students of their diminished social status. One former pupil related to the U.S. Congress what it was like to attend a public school in the 1950s as a religious minority student:

> Prayers and Bible passages were recited daily. Prayer is not a generic form of expression, and Bible passages and translations were not, are not, and should not be theologically neutral. The public school religion I encountered had in every case specific theological roots and forms. The prayers said in the public school I attended were distinctly Protestant in content. The students in the schools I attended were largely Jewish; the prayers exclusively Christian.
> . . .
> The use of Protestant religion was a part of a deliberate effort by the public schools to suggest to the American children of Jewish immigrants that these Protestant rituals represented true Americanism, that the rituals and rhythms of our parents' houses were alien and foreign, worse to children who desperately wished to be accepted, even "un-American." (Fraser, 1999, pp. 144–145).

In addition to the curriculum and religious practices endorsing a watered down form of Protestantism, educational administrations were expected to be Protestant. According to historians David Tyack and Elizabeth Hansot (1982):

> Religion provided an important informal criterion for selection to the superintendency. Being Protestant and an active church member was an important requirement for selection as superintendent, especially in small- or medium-sized communities. Among 796 superintendents who reported their religion in Frederick Bair's study in 1934, only 6 were Roman Catholic, none Jewish, and none agnostic; 93 percent reported that they attended church. (p. 169)

Another study from the 1950s found that in Massachusetts, superintendents and school boards overwhelmingly preferred white males as administrators, whereas a smaller number (but still a majority) preferred Protestants over Catholics and Jews (see Tyack & Hansot, 1982). Roughly from 1840 until the 1960s, the U.S. common school, and later the public school system, although officially secular, took on a largely Protestant tone.

Beginning in the early 1960s, the Supreme Court barred the official recognition of religious exercises in public schools and narrowed the legal definition of *secular*, moving away from vague and sometimes not so vague Protestantism, and toward a concept known as *neutrality* (Karst, 2003; Ryan, 2000; Zimmerman, 2002). Furthermore, the Court maintained that while public school students have a First Amendment right to their religious beliefs, these same students have a First Amendment right to be *free from religious imposition* while in the custody of state actors (see Karst, 2003). Consequently, public schools, because they are public institutions that essentially serve a "captive" audience (thanks to compulsory education laws) that is highly impressionable, must remain scrupulously neutral: School personnel, practices, and policies can neither promote religion nor inhibit it (Epstein, 1996; Greenwalt, 2002; Karst, 2003; Ryan, 2000).

This particular point, *neutrality*, has become increasingly salient for public schools when examining the accelerating rate of religious variation and innovation within the United States. Currently, roughly 2,000 differing faith systems are practiced in the United States, with over half of them forming *since* 1960 (French, 2003). Additionally, the percentage of religiously unaffiliated Americans has *doubled* since 1991 and currently stands at 14.1 percent (www.religioustolerance.org). Americans are far more likely than their European counterparts to choose a faith system that differs from the one in which they were raised. Consequently, religious life in the United States is marked by a high degree of innovation, individualism, eclectic and idiosyncratic practices (French, 2003; Lugg, 2004; Roof, 2003), marketing (Moore, 1994), and competition (Roof, 2003) for followers. The sheer religious diversity embodied by the student and staff populations can present a host of complex issues for educational leaders who work in historically weakly to strongly Protestant/Christian public schools (Tyack & Hansot, 1982).[1] Additionally, some educators who have been raised in and/or belong to various Christian denominations may not see long-standing public school practices, such as the annual Christmas or "Holiday" concert or various discipline policies, as potentially oppressive for religious minority students or for students who hold no religious beliefs (Greenwalt, 2002).

For example, in 1999 school personnel at Harrison Central High School in Gulfport, Mississippi, ordered Ryan Green to conceal his Star of David necklace (that his grandmother had given him) on the grounds that it was a gang symbol. However, school officials permitted Christian students at Harrison to wear visible crosses. The ACLU intervened, and after two weeks of intense national media scrutiny, the embarrassed school board relented (see CNN, August 20, 1999). Similarly, the Muskogee, Oklahoma, public school district was sanctioned in June of 2004 by a federal judge for banning the hijab, the head scarf worn by some Muslim girls and women as a mark of religious devotion. The district had maintained a blanket policy banning all head coverings as a way to prevent gang-related activity in schools. But the district refused to revise this policy in light of religious concerns, and the district twice suspended a Muslim sixth grader who wore the hijab to school (Associated Press, 2004). District officials could not see that such a blanket policy substantially interfered with a student's individual religious expression. And this specific expression had no discernable impact on either the learning environment or student safety and discipline. Consequently, the federal judge ruled that the policy was not religiously neutral, but was, in fact, hostile toward religion and one religion in particular: Islam.

This limit in administrative vision may further be encumbered depending on how compelled a given public school worker feels he or she must proselytize or share his or her faith with those who believe differently or those who hold no religious beliefs. Christianity, like Islam, but unlike Judaism or Buddhism (Armstrong, 1993, 2000), seeks converts to the faith as a matter of religious obligation. But public school personnel, teachers, administrators, counselors, janitors, and so on—regardless of their own individual religious preferences—are representatives of the state, and consequently they must remain religiously neutral when at work (Gey, 2000). Additionally, public school personnel have *fewer* free speech rights, and this includes religious speech, while at the school site than do students (MacGillivray, 2004). For Muslim and Christian educators, this means they must suspend the religious obligation of proselytization—sharing their faith— if they are to remain neutral and within Constitutional boundaries. The neutrality principle also extends beyond individual educator behavior. The Supreme Court has determined that many "traditional" public school practices violate the Establishment Clause because they promote a specific religion. The court has:

> . . . rejected arguments that school prayers and Bible readings promote moral values and an appreciation of literature; that the posting of the Ten Commandments educates students in the origins of the legal codes of Western Civilization; and that requiring creationism to be taught whenever evolution is taught furthers academic freedom. In each of these cases, the Court concluded that the actual purpose behind the activity was to promote religion and particular religious viewpoints. (Ryan, 2002, p. 1384, internal citations omitted)

Social-justice-oriented educators need to be sensitive to their own religious beliefs and be willing to refrain from engaging in or promoting religious activity, including religious-oriented speech, when they are functioning as a "state actor" (Gaddy, Hall, & Marzano, 1996; MacGillivray, 2004).

However, the situation confronting social justice educational leaders regarding religion and public education is even more complex. At times, public school administrators must violate the neutrality principle. Under U.S. law, school officials are obligated to *curtail* religious expression if the individual expression in question substantially interferes with the academic environment (Epstein, 1996; Harvard Law Review Association, 2002; Karst, 2003; MacGillivray, 2004; Ryan, 2000). Although students are permitted more latitude than public school workers in expressing their beliefs (religious as well as other beliefs), these expressions cannot interfere with the school's learning environment. For example, students are not permitted to spontaneously break into vocal prayer, song, and so on in the midst of a lesson, group project, class discussion, or assembly. Furthermore, in the case of Sikh children, they are not permitted to wear *kirpans* or ceremonial knives to school, although these knives are a marker of religious devotion (see Harvard Law Review Association, 2002). Such behavior is seen as disruptive to the learning environment, a threat to the safety of other students, and/or as a disciplinary infraction. Consequently, educators are expected to proscribe it (MacGillivray, 2004; Ryan, 2000).

However, the lines between neutrality and school discipline can blur, typically in cases where students are engaging in religious discussions during lunch, in the hallways, or on the playground. What feels like a stimulating debate for some students, may feel like religious-based harassment to others (Harvard Law Review Association, 2002; Greenwalt, 2002; MacGillivray, 2004). If improperly addressed, these situations can escalate into name-calling, harassment, or worse. At times, religious minority parents and their children, as well as religious majority parents and their children, have been treated insensitively by public school personnel in their attempts to resolve these matters (Baer & Carper, 2000; Fraser, 1999; Nord, 1995).

Another matter confronting social justice educators with regard to issues of religion and public education is the tendency to confuse *neutrality* with silence or selective silence (Gey, 2000). Over the past 20 years, researchers have documented the degree to which public school textbooks ignore religious influences on U.S. culture and politics (Greenwalt, 2002; Zimmerman, 2002). Typically, educators will claim they are not competent to address matters of religion in a way that is congruent with legal strictures covering public schools—so they avoid the matter entirely (Greenwalt, 2002; Nord, 1995). Religious omission by a public school curriculum might well be a defensible position if a given school district has been marked by religiously based political conflict or outright oppression of religious minorities by majorities (see Greenwalt, 2002).[2] However, many times, this silence is not neutral, because it distorts history, literature, economics, anthropology, and sociology, as well as the history of science (Greenwalt, 2002; Nord, 1995). As the Supreme Court has repeatedly noted, it is perfectly constitutional to teach *about* various religions. Public schools are only enjoined from teaching religious faiths as *truth* (Greenwalt, 2002; Karst, 2004; Ryan, 2000).

Besides silence, there is the ongoing matter of *selective silences* regarding religion and public education. Generally, if religion is covered by coursework and/or textbooks, the only faith that is examined is Christianity. Although many Christian parents object to how poorly Christianity is addressed (Greenwalt, 2002; Zimmerman, 2002), other religions typically receive no mention at all in the public school curriculum. As one Muslim public school student recently recalled:

> They never covered anything about Islam in high school. They never did. They never even brought it up. I learned about it when I was in college. It was never— in history books. They never even had it. Always had it with the United States presidents and mostly concentrated on United States than other Muslim countries. There was not even any Muslim country.—Fahima (Tabbaa-Rida, 2004, p. 313)

Given the high degree of religious pluralism in the United States, or what one scholar has labeled "hyper-pluralism" (see Herrington, 2000), the exclusion of other religious faiths from academic discussions is deeply troubling and probably mis-educative in the Deweyian sense (see Dewey, 1935; Chapter 2 this volume). Although Christianity has played an important role is shaping U.S. culture, so have other traditions, including nonreligious strains of thought, such as Freethinking, Taoism, and atheism. Their exclusion from academic exploration distorts what material is presented and alienates many contemporary students (Greenwalt, 2002).

The final point in this section deals with what could be called "religious offense." Public schools do cover material and subjects to which some people of faith may well object (e.g., sexuality education, evolution, sexuality explicit literature, and differing religious traditions). Some parents may wish to exempt or remove their children from certain classrooms or subjects to minimize their exposure to religiously objectionable information. Yet these religious concerns may be trumped by other pressing social and political concerns (Gutmann, 1987; Karst, 2003; MacGillivray, 2004). Under the "compelling state interest" rubric, states and local school districts can mandate certain classes, including courses covering human sexuality, regardless of parental religious objections, if this information is deemed critical to a child's well-being (see Lugg, 2003). It is under this rubric that many states mandated HIV/AIDS education during the late 1980s and early 1990s, although most of the information presented stresses abstinence in deference to the political clout of religious activists (Lugg, 2004). Nevertheless, the balance of religious liberty and compelling state interest is constantly shifting, and educational leaders need to pay attention to both sudden and subtle movements (see Karst, 2003).

Educational Leadership, Social Justice, and Religion in Public Schools

Educational leaders who are committed to social justice need to be cognizant of the various complexities involving religion and public education, as well as the local contexts in which issues of religious faith and practice can play out upon the public school political stage. First, they need to be informed about how diverse the U.S. religious landscape has been in the past as well as how diverse it is today. Although public schools, as organizations, have historically held a Protestant flavor, this distorts the rich and astonishingly diverse religious legacy of the United States (Ahlstrom, 1972). Furthermore, students and their parents hold a variety of religious beliefs, even within communities that may overwhelmingly be of one specific faith. Likewise, there is a rapidly growing percentage of Americans who hold no religious beliefs (www.religioustolerance.org). Second, educational leaders need to remember that some-to-many students may hold no religious beliefs at all, or that individual students may well hold religious beliefs that differ from their parents (Harvard Law Review Association, 2002). Third, if religion is addressed as an academic topic, it needs to be presented in a neutral manner by educators and cover a variety of faith systems (Greenwalt, 2002).

Additionally, leaders who are committed to social justice need to reexamine their discipline policies in light of religious liberty and establishment clause issues, navigating the gray areas between remaining neutral on religious matters and maintaining discipline. In particular, student dress codes should carefully be examined for any potential bias regarding a given faith. Nevertheless, social-justice-minded educational leaders also need to be cognizant that not all religious objections may be actionable. If there are pressing issues involving public health and/or student welfare, these objections may have to go unsatisfied.

Finally, educational leaders need to reflect on their own belief systems (both religious and nonreligious) to see if they are impermissibly shaping the culture and experiences within the public school walls (see Epstein, 1996). Educational leaders who are committed to social justice for all children need to evaluate their own values and actions to ensure that they are not unwittingly engaging in religious oppression.

As one can tell from this brief exploration, these are complex waters for educational leaders to navigate, particularly for those committed to expanding social justice within their own school's walls. Furthermore, this complexity varies from state to state, district to district, and school to school. But the results can be rewarding for all involved with public schooling if educational leaders are willing to explore more socially just ways of addressing issues of religion, religious belief, nonbelief, and expressions of both.

Discussion Questions and Activities _____

1. Have the U.S. public schools always been secular? Use examples to justify your answer

2. Has the meaning of the term *secular* changed over time? If so, how has it changed?

3. What does *secular* mean *today* regarding public schools and religion? What are the implications for socially just educational leadership?

4. What is religious *neutrality*? Does it mean that public school workers must remain silent regarding issues of religion? Give examples to support your opinion.

5. In your current work environment, how is religious neutrality manifested in daily practice?

6. In what situations might the neutrality principle be violated and yet your actions be considered socially just?

7. In another chapter in this book, Michael Dantley and Linda Tillman (Chapter 2) discuss moral leadership and its influence in shaping socially just, transformational

leadership practices. Does morality differ from religious faith? Why or why not? If it does differ, how does it differ? Can a moral educational leader be neutral toward religion? Why or why not?

8. After reading several of the publications listed in the "Further Reading" section, present the main ideas of these works to your work group or class, leading a discussion on the theories, the research findings, and points of view presented by the authors.

9. In the following two case studies, readers are invited to the tackle the challenges presented by the intersections of religious belief, student life, and public schools. Both cases are drawn from the research literature.

10. The following case study is drawn from Tabbaa-Rida (2004). Read the case study and then complete the activities that follow.

On Wednesday, Mr. Ernest, the school principal at Sunnydale Public High School, had finished his morning walk through the school's hallways and was heading back towards his office for his first appointment for the day. It was with a parent whose ninth-grade daughter, Mona, had claimed that she had experienced religious harassment at school a few days earlier. Dr. Kamal, the student's mother, had decided to convey her concerns about the school's hostile attitude toward her daughter's religious head covering, and possibly, hostility toward their Muslim faith. Mr. Ernest suspected it was more likely a "tempest in a teapot," that the harassment was, in fact, adolescent teasing that had gotten somewhat out of hand.

On Monday, while Mona was at her locker getting her books, someone had grabbed her flowery scarf and pulled it off. As it came off, she heard giggles and sarcastic comments from behind. Humiliated, Mona started crying and wanted to leave school as quickly as possible. She was unsure whether a teacher had witnessed the actual incident, because it happened so quickly, but there should have been at least one teacher in the area. Furthermore, Mona was disheartened and felt violated, particularly because the school's educators had repeatedly stressed their commitment to tolerance and diversity, although religious diversity was never mentioned. At Sunnydale, there were few Muslim students, and Mona was the only young woman who wore the hijab. She felt proud of her religious faith, but she often felt isolated. Later that day when she tearfully related the incident to her mother, Mona said, "Is this only the beginning? Am I going to be picked on again and again for wearing hijab? Do I really belong here?"

In her meeting with the principal, Dr. Kamal, a well-respected molecular biologist in the pharmaceutical industry, questioned Mr. Ernest about the meaning of a healthy school culture that ensures that all students have the right to learn and celebrate their individuality. Furthermore, she asked whether students' rights are equally protected and how that is reflected in the school vision, as well as in action. More pointedly, she asked, "Do you really embrace diversity? Or is diversity merely the school's slogan? Is it just a word?" Dr. Kamal related her own frustrations and concerns over the incident, noting that the larger cultural environment had become increasingly hostile toward U.S. Muslims since the 9/11 attacks.

Mr. Ernest was startled by Dr. Kamal's vehemence, but carefully listened to her concerns. At the end of the meeting, Mr. Ernest told Dr. Kamal that he would take the correct actions to protect his students, and this means all students—including religious minorities. After he bid Dr. Kamal good-bye, he sat down at his desk, took a deep breath, and began to think.

a. State the facts of this case study and define the main issues.
b. Is the school neutral toward religion? Why or why not? Explain your response.
c. What are some possible resolutions to this problem?
d. Should the principal be concerned about students' attitudes toward each other, particularly with regard to religious practices? Why or why not? Explain your response.
e. What is the school's responsibility in providing orientation programs and informative sessions to teachers, students, and their families to build a healthy school culture?
f. Working in teams, please develop the following:

- Write an action plan for Mr. Ernest.
- Write a response, which includes details of the action plan, to Mrs. Kamal.
- Make a chart showing the responses of a traditional managerial leader and those of a social justice leader. Discuss these differences with your team.

11. The following case study is drawn from MacGillivray (2004). Read the case study and then complete the activities that follow.

After a two-year-long battle with the local school board, Scott Miller had not only established a Gay–Straight Alliance (GSA), which met after school on Thursdays, but he had been elected its president. The threat of possible federal litigation had finally prompted the school board to relent and let the group meet on school grounds. Nevertheless, the community members of Happy Valley, Colorado, were distressed that such an organization existed in their beloved public school. Many of these residents were deeply religious, attending one of a handful of evangelical Protestant churches or the tiny Catholic Church, St. Luke's. This religiosity was somewhat reflected in the composition of the school board; three out of nine members were very vocal in their desire to uphold traditional values of morality, faith, and the traditional family.

Scott had come out as a gay teen while in ninth grade. After a miserable eighth-grade year of teasing, taunting, and low-grade physical bullying, he had decided if people were going to call him "fag" and harass him, they could do so more publicly. At the time he came out, he also requested that the school board recognize the GSA that he and a couple of his straight friends, who were upperclassmen, were trying to establish. He got more than he bargained for. He was promptly derided by some of his classmates, as well as more than a few adults in Happy Valley. The three traditional members of the board attacked the proposal, with one member publicly stating, "I believe the Bible is the literal word of God. And the Bible says God created Adam and Eve, not Adam and Steve. I believe that permitting the proposed GSA threatens the rights of Christian parents to raise their children as they see fit." It was quite clear that the traditional board members saw the GSA's existence as a threat to their Christian beliefs.

But Scott's successful battle for the GSA earned the respect of some teachers; his vice-principal, Mrs. Jamison; and more than a few community members who were impressed his persistence and sheer "cussedness." By the beginning of the fall of his senior year, the GSA was small, but it had a core membership of 10 students, one who was openly gay (Scott), five who were somewhat-to-deeply closeted, and the rest were straight allies.

With the arrival of the GSA, two members of the Fellowship of Christian Athletes began a campaign of trying to convert Scott to their Christian beliefs. Ralph was respectful of Scott's position, but persistent in stating that Scott's "chosen lifestyle was wrong" and that he "should think about what the Bible says." Jenny was more confrontational, claiming that Scott was "doomed to hell," and that he was recruiting younger students, particularly boys, into the GSA, thereby corrupting them.

Scott replied to both individuals that his sexuality was not "chosen" and that he was free to believe or not believe as they did. What he did was none of their business—they needed to "butt out" of his life and leave him alone. But neither did. They continued to address him and questioned his religious beliefs almost every chance they got at school. By November, Scott had had enough. After consulting with his parents and then an attorney, he wrote a letter to the building principal, Ms. Smith, stating that he was feeling harassed by Ralph and Jenny, and that the school was hostile towards him personally. Scott related everything that he had recently experienced in the letter and added some details when he met with Ms. Smith a few days later. In the meeting, Scott hinted at possible litigation for religious discrimination, but he did not state this in the letter.

The next day, Ms. Smith called Ralph, then Jenny, and then Sam, who was FCA president, into her office and questioned them as to events and details. Both Jenny and Ralph stated that they had talked with Scott, but that they had meant no harm, in fact, they wanted to keep him from all the possible harms they believed were headed his way. They also felt they had a right, under the First Amendment, to espouse their religious beliefs at school. They both thanked Ms. Smith for her concern but were firm that they had a religious obligation to save Scott from his ways. Although Sam felt much the same as Ralph and Jenny did, he did not think it was his or FCA's business to convert Scott. But he stated that Jenny and Ralph were free to express their own convictions.

After the meeting with Sam, Ms. Smith grabbed a few books from her bookcase, sat down at her desk, took a deep breath, and began to jot some notes.

a. State the facts of this case study and define the main issues.
b. Is the school neutral toward religion? Why or why not? Explain your response.
c. Are Sam, Jenny, and Ralph's religious claims all the same? If not, how do they differ? Are any of their actions grounds for disciplinary action? Why or why not?
d. In your opinion, what are some suggested resolutions to this problem.
e. Should the school be concerned with students' attitudes toward each other, particularly with regard to religiously motivated speech?
f. What is the school's responsibility in providing orientation programs and in-

formative sessions to teachers, students, and their families to develop a healthy school culture?

g. Working in teams, please develop the following:

- Write a memo to the school superintendent detailing the situation, potential problems, and possible solutions.
- Write an action plan for Ms. Smith.
- Make a chart showing the responses of a traditional managerial leader and those of a social justice leader. Discuss these differences with your team.

Annotated Readings

Sydney Ahlstrom's highly acclaimed *A Religious History of the American People*, remains the definitive history of religious life in the United States more than 30 years after it was in 1972. What is so remarkable about the book is that the author does not assume Christianity, and Protestant Christianity in particular, to be the only important story. Ahlstrom opens the book as follows:

> Only a minority of Americans have ever believed that Christianity holds the central ruling position in history, or considered themselves to be part of what Schaff called the objective, organized, visible Kingdom of Christ on earth. . . . Even this current consists of many quite discrete substreams, and from one or another of these separate confessional positions much of American's religious history has been interpreted in terms of heresy. (p. xii)

The book is massive (over 1,090 pages); the prose is dense, if wry; and the footnotes are extensive and wonderfully chatty. For researchers and those individuals interested in religion and public education, this is a "must-have" for their professional library.

Karen Armstrong's *The Battle for God* (2000) explores the influence of fundamentalism and globalization upon Christianity, Islam, and Judaism, as well as the cross-pollinations these faiths have had upon each other. As such, it is a global history, beginning in 1492 and shifting between the Middle East, Europe, and the Americas as events unfold. It should be read with James W. Fraser's book, *Between Church and State* (1999), which explores the politics of religion and public education in the United States, and Wade Clark Roof's sociological study, *Spiritual Marketplace* (1999), which examines the influence of "marketized" spirituality on American social life.

Steven Epstein's provocative law review article, "Rethinking the constitutionality of ceremonial Deism," (1996), explores the constitutionality of invocations of a divine in public settings—including public schools. He opens the article with the following:

> The year is 2096. Due to radically altered immigration and birth patterns over the past century, Muslims now comprise seventy percent of the American population, while Christians and Jews comprise only twenty-five percent, collectively. Elementary school students in most public school systems begin each day with the Pledge of Allegiance in which they dutifully recite that America is one nation "under Allah"; our national currency—both coins and paper—contains the inscription codified as our national motto, "In Allah We Trust"; witnesses in court proceedings and public officials are sworn in by government officials asking them to place one hand on the Koran and to conclude "so help me Allah"; presidential addresses are laced

with appeals to Allah; federal and state legislative proceedings begin with a formal prayer typically delivered by a Muslim chaplain in which supplications to Allah are unabashed; state and federal judicial proceedings—including proceedings before the United States Supreme Court—begin with the invocation "Allah save this Honorable Court"; and, pursuant to federal and state law, only Muslim holy days are officially celebrated as national holidays. (pp. 2084–85)

What unfolds will make most religious adherents, regardless of their individual faith, squirm. This should be read concurrently with Amy Gutmann's *Democratic Education* (1987), which explores the political purposes and tensions confronting U.S. public education, as well as Kenneth Karst's 2003 article, "Law, cultural conflict, and the socialization of children," and Steven Gey's 2000 article, "When is religious speech not 'free speech'?"

Related Readings

Barazangi, N. H. (1990). The education of North American Muslim parents and children: Conceptual change as a contribution to Islamization of education. *The American Journal of Islamic Social Sciences*, 7(3), 385–402.

Eisenlohr, C. J. (1996). Adolescent Arab girls in an American high school. In B. C. Aswad & B. Bilge (Eds.), *Family and gender among American Muslims: Issues facing Middle Eastern immigrants and their descendants* (pp. 129–142). Philadelphia: Temple University Press.

Esposito, J. (1998). Muslim in America or American Muslims. In Y. Haddad & J. Esposito (Eds.), *Muslims on the Americanization path?* (pp. 3–17). Atlanta: Scholars Press.

Gibson, M. A. (1988). *Accommodation without assimilation: Sikh immigrants in an American high school*. Ithaca, NY: Cornell University Press.

Gutmann, A. (Ed.). (1994). *Multiculturalism: Examining the politics of recognition*. Princeton, NJ: Princeton University Press.

Haddad, Y. Y. (1998). The dynamics of Islamic identity in North America. In Y. Y. Haddad & J. Esposito (Eds.), *Muslims on the Americanization path?* (pp. 21–56). Atlanta: Scholars Press.

Khan, S. (2002). *Aversion and desire: Negotiating Muslim female identity in the diaspora*. Toronto, Ontario: Women's Press.

Nyang, S. (1999). *Islam in the United States of America*. Chicago: ABC International Group Inc.

Peshkin, A. (1988). *God's choice: The total of a fundamentalist Christian school*. Chicago: University of Chicago Press.

Rhodes, A. L., & Nam, C. B. (1970). The religious context of educational expectations. *American Sociological Review*, 35(2), 253–267.

Sarroub, L. K. (2001). The sojourner experience of Yemeni American high school students: An ethnographic portrait. *Harvard Educational Review*, 71(3), 390–415.

Sears, J. R., & Carper, J. C. (Eds.) (1998). *Curriculum, religion and public education. Conversations for an enlarging public square*. New York: Teachers College Press.

Taylor, C. (1994). Comment. In A. Gutmann (Ed.), *Multiculturalism: Examining the politics of recognition* (pp. 25–73). Princeton, NJ: Princeton University Press.

Waugh, E., Abu-Laban, S., & Qureshi, R. (Eds.) (1991). *Muslim families in North America*. Edmonton, Alberta: University of Alberta Press.

Wuthnow, R. J. (1988). Sociology of religion. In Smelser, N. (Ed.) (1988). *Handbook of sociology* (pp. 473–509). Newbury Park, CA: Sage.

References

Ahlstrom, S. E. (1972). *A religious history of the American people*. New Haven, CT: Yale University Press.

Armstrong, K. (1993). *A history of God*. New York: Ballantine Books.

Armstrong, K. (2000). *The battle for God*. New York: Alfred A. Knopf.

Associated Press. (2004, June 12). Oklahoma school district changes dress code to settle lawsuit over religious head coverings. Retrieved June 13, 2004, from http://ap.tbo.com/ap/breaking/MGBBMNC5EVD.html

Baer, Jr., R. A., & Carper, J. C. (2000). "To the advantage of infidelity" or how not to deal with religion in America's public schools. *Educational Policy, 14*(5), 600–621.

Bennett, D. H. (1995). *The party of fear: The American far right from Nativism to the militia movement, Revised Edition*. New York: Vintage Books.

Button, H. W., & Provenzo, Jr., E. F. (1983). *History of education and culture in America*. Englewood Cliffs, NJ: Prentice-Hall.

CNN (1999, August 20). Mississippi school board to review Star of David ban. Retrieved December 5, 2004, from http://www.cnn.com/US/9908/20/miss.star.of.david/

Dewey, J. (1935). *Experience and education*. New York: Macmillan Publishing.

Epstein, S. B. (1996, December). Rethinking the constitutionality of ceremonial deism. *Columbia Law Review, 96*, 2083–2174.

Fraser, J. W. (1999). *Between church and state: Religion and public education in a multicultural America*. New York: St. Martin's Griffin.

French, R. R. (2003, Winter). Shopping for religion: The change in everyday religious practice and its importance to the law. *Buffalo Law Review, 51*, 127–199.

Gaddy, B. B., Hall, T. W., & Marzano, R. J. (1996). *School wars: Resolving our conflicts over religion and values*. San Francisco: Jossey-Bass.

Gey, S. G. (2000). When is religious speech not "free speech?" *University of Illinois Law Review, 379*–460.

Greenwalt, K. (2002). Teaching about religion in the public schools. *Journal of Law and Politics, 18*, 329–385.

Gutmann, A. (1987). *Democratic education*. Princeton, NJ: Princeton University Press.

Harvard Law Review Association (2002). Note: Children as believers—Minor's free exercise rights and the psychology of religious development. *Harvard Law Review, 115*, 2205–2227.

Herrington, C. D. (2000). Religion, public schools, and hyperpluralism: Is there a new religious war? *Educational Policy, 14*(5), 548–563.

Karst, K. L. (2003, July). Law, cultural conflict, and the socialization of children. *California Law Review, 91*, 967–1027.

Lugg, C. A. (2003). Sissies, faggots, lezzies, and dykes: Gender, sexual orientation, and a new politics of education? *Educational Administration Quarterly, 39*(1), 95–134.

Lugg, C. A. (2004). One nation under God? Religion and the politics of education in a post-9/11 America. *Educational Policy, 18*(1), 169–187.

MacGillivray, I. K. (2004). *Sexual orientation & school policy: A practical guide for teachers, administrators, and community activists*. Lanham, MD: Rowman & Littlefield.

Marshall, C. (2004). Social justice challenges to educational administration: Introduction to a special issue. *Educational Administration Quarterly, 40*(1), 5–15.

Moore, R. L. (1994). *Selling God: American religion in the market place of culture*. New York: Oxford University Press.

Nasaw, D. (1979). *Schooled to order: A social history of public school in the United States*. New York: Oxford University Press.

Nord, W. A. (1995). *Religion and American education: Rethinking a national dilemma*. Chapel Hill: University of North Carolina Press.

Religioustolerance.org (2004). Membership of US religious and spiritual groups. Retrieved December 5, 2004, from http://www.religioustolerance.org/us_rel1.htm

Roof, W. C. (1999). *Spiritual marketplace: Baby boomers and the remaking of American religion*. Princeton, NJ: Princeton University Press.

Ryan, J. E. (2000). The Supreme Court and public schools. *The Virginia Law Review, 86*, 1335–1433.

Tabbaa-Rida, Z. (2004). *Muslim women reflecting on American education. Exploring the question of educational identity*. Unpublished dissertation. Rutgers University.

Tyack, D., & Hansot, E. (1982). *Managers of virtue: Public school leadership in America, 1820–1980*. New York: Basic Books.

Zimmerman, J. (2002). *Whose America? Culture wars in the public schools*. Cambridge: Harvard University Press.

Endnotes

[1]Although the federal courts have been firm in disentangling religion and public education, local practice generally has not been as robust. How well a given public school respects the neutrality principle depends on the power of a local school board in following Constitutional principles, historically a problematic practice (see Karst, 2003; MacGillivray, 2004; Zimmerman, 2002).

[2]This can be a common feature in some communities, as was the case in Santa Fe, Texas (see Lugg, 2004).

8

Meeting All Students' Needs: Transforming the Unjust Normativity of Heterosexism

James W. Koschoreck

Patrick Slattery

"Instead of perpetually listening for conclusions, we might be more focused on the negotiations, the process, and the paradoxical oscillation between the claiming of an identity and the struggle to rework its meaning and effect on our lives." (Scholl, 2001, p. 158)

For years, researchers, sociologists, and social activists have alerted educators to the perils of the persistent failure of public schools to address the needs and concerns of lesbian, gay, bisexual, transgender, intersexual, and queer (LGBTIQ) students (Harris, 1997; Human Rights Watch, 2001; Lugg & Koschoreck, 2003; Macgillivray, 2004; Pinar, 1998; Rofes, 1989; Sears, 1991, among others). Yet despite nearly two decades of professional entreaties to transform public schools into nurturing, nonthreatening, nonviolent social spaces, prejudice, harassment, and discrimination continue to pervade the social experience of LGBTIQ students across the country. Neither the liberal, ethical appeals to goodness and fairness (e.g., see Chasnoff & Cohen, 1996), nor the more transgressive calls to queer our pedagogical practices (Britzman, 1995; Luhmann, 1998) have resulted in any large-scale systemic effects on the way public schools approach LGBTIQ issues. As Rofes (1997) stated, "the heteronormativity of schools remains intransigent, resisting reform as schools have long avoided pedagogical innovation"

(p. xiv). After nearly seven years—and in light of a rapidly expanding discourse on LGBTIQ issues that becomes more and more difficult to ignore—this statement is as true today as when Rofes wrote it.

Oftentimes, when confronted with the challenge of reforming their own political and pedagogical practices to be more socially inclusive of sexual minorities, even well-intentioned teachers and aspiring administrators bemoan the lack of programmatic guidance on how to address the needs of this particular group of students. Yet such programs and recommendations have been available for quite some time. In 1989, for example, Rofes discussed in detail two different programs focused on educational opportunities and support for LGBTIQ students. And as early as 1983, Sears suggested a list of resources for teachers that could be integrated into the school curriculum to introduce the topic of "homosexuality," as he then called it. More recently, the Human Rights Watch (2001) has enumerated detailed recommendations to school districts, school boards, teachers, counselors, and staff as well as to the state and federal governments to end the abuse that derives from "the substantial failure of the government at the local, state, and federal level to protect lesbian, gay, bisexual, and transgender students from human rights violations, including harassment, violence, and deprivation of the right to education" (p. 9).

If plans to meet the needs of LGBTIQ students have long been available, then our inquiry must rather focus on those forces of resistance *in schools and other educational institutions* that maintain the heteronormative status quo. Why are teachers and administrators so reluctant to engage in discourse that would allow them to transform public schools into safe, caring environments for LGBTIQ students? Why, given that few educators would tolerate openly racist utterances and behaviors (and often sexist, xenophobic, and disability prejudices as well), are so few willing to take a public stand when faced with blatantly heterosexist discrimination and harassment? Why, indeed, when our national discourse demands that *no child be left behind* do we not do whatever it takes to prevent the high levels of taunting, depression, suicide, and drop-out rates of LGBTIQ students across the nation? (Human Rights Watch, 2001).

Throughout our years of experience as academics in teacher and administrator preparation programs, we have heard a litany of excuses:

- *We hesitate to become more proactive with these issues because we fear the possible negative reactions from parents.*
- *"Sexuality" has no place in the public school curriculum; it more properly falls within the domain of parental responsibility.*
- *What can we do? We have to uphold the values, beliefs, and attitudes of the community.*
- *These are issues that belong in the private sphere; no good will come of making them public.*
- *What's the point of all the discussion and programming around issues of sexuality? Straight people don't constantly make issue of their sexuality. Why do LGBTIQ students feel it necessary to force this stuff down everyone's throat?*

- *I would like to do something, but I would be harassed and could lose my job if I address this issue.*
- *The LGBTIQ community needs to take the lead on these issues. I do not have the knowledge or power to take this on myself.*
- *Homosexuality is a sin and an unhealthy lifestyle, and we should be helping our students to reject this lifestyle rather than normalizing it.*
- *I hesitate to get involved in these issues because of my discomfort and lack of understanding.*
- *I am uncomfortable addressing issues of sexuality and homosexuality. I was raised not to discuss sexuality.*
- *I am sympathetic to gays and lesbians, but if I get involved with LGBTIQ issues then my sexuality and morality will be questioned, and I will be placed in an awkward environment.*
- *I am very empathetic because I am homosexual (bisexual, intersexual, questioning, etc.), but I am in the closet, and I do not want to draw attention to myself.*
- *Homosexuals flaunt their sexuality and deserve any negative reactions they provoke.*

These are the excuses we hear when we present LGBTIQ curriculum and leadership models and practices to our undergraduate and graduate students. We also hear some of the same rhetoric from colleagues. Despite the advancements in the American, British, Canadian, and global community in recent years—same-sex marriage, ordinations, U.S. Supreme Court decisions, political elections, organizations, etc.[1] (see Table 8.1)—the oppressive atmosphere for LGBTIQ students in K–12 schooling must be addressed forthrightly. The antagonism between the challenges to the heteronormative order in the broader community and the oftentimes brutal environments that LGBTIQ students face in schools creates an untenable conflict for many young people. On the one hand, the societal changes that challenge the hegemony[2] of heteronormativity encourage these youths to be honest about their lack of conformance to the expectations of the dominant order; on the other hand, the cultures in most public schools have not yet become the safe environments they should when nonheteronormative students make themselves seen and heard. In this chapter, we will reflect not only on the visibility of heteronormativity in K–12 schooling, but also challenge educators to move beyond the prejudices and fears reflected in the excuses for avoiding LGBTIQ issues.

Certainly, we do not mean to paint a picture of gloom and doom. Many administrators, teachers, and students regularly promote issues of social justice in their daily practices. For instance, it is not uncommon to hear comments of the following sort:

- *I am appalled at the level of teasing, harassment, and ridicule of LGBTIQ students, so I intend to say something to stop the language every time I*

TABLE 8.1   *Selected Societal Changes that Have Impacted the Hegemony of Heteronormativity*

Category	Example	Country of Origin	Year	Social Effect
Same-sex marriage	Supreme Judicial Court of Massachusetts recognizes same-sex marriage.	USA	2004	The redefinition of marriage to include same-sex partners represents a shift of historic proportion in the heteronormative paradigm.
	Supreme Court of Canada upholds Ontario Court of Appeals decision to change common law definition of marriage.	Canada	2003	
Religious ordination	Episcopalian House of Bishops consecrates Canon Gene Robinson	USA	2003	The consecration of an openly gay bishop to the high leadership of the Anglican church challenges the fundamental heteronormativity of religious doctrines.
U.S. Supreme Court decisions	*Romer v. Evans*, 517 U.S. 620 (1996)	USA	1996	U.S. Supreme Court overturns Colorado state legislation that would have discriminated on the basis of sexual orientation.
	Lawrence and Garner v. Texas, 539 U.S. 558 (2003)	USA	2003	Striking down state sodomy laws, U.S. Supreme Court protects right to sexual privacy.

TABLE 8.1 *Continued*

Category	Example	Country of Origin	Year	Social Effect
Political elections	In the United States, Elaine Noble was the first openly gay elected official; in 2004 there were more than 170.	USA	1974 to present	Public recognition and acceptance of openly gay elected officials helps to break down the barriers of stereotypes and bigotry.
	Klaus Wowerite	Germany	2001	First leading gay German politician wins landslide victory in public elections.
Organizations	GLSEN (Gay, Lesbian, Straight Education Network)	USA	1990	Activities promote safe school environments for *all* children.
	Stonewall	UK	1989	Professional lobbying organization works on policy development to promote equal rights.
Educational leadership	The board of education of Cincinnati public schools revises nondiscrimination policy to include sexual orientation as a protected category.	USA	1995	Discriminatory practices are held to be unconscionable at the highest level of local educational leadership.
	National Education Association forms the Gay, Lesbian, Bisexual, and Transgender Caucus	USA	1987	The caucus works to educate national and state education associations on issues of discrimination and sexual orientation.

hear it. And I also add positive words of encouragement for all minority students.

- *I mention positive role models of LGBTIQ persons at every appropriate opportunity in my classroom and in the curriculum.*
- *I invert heterosexism in subtle ways whenever possible. I use phrases like "domestic partner," "significant other," "partner," and "lover" instead of "husband," "wife," or "spouse" for straight and gay couples. And I never assume that when someone refers to a "date" that the person is of the opposite gender.*
- *I include books in my library, on my bulletin board, and on my Web page about gay and lesbian persons and issues along with all of my other multicultural literature.*
- *I speak positively about my LGBTIQ friends and family members and never try to hide my love and support for them.*

In addition to these individual acts and utterances that promote a greater sense of social justice, many courageous young people are blazing a trail for social consciousness and political activism. We think there of Brandon Fitzgerald, a high school senior who formed a Gay–Straight Alliance (GSA) in his high school in Cleveland, Ohio, in 2001. Brandon, like so many other LGBTIQ students and their straight allies, took the lead in educating administrators, teachers, and parents about the needs and contributions of gay youth. The GSA movement in high schools is proliferating, providing education and hope for thousands of young people. Brandon did not form the GSA without struggles. It was only one year earlier that he came out to his classmates and teachers in a very dramatic way. Brandon asked for permission to read a poem at a school assembly during his junior year, along with other students who were planning skits, poetry, and narratives for this assembly. Brandon was given permission by the moderator to read this poem:

Locked away minds of rainbow flags . . .
Faces hidden beneath paper bags . . .
Confused kids rolled away in body bags,
'Cause everyone else always called them fags.
They are the few, and they are often the crazed.
They are mere mortals of life's twisted maze.
They are fish in black water.
They are the victims of history's ongoing slaughter.
Years upon years
My face drowns in tears.
I shouldn't have to hide in fear
Or fade into the shadows and disappear.
For me each day is a rainy day,

In a world where being different is somehow not okay.
Don't try to make me go away,
'Cause I am who I am and that includes being gay.
—Brandon Fitzgerald (2001) (Slattery & Rapp, 2003, p. 126)

Brandon's maturity and courage inspire us. But as he states in his poem, life is not easy for those who are different from the cultural stereotyped norms. Others are not so fortunate, because hate can kill. Reread Brandon's poem while listening to lesbian musician and entertainer Melissa Etheridge's song "Scarecrow"—a poignant tribute to Matthew Shepard, the University of Wyoming gay student who was beaten mercilessly and left to die tied to an isolated ranch fence post (see p. 152). Matthew's only offense was being gay; his murderer's only excuse was homophobia and hatred. Unfortunately, Matthew's story is not an isolated event.

Heterosexism/Homophobia in Schooling

Schools can either be part of the solution or a part of the problem in addressing heterosexism and bigotry against LGBTIQ students, staff, and parents. As we know from many highly publicized incidents, such as the gay-bashing murder of Matthew Shepard in Wyoming, heterosexism can escalate beyond exclusion and taunting to violence and murder. Why does this happen, and how can educators be at the forefront of ending the violence?

Professor John Aston has studied gay bashing and murders and reports that the typical high school student hears antigay slurs 22.5 times a day. Furthermore, 69 percent of youths perceived to be either gay or lesbian experience some form of harassment or violence in school, with over half of these experiencing it daily, and over one-third of youth reported hearing homophobic remarks from faculty or school staff (Aston, 2001b). Additionally, Aston cited a 1993 Massachusetts Governor's Commission on Gay and Lesbian Youth study that reported that 85 percent of teachers oppose integrating gay/lesbian/bisexual studies within their curriculum (Aston, 2001a). Psychologist Karen Franklin's landmark study found thrill-seeking, peer dynamics, and societal permission and encouragement to be the primary motivations for

"We must arouse educators—if they are silent on the matter—to examine their complicity and silence on gay bashing, teasing, and violence against minorities and those perceived as different in schools and society. The constant harassment and marginalization that until recently were sanctioned by law and practices outside of schools produce the kind of psychic/psychological death . . . ."

For those unfamiliar with Etheridge's song, the lyrics are reproduced here (Etheridge, 1999).

Scarecrow

Showers of your crimson blood
Seep into a nation calling up a flood
Of narrow minds who legislate
Thinly veiled intolerance
Bigotry and hate

But they tortured and burned you
They beat you and they tied you
They left you cold and breathing
For love they crucified you

I can't forget hard as I try
This silhouette against the sky

Scarecrow crying
Waiting to die wondering why
Scarecrow trying
Angels will hold carry your soul away

This was our brother
This was our son
This shepherd young and mild
This unassuming one
We all gasp this can't happen here
We're all much too civilized
Where can these monsters hide

But they are knocking on our front door
They're rocking in our cradles
They're preaching in our churches
And eating at our tables

I search my soul
My heart and in my mind
To try and find forgiveness
This is someone's child
With pain unreconciled
Filled up with father's hate
Mother's neglect
I can forgive But I will not forget

Scarecrow crying
Waiting to die wondering why
Scarecrow trying
Rising above all in the name of love

antigay assailants (Franklin, 1997). If societal permission seems to be over-stated, consider the response in Dallas by The Constitution Party of Texas (CPT) that led a protest of the Texas State Legislature's consideration of bills to protect gay men and lesbians. The Texas Triangle (2001) reported:

> The men protesting, one who brought his five-year-old son to the event, believe homosexuality should be illegal, and ultimately punishable by death. They base their beliefs on the book of Leviticus in the Bible.
>
> "Well, we know punishing homosexuals by death would be extremely hard in today's society," said Larry S. Kilgore, the Dallas/Fort Worth chairman of the Constitution Party. "But we hope that we can help to drive it under ground so in about twenty or thirty years, the punishment can fit the crime."

This attitude of permission to hurt and even kill not only gay men and lesbians, but Jews, Blacks, immigrants, and other minorities, is promoted in several conservative political groups, churches, and Web sites today. A glance at www.americannaziparty.com or www.godhatesfags.com almost inevitably produces chills because of the hate rhetoric.

We show several films to our students to impress upon them the seriousness of this ethical nightmare: the dramatic fictional account of teenagers in Los Angeles in the film titled *American History X*, a must see for all educators concerned about hate crimes, *Licensed to Kill*, a documentary that interviews men in prison who killed gay men and lesbians, and *Jim in Bold*, the poignant story of Jim Wheeler, who was harassed in high school because he was gay and eventually killed himself (see www.jiminbold.com).

One of the most frightening aspects of these films that must give pause to critical educators, indeed, to any educator, is that the permission to kill is rooted in injudicious biblical interpretations, social conventions, church sermons, and hate-filled rhetoric learned in educational settings. Our convictions must direct us to counter hate speech in all of its manifestations. Whereas ignorance of the pervasiveness of this problem might be countered through education to produce an empathetic leadership, intentional silence in the face of hate crimes or hate speech is a moral failure of educators and citizens that amounts to complicity in the crime.

John Aston followed up on Karen Franklin's research with a case study of one young man from Houston who perpetrated violence on gay men in Houston, Texas, titled "Deconstructing heterosexism and homophobia in schools." Aston (2001b) writes:

> This investigation focuses on the internal and external factors that led to Jon Buice's murderous assault along with nine of his adolescent peers on a gay man, Paul Broussard, in Houston on the night of July 4, 1991. The study examines the societal sense of permission (Franklin, 1997) to harass and assault those who violate gender norms, with a particular focus on the role of schools as passively and sometimes actively contributing to a sense of permission. . . . This case study

shows that Jon was more typical than atypical of young male adolescents in our highly gendered and patriarchal society. He was driven by thrill-seeking and peer dynamics to attack societally-permitted targets rather than by any knowingly anti-gay ideology. The members of Jon's school and community may make convenient scapegoats of Jon and his companions, but this study indicates that we are all implicit in such acts, and ends with suggestions about ways to end our schools' complicity in such grim oppression. (pp. iii–iv)

We must arouse educators—if they are silent on the matter—to examine their complicity and silence on gay bashing, teasing, and violence against minorities and those perceived as different in schools and society. The constant harassment and marginalization that until recently were sanctioned by law and practices outside of schools produce the kind of psychic/psychological death that Brandon expresses and struggles against in his poem. Others, like Jim Wheeler, do not struggle successfully. As educators, we must stop making young people struggle to overcome and stave off psychological—and possibly actual—death. Aston's recommendations must become an integral part of teacher education workshops, administrative policy, and classroom practices. Aston (2001b) recommends the following:

> Establish and maintain gay–straight alliances, where students and staff, whether gay or straight, could get together for mutual support and understanding without being branded or labeled as one or the other. Include [GLBT] issues in the curriculum. Sadly, such [curricular materials and] alliances, I found, are frequently against school and/or district policy. Indeed any mention of homosexuality, whether in sex ed., health, history, or any other subject, is frequently not allowed. Stop the antigay language, even when kids say "that's so gay" . . . I would never again let another bit of such "language" go unchallenged, so help me God. I would speak up, and out, and add my voice to all those who seek full civil rights and liberty for the GLBT community. Finally, I would no longer remain silent, or in any way equivocate. (p. 71)

Can all educators take such a positive ethical stance as professors Aston and Franklin? We hope so!

This quote could be humorous if not so tragic:

> In a New England college where I taught, the presence of a few lesbians threw the more conservative heterosexual students and faculty into a panic. The two lesbian students and we two lesbian instructors met with them to discuss their fears. One of the students said, "I thought homophobia meant fear of going home after a residency." And I thought, how apt. Fear of going home. And of not being taken in. (Anzaldua, 1987, pp. 19–20)

Institutional Contributions to Heteronormative Oppression

There are many ways in which schools (often unintentionally) allow heteronormative oppression to create a climate of fear, hate, and violence and contribute to Aston and Franklin's "societal sense of permission" to marginalize, abuse, or assault gay men, lesbians, bisexuals, and transgendered individuals—or the children of LGBTIQ parents. For example, by selectively choosing not to intervene when students or others verbally express homophobia, such as "that's so gay" or "you faggot," teachers and administrators become tacitly complicit in endorsing a climate of intolerance. Similarly, a climate of fear, hate, and violence is reinforced when school leaders fail to intervene to put an end to verbal or physical assault on LGBTIQ students or children of LGBTIQ families. In fact, allowing taunts, ill-intentioned teasing, and bullying of any kind tends to marginalize and abuse young people in the schools. Other ways in which schools contribute to heteronormative oppression include:

1. Ignoring patriarchal, sexist, heterosexist, and homophobic remarks on the part of faculty or staff.
2. Denying that heterosexism and homophobia exist in a school despite clear evidence of the same.
3. Assuming that all students and their parents are heterosexual, as well as all staff, and expressing this assumption in school announcements, documents, and publications.
4. Failing to specifically include heterosexist harassment in faculty/staff training and in-service programs designed to counter sexual harassment.
5. Permitting discrimination against gay men or lesbians in hiring and/or retention policies.
6. Disallowing Gay–Straight Alliances or other programs or activities designed to assure the civil rights and safety of students perceived to be gay, lesbian, or children of the same.
7. Disallowing any mention of or discussion of LGBTIQ topics in the classroom, even in health or social studies classes.
8. Failing to include literature or other media dealing with the topics of gay men and lesbians in the school library, and failing to mention the sexuality of famous authors, scientists, and leaders in the school curriculum, even when such information is directly related to the topic of study, such as references to gay love or romance in poetry or literature by a gay author.
9. Failing to include the contributions of gay men and lesbians to history and culture or to include the LGBTIQ communities in multicultural curricula.

TABLE 8.2 *Ways in Which Schools Can Resist Heteronormative Oppression*

Type of Activity	*Recommendations*
Staff development	• Establish peer intervention and other student/staff training programs on bullying and nonviolent conflict resolution techniques.
	• Train faculty and staff to recognize and effectively intervene against heterosexist harassment. Also, train them in ways to assist students who are victims of this type of harassment.
	• Employ counselors who are trained in awareness of heterosexism and its effects on students. These counselors should be aware of and sensitive to the gender identity and developmental issues commonly found among adolescents.
Policy	• Permit and foster Gay–Straight Student/Staff Alliances on school campuses.
	• Establish clearly stated antiheterosexist harassment policies—for both students and staff—with clear penalties and consequences. These policies should be consistently enforced and should include specific penalties for failure to intervene on the part of faculty or staff.
Student support	• Establish connections with PFLAG (Parents and Friends of Lesbians and Gays), GLSEN (Gay Lesbian Straight Education Network), or similar organizations with outreach programs to families and communities.
Curriculum	• Offer resources such as library books and films that promote inclusion of gay men, lesbians, and gay and lesbian families.
	• Include the study of gay men, lesbians, bisexuals, intersexuals, and transgendered (LGBTIQ) persons and their current and historical roles in society in multicultural curricula.
	• Incorporate into the curriculum specific moral training in empathy, respect, and inclusion for all students, beginning at the primary grades. Focus specifically on cognitive, affective, and experiential components that include LGBTIQ students and families.

Schools can resist these institutional contributions to heteronormative oppression by helping to ensure the physical and emotional safety and well-being of all students, including gay or lesbian students or children of the same. They can accomplish these goals through well-defined staff development, policy, student support, and curriculum. For example, in designing staff development activities that would promote the safety and well-being of all students, educational leaders could train faculty and staff to recognize and effectively intervene against heterosexist harassment. In the area of policy, school leaders might permit and foster Gay–Straight Student/Staff Alliances on school campuses. Student support activities might include the establishment of connections with PFLAG (Parents and Friends of Lesbians and Gays), GLSEN (Gay Lesbian Straight Education Network), or similar organizations with outreach programs to families and communities to address the shared issues of heterosexism and homophobia in schools and society. Finally, in the area of curriculum, school leaders might insist that specific moral training be provided in empathy, respect, and inclusion for all school students, beginning in the primary grades. This would include cognitive, affective, and experiential components specifically designed to include LGBTIQ students and families. (See Table 8.2 for a summary of these and other recommendations.)

LGBTIQ Activism and Strategies for Collective Action

Lesbian, gay, and queer movements have, so far, depended on the involvement of individuals as the primary drivers of social action. Yet we know from the experience of past movements for social change (and particularly the experience of labor movements) that individuals need to have structural representation in order to maintain the energy needed for sustained opposition. Individuals working against their oppressors, whether in the workplace or neighborhood, cannot succeed without a mechanism that can play a larger role in incorporating them into communities of resistance where mutual recognition is present (Kirsch, 2000, p. 118).

Recently, one of us was invited to participate in a panel discussion at the Clark Montessori High School in Cincinnati. The event was organized with the specific aim of helping students to become effective agents for social change. Many of them had previously expressed frustration over the abstract classroom discussions of social injustices that left them with an unclear sense of what they could do.

In light of these expressed desires, the teachers and administrators of Clark Montessori convened a panel of social activists—some heterosexual and some from the LGBTIQ community—to share ideas about how high school students could become involved in helping to correct social inequities. The panelists included: a White, gay university professor engaged in educational policy research and LGBTIQ issues; a Latina youth activist and spoken word artist with the local Hispanic ministry center; an African American spoken word artist on the board of a local community council; and a White criminal justice activist who also coordinates the Hip Hop Youth Arts Center in Cincinnati.

After brief introductions by each panel member to the assembly of approximately 250 students from the ninth through the twelfth grades, the panelists addressed questions generated by the students. These questions included such topics as:

- *Why do you feel that art is the way to nurture the community?*
- *What are your beliefs concerning marriage?*
- *Why are you fighting for gay/lesbian rights?*
- *What are the biggest problems facing gay/lesbian teenagers in high school?*
- *What can we do as advocates for gay/lesbian rights?*
- *Should students be taught about gay/lesbian issues in high schools?*
- *What is your motivation for becoming a social activist?*

Though these questions were ordinarily directed to a particular panelist, several members on the panel often responded to the same question.

After about an hour of the moderated question–answer format, students broke up into smaller groups for follow-up discussions. Each group was facilitated by one of the teachers at Clark Montessori. During this time, the invited panelists were individually shepherded from group to group in order to engage in more informal discussions with smaller numbers of students. The chief aim of these break-out sessions was to discuss general issues of inequality—highlighting those that affect teenagers—and to strategize plans for direct community action.

This event serves as a model of the kinds of activities and experiences that school leaders can facilitate for their students in order to foster among young people a sense of involvement with issues of social justice. By bringing together community activists of different genders, races, ages, and social concerns, students can witness the similarities of the larger issues of gender, racial, and sexual oppression. Collaboration among coalitions of diverse groups can thus strengthen the efforts to create a more just society.

Heteronormativity and the Implications for Practice

Gay identity constructions reinforce the heteronormativity of the dominant hetero/homo sexual code. If homosexuality and heterosexuality are a coupling in which each presupposes the other, each being present in the invocation of the other, and in which this coupling assumes hierarchical forms, then the epistemic and political project of identifying a gay subject reinforces and reproduces this hierarchical figure (Seidman, 1993, p. 130).

In his introduction to *Fear of a Queer Planet: Queer Politics and Social Theory*, Warner (1993) posits the notion of heteronormativity as those elements of social expectations in which "the culture thinks of itself as the elemental form of human association, as the very model of intergender relations, as the indivisible basis of all community, and as the means of reproduction without which society wouldn't exist" (p. xxi). The pervasiveness of heteronormativity as an organizing social structure leads to the concession of bounteous privileges to those who understand themselves to operate within the limited parameters of heterosexualized norms of behaviors, attitudes, and beliefs. This heteronormative system of social organization is a self-perpetuating design that infuses all aspects of Western culture.[3] Sumara and Davis (1999) remark, however, that we cannot successfully interrupt heteronormative thinking and acting by continuing to pursue a line of educational and social research that focuses on the biographical and autobiographical narratives of nonheterosexual identities. As they state,

> Although we acknowledge the importance of the "coming out of the closet" literature and the work it accomplishes, we worry that it continues to participate in the ongoing subjugation, through representation practices of differentiation, of those identities that do not identify as ones that are structured by opposite-sex desire (Sumara & Davis, 1999, p. 193).

Clearly, by opting to focus on the social and lived realities of "the other," while at the same time disregarding a critical examination of the dominant power/knowledge regimes associated with heterosexual identities and failing to interrogate heteronormativity itself, researchers and practitioners actually contribute to the perpetuation of an inequitable social system that privileges some at the expense of others. Through this very omission, educators and others actually become parties to social inequity and injustice.

On the one hand, we—the authors—understand the power in the collective based on alternative sexual identities to organize political civil rights movements. The pages of recommendations by the Human Rights Watch (2001) to school districts, administrators, teachers, counselors, state legislatures, and other governmental bodies are all predicated on the notion of an identifiable minority sexual orientation or gender identity—whether essentialized or socially constructed—whose rights should include freedom from "human rights violations, including harassment, violence, and deprivation of the right to education" (p. 9). The current national discourse surrounding the issues of gay marriage is but one example of a group of sexual minorities joining together as an identity-based collective to demand the rights and privileges of the dominant group.

On the other hand, we are troubled by the epistemological[4] implications of a social collective that by its very existence continues to focus on and maintain the dualistic, hierarchical pattern of dominance and subordination that it seeks to topple. As Patton (1993) states,

> We once embraced the notion of inherent identities because it was strategically useful: we should question identity now not for formal reasons (Is it essentialist?) but because one form of identity rhetoric may fold us back into the same structures of "oppression," for lack of a better term. Indeed, the highly circumscribed

visibility that identity and its public representation afford seem to spawn sublime new oppressions—stereotyping of the severe dyke (arguing for abortion rights) and clean-cut (no doubt HIV-positive) fag lawyer, invisibility of most other forms of homosexual performance, hate crimes and their accounting. This is not just a problem of messy analytic categories: we live the political reality of our identity effects. (p. 175)

The challenge quickly becomes evident: How do we create equitable systems for social justice that do not reify subordinate identities and reproduce ontological[5] exclusions?

The history of sexual identity politics is rife with inequitable outcomes, unintended or otherwise. The materialist ambitions of an assimilationist gay rights movement, for instance, systematically exclude women within the movement as the power of the patriarchy pressurizes them into a subaltern status. And as Patton (1993) indicates, even among men a hierarchy of status and privilege is established that catapults gay or queer men who exhibit more visibly masculine characteristics to the top of the heap, leaving those others to wallow below amongst the social castaways whose existence and separateness are ontologically assured in current Western societies by the process of "othering"[6] (see also, for example, Connell, 1995).

Leaders with a penchant for social justice must be aware of these complexities. It is patently insufficient to declare support for an identity-based civil rights movement without understanding the philosophical inadequacies that such a movement entails. However, it also is unacceptable to stand back and do nothing because of the enormity of resisting heteronormativity.

Scholars working in the field of oppositional theory (see, for example, Britzman, 1995; de Castell and Bryson, 1997; Eribon, 2001; Sumara & Davis, 1999; Talburt & Steinberg, 2000) contend that continued efforts toward understanding identities and differences—in both dominant and subordinate subgroups—can have a vast influence on educational and leadership practices. Morris (2000) states categorically that

> Queer theory might seem completely irrelevant to education, but it isn't. Consciousness-raising about this new field might help teachers better educate their students about the complexities of identities. Perhaps queer theorists might help foster understanding and even empathy toward those who have been labeled in damaging, violent ways. Queer theory teaches that all identities are performances and these performances are interrelated and complicit in many ways, queer and nonqueer. The damaging effects of labels are still felt by many in the queer community. If anything, queer theory teaches that naming kills. Perhaps one day educators will queer up the field and "tilt the tower" (Garber, 1994) by joining the fight against the violence of naming, heteronormativity, hate crimes (p. 27).

Sumara and Davis (1999) suggest multiple approaches to "interrupting heteronormativity" in our educational practices. First, they suggest—as Sedgwick (1990) had done earlier—that sexuality underlies all forms of knowledge in the West and that through curriculum,

> ... by attempting to interpret the complex relations among knowledge, desire, and identities (and not just queer identities), these interpretive sites [yield] complex understandings of the ways in which knowledge/ignorance, queer/straight, and male/female always are articulated in and through one another. (pp. 203–204)

Second, they propose that our educational and curricular practices focus not on the interpretation of the identities of sexual minorities, but rather on the complexities and differences found amongst those who identify as heterosexual. The ostensible purpose of this is "to call into question the very existence of heterosexuality as a *stable* [original emphasis] category" (p. 204). Third, they believe that our "unit of analysis" for understanding differences ought to be the individual persons rather than categories of people. Such approaches are steps toward social change. As they state,

> Not only do these interruptions to heteronormative thinking assist in the important work of eliminating homophobia and heterosexism in society, but they also create some conditions for the human capacity for knowing and learning to become expanded. (p. 205)

Britzman (1997) asserts that the parameters of academic (and social) discourse commonly utilized to debate sexuality—that is, the nature-versus-nurture arguments—misguidedly lead us to irreconcilable discussions with no hope of resolution. She argues that in order to move toward a more equitable social reality, we ought instead to frame the arguments in terms of Sedgwick's (1990) minoritizing/universalizing orientations. As Britzman states,

> I believe these categories are relevant to educating educators. Minoritizing orientations approach the question of homosexual/heterosexual definitions as being relevant only to a "small, distinct, relatively fixed homosexual minority." This orientation shuts out the fact that identity is, first and foremost, a social relation. The logic and criteria of a minoritizing orientation compels educators to deem homosexuality as a separate and discreet category, relevant only to homosexuals. For a different vantage, those who take a universalizing orientation approach the divide between heterosexual and homosexual as a particular construction and "as an issue of continuing, determinative importance in the lives of people across the spectrum of sexualities." If educators are to be effective in working with every youth, they must begin to take a more universalizing view of sexuality in general and homosexuality in particular. So that rather than seeing questions of homosexuality as having to do with only those who are homosexual, one must consider how dominant discourses of heterosexuality perform their own set of ignorances *both* [original emphasis] about homosexuality and about heterosexuality. (pp. 202–203)

Conclusions

As this chapter has shown, LGBTIQ persons regularly experience harassment, violence, and abuse within our educational systems. Students, teachers, administrators, parents, and other community members are all complicit in maintaining heteronormative social structures that stigmatize sexual minority individuals. Awareness of these issues is only the first step toward changing our beliefs and practices.

Recommendations for action are complex. Some proponents for social change with sexual minorities argue that the most appropriate course of action is one that is modeled on the civil right movements of African Americans and women. Others contend that we cannot become a just society until we have managed to eliminate the hierarchical, dichotomous—and inherently unequal—social categories that operate at an ontological level. These categories include heterosexual/homosexual, male/female, white/not white, young/not young, knowledge/ignorance, and so on.

Whatever actions we choose to pursue, it is abundantly clear that the determination of a socially just community must occur both at the individual and at the institutional levels. *Every* person within our schools must be valued with regards to the fullness of all the characteristics and differences that that person exhibits. Every teacher and administrator has the capacity and the responsibility to effect the social changes required to serve the needs of these students. Whether it be through the kindness and understanding of individual acts or through systemic institutional changes that eradicate discriminatory practices, it is incumbent upon all school leaders to eliminate the homophobia and heterosexism within our educational systems. Though this can certainly begin in college and university discussions and professional preparation activities, it will only make a difference to young people like Brandon, Jim, and Matthew if it is also enacted and made to happen through the leaders' actions in schools.

Discussion Questions and Activities _____

1. Discuss ways in which teachers and administrators might effectively dismantle the stronghold of heterosexism in their schools.

2. Assuming you were a high school principal, how would you react if a group of students approached you with a petition to establish a Gay–Straight Alliance in your school? What constraints, if any, might need to be addressed? How would your response differ if there were an organized community opposition to such an alliance?

3. Working in small groups, create a mission statement for an imaginary ideal school that would seek to combat the normativity of heterosexism. Once you have established the mission statement, make a list of strategies—both in terms of policy and of curriculum—that would help you accomplish your goals.

4. Examine the policies and activities in your school building and or district with regards to antidiscrimination on the basis of sexual orientation. How do these policies advance or inhibit the rights of students to a safe, democratic multicultural education?

5. As a class, use Brandon Fitzgerald's poem to complete the following activities:

   a. Do a close reading of the poem alone to foreground the message(s).
   b. Discuss the meaning of these messages at the affective level. What do they communicate about how it feels to know and accept yourself when others do not?
   c. Discuss the meaning of these messages at the cognitive level. What lessons is the author attempting to teach to others about who he is, the way heteronormative exclusion makes him and others feel, and about the toll of unabated violence based on sexual orientation?

6. Listen to the lyrics of Melissa Etheridge's "Scarecrow" in class.

   a. Discuss the "societal permission" that we seem to give young people to perpetrate violence on others because they do not fit a heteronormative sexual paradigm.
   b. Strategize and develop an action plan about what schools and educators can do to ensure that outspoken and self-aware students like Fitzgerald do not become subject to the physical violence perpetrated on Matthew Shepherd or the psychological violence of name-calling and teasing that is more prevalent in schools.

7. Discuss the real-world consequences to educators when they advocate justice and inclusion of all students, notwithstanding their sexual orientation. How does one handle the resistance to changes in school cultures and practices that are heteronormative? What strategies facilitate change? How can school leaders avoid the accusation of appearing to "promote an alternative lifestyle"?

Annotated Readings

Kevin Kumashiro's (2002) *Troubling Education: Queer Activism and Anti-oppressive Pedagogy* provides practical guidance for teachers who want to be proactive in the transformation of their classrooms. Through a combination of interviews, poetry, narrative, and careful analysis, Kumashiro crafts a postmodern collage that interrogates the complex role of activism in our pedagogy, troubles our educational research practices, and demonstrates how certain groups in society are privileged and certain identities are normalized.

The Human Rights Watch (2001) report, *Hatred in the Hallways: Violence and Discrimination against Lesbian, Gay, Bisexual, and Transgender Students in U.S. Schools*, uses qualitative research methods to construct a compelling indictment of the public school system and its failure to protect LGBTIQ students from harassment and violence. Moving beyond the language of condemnation, however, this report offers practical recommendations for teachers, administrators, and government officials to help them to end the multiple abuses experienced by LGBTIQ students.

In a broad effort "to help make gay, lesbian, bisexual, and transgender experiences part of this nation's vision of democratic multiculturalism" (Lipkin, 1999, p. xv), *Understanding Homosexuality, Changing Schools* explores the theories of homosexuality, the problems of homophobia and heterosexism, and developmental models of identity formation. More importantly for the practitioner, Lipkin provides specific strategies for changing the attitudes and behaviors of school administrators, teachers, and community members by focusing on ways in which policy reform efforts can effectively address oppositional tactics designed to maintain oppressive, heterosexist social systems.

Queering Elementary Education: Advancing the Dialogue about Sexualities and Schooling (Letts & Sears, 1999) is an anthology of essays that collectively call on educators to question their pedagogical practices in order to discover ways in which the values of social justice might infuse our notions of democratic multiculturalism by including individuals of all gender and sexual identifications. Underlying all the articles in this book is a belief that children must be taught to move beyond the traditions of dualistic thinking in order to break free of the chains of abuse and oppression that are wrought upon all of us by presumptive heterosexuality.

William Pinar's *Queer Theory in Education* (1998) is a highly significant collection of scholarly essays and research that aims to expose the homophobic and heterosexist silliness that pervades educational systems. Pinar's characteristically insightful commentary wraps this compilation of thought-provoking theoretical inquiries with a sense of urgency and a bit of hope that by focusing on the difference that "queer" represents, we might start seeing an as yet unimaginable new world order.

References

Anzaldua, G. (1987). *Borderlands/La Frontera: The new mestiza*. San Francisco: Aunte Lute Books.

Aston, J. (2001a). Autopsy of hate: Ten years later. *Outsmart, 8*(6), 64–69.

Aston, J. (2001b). *Deconstructing heterosexism and homophobia in schools: Case study of a hate crime by an adolescent offender*. Unpublished doctoral dissertation, Texas A&M University, College Station, Texas.

Britzman, D. P. (1995). Is there a queer pedagogy? Or, stop reading straight! *Educational Theory, 45*(2), 151–165.

Britzman, D. P. (1996). "On becoming a little sex researcher": Some comments on a polymorphously perverse curriculum. *Journal of Curriculum Studies, 12*(2), 4–11.

Britzman, D. P. (1997). What is this thing called love? New discourses for understanding gay and lesbian youth. In S. de Castell & M. Bryson (Eds.), *Radical in<ter>ventions: Identity, politics, and difference/s in educational praxis* (pp. 103–107). Albany, NY: SUNY Press.

Chasnoff, D. (Director/Producer), & Cohen, H. S. (Producer). *It's elementary: Talking about gay issues in school* [Videotape]. San Francisco: Women's Educational Media.

Connell, R. W. (1995). *Masculinities*. Berkeley: University of California Press.

de Castell, S., & Bryson, M. (Eds.). (1997). *Radical in<ter>ventions: Identity, politics, and difference/s in educational praxis*. Albany: SUNY Press.

Eribon, D. (2001). *Reflexiones sobre la cuestión gay* (J. Zulaika, Trans.). Barcelona: Editorial Anagrama. (Original work published 1999.)

Etheridge, M. (1999). "Scarecrow." On *Breakdown* [CD]. Island Records.

Fitzgerald, B. (2001). *Locked away minds of rainbow flags*. Unpublished poem.

Garber, L. (Ed.). (1994). *Tilting the tower*. New York: Routledge.

Franklin, K. (1997). *Hate crime or rite of passage? Assailant motivations in antigay violence*. Unpublished doctoral dissertation, California School of Professional Psychology, Berkeley/Alameda.

Harris, M. B. (1997). *School experiences of gay and lesbian youth: The invisible minority*. New York: Harrington Park Press.

Human Rights Watch (2001). *Hatred in the hallways: Violence and discrimination against lesbian, gay, bisexual, and transgender students in U.S. schools*. New York: Author.

Kirsch, M. H. (2000). *Queer theory and social change*. New York: Routledge.

Kumashiro, K. (2002). *Troubling education: Queer activism and antioppressive pedagogy*. New York: RoutledgeFalmer.

Letts IV, W. J., & Sears, J. T. (1999). *Queering elementary education: Advancing the dialogue about sexualities and schooling.* Lanham, MD: Rowman & Littlefield.

Lipkin, A. (1999). *Understanding homosexuality, changing schools.* Boulder, CO: Westview Press.

Lugg, C. A. (2003). Our strait-laced administrators: The law, lesbian, gay, bisexual, and transgendered administrators, and the assimilationist imperative. *Journal of School Leadership, 13*(1), 51–85.

Lugg, C. A., & Koschoreck, J. W. (Eds.). (2003). The final closet [Special issue]. *Journal of School Leadership, 13*(1).

Luhmann, S. (1998). Queering/querying pedagogy? Or, pedagogy is a pretty queer thing. In W. F. Pinar (Ed.), *Queer theory in education* (pp. 141–155). Mahwah, NJ: Lawrence Erlbaum Associates.

Macgillivray, I. K. (2004). *Sexual orientation and school policy: A practical guide for teachers, administrators, and community activists.* Lanham, MD: Rowman & Littlefield.

Morris, M. (2000). Dante's left foot kicks queer theory into gear. In S. Talburt & S. R. Steinberg (Eds.), *Thinking queer: Sexuality, culture, and education* (pp. 15–32). New York: Peter Lang.

Patton, C. (1993). Tremble, hetero swine! In M. Warner (Ed.), *Fear of a queer planet: Queer politics and social theory* (pp. 143–177). Minneapolis: University of Minnesota Press.

Pinar, W. F. (Ed.). (1998). *Queer theory in education.* Mahwah, NJ: Lawrence Erlbaum Associates.

Rofes, E. (1989). Opening up the classroom closet: Responding to the educational needs of gay and lesbian youth. *Harvard Educational Review, 59*(4), 444–453.

Rofes, E. (1997). Schools: The neglected site of queer activists. In M. B. Harris (Ed.), *School experiences of gay and lesbian youth: The invisible minority* (pp. xiii–xviii). New York: Harrington Park Press.

Scholl, L. (2001). Narratives of hybridity and the challenge to multicultural education. In K. K. Kumashiro (Ed.), *Troubling intersections of race and sexuality: Queer students of color and anti-oppressive education* (pp. 141–161). Lanham, MD: Rowman & Littlefield.

Sears, J. T. (1983). Sexuality: Taking off the masks. *Changing Schools, 11,* 12–13.

Sears, J. T. (1991). Helping students understand and accept sexual diversity. *Educational Leadership, 45*(1), 54–56.

Sedgwick, E. (1990). *Epistemology of the closet.* Berkeley: University of California Press.

Seidman, S. (1993). Identity and politics in a "postmodern" gay culture: Some historical and conceptual notes. In M. Warner (Ed.), *Fear of a queer planet: Queer politics and social theory* (pp. 105–142). Minneapolis: University of Minnesota Press.

Slattery, P., & Rapp, D. (2003). *Ethics and the foundation of education: Teaching convictions in a postmodern world.* Boston: Allyn and Bacon.

Sumara, D., & Davis, B. (1999). Interrupting heteronormativity: Toward a queer curriculum theory. *Curriculum Inquiry, 29*(2), 191–208.

Talburt, S., & Steinberg, S. R. (2000). *Thinking queer: Sexuality, culture, and education.* New York: Peter Lang.

Texas Triangle. (2001, December 28). Protesters ultimately want death for homosexuals. Retrieved February 20, 2004, from www.txtriangle.com/archive/1012/coverstory.htm

Warner, M. (Ed.). (1993). *Fear of a queer planet: Queer politics and social theory.* Minneapolis: University of Minnesota Press.

Endnotes

[1]For a thorough listing of seminal U.S. state and federal legislation and court actions that affect the lives of LGBTIQ persons and the educational system, see Human Rights Watch (2001) and Lugg (2003). The following are of particular note for teachers and other educational leaders:

- *Nabozny v. Podlesny*, 92 F.3d 446, 458 (7th Cir. 1996) in which the federal court prohibited the right of any student to assault another on the basis of sexual orientation.

- Massachusetts *Discrimination in Education Prohibited (Annotated Laws of Massachusetts, chapter 76, section 5)*. This provision states, in part, that "no person shall be excluded from or discriminated against in admission to a public school of any town, or in obtaining the advantages, privileges and courses of study of such public school on account of race, color, sex, religion, national origin or *sexual orientation*" [italics added] (Human Rights Watch, 2001, pp. 202–203).

[2]The term *hegemony* refers to the predominant influence or authority over another or a group of others. Though in its original meaning it applied to the dominant influence of one state over another, it has come to denote a prevailing consciousness that becomes internalized in the values, beliefs, and attitudes of a society in such a way that this consciousness becomes normalized.

[3]Britzman (1996) helps us to understand just how extensive these organizing heteronormative social structures are when she states that "the work of the apparatuses of *education, law, and medicine* [italics added] become occupied with normalizing sexuality to the confines of proper object choice" (p. 6).

[4]*Epistemology* refers to the branch of philosophy that studies the nature of knowledge.

[5]*Ontology* is the branch of philosophy that examines the nature of being.

[6]*Othering* refers to a process whereby one secures his or her own positive sense of identity by stigmatizing others.

9

Teaching Strategies for Developing Leaders for Social Justice

Madeline M. Hafner

Introduction

Many university-based leadership preparation programs around the country now include specific coursework or program emphasis on issues of diversity, equity, and social justice. Although highly individualistic, each of these initiatives provides evidence that

> . . . a growing force of professors of educational administration are expressing interest in transforming administrator preparation to focus on social justice. These professors want to move beyond merely describing demographic shifts in our country. Instead they are developing and seeking teaching strategies and curriculum materials that uncover individual and institutional oppression and that reveal concrete actions school leaders can take to alleviate this oppression. (Hafner & Young, 2003, p. 1)

In response to this call from the field, an instructional resource that outlines teaching strategies and curriculum issues that inform the development of leaders who can "promote and deliver social justice" (Grogan & Andrews, 2002, p. 250) is both timely and valuable. The purpose of this chapter, then, is to provide individuals in educational leadership preparation programs and practicing school administrators with action-oriented instructional strategies and concrete curricular information that can be utilized in developing leaders for social justice.

This chapter provides a brief overview of the growing knowledge base that informs the practice of leadership for social justice. This is then followed by an extensive overview of instructional and curricular resources from different areas of education that are available to individuals engaged in teaching for social justice within the context of leadership preparation and development. Lastly, two specific teaching strategies are presented—"Social Justice Education Practice" and "Social Reconstructionist Schooling"—that can be utilized to develop leaders for social justice.

Leadership for Social Justice—A Growing Knowledge Base

As demonstrated by the publication of a book of this nature, the field of educational leadership has developed a growing knowledge base regarding issues of diversity, equity, and social justice (Capper, 1993; Dantley, 2002; Foster, 1986; Grogan, 1999; Larson & Ovando, 2001; Lyman & Villani, 2002; Reyes, Scribner, & Scribner, 1999; Rusch, 2003; Scheurich & Skrla, 2003; Scheurich & Young, 1997; Young & Laible, 2000, and others). Several of these publications offer a comprehensive overview of the empirical and theoretical work that contributes to what we know about leadership for social justice and contextualizes this information in terms of leadership preparation program design. It is important to note that throughout these articles social justice is conceptualized as both a "means and an end" (Pounder, Reitzug, & Young, 2002, p. 262) in the quest for school improvement. Three publications in particular have influenced the diverse instructional practices and curriculum issues involved in developing leaders for social justice.

Colleen Larson and Khaula Murtadha (2002) provide a thorough review of the literature to date in the area of leadership for social justice. They describe how school leaders and "researchers in educational administration who believe that injustice in our schools and communities is neither natural nor inevitable loosely coalesce under an umbrella of inquiry called leadership for social justice" (p. 135). From this "umbrella of inquiry," the authors discuss three areas of study that inform what we know about leadership for social justice: "deconstructing existing logics of leadership; portraying alternative perspectives of leadership; and constructing theories, systems, and processes of leadership for social justice" (p. 137).

Additionally, Diana Pounder, Ulrich Reitzug, and Michelle Young (2002), in their book chapter entitled "Preparing School Leaders for School Improvement, Social Justice, and Community," directly situate the leadership for social justice discourse within leadership preparation programs. As they explore the relationships among school improvement, democratic community, and social justice, Pounder et al. (2002) offer both theoretical and practical responses to two reflective questions being posed to leadership preparation programs today: ". . . What [do] school and district leaders need to know and be able to do to promote social justice in their schools, and . . . how [can leadership preparation] programs develop leaders to champion and support social justice?" (p. 272).

Carolyn Riehl's (2000) review of literature chronicling the "role of the school administrator in responding to the needs of diverse students" (p. 55) includes historical, empirical, and theoretical literature influencing the practice of school leadership. Riehl clearly articulates that an "inclusive administrative practice is rooted in the values of equity and justice" (p. 55) and that the values of equity and justice are lenses through which leadership practices can be considered inclusive or transformative. She outlines three broad leadership "tasks" that shape how school leaders respond to racial and ethnic diversity in schools. These tasks include: (1) "fostering new meanings about diversity," (2) "promoting inclusive practices within schools," and (3) "building connections between schools and communities" (p. 59). Riehl goes on to provide examples of what each of these tasks looks like in the everyday practice of school leadership.

As demonstrated by the works briefly described here and discussed at length in other areas of this text, a compelling knowledge base focusing on leadership for social justice has emerged. The number of empirical studies that guide our understanding of what leaders who possess a deep commitment to social justice think and do is growing (Riester, Pursch, & Skrla, 2002; Scheurich, 1998; Strachan, 1999). Scholars and practitioners in the field of educational leadership have made it clear that issues of diversity, equity, and social justice must find a permanent home in leadership preparation programs. But how do we teach social justice? What teaching strategies can be helpful in developing leaders for social justice? The remainder of this chapter responds to these questions and provides an overview of different teaching strategies and curriculum issues that can be utilized in leadership preparation programs and in school districts to develop leaders for social justice.

Overview of the Literature on Teaching for Social Justice

Compared with other areas of study, educational leadership has come to the "teaching for social justice" dance relatively late. The field of teacher education in particular has contributed significantly to the development of and research on teaching for social justice. Many of the instructional strategies described in this overview on teaching for social justice speak directly to educators' work within K–12 school settings, whereas others are situated within higher education or adult learning arenas. Additionally, although small in number, several resources directly address teaching for social justice within leadership preparation programs and in terms of professional development of practicing school administrators.

Teacher Education

The field of teacher education has, over time, advanced powerful discourses relative to issues of diversity, equity, and social justice (see, for example, Allen, 1999; Ayers, Hunt, & Quinn, 1998; Christensen, 1999; Delpit, 1993; Dilg, 1999; Gay, 2000; Giroux, 1988; Kumashiro, 2000; Ladson-Billings, 1995, 2000; Nieto, 1999; Perry, 2000; Rethinking Schools, 1994, 2001; Wallace, 2000; and others). For many in the field of teacher education, *how we come to know how to teach* is only one piece of the educational puzzle. *To what ends do our teaching methods serve* is the other. The concept of the teacher as an agent of social change is rooted in the work of critical theorists such as Paulo Friere, bell hooks, Lisa Delpit, Michael Apple, Geneva Gay, Carl Grant, Maxine Greene, Gloria Ladson-Billings, and Christine Sleeter. The idea of "education as the practice of freedom" (hooks, 1994, p. 1) grounds much of the teaching for social justice literature in the field of teacher education, including the areas of multicultural education, culturally responsive pedagogy, and anti-oppressive education.

One text in particular, *Teaching for Social Justice*, edited by William Ayers, Jean Ann Hunt, and Therese Quinn (1998), offers firsthand accounts of social justice work within teacher education programs. Personal stories from social justice educators, defined broadly to include teachers, students, parents, school leaders, community organizers, and researchers, provide a rich framework for understanding what teaching for social justice means in the everyday world of people's lives. Although the text does not include specific instructional strategies or curriculum issues, it does connect readers more intimately with people engaged in social justice work, and in doing so, offers them the opportunity to reflect on their own work in developing leaders for social justice.

Other Fields of Study

Authors from other fields of study, including women's studies, gender studies, and ethnic studies, have developed multiple curriculum resources and pedagogical tools that can be utilized by individuals developing leaders for social justice (see, for example, Adams, Bell, & Griffin, 1997; Derman-Sparks & Phillips, 1997; Ellsworth, 1989; hooks, 1994). Two texts in particular outline specific instructional strategies and curriculum issues that can be applied for use in leadership preparation programs or school districts: *Teaching for Diversity and Social Justice: A Sourcebook* by Maurianne Adams, Lee Anne Bell, and Pat Griffin (1997) and *Teaching/Learning Antiracism: A Developmental Approach* by Louise Derman-Sparks and Carol Brunson Phillips (1997).

In their transformative text, *Teaching for Diversity and Social Justice: A Sourcebook*, Adams et al. (1997) provide readers with foundational information relative to social justice education. Describing social justice education as "both a process and a goal" (p. 3), the authors explain:

> The goal of social justice education is full and equal participation of all groups in a society that is mutually shaped to meet their needs. Social justice includes a vision of society in which the distribution of resources is equitable and all members are physically and psychologically safe and secure.... Social justice involves social actors who have a sense of their own agency as well as a sense of social responsibility toward and with others and the society as a whole. The process for attaining the goal of social justice we believe should also be democratic and participatory, inclusive and affirming of human agency and human capacities for working collaboratively to create change. ... This book focuses on developing educational processes for reaching these goals. (pp. 3, 4)

After introducing the reader to their definition of social justice education Adams et al. go on to provide a comprehensive and reader-friendly description of the theoretical underpinnings that support their work.

One of the most significant contributions of the *Teaching for Diversity and Social Justice* text is the authors' conceptualization of a pedagogical framework for social justice education. The "Major Elements of Social Justice Education Practice" framework for teaching asks educators to:

1. Balance the emotional and cognitive components of the learning process;
2. Acknowledge and support the personal (the individual student's experience) while illuminating the systemic (the interactions among social groups);
3. Attend to social relations within the classroom;
4. Utilize reflection and experience as tools for student-centered learning; and
5. Value awareness, personal growth, and change as outcomes of the learning process. (p. 42, 43)

These elements provide a pedagogical approach that has been found exceptionally useful in developing leaders for social justice (Brown, 2004; Hafner & Young, 2003; Ropers-Huilman, 1999; Young & Laible, 2000) and will be discussed at length later in this chapter.

After introducing readers to the Major Elements of Social Justice Education Practice, the *Teaching for Diversity and Social Justice* text provides specific curricula that can be utilized to teach about different forms of oppression. These curriculum design chapters address different forms of oppression experienced in the United States, including racism, sexism, heterosexism, anti-Semitism, ableism, and classism. A detailed instructional outline is provided within each chapter. These outlines include information about important conceptual issues and historical information relative to the form of oppression being discussed, overall goals and key concepts that inform the different instructional modules presented in the chapter, and specific course activities and expected time frames for each activity.

In addition to the curricular and instructional information outlined in each of these chapters, Adams et al. include insights from their own teaching experiences that shed light on the interpersonal and intrapersonal dynamics that occur when educating for social justice. They highlight specific areas of the curriculum where instructors may encounter participant resistance and discuss examples of participant reactions and classroom dynamics that typically occur when discussing complex and provocative issues such as oppression, racism, and privilege. In essence, the curriculum design chapters in *Teaching for Diversity and Social Justice* provide readers with multiple examples of how a pedagogical framework for social justice education actually plays out within different instructional contexts.

A second resource that provides specific instructional strategies and curriculum issues that can be utilized by individuals developing leaders for social justice is the text *Teaching/Learning Antiracism: A Developmental Approach* by Louise Derman-Sparks and Carol Brunson Phillips (1997). Unlike the Adams et al. (1997) text, *Teaching/Learning Antiracism* focuses on a single form of social group oppression—racism.

Teaching/Learning Antiracism offers individuals working to develop leaders for social justice a detailed curriculum regarding antiracist education and specific instructional strategies for implementing that curriculum. For example, the authors provide a detailed overview of how to introduce the concept of antiracist identity. In addition to instructional strategies for teaching specific content, the authors provide instructional strategies to assist the reader in making sense of the affective issues that arise when teaching for social justice. The authors include helpful sections on teaching challenges and student responses to course content.

Educational Leadership

Although limited in number and scope, several resources within the field of educational leadership directly address the topic of teaching strategies for developing leaders for social justice. Several of these resources speak directly to

"The number of empirical studies that guide our understanding of what leaders who possess a deep commitment to social justice think and do is growing (Riester, Pursch, & Skrla, 2002; Scheurich, 1998; Strachan, 1999). Scholars and practitioners in the field of educational leadership have made it clear that issues of diversity, equity, and social justice must find a permanent home in leadership preparation programs. But how do we teach social justice? What teaching strategies can be helpful in developing leaders for social justice?"

developing leaders for social justice within leadership preparation programs (see Brown, 2004; Ropers-Huilman, 1999; Young & Laible, 2000), whereas others focus on developing leaders for social justice within the context of professional development (see Henze, Katz, Norte, Sather, & Walker, 2002; Lindsey, Robins, & Terrell, 2003). Although each of these resources can be utilized in a variety of ways to prepare school leaders "to promote and deliver social justice," the work of Young and Laible (2000) and Brown (2004) provides specific instructional strategies that individuals in leadership preparation programs and school districts can utilize to develop leaders for social justice.

White Racism, Antiracism, and School Leadership Preparation by Michele Young and Julie Laible (2000) is a seminal work in the field of educational leadership regarding developing leaders for social justice. Through their work as professors in leadership preparation programs, the authors advance the notion that ". . . school leaders must be prepared to work against all forms of oppression that exist in our schools today and to work for social justice" (p. 375). To this end, the authors advocate for promoting antiracist education within leadership preparation programs.

Young and Laible (2000) articulate four goals of teaching and learning antiracism vis-à-vis the Derman-Sparks and Phillips (1997) text *Teaching/Learning Antiracism*. These include:

(a) to have students learn about themselves and their own racial and cultural identity; (b) to have students learn about White racism, how it works, and how it affects policies, programs, and practices; (c) to have students learn about and appreciate the knowledge, experiences, and histories of racial and ethnic groups that differ from their own; and (d) to have students develop the capabilities and mind frame necessary to work for change. (p. 392)

Citing the " 'WASP suburban bias' of most administration programs (Parker & Shapiro, 1992, p. 24)" (p. 387), the authors go on to outline a rationale for including antiracist education within leadership preparation programs. They assert:

More attention needs to be given to future school and district leaders' (particularly White leaders') understanding of racial oppression and ability to support the education of all children. Opportunities must be provided for leaders to examine and reflect on the meaning of their cultural background, their skin color, and their belief systems as well as the relationship between these attributes and their personal and professional practice. Future school leaders should not be granted licensure or graduate from their preparation programs without an understanding of racism, racial identity issues, racial oppression, and how to work against racism in their schools. (pp. 387, 388)

In terms of preparing leaders for social justice, Young and Laible (2000) believe that antiracist education can be an "oppositional and a transformational force to White racism" (p. 390).

In addition to providing a strong rationale for including antiracist education within leadership preparation programs, Young and Laible (2000) delineate six instructional strategies relative to developing leaders for social justice. These include: "know [y]our students, create a classroom environment that is safe and positive, examine racism as a system of oppression, facilitate students' self reflection, provide opportunities for students to dialogue with their peers, and engage students in antiracist activity" (p. 395). A brief overview of these instructional strategies is presented next.

The Knowing [Y]our Students instructional strategy involves a process of recognizing and exploring "the unique identity of all class members . . . and what role [culture, race, and ethnicity] plays in their lives" (p. 395). Creating a Positive Classroom Environment includes creating a "classroom climate in which students feel they will be supported and in which they, in turn, have a responsibility to support their classmates (Bell & Griffin, 1997)" (p. 396). Focusing on the Systemic Nature of Racism involves a methodical analysis of racism at multiple levels—"from the individual level to the societal level (Scheurich & Young, 1997)" (p. 397). To encourage Individual Reflection, the authors require students to actively "reflect on their own racial identity" (p. 397) utilizing specific models of racial identity. Group Reflection involves sharing the results of reflective exercises with classmates in a manner that is "nonthreatening and allow[s] the students to decide how revealing they want to be" (p. 400). Finally, through Taking Antiracist Action students are asked ". . . to apply their new understandings by taking meaningful action, to see themselves as agents of change, capable of acting on their convictions and in concern with others against the injustices they see" (Bell & Griffin, 1997, p. 48) (p. 402).

Many of the instructional strategies utilized by Young and Laible (2000) are supported by the work of Kathleen Brown (2003, 2004). In her article "Leadership for Social Justice and Equity: Weaving a Transformative Framework and Pedagogy," Brown (2004) provides a comprehensive overview of eight instructional strategies she utilizes in her work with preservice and practicing administrators. These strategies include: (1) Cultural Autobiography, (2) Life Histories, (3) Prejudice Reduction Workshops, (4) Reflective Analysis Journals, (5) Cross-Cultural Interviews, (6) Educational Plunge, (7) Diversity Panels, and (8) Activist Action Plans. Brown asserts that there is transformation power in teaching strategies that are focused on developing leaders for social justice. She argues,

> By being actively engaged in a number of assignments requiring the examination of ontological/epistemological assumptions, values and beliefs, context and experience, and worldviews, students are better equipped to work with and guide themselves and others in translating their perspectives, perceptions, and goals into agendas for social change. The exploration of new understandings, the synthesis of new information, and the integration of these insights throughout personal and professional spheres can lead future educational leaders to a broader, more inclusive approach in addressing equity issues. (p. 101)

Brown's empirical research (2003) exploring the relationship between these instructional strategies and leaders' awareness and actions represents a missing link in the discourse on teaching strategies and program design for developing leaders for social justice. Her study, and other preliminary research studies like it (Anderson, 2003; Hafner, 2005; Rusch, 2003; Szabo et al., 2002), must be an integral part of any leadership program evaluation and transformation. Young, Peterson, and Short (2002) provide a clear reminder to each of us who have invested our lives in the preparation and development of school leaders—"We do not have a lot of reliable data on which to base our program enhancement efforts" (p. 151).

Although a handful of research studies provide preliminary evidence as to how practicing school leaders promote social justice in their schools, the influence of leadership preparation coursework, program emphasis, or professional development on school leaders' commitment to social justice has not been investigated. Furthermore, understanding how school-based outcomes are influenced by leadership for social justice is another area of research that has only recently been considered in the field of educational leadership. Given this inadequacy and the growing call from the field of educational leadership for leaders who can "promote and deliver social justice," it is imperative that further research be conducted to better understand the relationship between specific instructional strategies and the development of leaders for social justice.

In addition to the information offered by Young and Laible (2000) and Brown (2004), which address teaching for social justice within leadership preparation programs, two texts from the educational leadership literature focus on developing leaders for social justice through professional development: *Leading for Diversity: How School Leaders Promote Positive Interethnic Relations* (2002) by Rosemary Henze, Anne Katz, Edmundo Norte, Susan E. Sather, and Ernest Walker and *Cultural Proficiency: A Manual for School Leaders* (2003) by Randall B. Lindsey, Kikanza Nuri Robins, and Raymond D. Terrell. Written with field-based practitioners in mind, Henze et al. (2002) focus on developing cultural proficiency in school leaders; Lindsey et al. (2003) concentrate on fostering leadership that promotes positive interethnic relations within the context of schools. The purpose of both texts is best summarized by Henze et al., "Our intent is to bring a number of different tools and theories to the attention of practitioners in a way that enables them to use these resources to solve problems and improve schools" (p. 16).

Focusing specifically on issues of race and ethnicity, *Leading for Diversity: How School Leaders Promote Positive Interethnic Relations* (Henze et al., 2002) outlines a "Framework for Developing Positive Interethnic Communities" (p. 15) based on 21 case studies of schools across the United States where leadership played a key role in diffusing racial and ethnic tension. Each chapter is framed by a different step or stage within the Framework for Developing Positive Interethnic Communities, which is similar to what Scheurich and Skrla (2003) describe as an "equity audit" [see also Capper, Frattura, & Keyes (2000) and Johnson (2002) for other examples of equity audits]. As leaders work through each step of the framework, they engage in a process of data collection, action planning and implementation, and evaluation in terms of school and district level "supports or restraints that can encourage positive interethnic relations" (p. 28). Reflective activities and case studies also are provided.

In *Cultural Proficiency: A Manual for School Leaders*, Lindsey et al. (2003) provide readers with "a strong conceptual understanding of cultural proficiency and give specific, practical, field-tested applications of those same concepts" (p. xxi). Each chapter addresses one of the key elements of the authors' approach to building cultural proficiency. The elements needed to build cultural proficiency in school leaders include: (1) "the four tools for developing one's cultural competence," (2) "the cultural proficiency continuum that indicate unique ways of seeing and responding to difference," (3) "the essential elements of cultural proficiency [that] provide the standards for individual behavior and organizational practices," (4) "the guiding principles: the core values, the foundation on which the approach is based," and (5) "the barriers" to cultural proficiency (pp. 6, 7). Imbedded throughout the text is a complex case study that affords readers a common context for discussion. In addition, each chapter ends with a set of structured activities to reinforce new learning and apply content to practice.

Whether focusing specifically on teaching strategies for developing leaders for social justice, leadership for diversity, or culturally proficient school leaders, each resource described in this chapter provides readers with a variety of instructional strategies that can inform leadership preparation programs and school districts working to develop leadership for social justice. The authors of each resource, however, are firm in their common caveat regarding how their work is utilized: *The ideas and instructional methods included in these articles and texts are not quick fixes or one-shot professional development models.* The authors emphasize that their work "is not a magic formula, a silver bullet, or a panacea" (Lindsey et al., 2003, p. xxii). They challenge each of us in leadership preparation and development when they remind us: "You have to do the work. Schools have been designed for some students to be successful. It will take great effort and hard work to make schools places where all students will be successful" (p. xxii). The next section of this chapter describes two specific teaching strategies that can assist individuals in leadership preparation programs and school districts make schools "places where all students will be successful."

Teaching Strategies for Developing Leaders for Social Justice

Two strategies that can serve to scaffold the teaching and learning process in developing leaders for social justice are the Elements of Social Justice Education Practice and Social Reconstructionist Schooling. Presented earlier in this chapter, the Elements of Social Justice Education Practice is a pedagogical framework conceptualized by Adams et al. (1997) that guides each facet of the instructional process. Social Reconstructionist Schooling is a conceptual tool that can be applied to the work of school leaders (Capper, 1993) across courses and content areas within leadership preparation programs and professional development. In this section, I describe these two teaching strategies and then provide examples and illustrations of how each has actually played out in my own work and the work of others in the field of educational leadership as we have engaged in the process of teaching for social justice.

Social Justice Education Practice: A Pedagogical Tool for Developing Leaders for Social Justice

As a pedagogical tool, the Elements of Social Justice Education Practice structures the approach to teaching that many of us in the field of educational leadership take within our own work and provide one example of how social justice education is both a process and goal. This framework reminds educators that the process of teaching for social justice models the goals of social justice education. Essentially, the process of teaching for social justice involves a different way of thinking about teaching, specifically in terms of who we are as teachers. The following text outlines how each element shapes the teaching and learning process, and in doing so, models the goals of social justice education.

(1) Balance the emotional and cognitive components of the learning process: Teaching that pays attention to personal safety, classroom norms, and guidelines for group behavior. As an educator for social justice, I recognize that the teaching strategies utilized to establish classroom norms, group behavior, and emotional and intellectual safety in the classroom must mirror the principles of social justice about which I am teaching. One of the first activities I facilitate in the courses I teach can be described as a *Safe and Successful Learning needs assessment*. In a large group, I ask each class participant to identify what they need from the group in order for our class to be a safe and successful learning environment. I write each need on chart paper so that I can type up the list and distribute it to each member of the class. The list becomes a shared reference point concerning social interactions, emotional safety, and classroom norms and behaviors.

Some needs identified by class participants are concrete and self-explanatory, for example, "I need to be able to bring dinner to class" or "I can only pay attention to one conversation at a time." Other needs, however, are not as straightforward or observable. In those cases, I encourage participants to operationalize the need they have identified. For example, if a participant says, "I need to be heard and not judged," I ask that person to describe what being heard and not judged would actually look like within the context of the class. The participant then articulates for the class attitudes and be-haviors that would need to occur for this need to be met. For example, the participant might operationalize the need of being heard and not judged by saying, "Well, if you don't like what someone has to say, if you think it's wrong or dumb, you can't just shout out at them 'How can you say that?' or 'You don't know that!' or 'You're wrong—you're way off base.' Rolling your eyes is just as bad and it sends the same message." The process of articulating needs for a safe and successful learning environment naturally leads into a conver-sation about the need for emotional safety when discussing issues inherent in the topic of social justice such as racism, homophobia, institutionalized op-pression, power, or agency. In the example provided, I then ask class partici-pants to identify several attitudes and behaviors they could employ when they disagree with a statement made in the class that would not be perceived as judging. Participants typically share strategies they have developed or utilized in other contexts, for example, using "I statements" to communicate how they feel or keeping the conversation focused on the content being discussed, not individual opinions. Revisiting the list of needs throughout the semester also is helpful as class participants take ownership in monitoring the safety of the environment and ensuring that positive practices negotiated by the group are reinforced.

(2) Acknowledge and support the personal (the individual student's experience) while illuminating the systemic (the interactions among social groups): Teaching that calls attention to the here-and-now of the classroom setting and grounds the systemic or abstract in an accumulation of concrete, real-life examples.   Many of us will never have the opportunity to discuss issues such as social group oppression or internalized racism with individuals from backgrounds and experiences different than our own. One of the most powerful teaching tools I have utilized to provide class participants insight into this type of a conversation is a structured viewing of the video *The Color of Fear* (1995). Viewing *The Color of Fear*, a documentary by diversity trainer Lee Mun Wah, allows class participants to witness an intimate dialogue regarding the impact of racism and privilege on the lived experiences of individuals from different racial and ethnic groups. After viewing this documentary, many class participants, particularly White participants, are more able to apply abstract information presented to them through course readings, activities, and discussions to the personal, lived experiences of individuals and connect that new learning to the here-and-now classroom setting. In addition, through participating in a follow-up application-to-practice class participants relate the concepts and experiences learned through course readings, discussed in the documentary, and reflected on in class to issues that challenge their individual school settings. An outline of this activity (Creating Antiracist Schools) is provided in Figure 9.1.

text continues on p. 182

FIGURE 9.1   *Creating Antiracist Schools*

The Color of Fear (A documentary film by Lee Mun Wah)

Class participants have already read several articles introducing the ideas of privilege, racism, White racism, oppression, levels of oppression, and the concepts of target and ally.

Introduction

Right before we begin watching the documentary, I set up the role the video plays in our larger discussion about leadership, diversity, and social justice. We then review the two objectives for the class session: (1) increasing our awareness of privilege and (2) moving our thinking about racism into action. I explain to the students the following points about the video:

- This is a documentary about individuals' experiences with racism.
- The individuals in the video are not actors.
- Our role is not to critique the film.
- Each participant was chosen to be part of the film for their honesty, directness, sincerity, and their work against racism.

Documentary: 90 minutes (View documentary with no interruptions)

Reflective Questions

I usually wait 20 seconds or so before I ask any reflective questions.

- What was it like for you to witness this conversation?
- What are the emotions that play into/influence this discussion of racism?
- Open up discussion. Questions might include: What parts of the film are difficult to watch? Why? What parts caused you to pause?

Next Steps—Action Steps

Ultimately, we must ask ourselves the question "How can we as school leaders use our privilege well?"
Using a Think–Pair–Share cooperative structure, ask participants to respond to the following questions:

What actions will we take to create antiracist schools? Specifically,
   What actions will we stop?
   What actions will we start?
   What actions will we continue?

(continued)

FIGURE 9.1   *Continued*

After I ask these action questions, participants move into small groups and spend 20–30 minutes filling in the following chart:

What actions will we take to create antiracist schools?

_____

_____

What actions will we stop?

_____

_____

What actions will we start?

_____

_____

What actions will we continue?

_____

_____

After all groups are done constructing their lists, create one large list on chart paper asking each group to contribute. When finished, type the chart paper up and distribute it to the class as a visual reminder of their commitment to action.

Sample Responses:

Actions we will take to create anti-racist schools . . .
We will stop . . .

Ignoring the problem of not enough minority representation on our community councils.
Treating people like they are invisible.
Being silent and become a voice *for* equity.
Blaming "groups" (poor/minority) and see individuals; seek methods to make changes.
The "-ism" comments.
Negative perspectives through "teachable moments."
Cultural stereotypes.
Racist language-jokes, derogatory tales, etc.
Non-inclusive practices.
Deficit oriented faculty room conversations.
Overt, racist practices (e.g., grouping, testing, placements).
Volunteer testing for GT in a magnet site.
Talking about areas in the district as the "low" or "high" achieving school.

FIGURE 9.1 *Continued*

We will start ...

Collecting data about college bound students and disaggregate the data.
Recognizing White privilege and thinking about how to be an ally.
Recruiting individuals of color (parents or members of community) to serve on community councils.
Convincing students to become allies.
Being aware and confronting demeaning/labeling language.
Talking to colleagues about language policies.
Interrupting racist and deficit thinking remarks.
Questioning dominant assumptions.
Pointing out privilege.
Seeking out information on racial issues in order to understand, confront, and educate. (Study leadership of marginalized groups.)
Acknowledging "spirituality" as leadership vision (e.g., compassion, looking inward, etc.).
Actively recruiting teachers to represent diversity.
Asking clarifying questions.
Being conscious of deficit thinking/racist thoughts (preconceptions).
Start taking risks!!
Sitting by someone you wouldn't normally sit by.
Looking at self and own beliefs.
Ensuring student activities are accessible to all students (i.e., GT, after-school, student body officer).
Building in time to dialogue.
Talking about placing highest performing teachers in lowest performing schools.

We will continue ...

Going to different universities to recruit teachers, specifically teachers with an ESL endorsement and/or teachers of color.
Service learning projects that don't reinforce stereotypes or deficit thinking.
Discussions on the issue of oppression.
Professional development on social justice, racism, cultural awareness.
Collecting data on %, ratio of students of color in GT, honors, resource classes and act for equity here.
Using our positions in our community to teach and nurture equity (without being fired).
Being visible in the community.
"Making it public;" making people aware of derogatory statements.
Being aware of seating arrangements.
Collecting data on attrition in GT strands.

(3) Attend to social relations within the classroom: Teaching that helps students name behaviors that emerge in group dynamics, understand group process, and improve interpersonal communications, without blaming or judging each other. In addition to the class establishing a shared set of norms and behaviors outlined through the Safe and Successful Learning assessment described previously, I also utilize my role as teacher/facilitator to moderate and model behaviors that assist class participants in recognizing and understanding the impact of individual behaviors as well as group dynamics. [For a thoughtful discussion of teacher influence on group dynamics and issues of power that reinforce or counteract the goals of social justice education see hooks (1994) and Ropers-Huilman (1999).]

From constructing course syllabi to moderating course discussion, I am conscious to guide group processes and social relations within the course to reflect the goals of social justice education. For example, in the course syllabus developed for the Leadership, Diversity, and Social Justice course that I teach, I outline specific behaviors that lend themselves to constructive class discussion that is cognizant of issues of power and privilege. (This syllabus can be located at http://ed.utah.edu/~mhafner/.) Constructive behaviors include: contributing interesting, insightful comments; presenting good examples of the comments at hand; building on the comments of others instead of repeating ideas previously shared; raising good questions; listening and responding appropriately to others; being sensitive to levels of participation and making attempts to increase or decrease if necessary; and voicing thoughts and opinions in a way that is respectful of other individuals. In addition, I typically keep a speaker's queue during class as a way to bring attention to and moderate the amount of verbal space utilized (or not utilized) by class participants. By naming behaviors that guide group interactions, I highlight the idea that sometimes, what appears to be a benign function or task—in this case participating in class discussion—can serve to reinforce or resist power imbalance and privilege.

(4) Utilize reflection and experience as tools for student-centered learning: Teaching that begins from the student's world view and experience as the starting point for dialogue or problem solving. One teaching strategy that encourages a student-centered learning approach is an adapted "Corners" cooperative learning structure (Kagan, 1990, in Bennett, Rolheiser, & Stevahn, 1991). What I call a *Four Corners Activity* is a cooperative learning structure that utilizes students' individual and collective ideas and experiences as the basis of class discussion.

In a Four Corners Activity, each class participant is asked to respond verbally to a guiding question. The facilitator or instructor lists each response on chart paper or whiteboard and then makes conceptual links among responses as appropriate. After all of the participants have responded to the given question, the facilitator summarizes the responses and categorizes them into four main issues or topics that directly respond to the guiding question. These four issues are then listed on chart paper and posted in each of the four corners of the classroom. Once posted, class participants select one of the four issues to explore more thoroughly based on their level of interest in the topic, and physically move to that corner of the room.

While in their small group, students share a brief story that illustrates why the identified issue is compelling to them and how that issue plays out in their own school or district. After each group member shares his or her story, the group discusses how the information presented in course readings and class discussion might assist them in addressing the identified issue. Finally, the group brainstorms, chronicles, and shares with the entire class specific actions that a leader could take in her or his own school setting to address the identified issue. (A detailed example of how a Four Corners Activity can be utilized to facilitate a conversation about inclusive education in relationship to students with dis/abilities is provided in Figure 9.2.)

By encouraging different viewpoints and perspective regarding the same topic and linking new learning to individual lived experiences, a Four Corners teaching strategy allows participants the opportunity to identify *why* course content matters to them personally and *how* course content actually plays out in their particular school settings. It moves participants from merely connecting intellectually with the information presented in class to actual problem solving in relationship to their own work in schools.

(5) Value awareness, personal growth, and change as outcomes of the learning process: Teaching that balances different learning styles and is explicitly organized around goals of social awareness, knowledge, and social action, although proportions of these three goals change in relation to student interest and readiness. In addition to utilizing teaching strategies that take into consideration different learning styles and needs (e.g., cooperative learning structures or individual and group reflection), one of the most powerful teaching tools I have utilized to facilitate the goals of social justice education is the "Action Continuum" (Adams et al., 1997, p. 109). The Action Continuum (see Figure 9.3) provides a visual representation of the relationship between an individual's "social awareness, knowledge, and social action" (p. 109). Furthermore, it delineates how different types of thoughts and actions serve to move us in one direction or another along this continuum—either moving us in the direction of supporting oppression or confronting oppression.

In addition to providing individuals with a mental model from which to understand how their actions support or confront oppression, the Action Continuum also provides participants with a nonthreatening assessment tool regarding the direction their behaviors and attitudes are moving in terms of social justice work. Individuals are able to locate where their behaviors and attitudes fall within the Action Continuum, evaluate how these behaviors and attitudes support or confront oppression, and envision what changes might need to be made in order to facilitate their movement along the continuum.

FIGURE 9.2   *Four Corners Activity*

Creating Inclusive Schools

One social group that has experienced individual, societal, and institutionalized oppression are individuals with dis/ability labels. After reading several articles on the history of special education in the United States, the social construction of dis/ability, promising practices and barriers to inclusive education, and the principal's role in including students with dis/ability labels, class members are asked to participate in a "Four Corners" activity regarding building an inclusive school.

Ask participants to respond to the following question:

What is the most significant barrier you are facing in your school or district as you work to create a school inclusive of students with dis/abilities?

Collapse responses that are similar and then rank barriers in terms of relevancy to class as a whole. Write the topic of the top four barriers to inclusive education on chart paper and post in the four corners of the room.

Provide the following information:

1. Determine which of the four barriers to creating an inclusive school you would like to explore more deeply and move to that corner of the room.

Once in that group . . .

2. Each tell a brief story that illustrates why that identified barrier is compelling to you.
3. Share examples of how this barrier plays out in your own school/ district.
4. As a group, discuss how the information in course readings and class discussion will assist you as a school leader in overcoming the identified barrier.
5. Be prepared to share three (3) specific leadership actions you and your colleagues can take as you work to dissolve the identified barrier to inclusive schooling.

(Note: It is not by chance that the first question of this activity asks participants to identify barriers to inclusive education. Barriers are addressed first in order to move class members' thinking beyond simply regurgitating a laundry list of strategies that "haven't" or "couldn't possibly" work, to thinking concretely about what *is* possible and *is* currently happening in successful inclusive settings.)

Finally, scribe each of the leadership actions articulated by the four groups creating a list of "next steps" that address the barriers discussed in class. Copy this list and distribute to the entire class. The list serves as a physical reminder of what *is* possible in moving toward, in this case, more inclusive schooling experiences for students with dis/ability labels.

FIGURE 9.3 *The Action Continuum*

| *Actively Participating* | *Denying, Ignoring* | *Recognizing, No Action* | *Recognizing, Action* | *Educating Self* | *Educating Others* | *Supporting, Encouraging* | *Initiating, Preventing* |

Supporting Oppression ◄──────► **Confronting Oppression**

Actively Participating: Telling oppressive jokes, putting down people from target groups, intentionally avoiding target group members, discriminating against target group members, verbally or physically harassing target group members.

Denying: Enabling oppression by denying that target group members are oppressed. Does not actively oppress, but by denying that oppression exists, colludes with oppression.

Recognizing, No Action: Is aware of oppressive actions by self or others and their harmful effects, but takes no action to stop this behavior. This inaction is the result of fear, lack of information, confusion about what to do. Experiences discomfort at the contradiction between awareness and action.

Recognizing, Action: Is aware of oppression, recognizes oppressive actions of self and others and takes action to stop it.

Educating Self: Taking actions to learn more about oppression and the experiences and heritage of target group members by reading, attending workshops, seminars, cultural events, participating in discussions, joining organizations or groups that oppose oppression, attending social action and change events.

Educating Others: Moving beyond only educating self to question and dialogue with others too. Rather than only stopping oppressive comments or behaviors, also engaging people in discussion to share why you object to a comment or action.

Supporting, Encouraging: Supporting others who speak out against oppression or who are working to be more inclusive of target group members by backing up others who speak out, forming an allies group, joining a coalition group.

Initiating, Preventing: Working to change individual and institutional actions and policies that discriminate against target group members, planning educational programs or other events, working for passage of legislation that protects target group members from discrimination, being explicit about making sure target group members are full participants in organizations or groups.

Source: Created by P. Griffin and B. Harro (1982) from Adams, Bell, & Griffin (1997), p. 109.

Social Reconstructionist Schooling: A Conceptual Tool for Developing Leaders for Social Justice

The second instructional strategy I have found helpful in developing leaders for social justice is the notion of Social Reconstructionist Schooling. Originally developed as a philosophical lens through which to view educational practices, education that is "social reconstructionist" in nature (Sleeter, 1991) directly teaches about social group oppression and challenges individuals to see themselves as change agents in terms of social inequities. Specifically applying the notion of "social reconstructionism" (Sleeter & Grant, 1987) to the practice of educational leadership, Colleen Capper (1993) describes "Social Reconstructionist Schooling" (p. 288) as a reflective and action-oriented process that challenges educational leaders to identify and remedy areas of inequity within individual educational environments. Social Reconstructionist Schooling is a conceptual tool that can assist school leaders in not only thinking about, but also changing current practices and structures within educational organizations that overtly or covertly perpetrate inequity.

Essentially, Social Reconstructionist Schooling is a two-step process: deconstruction and reconstruction. According to Capper (1993),

> Deconstruction seeks to expose "the silences and gaps between that which is valued and disvalued" (Cherryholmes, 1988, p. 161), or to "set up procedures to demystify the realities we create" (Lather, 1991, p. 13). Reconstruction . . . suggests the "putting back together" in a different form, perhaps with different pieces. (p. 290)

During deconstruction, class participants are asked to unpack school policies, practices, and procedures in light of issues of "invisibility/imbalance," "stereotyping," and "fragmentation/isolation" (Capper, 1993, p. 291). Deconstruction prompts leaders to reflect on and critique the everyday practices of schooling (e.g., curriculum content, instructional practices, teaching assignments, etc.) and then ask the following reflective questions: *"Why are things done this way?"* and *"Who does 'doing things this way' serve?"*

Class participants generally identify areas of *invisibility/imbalance* in their schools and districts in relationship to issues of access. For example, participants review democratic characteristics of students in AP classes and receiving special education services or issues of access concerning partner health benefits. Locating examples of *stereotyping* typically involves asking questions about how individuals and groups are perceived in schools and how those per-

---

"Originally developed as a philosophical lens through which to view educational practices, education that is 'social reconstructionist' in nature (Sleeter, 1991) directly teaches about social group oppression and challenges individuals to see themselves as change agents in terms of social inequities. Specifically applying the notion of 'social reconstructionism' (Sleeter & Grant, 1987) to the practice of educational leadership, Colleen Capper (1993) describes 'Social Reconstructionist Schooling' (p. 288) as a reflective and action-oriented process that challenges educational leaders to identify and remedy areas of inequity within individual educational environments."

ceptions are formed. For example, participants ask questions about representation of individuals from particular racial and ethnic groups on sports teams, in AP classes, on student council, and in other extracurricular activities. Additionally, class participants probe how *fragmentation/isolation* occurs in schools when "minority issues" are discussed separate from the core functions of schooling. For example, school leaders might consider the strengths and weaknesses of an annual "multicultural celebration" and the overt and covert message a stand-alone event sends to the school and community.

Once issues of inequity are unearthed, educational leaders re-create or reconstruct policies, practices, and procedures in order to remedy different inequities discovered during deconstruction. Through the process of reconstruction, leaders commit to rebuilding school practices in a way that well serve each and every student in our care. Although the terminology used to define Social Reconstructionist Schooling is sometimes intimidating to class participants, once the processes of deconstruction and reconstruction are described and applied, individuals connect the two processes naturally.

I utilize the notion of Social Reconstructionist Schooling in every course I teach. One example of an instructional activity that has at its core a Social Reconstructionist Schooling framework and that has been particularly useful to class participants is a three-step, data-based action planning process I refer to as an *Equity Action Plan*. This type of process involves collecting different forms of data, evaluating or auditing that data in terms of issues of equitable access and outcomes, and developing an action plan for change relative to areas of need identified through the auditing process (see Chapter 13 in this text by Skrla, Scheurich, García, and Nolly for a detailed description of equity audits).

During this three-step process, participants first gather information from their individual school and/or district relative to curriculum, instruction, and climate as well as issues of access and outcomes. In order to guide their thinking, participants complete the "Demographic Data Questionnaire" outlined in *Meeting the Needs of Students of All Abilities: How Leaders Go Beyond Inclusion*, a user-friendly text by Colleen Capper, Elise Frattura, and Maureen Keyes (2000, pp. 177–180). The Demographic Data Questionnaire challenges class participants to ask significant questions relative to a variety of educational issues, including academic performance, discipline issues, placement rates in special education, access to Advanced Placement courses, teaching appointments, curriculum representation, and other areas of daily school life. At times, data of this nature are not readily available, and frustration levels can build. However, the process of data collection is as useful as the product. A lack of data, or even a lack of access to data, is data itself.

It is important to note that both data collection and analysis are essential components of this activity. Using the results of the Demographic Data Questionnaire, class participants analyze or *deconstruct* their data in terms of strengths, weaknesses, and recommendations for change.

Once inequities are identified, participants move into the *reconstruction* phase of the project—developing an action plan for implementing school level change. The following guidelines for the development of the action plan are outlined for class participants: clearly describe the purpose of the actions to be taken, link action plan to one of the current goals of your school improvement plan, describe both reactive and proactive components of action plan, and include an evaluation method by which to measure progress. The action plans developed by class participants include practical "What am I going to do on Monday morning?" ideas that can be implemented within their current leadership practice. By participating in this type of action planning activity, class participants have engaged in the process of Social Reconstructionist Schooling. They deconstruct current conditions in light of issues of imbalance/invisibility, stereotyping, and fragmentation/isolation. Then, they reconstruct school conditions in order to serve all students in an equitable manner. (The Creating Antiracist Schools activity described earlier in this chapter is another example of how a Social Reconstructionist Schooling approach can be used to develop leaders for social justice.)

Remembering that the notion of Social Reconstructionist Schooling is rooted in multicultural education and critical theory, a fundamental belief at the center of this instructional tool is that educators are agents of change. How we choose to use that agency—to perpetuate the status quo or to advocate for educational equity and social justice—is up to us. By engaging in activities rooted in the process of Social Reconstructionist Schooling, school leaders reflect, analyze, and re-create educational organizations to serve all students well. As an ongoing practice, Social Reconstructionist Schooling demands a commitment to action by educational leaders. And in this action lies hope—hope that schools, as social structures, might generate and reinforce policies and practices that clearly demonstrate a commitment to social justice.

Conclusion

The call put out by the field of educational leadership to develop leaders who can "promote and deliver social justice" is clear. It is my hope that this chapter has provided individuals in educational leadership preparation programs and practicing school administrators with a brief glimpse into the possible teaching strategies and curriculum issues that can move leaders to respond to this call by thinking more concretely about what it means to participate in social-justice-oriented work. Many resources are available to assist us in this work. Theoretical, empirical, conceptual, and practitioner-oriented articles and texts can each inform the work we do in leadership preparation programs and in school districts. However, as noted earlier, no one instructional strategy, conceptual model, tool, or text offers a one-size-fits-all technique for equitable reform or a step-by-step recipe for developing leaders for social justice. At the core of teaching for social justice is the hard work of consistent self-reflection in relationship to issues of privilege and oppression, access and outcomes, resistance and hope. It is essential that we remember that teaching for social justice is not only about *what we teach*, but also about *how we teach* and *who we are* as individual school leaders.

Discussion Questions and Activities

1. Several teaching strategies for developing leaders for social justice were identified in this chapter. Choose one strategy and discuss how you might incorporate it in your current professional practice (e.g., professional develop opportunities, faculty meetings, etc.).

2. Review the "Action Continuum" described on page 185. Identify everyday practices, policies, or procedures that occur in your school or district that are examples of movement toward "Supporting Oppression." What actions can you take as a school leader to assist individuals as well as the organization in moving toward "Confronting Oppression"?

3. How might district level staff development directors incorporate the teaching strategies described in this chapter into their current practice? What are possible objections or barriers to using these teaching approaches? Identify how you would work through these objections or get past these barriers.

4. When policy discussions arise in your school or district how can the notion of *Social Reconstructionist Schooling* inform your thinking (e.g., zero tolerance or harassment policies, entrance criteria for gifted programs)? What would these discussions actually look like?

5. As noted earlier, the teaching strategies outlined in this chapter offer no quick fixes and are ". . . not a magic formula, a silver bullet, or a panacea" (Lindsey et al., 2003, p. xxii). How, then, can the strategies and topics described in this chapter assist you in the long-term process of leadership for social justice?

6. What does the statement "social justice is both a process and a goal" (Adams et al., 1997) mean to you? What might this statement mean for your current leadership practice?

7. Given that teaching for social justice is not only about *what we teach* or *how we teach* but also *who we are* as individuals, how might the principles of *Social Justice Education Practice* described in the chapter be useful to you as you interact in one-on-one situations with colleagues, friends, or family members who challenge you with a lack of awareness of social justice issues?

8. Build a case, as if presenting it to a school board, to argue that the district personnel and the board should invest in this kind of social justice immersion. Do the same, as if presenting to a traditional educational leadership faculty.

Annotated Readings

Resources across various fields of study inform the topic of teaching strategies for developing leaders for social justice. Many of these resources speak directly to developing leaders for social justice within leadership preparation programs, whereas others focus on developing leaders for social justice within the context of professional development.

Teaching for Diversity and Social Justice: A Sourcebook by Maurianne Adams, Lee Anne Bell, and Pat Griffin (1997) provides readers with foundational information relative to social justice education. After introducing the reader to their definition of social justice education, Adams et al. go on to provide a comprehensive and reader-friendly description of the theoretical underpinnings that support their work as well as specific curricula that can be utilized to teach about different forms of oppression. Information regarding important conceptual issues and historical information relative to the form of oppression being discussed, the overall goals and key concepts, and specific course activities are clearly delineated. In essence, *Teaching for Diversity and Social Justice* provides readers with a pedagogical framework from which to teach for social justice and multiple examples of how this instructional framework actually plays out across different curricular contexts.

Through their work as professors in leadership preparation programs, Michelle Young and Julie Laible (2000) and Kathleen Brown (2004) provide specific instructional information for educators working to develop leaders for social justice. In *White Racism, Antiracism, and School Leadership Preparation*—a seminal resource in terms of educating leaders for social justice—Young and Laible (2000) advocate for promoting antiracist education within leadership preparation programs. In addition to providing a strong rationale for including antiracist education within leadership preparation programs, the authors outline six instructional approaches they have found helpful in developing leaders for social justice: (1) Knowing [Y]our Students, (2) Creating a Positive Classroom Environment, (3) Focusing on the Systemic Nature of Racism, (4) Self-Reflection, (5) Group Reflection, and (6) Antiracist Activity. In her article "Leadership for Social Justice and Equity: Weaving a Transformative Framework and Pedagogy," Kathleen Brown (2004) provides a comprehensive overview of eight pedagogical strategies that can be utilized in leadership preparation programs. These include (1) Cultural Autobiography, (2) Life Histories, (3) Prejudice-Reduction Workshops, (4) Reflective Analysis Journals, (5) Cross-Cultural Interviews, (6) Educational Plunge, (7) Diversity Panels, and (8) Activist Action Plans.

In addition, two practitioner-oriented texts add to the work of preparing leaders who can promote and deliver social justice. Written with field-based practitioners in mind, *Leading for Diversity: How School Leaders Promote Positive Interethnic Relations* by Rosemary Henze, Anne Katz, Edmundo Norte, Susan E. Sather, and Ernest Walker (2002) concentrates on fostering leadership that promotes positive interethnic relations within the context of schools. *Cultural Proficiency: A Manual for School Leaders* by Randall B. Lindsey, Kikanza Nuri Robins, and Raymond D. Terrell (2003) focuses on developing cultural proficiency in school leaders. The purpose of both texts is best summarized by Henze et al., "Our intent is to bring a number of different tools and theories to the attention of practitioners in a way that enables them to use these resources to solve problems and improve schools" (p. 16).

Acknowledgments _____

In addition to my sincere appreciation to the editors of this book, I would like to thank Colleen Capper, Michelle Young, Cryss Brunner, and Kathleen Brown—instructors who walk their talk in terms of leadership for social justice. Much of their work, including conversations, publications, teaching techniques, and course syllabi, informs my own. Their modeling of what it means to teach for social justice cannot go unacknowledged. With sincere gratitude for each of you and your work . . . thank you.

References

Adams, M., Bell, L. A., & Griffin, P. (1997). *Teaching for diversity and social justice.* New York: Routledge.

Allen, J. (1999). *Class actions: Teaching for social justice in elementary and middle schools.* New York: Teachers College Press.

Anderson, G. L. (2003). *Can we effectively build credential programs for educational administrators on principles of social justice? A case study.* Unpublished manuscript.

Ayers, W., Hunt, J. A., & Quinn, T. (1998). *Teaching for social justice.* New York: Teachers College Press.

Bennett, B., Rolheiser, C., & Stevahn, L. (1991). *Cooperative learning: Where heart meets mind.* Toronto: Educational Connections.

Brown, K. M. (2003, November). Assessing preservice leaders' beliefs, attitudes and values regarding issues of diversity, social justice, and equity: A review of existing measures. Paper presented at the annual meeting of the University Council of Educational Administration, Portland, OR.

Brown, K. M. (2004). Leadership for social justice and equity: Weaving a transformative framework and pedagogy. *Educational Administration Quarterly, 40*(1), 79–110.

Capper, C. A. (Ed.) (1993). Administrator practice and preparation for social reconstructionist schooling. In Colleen A. Capper (Ed.), *Educational administration in a pluralistic society* (pp. 288–315). Albany, NY: SUNY Press.

Capper, C. A., Frattura, E., & Keyes, M. W. (2000). *Meeting the needs of students of all abilities: How leaders go beyond inclusion.* Thousand Oaks, CA: Corwin Press.

Christensen, L. (1999). 'High-stakes' harm. *Rethinking Schools, 13*(3), 14, 18.

Dantley, M. E. (2002). Uprooting and replacing positivism, the melting pot, multiculturalism, and other impotent notions in educational leadership through an African American perspective. *Education and Urban Society, 34*(3), 334–352.

Delpit, L. (1993). The silenced dialogue: Power and pedagogy in educating other people's children. In Lois Weis & Michelle Fine (Eds.), *Beyond silenced voices: Class, race, and gender in United States schools.* Albany, NY: SUNY Press.

Derman-Sparks. L., & Phillips, C. B. (1997). *Teaching/learning antiracism: A developmental approach.* New York: Teachers College Press.

Dilg, M. (1999) *Race and culture in the classroom: Teaching and learning through multicultural education.* New York: Teachers College Press.

Ellsworth, E. (1989). Why doesn't this feel empowering? Working through the repressive myths of critical pedagogy. *Harvard Educational Review, 59*(3), 297–324.

Foster, W. P. (1986). *Paradigms and promises: New approaches to educational administration.* Amherst, NY: Prometheus Books.

Gay, G. (2000). *Culturally responsive teaching: Theory, research, and practice.* New York: Teachers College Press.

Giroux, H. (1988). *Teachers as intellectuals: Toward a critical pedagogy of learning.* Westport, CT: Bergin & Garvey.

Grogan, M. (1999). Equity/equality issues of gender, race, and class. *Educational Administration Quarterly, 35*(4), 518–536.

Grogan, M., & Andrews, R. (2002). Defining preparation and professional development for the future. *Educational Administration Quarterly, 38*(2), 233–256.

Hafner, M. M. (2005). *Preparing school leaders to ensure equity and work towards social justice: An exploratory study of leadership dispositions.* Paper presented at the Annual Meeting of the American Educational Research Association, Montreal, Quebec.

Hafner, M. M., & Young, M. D. (2003, November). Teaching strategies for developing leaders for social justice. Interactive Symposium Session at the University Council of Educational Administration Annual Convention, Portland, OR.

Henze, R., Katz, A., Norte, E., Sather, S. E., & Walker, E. (2002). *Leading for diversity: How school leaders promote positive interethnic relations.* Thousand Oaks, CA: Corwin Press.

hooks, b. (1994). *Teaching to transgress: Education as an act of liberatory freedom.* New York: Routledge.

Johnson, R. S. (2002). *Using data to close the achievement gap: How to measure equity in our schools.* Thousand Oaks, CA: Corwin Press.

Kumashiro, K. K. (2000). Toward a theory of anti-oppressive education. *Review of Educational Research, 70*(1), 25–53.

Ladson-Billings, G. (1995). But that's just good teaching! The case for culturally relevant pedagogy. *Theory into Practice, 34*(3), 159–165.

Ladson-Billings, G. (2000). Racialized discourses and ethnic epistemologies. In Norman K. Denzin and Yvonna S. Lincoln (Eds.), *Handbook of qualitative research* (2d ed.) (pp. 257–278). Thousand Oaks, CA: Sage.

Larson, C. L., & Murtadha, K. (2002). Leadership for social justice. In Joseph Murphy (Ed.), *The educational leadership challenge: Redefining leadership for the 21st century* (pp. 134–161). Chicago: University of Chicago Press.

Larson, C. L., & Ovando, C. J. (2001). *The color of bureaucracy: The politics of equity in multicultural school communities.* Belmont, CA: Wadsworth.

Lee, Mun Wah (1995). *The color of fear.* Oakland, CA: Stir Fry Seminars & Consulting.

Lindsey, R. B., Robins, K. N., & Terrell, R. D. (2003). *Cultural proficiency: A manual for school leaders.* Thousand Oaks, CA: Corwin Press.

Lyman, L. L., & Villani, C. J. (2002). The complexity of poverty: A missing component of educational leadership programs. *Journal of School Leadership, 12*, 246–280.

Nieto, S. (1999). *The light in their eyes: Creating multicultural learning communities.* New York: Teachers College Press.

Parker, L., & Shapiro, J. P. (1992). Where is the discussion of diversity in educational administration programs? Graduate students' voices addressing an omission in their preparation. *Journal of School Leadership, 2*(1), 7–33.

Perry, M. (2000). *Walking the color line: The art and practice of antiracist teaching.* New York: Teachers College Press.

Pounder, D., Reitzug, U., & Young, M. D. (2002). Preparing school leaders for school improvement, social justice, and community. In Joseph Murphy (Ed.), *The educational leadership challenge: Redefining leadership for the 21st century* (pp. 261–288). Chicago: University of Chicago Press.

Rethinking Schools (1994). *Rethinking our classrooms: Teaching for equity and justice.* Milwaukee: Rethinking Schools.

Rethinking Schools (2001). *Rethinking our classrooms: Teaching for equity and justice, Volume 2.* Milwaukee: Rethinking Schools.

Reyes, P., Scribner, J. D., & Scribner, A. P. (Eds.). (1999). *Lessons from high-performing Hispanic schools: Creating learning communities.* New York: Teachers College Press.

Riehl, C. (2000). The principal's role in creating inclusive schools for diverse students: A review of normative, empirical, and critical literature on the practice of educational administration. *Review of Educational Research, 70*(1), 55–81.

Riester, A. F., Pursch, V., & Skrla, L. (2002). Principals for social justice: Leaders of school success for children from low-income homes. *Journal of School Leadership, 12*, 281–304.

Ropers-Huilman, B. (1999). Social justice in the classroom. *College Teaching, 47*(3), 91–96.

Rusch, E. (2003). *Social justice in New Jersey: Equity issues and beginning principals.* Unpublished manuscript.

Scheurich, J. J. (1998). Highly successful and loving, public elementary schools populated mainly by low-SES children of color. *Urban Education, 33*(4), 451–491.

Scheurich, J. J., & Skrla, L. (2003). *Leadership for equity and excellence: Creating high-achievement classrooms, schools, and districts.* Thousand Oaks, CA: Corwin Press.

Scheurich, J. J. & Young, M. D. (1997). Coloring epistemologies: Are our research epistemologies racially biased? *Educational Researcher, 26*(4), 4–16.

Sleeter, C. E. (1991). *Empowerment through multicultural education.* Albany, NY: SUNY Press.

Sleeter, C. E., & Grant, C. A. (1987). An analysis of multicultural education in the United States. *Harvard Educational Review, 57,* 421–444.

Strachan, J. (1999). Feminist educational leadership: Locating the concepts in practice. *Gender and Education, 11*(3), 309–322.

Szabo, M. A., Hoagland, G., Lambert, L., Lopez, J., Starnes, L., Stern, J., Storms, & Vieth, R. (2002, April). Developing bold, socially responsible leadership: Strategies for administrative preparation programs. Paper presented at the annual meeting of the American Educational Research Association, Seattle, WA.

Wallace, B. C. (2000). A call for change in multicultural training at graduate schools of education: Educating to end oppression and for social justice. *Teachers College Record, 102*(6), 1086–1111.

Young, M. D., & Laible, J. (2000). White racism, antiracism, and school leadership preparation. *Journal of School Leadership, 10*(5), 374–415.

Young, M. D., Peterson, G. J., & Short, P. M. (2002). The complexity of substantive reform: A call for interdependence among key stakeholders. *Educational Administration Quarterly, 38*(2), 137–175.

10

Learning from Leaders'
Social Justice Dilemmas

Catherine Marshall

Laurence Parker

Introduction

Too often, educational leaders are encouraged to ignore social justice concerns. Protective mentors may show them how to avoid and evade dilemmas,
encouraging a sweep-it-under-the-rug management style. In their internships,
and perhaps on licensure examinations and at job interviews, they may be rewarded when, in their talk and their actions, they simplify issues.

Leaders relegate dilemmas into legal or bureaucratic niches or assign
them as tasks for the district multicultural consultant. Current federal policy,
such as No Child Left Behind, directs leaders to hone in on children's learning outcomes in specific subjects. Locally, leaders' colleagues, professors, communities, and boards, too, may expect them to emphasize efficiency, order,
competition, and achievement above all, ignoring the deep societal, cultural,
historical, and economic forces that have created inequities. Historians of education remind us of the long tradition of expecting school leaders to embed
the individualistic and competitive forces in American culture into the structures of schooling (Labaree, 1997). But children do get left behind and fall
through the cracks, and children's needs cannot be met by simply delivering
a curriculum.

Educators see children's needs for nutrition, sex education, caring role
models, validation, and adults who will notice them; they intervene when children are bullied; and administrators will argue until they are fired over funding
inequities. Therefore, social justice leaders in training; those whose tendencies,

actions, and beliefs veer from dominant policy directions; those who would use school resources and educators' time "off task" to take care of children's wider needs; and those who intervene to correct inequities and make schools psychologically safe will need plentiful practice and reinforcement to buck these trends. Educators must practice seeing dilemmas, arguing with themselves and others, and trying out possible strategies for engaging dilemma-laden situations. This chapter demonstrates the use of the case method of training, offering dilemma-laden cases as a way to engage school leaders and practice puzzling through dilemmas and enacting social-justice-leader stances and actions.

Erroneous and Short-Sighted Approaches to "Managing" Social Justice Issues

Educators, families, and policy makers often make decisions based on unexamined traditions. First, educational systems are structured so that problems can be assigned to specialists, such as counselors, social workers, multicultural trainers, special education experts, and the like. Once the problem has been assigned, it is considered to be "fixed." This traditional pattern appears to be efficient, but every parent whose child's needs have gone unmet and every teacher and principal who has witnessed examples of persistent inequities know that such bureaucratic efficiency cannot meet the needs of children living with the consequences of deep social and economic inequities. Further, social justice challenges must be addressed systemically, not with quick fixes.

Second, social justice often is translated into educational decisions based on the idea that students from diverse backgrounds can and will be "educated" so that they can be "just like us" (i.e., White Euro-American, upper middle class, suburban). The tradition of schooling for assimilation, making all students and learners the same, undermines social justice efforts.

Third, dominant policy approaches now emphasize testing. Such testing documents evidence of inequality of learning outcomes and holds educators accountable for classroom performance. Proponents of testing assert that a market-based system of families choosing schools (e.g., charters, vouchers, higher performing schools) will equalize opportunity (Vincent, 2003). Such policies place responsibility on children and educators to work hard, overcome obstacles, and focus on specified, measurable learning outcomes. These approaches ignore the sociopolitical and economic contexts affecting educators' and children's daily struggles. They push aside, ignore, and suppress the need for educators to consider children's cultural identities and their experiences of mistreatment and exclusion. Policymakers assert that accountability systems are the instruments toward the common goal of "leaving no child behind," or educating all children, as if solving inequities were so simple.

School leaders and policymakers often promote such comfortable traditions—reliance on standard operating procedures, bureaucratic policy, and the use of language to place complex issues onto simple, more manageable categories (children at risk, no child left behind) to make people feel that problems have been solved. However, this pulls the rug over certain realities, such as how school personnel make decisions (or do nothing) that result in a disproportionate group of students receiving inequitable treatment (Anderson, 1990) and the persistence of inequitable resources so that the schools and children with least resources continue to get the least-qualified teachers (Zeichner, 2003). Ignoring these realities results in wider disparities between students who have access to a bright future through education and those who do not. For example, schools and school leaders advocating social justice cannot claim to promote excellence in education and then tolerate and explain a special education placement rate of 47% of their African American students in behavior/emotional disorder classes, even though they constitute only 31% of the student population in particular school districts, by asserting that the intractable problems are within the cultural deficits of families or poverty in low income communities (Peterkin & Lucey, 1998). For another example, girls' high academic performance can easily be undermined by peer harassment or unequal athletic playing fields or women educators who have learned that career survival depends upon their acceptance of male dominance in school leadership. Nor, for example, can school leaders claim that they are for all students in their schools when they deny the legal rights of gay, lesbian, and transgendered students and their allies to form after-school clubs because of the potential disruptive influence they may have on the general school population and larger community.

So, social justice leaders must build their skills in critiquing tradition and trite policy assertions. They must be able to argue and demand that inadequate policies and programs be reframed (Marshall & Gerstl-Pepin, 2005). They must be able to present arguments that educational excellence means moving beyond test scores and working with parents and communities to build inclusive, safe, and trusting spaces. As stressed by Goldfarb and Grinberg (2002), educational excellence requires more than simply "assessing needs, or providing services in order to mainstream marginalized populations with dictated services and program content" (p. 170). Rather, a social justice perspective in educational administration also calls for school leaders to search to discover existing models of how social justice is attempted and actualized in schools. It requires them to identify ways to lead with core beliefs and create organizational structures that promote social justice. They need to seek examples and learn from the practices of principals and superintendents who work with teachers, parents, and children to build schools that are connected to communities and that emphasize high performance for each child in a passionately committed and loving way (Scheurich & Skrla, 2003). Traditional training through internships and graduate courses in law and organizational theory and wisdom learned from the profession's "good ole boys" about how to manipulate the community will not provide social justice leaders with the skills they need.

The Need for Preparatory Practice and Models for Social Justice in Action

Although new literatures, theories, models, policies, and training experiences are emerging, educational leaders have had few opportunities to develop the values, skills, comfort, and courage to intervene to make social justice happen. Policymakers, as shown in Chapter 6, are hesitant to take forceful stands for social justice training. People in charge of national professional associations are hesitant and worried about whether educational administrators are willing to move quickly on all social justice agendas (Marshall & Ward, 2004). Many professors of educational administration still avoid or only give lip service to diversity and equity issues and experience discomfort—even fear—over the conflicts that would ensue from frank and open faculty or classroom discourse about privilege and inequities (Rusch, 2004). As Rusch says, "talk about equity demands debate about emotional and value-laden issues such as privilege, meritocracy, affirmative action, gender, race, ethnicity, and sexuality" (p. 43). The tendency is to submerge such controversial yet important talk. Educational leaders learn to sweep social justice issues under the rug, when they really need to be shaking the dirt out of the rug. What is needed is a safe, yet challenging way to move practitioners, students, staff development coordinators, policymakers, and professors to work toward a comfort level with social justice dilemmas. The case method of training, originally developed for prospective business managers, if used well, can show the way for educators.

Applying the Case Study Method for Social Justice Training

The use of the case study method has a long tradition in business, law, and educational administration. People use case studies to prepare for uncertain situations; to identify the implications of assumptions held by central characters, as well as to determine their values and commitments (and those of the analyst, too); to critique how educators typically practice their craft; and to identify a range of options (Ashbaugh & Kasten, 1991; Brookfield, 1992; Harrington and Garrison, 1992; Schön, 1983). According to Harrington and Garrison (1992), "Cases provide opportunities for inquiry . . . bounded by experience, framed by theory, generating possibilities, and transforming practice" (p. 721).

In education, cases and vignettes are stories and narratives of practice that are useful for bringing forth social justice dilemmas. These narratives not only tell a story to readers, but also lay out the perspectives and positions of the participants involved. Social justice cases are best used to pose dilemmas that will help school leaders to develop their analytical skills, producing evidence and rehearsing messages and reasoning to support recommendations, platforms, stances, and actions.

When using case studies, trainers and trainees should use the following general guiding questions to interrogate issues of social justice:

1. What is the dilemma described in the vignette?
2. What other information would you need to make a decision in this case?
3. Would this be a dilemma for you?
4. What direction does existing policy indicate?
5. How would your immediate supervisors and mentors tell you to manage this dilemma?
6. What are the assumptions inherent in policy and practitioner options?
7. If your full-time job were to make all school practices equitable, how would you plan to work on this situation?
8. How would you take this dilemma from a small, confined, and manageable situation to the larger arena where this dilemma could be used to illustrate persistent societal inequities?
9. What theories, models, research, and extant practices provide you with ways to think imaginatively about taking a stand in this kind of situation?
10. What professional, moral, political, or philosophical stances guide your own assumptions and decisions about possible actions to take in such a situation?
11. What are the constraints to taking a social justice stand and how can you move beyond them?
12. What decision would you advocate and why?

For participants and instructors in staff development and in education administration classes, cases provide the opportunity to defend arguments and analyses in the safety of the classroom without the pressure of an angry crowd, a threatening school board member or Rotary Club, or the worry of letting a child drop through the cracks. We feel that the use of particular types of cases that contain specific social justice issues and dilemmas serves an important educational goal. Typically, students tend to read and discuss cases, particularly those with moral or ethical dilemmas, by simply stating what should be done (Strike, Haller, & Soltis, 1988). If students generate multiple responses to the case analysis and solutions, the students often conclude on their own that the issue cannot be resolved and a relativist approach is assumed to accommodate different opinions. From a social justice perspective, we wish to add to the tradition of using cases by highlighting the importance of encouraging students to think about ways in which social justice leadership may be applied. For example, Theoharis (2004) posits that education administrators range in how they view social justice and how it can be operationalized in critical situations, from those who possess a consciousness and passion for justice and the knowledge and skills of implementation to those who lack the social justice consciousness and may not have the knowledge and skills to seek equitable policy solutions to problems in their schools. Figure 10.1 illustrates the range in administrators' consciousness and skills.

Assuming that many students in educational administration are operating between these frameworks of thinking and reasoning, we feel that social-justice-orientated case analysis can be used to help students become more aware of social justice perspectives and engage in sophisticated moral reasoning.

Participants can use real-life dilemmas to try out theories and frameworks of analysis and see how research and "best practices" can or cannot be applied to actual administrative practice (Honan & Rule, 2002, p. 3). When using cases to practice scenarios, participants can discuss the realities of their own policy processes, their own power, and their own values stances, and they can critique a range of policy solutions/alternatives. Too often, the novice assistant principal or administrative intern is thrown into situations that are laden with dilemmas (Marshall & Mitchell, 1991). On the surface, they may appear to be straightforward find-the-policy-and-follow-it situations, be they handling fights on the school bus, assigning the number of hours for detention, or finding placements for the less effective teachers. However, every educator knows that he or she *should* and *want* to be able to deal with issues raging below the surface, such as addressing poverty, ensuring children's equal access to the best teachers, and creating caring and constructive strategies for students in trouble.

Cases are short, context-full stories that are used as teaching devices for moving discussion and leadership training below the surface. As demonstrated in Table 10.1, the analysis of critical incidents and cases forces people to go

FIGURE 10.1 *Social Justice Leadership Matrix*

A	B
Possess consciousness and passion for justice. Possess the skills and knowledge to do the work.	Possess consciousness and passion for justice. Lack the skills and knowledge to do the work.
C	D
Lack consciousness and passion for justice. Possess the skills and knowledge to do the work.	Lack consciousness and passion for justice. Lack the skills and knowledge to do the work.

Source: Adapted from Theoharis (2004).

TABLE 10.1   *Kinds of Judgment and Analysis*

Kind of Judgment	Information Required	Questions Asked	People Involved
		Kinds of Analysis	
Practical	Procedural	What should I do? How? When? Where?	For and/or with whom?
Diagnostic	Descriptive	What happened?	Who was involved?
	Causal	What made it happen	Who Acted?
	Effectual	What does it do?	For whom?
	Affectual	What does it feel like?	For whom?
	Semantic	What does it mean?	To whom?
	Explanatory	Why did (does) it occur?	With whom?
Reflective	Personal	Do I like it?	Do others like it?
	Evaluative	Is it a good thing?	For whom?
	Justificatory	Why?	
Critical	Classificatory	What is it an example of?	Whose classification?
	Social	Is it just?	For whom?

beyond the quick-fix response. Incidents are broken down from their complexities into simpler parts, and then the analysts decide what kind of judgment they must make (practical, diagnostic, reflective, or critical) in their particular leadership position.

This chapter presents two cases of social justice dilemmas that demonstrate how to facilitate conversations and raise awareness of critical issues in our schools. When reading and analyzing these cases, the reader should focus on the use of cases in building leaders' skills to intervene with the strategic use of power to stop discrimination and inequity. The cases bring forth the realization that social justice in education requires active work on the part of leaders to change within school and out-of-school environmental circumstances that have a deleterious impact on the cognitive and emotional development of children. Of particular concern are those who have been underserved or "written off" by society at-large because of their race/ethncity, gender, class background, disability, language, national origin, sexual orientation, and so on (Mirón, 1997).

The two cases can also serve as models for the development of other cases generated from the experiences of students, professors, school practitioners, and policymakers. The development of cases should follow the example discussion questions and suggested implications for administrative practice as demonstrated in this chapter.

Two Case Examples

Read and use the two cases that follow as examples of reality-based situations that evoke emotions and demand intervention. The discussion questions and the expansions into sections entitled "Implications for Practice" should serve as models for, first, demanding that readers confront any desire to simply manage the immediate situation, to sweep it under the rug. Readers must engage, shake out the rug, and then connect the case to the "big picture" of theory, policy, practice, and societal patterns that shape the situations described in the cases. Read the cases, choose and discuss questions most useful for engaging your group, and generate lists of social justice dilemma-laden situations that your group has experienced. To move your group from the relatively safe discussion, choose several of the situations and form task groups to make plans and intervene as social justice leaders.

Case 1: Where Should He Be Placed?

"Excuse me, are you Dr. Davis?" asked Sonia Nevarez as she walked through the hallway. Ms. Nevarez had just come from registering her son for first grade at the elementary school in the town of Plainview. Few parents had met the new principal, who had come from the New York City school system to lead Kennedy Elementary. Newspaper stories had recounted her experience leading an innovative bilingual–bicultural education program located in a multiracial/ethnic district. She had won awards from various bilingual education groups for her work to raise the standardized test scores of immigrant students; parent groups praised her efforts to foster community connections with the school and to the native culture of the students and families. Dr. Davis's philosophy was that all students could learn English and still keep their native culture and language. She did not buy into some teachers' complaints that they could not teach classes with so many different languages spoken and had found ways to get parent and community help to overcome these barriers with teachers.

Sonia Nevarez felt confident, therefore, that she would be heard. She was unsettled because her son had just been placed in a special education (mental impairment) class and would be part of a pull-out ESL group at the Kennedy school. This was a shock, because there had been no clues until registration that day; therefore, she was quite forceful as she approached Dr. Davis, saying, "Dr. Davis, I want to have a word with you about the registration of my son at this school and where he was placed."

Calmly, Davis said, "Sure, do you want to go to my office and talk?"

As they entered Dr. Davis's office, Ms. Nevarez began to make her feelings known to the new principal, saying, "I just don't think it is right the way this school has placed my child. I feel that Alberto is being placed in the wrong class for first grade. The people at the registration said that he is being placed in a special education class and that he is going to be in a special ESL pull-out class. I don't feel he needs that. He needs to be in a regular class. Plus they did not give me a reason why they are doing this since we are new in this district."

Dr. Davis asked, "What exactly happened when you went to register your son Alberto today?"

"They looked at the forms I filled out, and then they told me to go to a different part of the gym to have my son registered. When I went to that different section, they said that we can't place your son in a regular classroom but that our special education class in combination with our ESL class will definitely have him ready for second grade next year, and that this would be the best possible education for your child," Ms. Nevarez replied.

Ms. Nevarez continued, "Plus they gave me no reason for this placement; they just went ahead and said this is what No Child Left Behind federal policy and state ESL and special education laws say we have to do to provide your son with the best services. But I don't want this for him. We just moved here from Texas, but we lived in Mexico before that. I worked with my son on his English and his reading, and I have his records from his kindergarten class and the teachers said he was a bright student, but they did not even want to look at my papers for Alberto." At this point Ms. Nevarez was in tears and began crying.

Dr. Davis sought to comfort her and offered, "Ok let me see these papers that you have. This does not sound right to me, and I will look into the situation and see if I can make a change in placement for Alberto. Today is Thursday, and school starts right after the Labor Day holiday, so you will hear from me about this before school starts that Tuesday."

Discussion Questions

1. Given Dr. Davis's previous expertise in bilingual education and her personal social justice beliefs, what should be her first steps in investigating the situation regarding Alberto's placement?
2. Speculate as to how models of efficiency and power in leadership and decision making directed the actions of school personnel who placed Ms. Nevarez's son in the ESL class. Discuss how these models undermine social justice principles and harm families.
3. Should Dr. Davis have voiced her opinion that "this does not sound right to me" to a parent before talking the situation over with the teachers or those who did the registration to hear their side of the story? Was this good leadership practice? Why or why not?
4. From a parental point of view, was Ms. Nevarez justified in demanding an immediate audience with the principal? Should there be restrictions as to when parents should or should not go to the principal with their concerns?

5. How many details of special education law and bilingual education regulations should educators be familiar with when making student placements? How could No Child Left Behind be used as a pretext to undermine social justice for children whose second language is English and whose parents (or the students themselves) are immigrants?

Implications for Practice. The Harvard Civil Rights Project (2002) issued a report on the overrepresentation of students of color in special education classes nationally. For example, in 1998, of approximately 1.5 million children identified in the classifications of mental retardation, emotional disturbance, or learning disabled, more than 876,000 of these children were African American or Tribal Nation students. In addition, the summary of the national data indicates that in some areas Latino and Asian American students are being underidentified in cognitive disability categories compared to whites, but overrepresented in other special education categories. How typical are Kennedy Elementary School's current, and perhaps past, problems with special education placement? Has the school district performed an equity audit with regard to racial and language minority student placement in special education?

Guided by critical race theory, Auerbach (2002) analyzed the narratives of Latino/Latina parents who voiced concern and frustration with school policies and procedures and personnel who systematically ignored parental and student requests for high-track placement for high-achieving Latino students. Auerbach's analysis reveals the following implications for practice as principals and superintendents work with the school and the district:

1. Ensure that all teaching staff members screen students.
2. Keep appropriate records.
3. Provide appropriate training on an annual basis.
4. Review placement criteria and ensure racial, ethnic, and gender balance.
5. Recruit and hire more African American, Latino, and Native American teachers, psychologists, and social workers.
6. Enlist independent evaluation of the effectiveness of the building-level teams and committees for adherence to state and federal guidelines.

But beyond such monitoring, how, and why, would school administrators talk with parents of color, listen to their concerns, and act on them to promote equity? What training do school leaders need to learn how to engage in activities to promote communication and equity? Administrators can promote communication by going into the Latino community to address parent's issues related to their children's education and making necessary staff changes. Other activities would include talking to students in ESL classes to find out what their experiences have been and what changes could be made to improve the program. School leaders could seek out local immigration services and churches and speak to those involved about providing services for newly arrived immigrant students, working with these facilitators and parents to determine what would make the schools seem more welcoming to new immigrant students. Administrators should also work to provide an academic and social environment that will promote student achievement and ensure respect for the children's family background.

Such assertive and interventionist leadership stems from what Larson and Ovando (2001) call "double-loop learning" (p. 183), in which school leaders examine the social context of the decision-making and policy operations in the school or district and then question whether the operating norms and logics are appropriate. Double-loop learning is important, because decisions are analyzed not only for their impact on teachers and their placement evaluations, but also for their effects on language minority students and parents and larger school–community relations. Thus, in this case, by using Ms. Nevarez's resistance to her child's placement as a critical feedback loop of analysis, the administrator can use the opportunity to engage in more equitable practice for student placement decisions.

Nearly 40% of school administrators' time is now consumed with special education placement issues. Therefore, school leaders have numerous opportunities to practice leadership based on a "strong ethical and moral core focused on equity and excellence as the only right choice for schools in a democracy" (Scheurich & Skrla, 2003, p. 100). This type of leadership is grounded in the larger historical struggle for civil rights and equity for working poor people, racial and ethnic minorities. Such leadership views the attainment of an adequate education as a fundamental right in U.S. society (Scheurich & Skrla, 2003).

School leaders can resist discrimination and create "a moral politics that affirm institutional commitment to the principles of racial equality, social class equity, and other principles of social justice at the level of daily practice" (Mirón, 1997, p. 110). Part of this also involves challenging the color-blind perspective of special education placement, in which race and racism are ignored in special education research and teaching and teachers are socialized to not see race with respect to placement decisions, even though there are racial disparities between minority and majority students in special versus regular education classes (McCray & Garcia, 2002).

Administrators working from a social justice perspective work with teachers, social service agencies, and parents to create better learning and social opportunities and results for children. This includes support for early literacy and math skills/knowledge and family literacy as well as recognizing the importance of the social well-being of the child and family. From a social justice perspective, this can be done through culturally responsive teaching so that the instructional strategies reflect the cultural values, traits, and socialization of African American and other minority students (Gay, 2002).

What theories, assumptions, and moral and ethical principles guide education leaders? What day-by-day and minute-by-minute displays must leaders make to pull all school personnel along, to lead them, toward prevention of race-based placements?

Case 2: My Name Is Jasmine (Diem, 2003)

Jasmine came off the school bus sobbing, ran up the parking lot, flung the metal door open like it was made out of papiermâché, and ran straight to her room. Jasmine was a child who generally went with the flow and didn't get too visibly upset by things, so this type of behavior was alarming. She had seen and experienced a lot in her short life, so it took a lot to get her emotions going. But this was one of those things. This was one of those things that would remain with her for the rest of her life, or at least shape her feeling of self-worth as she wandered through the rugged terrain of adolescence. Jasmine had never actually experienced physical pain, but she had been hurt by what she saw, and now was hurt by what she heard.

Being a witness to domestic violence is something that stays with you forever. Watching your mother get beat on, physically and emotionally, throws your whole world into a state of turmoil. You have no sense of what is right, whom you can trust, or what it feels like to be safe. To witness a man, who one minute tells your mother that he loves her and take his fist to her face the next, throws any sort of order and sense making out the window. And to witness all of this from the age of 8 until your mother finally gathers up the strength and courage to leave when you are 11, leaves a scar that no one can see but that penetrates far deeper than the lasting reminder of a severe cut. And when the result of your mother having the courage and wherewithal to leave comes with the price of becoming homeless, you begin to see the world a lot differently than many 11-year-old children. This was Jasmine's life, and that is how she saw the world.

When Jasmine slammed the door to her family's room closed, she was trying to close herself off from the world. She was tired of living in a world that distinguished her mother, sister, and herself from the rest of society as being different, as unusual. She was fed up with a world that seemed to punish women for having the courage to do what they knew they should, but at a great cost. She was tired of being homeless, of being a survivor of domestic violence, and of being Black in a society that talked a lot about equality, but far too often seemed to limit the issue to talk without real action. But most of all, she was tired of just being noticeably different. She wanted to blend into the scene and not cause a stir. Jasmine was 11, and life had already worn her out.

The parking lot Jasmine ran through was that of the transitional housing program for homeless families where she lived with her mother and older sister. It was not a shelter, but she still knew she was homeless. She knew her family would not be leaving soon, but she knew that this dwelling was not really home. More important to this story, the other kids on the school bus knew all of this, too. They might not have known the details, but they saw the big picture. They saw that they wore outfits that cost about as much Jasmine's mom made in 3 to 4 days at work, while Jasmine wore clothes that were obviously not in vogue. Jasmine attended school in a nationally recognized school district in a very affluent college town. But with the exception of their test scores and family incomes, the children in these schools were very much the same as children in any other school in the country. That is to say that they were often cruel to each other. Jasmine was in fifth grade, and on this day the children on her bus had finally noticed her and where she was picked up and dropped off for school, and they labeled her with a new nickname—Sheltergirl.

Jasmine unloaded her feelings to the Home's director, saying, "I hate going to school. I hate riding the bus. I hate that all the other kids call me names, and laugh behind my back. Sometimes they laugh right in front of me, but a lot of times they try to do it so I don't hear. But I do. I hate the reasons they laugh at me. They've never seen their mom get beat up. They've never had to sneak away from their house at night, without any of their favorite stuff. They've never had to ask where they were going to sleep or if they were going to have dinner that night."

Jasmine continues in a manner that makes her seem closer to 21 than 11: "I hate that the only kids I can be friends with are the other kids that no one else wants to be friends with. And some of *them* won't even talk to me. I hate being called Sheltergirl! Why can't they just leave me alone?"

Jasmine asks some important, but difficult questions. She asks the types of questions that people have been trying to answer for years: "They don't know how hard it is. I see the houses they live in. I see the cars their parents drive. I know they get to go buy whatever clothes they want, and we have to shop at Wal-Mart or wear the donations. Why do the other kids call me Sheltergirl? My name is Jasmine, not Sheltergirl! Don't they know how that makes me feel? And when I do get mad, or start crying, they smile. Then they do it more. I try not to get mad because I know that's what they want. But it's hard. I just want them to leave me alone. If they're not going to be my friends, why can't they just leave me alone?"

Jasmine is asked about what she thinks about the teachers and administrators in her school and her tone changes somewhat: "I think that most of the grown-ups at my school are nice. I think they're nice, but I don't think they really know what my mom and sister and I have done. But they try. They are always nice to me and help my mom and me when they can. But sometimes we don't want their help. If they help us then the other kids know we need help. I don't want anyone to know. The only help I want is for them to make the other kids be nicer. The other kids don't say stuff when we're in class or when they're around. But during recess, or at lunch, or on the bus, there's no one there so they say what they want. If they knew what it is like they wouldn't say anything. But they don't. They don't care. I hate 'em!"

Jasmine may only be 11, but her life experiences have forced her to grow up faster than most kids. She has an understanding of issues that many adults never have. Jasmine understands that her life has not been typical. She knows that the other kids don't have the same type of worries that her family does. She knows that the other kids have no idea what she's seen, or that that kind of stuff even exists. She realizes how hard she has it, while the other kids have no idea how easy they have it. She knows all of this and she is 11. Unfortunately, her understanding and maturity have come out of necessity. Jasmine would much rather be immature. She would much rather not have the worries she has. She would like to be able to laugh and make fun of the other kids, but she never would: "I know how bad I feel when they laugh at me. I would never do that." While many might think of vengeance, Jasmine can't. She has been hurt over and over, in many ways, and she just wants the pain to end—for everyone.

Discussion Questions

1. How should a school attempt to identify issues that students may be dealing with at home (e.g., homelessness, family violence/addiction in the home, health needs)? When do the attempts of school personnel invade personal rights, privacy, and the prerogative of other government agencies? When the answers to these questions are not clear, how should a school leader proceed? How much time and other resources should be invested?

2. Do you think schools should have services (beyond guidance counselors) to help their students deal with these types of issues? What kinds of services do you think would help Jasmine?

3. Does your school or district have someone on staff whose primary job responsibility is to ensure that the needs of homeless students are being met?

4. How does your school handle/monitor bullying?

5. How do you feel about the bus picking Jasmine up and dropping her off right in front of the transitional housing program where she lives? What alternatives do you think could be put in place?

6. How could you be proactive in addressing issues such as income disparities among students in the same school? Do you think it can/should be done by school leaders?

7. Jasmine says she doesn't want to be helped because then other children will know more about her situation. Should you help someone who doesn't want help, but needs it? If so, how do you attempt to do this without conveying a sense that you know what they need better than they do?

8. Have you ever had to deal with a situation similar to this one? How did you handle it?
9. How could you present this situation to the superintendent and the school board in a way that would result in better school environments for students like Jasmine?

Implications for Practice.   Class and income disparities affect judgments made by school personnel and students. When class divisions in the local community are reflected in the school, students will often play out class divisions in how they dress, how they look, how they treat and relate to each other. Such divisions often are reflected in the placement of students in academic, general, and vocational classes. What should a school leader operating from a social justice position do to reject these divisions? Children's identity development occurs within and outside school environments. How far outside of school walls should school leaders go to prevent unhealthy and unjust influences on their students' identity development?

Creative and assertive intervention by school leaders can address class issues in schools. For example, one principal in a Pennsylvania district with high employment, two major factories, and a large service industry lobbied employers to change work schedules and allow for flexible hours for parent–teacher nights or other special school district activities so that parents could participate in their children's academic and social program (personal communication by M. Leonard with Parker, June 15, 1994). Such lobbying and negotiating is creative leadership, but deeper societal inequities will persist. Should school leaders lobby for more funds from local businesses from property taxes? What can school leaders do to change the economic structures that lead to homelessness? Should principals and superintendents protest if state and local communities give tax breaks to companies such as Wal-Mart for the promise of jobs and economic development, when financially stressed school districts are left with the social, economic, health, emotional, *and* educational needs of all the Jasmines who are left behind from this economic boom?

What are school leaders' roles, both legal and moral, when confronted with the issue of domestic violence and abuse, either with students and their families or with staff? Critical choices have to be made with follow-up action to deal with these problems when they arise, linking with the proper social service agencies and law enforcement authorities. Chapter 2 posed democratic and transformative leadership models that provide guidance and direction for school leaders (see also, Laible, 2000). Critical feminist theory, too, reframes such issues by demanding that leaders and politicians look holistically at education policy issues and also incorporate the issues and needs of women and girls (Marshall, 1997). Feminist insights and alternative leadership perspectives were raised in Chapter 3 and in other chapters of this book. How could the needs of girls like Jasmine be better served by school leaders whose knowledge, skills, and values incorporate such insights?

Insights from the Case Method

The two cases, with their associated follow-up discussion and implications, model one method for preparing leaders for social justice action. By practicing with case studies, administrators can envision and enact more imaginative and constructive interventions when faced with difficult situations with children, families, staff, professors, political and community pressures, and with policies that force them to grapple with a range of intersecting inequities concerning race/ethnicity, gender, sexual orientation, religion, language, immigrant status, disability, age, and lifestyles.

This chapter should be seen as an introduction to thinking about how educators can debate ways in which standard operations and policies can be rethought from a social justice perspective(s). Cases and subsequent discussion can be used to explore different ways of thinking and crafting action on policy issues related to social justice.

Case studies can be used to explore a myriad of social justice topics. For example, educators can develop their own cases to explore some of the following issues:

- The efficiency of closing a school in a low-income neighborhood versus the pressing needs of the stressed families
- The desire to take charge of the teenage girl who keeps seeking affirmation through promiscuity, having her second child by age 15
- Frustration with a school board that refuses to address gay bashing
- The first-in-his-district African American principal who knows that community members and the board want *no* trouble, but who can't help but see the need to take a strong stand against districtwide racist structures
- The central office budget manager who has already been told to "just do your own job" but who knows that the Director of Special Education has devised ways of reporting district special education data so as to cover up long-standing practices of giving better services to wealthier families
- The woman assistant principal who wants to quit in disgust after seeing her white male peers' careers advance ahead of hers, seemingly because of their hanging out together in golf games, sexist joking, and the like
- The principal who sees through the shallowness of the district's 2-hour diversity training, knowing that personnel are inadequately prepared for comments he hears about Muslims, jealousies about some Asian students' scholarships, and kids who see gangs as their best chance for feeling "in"

School leaders have choices to make. Administrative decisions are never neutral, and all involve making conscious choices that have an impact on children, parents, teachers, and other community members. Without practice, leaders will avoid and evade dilemmas due to their unfamiliarity with such problems, lack of support, and uneasiness. Making the choice to do nothing when a problem arises has major implications for social justice. Cases, discussed with supportive colleagues, will strengthen the courage and ability of school leaders to confront and intervene to make social justice happen.

Discussion Questions and Activities

1. Write a case based on the most dilemma-laden situation you have dealt with in your career. Read the case to your colleagues and discuss how you reacted and why. Create and implement politically astute strategies for preventing a similar situation.

2. Identify (use your best guess) the most social-justice-oriented professor and school leader in your work or university context. Interview this person by asking the following questions: "What experiences/knowledge/values prepared you to care about social justice?" and "What obstacles have you faced and how have you overcome them and taken stands for social justice?" You may wish to expand on these questions using insights gained from previous chapters, especially Chapters 3 and 5.

3. In the four levels of transformative learning, "action" is the highest and most complex level. Theoharis (2004), for example, developed a social justice leadership matrix in which this highest level is characterized by school administrators who possess a passion for social justice and who also have the abilities, skills, and knowledge to actualize "actions" with others (e.g., teachers, parents, students) regarding social justice issues. A great deal of social justice leadership can take place within schools and the curriculum, which can be seen as the third level of transformation—within schooling. The fourth level, leading to social transformation, connects to community activities. This takes social justice outside of traditional boundaries of what educators "should" do. This is the most risky level of action. Discuss with your peers a situation in which you took action (or almost took action) with community members to confront a social justice dilemma.

4. Too often, educators and schools are held responsible for student outcomes (e.g., students' poor performance, dropping out, acting out). Identify instances in current federal, state, and local policies and political rhetoric that display these strong arguments. How can you, as a social justice leader, take on these forces in the media, forming coalitions and using other political strategies to "illuminate how economic and political decisions by others—over many decades" (Anyon, 1997, p. xix) have created a context full of inequities, exclusions, and inadequacies that require concerted social action by all, not just by educators and in schools, to change, rather than blame students, parents, or school personnel for their actions.

5. Some have argued that blatant discrimination no longer exists in our society. They argue that we live in a color-blind world where all races, ethnic groups, men and women, and all immigrant groups have equal opportunity and that only lack of hard work or bad cultural habits keep individuals from using education to get ahead. Furthermore, some polls have reported that Euro-Americans resent "special programs" for racial minorities to make up for past discrimination

(Bonilla-Silva, 2001). Given these attitudes, which are prevalent in many communities, what actions can you, as a social justice leader, take to move your community and fellow educators to identify *when racial disparities are the result of discrimination and when are they not due to discrimination* based on historical and social science evidence and political and economic decisions (as explored in the article by Roslyn Mickelson, 2003, pp. 1074–1076)? Similarly, what will you do to move your community and fellow educators to care about other social justice issues, such as bias against homosexuals and the ways girls' futures are limited by messages from the media, families, and religious groups?

Annotated Bibliography

Auerbach's (2002) article in the *Teachers College Record* uses critical race theory to highlight the importance of Latina–Latino parent narratives and of speaking back to education polices and processes that ignore the needs of Latino students. Auerbach's research documents that Latino parents want academic success for their children in high school, but are often blocked from doing so by school administrators and teachers who recommend low-track placement and do not offer the salient information needed for college applications. Auerbach offers specific policy recommendations for administrators to address Latino parent concerns.

Lopez's (2001) article in the *Harvard Educational Review* examines the typical ways in which parent involvement is accepted and expected in public schools. The traditional means of parent involvement center on parent–teacher associations or individual parents engaging with teachers about their specific child's educational needs. Lopez documents how some Latino migrant parents do not fit into these normative expectations of school–parent relations and involvement. Yet these parents are very committed to their children's education, and often serve as a parental example as to why education is important to gain the academic knowledge needed to potentially move into the middle class through future employment opportunities. School officials in many locations that have seen a large influx of Latino migrants often hold negative views of this population, but Lopez's research urges school leaders to see other ways that these immigrant/migrant parents participate in their children's education and to think of new ways in which schools can meet their needs.

McKenzie and Scheurich's (2004) article in the *Educational Administration Quarterly* is a follow-up to Scheurich's November 1998 article that was published in *Urban Education* on highly successful schools with low SES students of color. McKenzie and Scheurich lay out social justice suggestions and multiple paths for new principals to follow in terms of trying to lead their staff to establish a set of core beliefs and organizational culture characteristics that are undergirded by the belief that all children can succeed at high levels and that value the racial, language, and cultural diversity of the parents and community. They present commonly heard resistance statements to social justice and change by teachers and then draw from their own experiences and research on schools that have made equity changes to highlight ways in which the social justice thinking of teachers can begin to be changed.

Pillow's (2004) book, *Unfit Subjects: Educational Policy and the Teen Mother*, traces the policy discussions surrounding Title IX and how it has been used and ignored in the area of teen pregnancy and the education of girls in public schools. Pillow notes the racial, social class, and gender discourse connected to the control of teen sexuality and pregnancy and explores how race is connected with other policy arguments related to welfare. This book is useful from a social justice perspective in understanding ideology and its impact on sexuality and policy and how it has affected schools in terms of teen pregnancy. It is also useful in prompting administrative policy discussions about race and class issues related to the education of teen girls.

Acknowledgments

Special thanks to Josh Diem and Stacey Cutbush for assistance in generating cases and to Amy Anderson for editing assistance. All were graduate students at the University of North Carolina at Chapel Hill.

References

Anderson, G. L. (1990). Toward a critical constructivist approach to school administration: Invisibility, legitimation, and the study of nonevents. *Educational Administration Quarterly, 26*(1), 38–59.

Anyon, J. (1997). *Ghetto schooling: A political economy of urban educational reform.* New York: Teachers College Press.

Ashbaugh, C. R., & Kasten, K. L. (1991). *Educational leadership: Case studies for reflective practice.* New York: Longman.

Auerbach, S. (2002). Why do they give the good classes to some and not to others?: Latino parent narratives of struggle in a college access program. *Teachers College Record, 104,* 1369–1392.

Bonilla-Silva, E. (2001). *White supremacy & racism in the post-civil rights era.* Boulder, CO: Rienner Publishers.

Brookfield, S. (1992). Uncovering assumptions: The key to reflective practice. *Adult Learning, 3,* 13–18.

Diem, J. (2003). *My name is Jasmine.* Unpublished manuscript. University of North Carolina, Chapel Hill.

Gay, G. (2002). Culturally responsive teaching in special education for ethnically diverse students: Setting the stage. *International Journal of Qualitative Studies in Education, 15,* 613–630.

Goldfarb, K. P., & Grinberg, J. (2002). Leadership for social justice: Authentic participation in the case of community center in Caracas, Venezuela. *Journal of School Leadership, 12,* 157–173.

Harrington, H. L., & Garrison, J. W. (1992). Cases as shared inquiry: A dialogical model of teacher preparation. *American Educational Research Journal, 29,* 715–735.

Harvard Civil Rights Project (2002, June). *Racial equity in special education: Executive summary for federal policymakers.* Retrieved December 11, 2004, from www.civilrightsproject .harvard.edu/research/html

Honan, J. P., & Rule, C. S. (2002). *Using cases in higher education: A guide for faculty and administrators.* San Francisco, CA: Jossey-Bass.

Labaree, D. F. (1997). Public goods, private goods: The American struggle over educational goals. *American Educational Research Journal, 34,* 39–82.

Larson, C. L., & Ovando, C. J. (2001). *The color of bureaucracy: The politics of equity in multicultural school communities.* Belmont, CA: Wadsworth.

Laible, J. C. (2000). A loving epistemology: What I hold critical in my life, faith, and profession. *International Journal of Qualitative Studies in Education, 13,* 683–692.

Lopez, G. R. (2001). The value of hard work: Lessons on parent involvement from an (im)migrant household. *Harvard Educational Review, 71,* 416–437.

Marshall, C. (Ed.). (1997). *Feminist critical policy analysis: A perspective from primary and secondary schooling.* London: Falmer Press.

Marshall, C., & Gerstl-Pepin, C. (2005). *Reframing educational politics for social justice.* Boston: Allyn & Bacon.

Marshall, C., & Mitchell, B. (1991). The assumptive worlds of fledgling administrators. *Education and Urban Society, 23*(4), 396–415.

Marshall, C., & Ward, M. (2004). "Yes, but . . .": Education leaders discuss social justice. *Journal of School Leadership, 14*(5), 530–563.

McCray, A. D., & Garcia, S. B. (2002). The stories we must tell: Developing a research agenda for multicultural and bilingual special education. *International Journal of Qualitative Studies in Education, 15,* 599–612.

McKenzie, K. B., & Scheurich, J. J. (2004). Equity traps: A useful construct for preparing principals to lead schools that are successful with racially diverse students. *Educational Administration Quarterly, 40,* 601–632.

Mickelson, R. A. (2003). When are racial disparities in education the result of racial discrimination? A social science perspective. *Teachers College Record, 105,* 1052–1086.

Mirón, L. (1997). *Resisting discrimination: Affirmative strategies for principals and teachers.* Thousand Oaks, CA: Sage.

Peterkin, R., & Lucey, J. (1998, June 30). Educational audit for Champaign, Illinois, schools Unit #4: Findings & recommendations. Champaign, IL: Champaign Board of Education.

Pillow, W. S. (2004). *Unfit subjects: Educational policy and the teen mother.* New York: RoutledgeFalmer.

Rieseter, A. F., Pursch, V., & Skrla, L. (2002). Principals for social justice: Leaders of school success for children from low-income homes. *Journal of School Leadership, 12,* 281–304.

Rusch, E. (2004). Gender and race in leadership preparation: A constrained discourse. *Educational Administration Quarterly, 40*(1), 16–48.

Scheurich, J. J. (1998). Highly successful and loving, public elementary schools populated mainly by low SES children of color: Core beliefs and cultural characteristics. *Urban Education 33*(4), 451–491.

Scheurich, J. J., & Skrla, L. (2003). *Leadership for equity and excellence: Creating high achievement classrooms, schools, and districts.* Thousand Oaks, CA: Corwin Press.

Schön, D. A. (1983). *Educating the reflective practitioner.* San Francisco: Jossey-Bass.

Skrla, L., & Young, M. (2003). Reconsidering feminist research in educational leadership. In M. Young & L. Skrla (Eds.), *Reconsidering feminist research in educational leadership* (pp. 1–5). Albany: SUNY Press.

Strike, K. A., Haller, E. J., & Soltis, J. F. (1988). *The ethics of school administration.* New York: Teachers College Press.

Theoharis, G. T. (2004). *At no small cost: Social justice leaders and their response to resistance.* Unpublished dissertation, University of Wisconsin-Madison.

Vincent, C. (Ed.). (2003). *Social justice, education, and identity.* London: Routledge-Falmer.

Zeichner, K. M. (2003). The adequacies and inadequacies of three current strategies to recruit, prepare, and retain the best teachers for all students. *Teachers College Record, 105,* 490–519.

11

Disrupting Identity: Fertile Pedagogy for Raising Social Consciousness in Educational Leaders

C. Cryss Brunner
Christen Opsal
Maricela Oliva

How could I get my students to reconsider their ways of viewing the world? How could I awaken students from their slumber, their limited consciousness, without being impositional? I asked myself the questions posed by Bridges and Hartman (1975): How can the teacher, as problem poser, reflect student reality back to the student in a nonthreatening, problematic way that will induce self-examination and critical questioning—without imposition? In effect, how can teachers use their power and authority to *abolish* power and authority? This is the major contradiction of teaching from a critical and dialogic perspective. (Ahlquist, 1991, p. 165, emphasis in original)

Imagine that you and 14 other people are taking a class in the field of education. It doesn't really matter which one. What matters for the purposes of this particular class are the following conditions: You don't meet your classmates or learn much about them until a month into the semester. In the interim, the 15 of you "meet" in a chat room where you must solve a problem or accomplish a task together—while maintaining this near-total ignorance of each other. In your contributions to your class's three lengthy chat "conversations," you cannot reveal your name, age, gender, occupation, expertise, or any other type of personal information—in short, you must hide your identity, holding these characteristics as close to your chest as a poker hand.[1]

In everyday life, we may reveal deep personal information to complete strangers—"Hi, my name is Bob, and I'm an alcoholic"—or at least play our cards freely with friends and strangers alike. Moreover, our physical selves (i.e., dress, speech, carriage) reveal things about us to others and/or are interpreted and judged by them as meaning particular things before we even place our "hidden" identities (such as occupation and expertise, in most cases) on the table. These factors function in personal "zones of influence" (Oliva, 2000) through which communication messages are both transmitted and received and that constitute elements of understanding that in individual communication exchanges exceed the message itself (see also, Gardiner, 1992; Holquist, 1981).[2]

Being asked to keep one's hand to oneself while simultaneously being deprived of physical indicators is deeply unsettling. Noting that later in this chapter we will discuss the process of Experiential Simulations (ES),[3] continue to imagine yourself in this situation while turning your attention to the following questions:

1. What possible purpose could such an experience serve?
2. Why might *you* be asked to go through an experience like this?
3. What does this experience have to do with leadership, if anything?
4. What does the experience have to do with schools and education, if anything?
5. Would you have trouble communicating and/or getting work done with your identity hidden as described?
6. How would this modify or change the way that you interact and work with others?

If possible, jot down your answers to these questions before reading further.

By thinking about and answering these five questions, we hope that you come to understand that you and your peers' identities play a large part in your relationships with each other—and with others—for a myriad of reasons. Further, for often inexplicable reasons, your perceptions of others' identities feel too important to give up, at least for very long. Identity, it seems, shapes our interactions in ways that make those interactions "work" in particular ways so that they become familiar, and even cherished, over time. Can we function without them? And ultimately, for our purposes, do they get in the way of interpersonal understanding, true dialogue, and "justice-oriented" interaction? These last questions lead us into a brief discussion of mental models and how they unconsciously shape our interactions.

Our Perception of Others

"... our a priori schematic perceptions (those that form our identities and how we identify others) of ourselves and others—which include selective seeing—can be said to be our biases. 'Human beings consistently sort and classify women, men, rich, poor, and all people of color by schemas that reduce individuals and groups to social and cultural stereotypes. These stereotypes ... perpetuate inaccurate constructions of "the other" ' (Larson & Ovando, 2001, p. 77)."

Cognitive Schemas and Constructed Perceptions

Colleen Larson and Carlos Ovando (2001) observed the following in their book:

> We tend to see ourselves and others in particular yet partial ways. Human beings rely upon mental constructs, or schemas, to help make sense of individuals, groups, situations, or events that they encounter.... Cognitive schemas are necessary to human thought. They help us to organize and classify our world (Valian, 1998).... For example, we have schematic constructions for family, parties, men, women, racial groups, friendships, community, schools, and the roles of professionals within it. We even have a schema of ourselves—as persons, as teachers, or as administrators. Schemas develop very early in our lives. These schemas are helpful in that they enable us to organize our world, but they can also frame and limit our perceptions and expectations of others. (p. 74)

Larson and Ovando (2001) made it clear that our schemas make up our constructed identities of self and of others, and they conclude that although our schematic identities are important, they can also limit our thinking. Later in the same discussion, Larson and Ovando confronted their readers with the statement: "When an individual's behavior does not align with our schematic expectations, our inclination is to conclude that something is wrong. We struggle to fit this person into our own image of him or her, and if we can't, we conclude that it is the person, *not our* schema that is in question" [authors' emphasis] (p. 75). In other words, we rarely consider our own schematic perceptions as the possible problem. Furthermore, our a priori schemas serve as "zones of influence" that themselves filter and shape our experiences of and with others. In other words,

> The discourses of distinct communicators create particular zones of influence that then interact with the zones of influence of others. Through the interaction of language (discourse's primary medium) through zones of influence, the meaning of language is refracted in ways that bend and distort the meaning of communication arising out of different zones. (Oliva, 2000, p. 38)

Our distorted perceptions of those exchanges limit our capacity to see others as who they are rather than as a reflection of what we ourselves partially project. Those distorted perspectives and projections, as a consequence, change our interactions (all kinds of communications) with others (Valian, 1998; cited in Larson & Ovando, 2001). Thus, our a priori schematic perceptions (those that form our identities and how we identify others) of ourselves and others—which include selective seeing—can be said to be our biases: "Human beings consistently sort and classify women, men, rich, poor, and all people of color by schemas that reduce individuals and groups to social and cultural stereotypes. These stereotypes . . . perpetuate inaccurate constructions of 'the other' " (Larson & Ovando, 2001, p. 77).

In our view, the discussion in this section is one of the most important reasons we ask participant learners to go through the ES process. Revisiting the questions asked in the previous section, did the above discussion appear in any of your answers? Can you use this discussion to provide at least a partial answer to the questions?

Through ES (as well as other available methods), we offer participant learners a controlled simulation of otherness and at the same time incorporate reflective awareness during learning that can lead to new self-awareness and reflective practice. We have created a virtual environment where it becomes clear how individuals: (1) represent their and/or others' identities and communicate through them, (2) construct understandings of people from visual referents that categorize them as members of certain groups, and (3) use the artificial and inherently biased categories to filter and make decisions about other individuals' communications. This demonstrates that the impact of identity constructions on our communications and actions is profound. In sum, what Brunner's process does is move participant-learners out of their taken-for-granted racialized, gendered, constructed ways of interaction that often privilege "leaders" and get in the way of social justice leadership. Technology allows the instructor and participant learners to break down and deconstruct these taken-for-granted interactions to reconstruct identity and communication in more critically conscious ways.

Therefore, the purpose of this chapter is to illustrate how identity shapes both our communication and our perceptions of communication in ways that create obstacles to equitable practices/experiences for all learners and communities. Ways of thinking and acting that are not critically reflected upon by school leaders do not allow room for alternative voices or explanations and interpretations of experience. They crowd out or marginalize all but the centered and power-laden discourses of mainstream authority. In so doing, unquestioned discourses and ways of thinking can contribute to inequity and diminished social justice. As a response to that, the pedagogical processes described here can be used to make aspiring educational leaders experientially, as well as cognitively, aware that a marginalizing monologic[4] interaction with others does not necessarily require a willful and badly intentioned imposition of power on their part. It can also simply be embedded in the unquestioned practices established by and for those in authority. Such practices can include the processes routinely established by leaders for decision making; the platform of constraint and freedom within which stakeholders, such as parents, students, and teachers, are allowed to construct their identity and role; and in the narratives (whether of "service to a school community" or of "management") within which they organize their site leadership (e.g., see Merryfield, 2001; Schoorman, 2002; Sullivan, 2002; Warschauer, 1996, 1999).

Heidi Writes about Her ES Experience: Narrative Data in Original Form

Thus, with the purpose of ES and this chapter explicit, we return to our earlier request that you think about how you might react if you were put in a class with certain restrictions on the disclosure of your own and others' identities. In this section, we provide an example of one student's written reactions to hiding her identity during the ES process. We refer to her as Heidi (pseudonym), and her reactions are provided in the following text.

> *Without meaning to, I revealed something about myself in my very first chat room contribution. Almost everyone having checked in at the beginning of our first class chat session with an "I am here" message, we were given a few minutes to familiarize ourselves with the medium. During a preliminary conversation in which we shared our feelings about "chatting," I typed, "I'm glad to be back in school again . . ." inadvertently revealing that this was not my first semester of post-secondary education. A few lines later, one of my classmates acknowledged my gaffe: "Welcome back to school, 'H'!!!" Oops. This was not going to be easy.*
>
> *As I redoubled my efforts to "mask" my identity, I discovered a handful of types of remarks I could safely make. I began completing other people's sentences. I shared incontrovertible [sic] opinions:*
>
> - *technology can also be very isolating*
> - *[the assignment is] pretty vague, could be good or bad. (my perception of our "task")*
> - *. . . yes, the class has been very methodically prepared . . .*
> - *we seem to be doing pretty well "conversing" so far . . .*
>
> *I proposed group norms:*
>
> - *should we all agree not to judge each other on spelling etc.?*
> - *maybe we need to adopt chat aliases, like "Red Hot Momma"*
>
> *I puzzled aloud through the logistics of the chat room:*
>
> - *why does that say "private msg" before it?*

- *actually, I don't see where on pg 3 [of the syllabus] it says we can begin the task . . .*
- *are we supposed to stop or keep chatting?*

And I offered questions to get a discussion started:

- *as I was preparing for class tonight, I was thinking, is this technological approach to class biased in favor of people who are wealthy enough to own computers?*
- *or biased in favor of those who can read, type, and think fast?*

For the rest of our time in the chat room, I employed such tactics and succeeded in holding my cards close. Regardless, you may be able to infer some things about me simply from the remarks given above—like that I can type fast, or that I can be pretty concerned with following professors' instructions. However, think of how much more you would know about me if the 11 contributions given above were personal details instead of all those other types of remarks. In 11 short phrases, you could know (1) name, (2) gender, (3) race/ethnicity, (4) age, (5) occupation, (6) the degree I am pursuing/the department I'm in, (7) how close I am to getting a degree, (8) marital status, (9) political persuasion, (10) religion, and (11) hobbies. That's a significant amount of personal information! And you can bet that most of these were on the tip of my tongue at some point during my time in the chat room.

My classmates felt equally "stifled" by the requirement to hide identity, as evidenced by their success and failure in doing so. During a discussion of leadership, we had been brainstorming names of leaders when someone mentioned Mother Teresa. Another student, who we later learned was an instructor in the women's studies department, could not contain her political/social beliefs regarding poverty and oppression during the conversation that ensued. The following are comments she contributed to that conversation:

- *mother teresa was a wonderful woman, but i don't believe she influenced change*
- *she showed compassion and allowed people to die with dignity . . . but she did not create social change*
- *people gave to the needy before mother teresa—sorry but another example of giving rather than sharing—seeing what already existed*
- *does free medical care change the reason that there is so much disease in those countries in the first place?*
- *does it change their status as poor countries when they had the richest mineral resources?*
- *people in calcutta were creating social change before mother teresa and i can provide examples if people would like*
- *i guess i'm just saying that easing suffering—while one of the most noble things to do—is distinct from creating social change. and while she might have eased suffering in her immediate surroundings and inspired people all over the world, she did not impact the structural, systematic oppression of third world and indigenous peoples.*

Hiding one's identity, especially in the context of emotionally charged topics, is extraordinarily difficult.

As we can see from Heidi's comments, it was difficult for the participants to interact without the identity and persona that she and others had been assigned or had previously constructed for themselves through their prior socializations and experiences. Despite the foregrounded "fictive" nature of even these communicative selves, they depended, as most of us do unthinkingly, on their identity as a crutch against which they launched their reflections, educational practice, and interaction with others.

A Description of Experiential Simulations

Experiential simulations (ES)[5] is the name of an innovative pedagogical process designed and used by Brunner in school leader preparation courses. The core element of ES is the "modified persona" (MP) created by the professor and utilized by participant learners with computer technology. The MP is provided to participant learners and taken on by them as part of the learning process. The assignment of an MP serves four main purposes:

1. To socially position students differently during communications with others in a virtual, technological communication space than how they are actually positioned in real life.
2. To allow the participant learner a nontypical response from the "receiver(s)" of their communications other than what would be obtained if the audience knew the person's actual identity and appearance.
3. To provide the participant learner immersion in an interactive communication learning experience pertinent to their leadership work in democratic and socially just cultures.
4. To potentially complicate, and therefore diversify, the range of leadership and communication interaction options to which educational leaders can resort in their practice.[6]

Does it work? That is to say, does experience in ES cause participant learners of educational administration to take a hard look at their own identities and the effect of identity on decision making, communication, and other social interactions? Do participant learners develop a more salient understanding of their roles as leaders for social justice in education?

Based on participants'[7] answers to the reflection questions, the answer appears to be "yes." For example, before they were shown either the real or fake photos and videos that positioned them through identity, participant learners fretted about their lack of knowledge of their classmates. In their responses to the reflection questions, they wondered aloud if knowing another's gender, race, or other identity actually caused them to deliberately treat that person more or less "justly." One student, a woman of color, noted her discomfort in an environment without social identity "markers," stating that she felt she needed such markers to be "fair":

I may be judging [my classmates] on written communication that does not do them justice. I simply need some social interaction in order to be fair. (PI1: N4)

A number of the White participant learners agreed, making comments similar to this one:

I feel also that I may need to know about some of the individual's backgrounds, in order for me to be more compassionate and sensitive to where they are coming from, in order to put some of their attitudes and beliefs into perspective. (PI1: F4)

By "background," some meant gender:

I guess I personally would like to know the sex of the people I was talking to, and I'm honestly not sure why. I think it is somehow programmed in my brain that life will be out of balance if I don't know the sex of whom I am talking to! It just seems unnatural and out of order for me to not know whom I am speaking to. (PI1: L5)

Others noted sexual preference and religion:

I am concerned that I might say something to offend someone because they belong to a certain culture, religion, or sexual preference. That person is going to hate me later because I may seem insensitive. (PI1: N1)

It was also difficult to discuss with people when you do not know their gender or their race. When the issue of religion [a]rose, I was concerned that some people may not even believe in god, or have a different god for that matter. (PI1: I3)

However, not everyone agreed that fair treatment of others increases with knowledge of them. One student questioned the concept of "objectivity" and articulated the difficulty often faced by victims of bias when they wish to draw attention to their experiences:

I prefer [being anonymous in a chat room], because usually people dismiss my views regarding women and people of color as being because I am a woman of color. In other words, my gender and ethnic identity bias me, but theirs do not bias them. Being White and/or male, they can ostensibly be "objective." (PI1: K1)

One participant noted the value of the "identity-free" environment from the perspective of her classmates:

I liked not knowing or identifying others. I felt that my classmates had the opportunity to contribute to the process and my learning without my expectations being imposed on them. (PI1: D1)

Another student, concerned that personalities were surfacing despite the anonymous medium, wished that identity could be completely erased for the sake of openness and freedom of expression:

> If one thinks/feels that one wants to know more information about others in order to openly discuss, then I think one would be guilty of wanting to classify or put people into a category for one's own comfort level. In other words, that person would be too controlling. I don't feel a need to know anything more about others. In fact, I wish their personalities would remain blank for a longer period of time so more people could express openly their thoughts. (PI1: O5)

Because of their experiences in the chat room, these participant learners questioned the role of identity in social interaction, expressing divergent views about the value of knowing more about others.

After seeing the "pseudo" photos, however, participant learners were clear that the photos would have an effect on their work together. Student responses to the reflective questions have been summarized in Table 11.1. The column on the left contains answers written after the first online class, before participant learners saw the "pseudo" photos. The column on the right contains answers written after participant learners were shown their own photo among a class of "pseudo" photos. Both questions are basically the same. However, participant learners' answers changed significantly in their focus. In the first set of answers, only three of the participant learners noted constructions of identity (e.g., gender, race, religion, power dynamics, professional interests). Yet, in the second set of answers, most participant learners conveyed their opinion that constructions of identity create various barriers, misunderstandings, cautions, and limitations. The one student who answered the question with a "no" nevertheless stated that people would be more careful in their text messages.

After all online classes were complete, participant learners were asked to reflect on their experiences with the experiential simulations and what they had learned about the relationship between working with and "knowing" others. Several participant learners were pleasantly surprised by the group's productivity in the absence of "identity." Moreover, two of these participant learners noted feelings of goodwill toward their classmates, despite having only recently just "met" them:

> The most important aspect of the chat room sessions for me was looking into and participating within a different type of communication and community. It was amazing to see what people can do and learn from each other, and about themselves, strictly by communicating through technology and never meeting face-to-face. (PI6: E11)

> I was surprised how well our Task Force [class] worked together and met our goal and the sense of camaraderie I'm feeling toward the group. (PI6: G11)

Table 11.1 *Comparing Stage One and Stage Two Narratives: Identity and Task*

Participant	Answers After the First Chat: "Did the lack of identity affect the task force work that has to be accomplished?"		Answers After Photos Were Revealed: "Will the photo identities affect the task force work in any way? If so, how? If not, why not?"
	Yes	A	Yes—we will be more careful about what we say. I will be more careful because of others' gender and race.
	No—the chat room usage did that, information overload.	B	Not very much, but we may be more careful about what we say. There may be a tendency to classify our comments as male or female.
	Not as much as I expected. People did a good job remaining anonymous.	D	Yes—dominant culture norms will dictate behavior. I expect to be treated as dumb. I also expect that some of the group members will be given power by group members because of sex.
	Hard to say. I think we may have accomplished more because people were not jockeying for position.	E	Yes—hopefully positively, hopefully we won't offend each other by asking for particular perspectives (like male, female, racial perspectives) or dismiss certain people's comments because of who they are.
	Yes—because we couldn't identify what fields we are in or interested in.	F	Yes—makes us curious about backgrounds, can ask for particular perspectives.
	No—the chat room did. It is harder to get the work done. Our communication is not natural.	G	Yes—physical attributes definitely impact how persons are perceived.
	No—we could still share knowledge. The task would be difficult in face-to-face discussion too.	H	Yes—may confuse/mislead us [skeptical about photos being "real"]. We may assume things about them that may not be true.
	Yes—Hard to discuss without knowing gender, race, religion.	I	Yes—I will be more attuned to males' comments. I was surprised by the ages.

(continued)

Table 11.1 *Continued*

Participant*	Answers After the First Chat: "Did the lack of identity affect the task force work that has to be accomplished?"	Answers After Photos Were Revealed: "Will the photo identities affect the task force work in any way? If so, how? If not, why not?
J	Maybe—or could've been chat room. It was hard to keep track of individuals. It was confusing.	Yes—I may have these pictures in mind during next chat. It seems much less liberating after seeing the photos.
K	Yes—hard to keep track of what people said.	Yes—will complicate and perhaps hinder our work. I was disappointed to see photos so soon. Class is more diverse than I thought it would be.
L	Not sure. Natural leaders came forward.	Yes—age factor may make people dismiss me.
N	No—we became a group with a purpose.	No, but I will know when I must be considerate.
O	Yes—it allowed people to be irresponsible.	Yes—now stereotypes come into play.

Note: Letters C and M are missing because they were assigned to participant learners who had to drop the course before the ES process began.

> I was pleasantly surprised that we were able to organize ourselves and actually approach the task in a systematic way, and yet come up with a creative and personalized product. I wasn't sure it could be done. I came off our second session feeling very excited about the project, the medium, and my classmates, whoever they were. I hope we can have that synergy and consensus when "live"! (PI6: H11)

Can groups of people experience productivity and camaraderie in the absence of identity's trappings, those physical and psychological referents that bias our interactions and the reception of others' messages? These participant learners' reflections suggest the possibility.

People can get work done and even generate some feelings of rapport without knowing much about each other. However, this does not change the reality that, as one student put it, "Identity and gender are very influential in this life." The questions that follow are: (1) How are they influential? and (2) Who benefits from which categories? In their final set of chat reflection questions, several participant learners noted their *personal* discomfort with having their identity "replaced" by someone else's and their perceptions of others' reactions to them because of this replacement:

> I was also surprised that my [MP] identity was a non–Caucasian man. My feelings about being identified as a man were upsetting to me. I didn't realize how attached I am to being a woman/womyn!! (PI6: D11)

> I was surprised that I really began to question whether I was being discounted at times because of my perceived color [MP identity]. (PI6: F11)

> I may have overestimated people's reaction to me based on my physical appearance. Without yet having scrutinized the transcripts word for word, I didn't notice any changed reaction to me specifically except, perhaps, somewhat once our "real" identities were unveiled. (PI6: K11)

These participant learners' remarks raise the question of whether our identities are more important to others or ourselves. Either way, it is clear that identity—or the lack thereof—has a profound effect on collaborative work and on potential school administrators' reflective disposition to social justice leadership in real-world practice. (For more on the real-world challenges for developing such dispositions in practice, see Chapter 14.) Two additional excerpts from student reflections illustrate how participant learners who participated in Experiential Simulations became self-conscious about constructions of identity and the impact of these constructions on collaborative and social justice work:

> [This has been] a fascinating experiment that has made me question my own assumptions, and question assumptions in others. Where I didn't think that race/age might negatively impact how others are perceived, I know that this happens. (PI6: F11)

> I learned a lot about myself and others during the first three sessions. I—probably like most people—base more guesses about people's lives on their physical appearance than even what they tell us about what they think and believe. (PI6: K11)

For the educational leaders who participate in ES, the experience and lessons of displaced identity are profound and lingering.

Discussion

The ES process compelled the student participants to foreground what is usually in the background of their real-world interaction: That their interactions with others are unavoidably shaped by beliefs about who they and others are, by their categorical group membership in privileged or marginalized groups, and by the a priori assumptions about those and other characteristics that bias their interaction. In other words, ES was both about how individual students represented their identities and communicated through them as much as it was about how they also constructed understandings of people from the visual referents that categorized them as members of certain groups and that subsequently served to filter communications through considerably artificial and inherently biased (positively and/or negatively) constructs. We can say that in the ES process the students' identities were removed for the explicit purpose of education—an education that focused on the learning of intangible lessons that are not often available to educators in classrooms. The lessons allowed Brunner and her students to address several questions that are key to social justice leadership and leader development, including:

- How does one teach and learn the lessons of privilege and marginalization that school leaders must be aware of as they do their day-to-day work?
- How is an awareness of the experience of "otherness" experienced affectively as well as cognitively so that school leaders "see" or "get it" in lasting ways?
- How might such an experience help them to better understand how to appropriately address communicative or monologic bias when it has negative consequences for some students or otherwise shapes campuses and classrooms in ways that work against social justice?

As we have seen, the visceral experiences made possible by the Experiential Simulation process moved individuals out of their taken-for-granted racialized, gendered, constructed ways of interaction that seemed to privilege and marginalize them in unique ways. This included privileging some of the participants as potential "leaders" more than others. Uncritical and unreflective thinking of this nature and a lack of knowledge of these processes gets in the way of social justice work and action. So that it does not impede leaders and educators' advocacy on behalf of marginalized and underserved communities, it is important that educators find ways to learn these lessons.

Furthermore, this process implodes the general idea that communication is neutral and objective, forcing us to take into account our need, as school lead-

"Although instructors can create opportunities for . . . experiential learning, they cannot anticipate the zones of influence from which students interact, how those will connect with others in the class, nor foresee the individual and group pathways that must be cleared and navigated for lessons of this kind to be learned."

ers and educators, to defamiliarize and more closely attend to the day-to-day, taken-for-granted interactions in which we routinely participate. In this much more attentive communication process, educators are better able to listen, hear, and participate in communicative exchanges, to act more equitably, and to even reconstruct interactions so that they lead schools in more socially just ways.

Implications for Practice

Experiential simulations yield a wide array of implications for practice—an array as varied as the individual participant learners who take part in the experience. Participant learners report unique and individual effects on their lives and practices as a result of participation in ES. One student reported that she had "misjudged" White women and intended to give them the "benefit of the doubt" in her practice. She was embarrassed to have realized that some of her experiences of marginalization came from her own imagination and expectations. Other participant learners (months after the semester ended) reported that they thought about their experiences with ES "every day" in ways that created new behaviors and new eyes. Given these unique and varying comments, Brunner concludes that learning of this type is highly personal and largely idiosyncratic; therefore, it *must* be organized in ways that keep it largely in the hands of the learner. Although instructors can create opportunities for experiential learning, they cannot anticipate the zones of influence from which students interact, how individuals will connect with others in the class, nor foresee the individual and group pathways that must be cleared and navigated for lessons of this kind to be learned.

Discussion Questions and Activities _____

The following are three activities related to identity and power. These activities can be assigned to participant learners for use during face-to-face sessions or may be adapted for online or out-of-class work.

1. Disrupting Identity Face to Face

   Instructors who wish to work with constructions of identity in their classrooms can do so in fairly simple yet somewhat effective ways. For example, in order to teach about identity, instructors can lead participant learners through classroom-based experiences in which participant learners are asked to creatively alter their own personal backgrounds (names, education, family, professional position, degree program, occupation) in order to escape myriad constructions of difference when introducing themselves to others in the class. They are asked to remain within their created identities for as long as possible. Participant learners who take part in such activities note that typical classroom hierarchies are not established and that as a result they feel freer to speak and participate and come to know their classmates in substantive ways.

2. Power Plays
Participant learners are asked to define "power" in magic marker on a piece of paper. They do not put their names on their definitions. Papers are taken up and saved for another class session much later in the semester. After time has passed, papers are randomly handed out and participant learners are asked to sort the definitions into categories, to label the categories, and to defend the placement of the definitions. After this part of the exercise, a discussion of power and its various conceptions is conducted. In addition, enactments of power and their relationships to conceptions of power are also discussed. Finally, participant learners identify which definitions of power belonged to them and conduct an analysis of gender and race as they relate to conceptions of power. Often, it becomes clear that marginalized groups tend to agree on how power is conceived and enacted. For the full discussion of this exercise, see Brunner (2002).

3. Voice, Identity, and Leadership
As participant learners analyze transcripts of their ES discussions, they begin to note how much they talk or do not talk; what they say (write), how they say it, and why; and how well they communicate their own ideas. Some note that they are accustomed to "being heard," and that they are missing their usual places of prominence and privilege. In face-to-face settings, participant learners can engage in different aspects of this ES experience. For example, participant learners can be asked to identify themselves as "quiet" or "talkative." In this exercise, after their self-identification, the other participant learners are asked to verify others' self-identifications. Once everyone self-identifies and has received verification, the "talkers" are sent to one room and the "quiets" are sent to another. They are asked to have a discussion about the strengths and weaknesses of their categories and to list them all on a flip chart.
Finally, they all come back together for another discussion of shared/relational leadership. Characteristics of these types of leadership are listed on yet another flip chart. At this point, the lists from the "talkers" and the "quiets" are hung up next to the chart of leadership characteristics. Almost without fail, it is the list from the "quiets" that most closely aligns with the chart of leadership traits. A rich discussion follows this somewhat rankling exercise.

Annotated Readings

In his article, "Toward authentic participation: Deconstructing the discourses of participatory reforms in education," which is appropriate for both instructors and participant learners, Gary Anderson (1998) problematizes the notion of collaboration and participation as currently understood in public schools. It is clear that most participatory reforms have missed the mark. In ES environments, participant learners come to understand the nature of participation by analyzing transcripts of their collaborative decision-making sessions. This article also provides guidance for transcript analysis.
In their book, *Ethics and the Foundations of Education: Teaching Convictions in a Postmodern World*, Slattery and Rapp (2003) use the perspectives of critical theory, the democratic community, aesthetics, ecology, hermeneutics, and constructive postmodernism to explore ethical issues in schools and society. The book includes discussions of social

constructions of reality and the contribution of postmodern theories to compassion, social justice, and ecological sustainability within the context of global society. The authors use their own life experiences, personal convictions, and narrative and write in an autobiographical style—making the book immensely accessible to readers.

A special issue of the *Educational Administration Quarterly* (2004), edited by Marshall, provides a foundation for professors, instructors, participant learners, and professional educators in the field of educational administration who wish to "take an activist and pro-social justice stance" (Marshall, 2004, p. 5). Topics of gender, race, ecological analysis, transformation, and equity audits are addressed in six scholarly articles. New ideas, approaches, and perspectives are provided for anyone interested in moving social justice to the center of the field.

It is somewhat difficult to convey to learners that communicative interaction, to use Bakhtin's terms, can be monologic—one-way, autocratic, and power-laden, regardless of how pleasantly or politely it is delivered—or dialogic—two-way, equitable, and context specific. Gardiner's (1992) *The Dialogics of Critique* is masterful in describing and explaining Bakhtin's ideas in ways that are easily accessible. For those interested in developing a more in-depth understanding of Bakhtin's theories and how they relate to ES, supplementing Gardiner with Holquist's (1981) edition of four of Bakhtin's essays helps to convey the power of these ideas. Bakhtin's essays focus on the subject in which he specialized—literature—but the utility of those ideas to the social sciences and to education is quickly evident. The four essays are titled: (a) "Epic and novel," (b) "From the prehistory of novelistic discourse," (c) "Forms of time and of the chronotype in the novel," and (d) "Discourse in the novel." Oliva's (2000) application of Bakhtin's ideas to a study of North American cross-cultural educational coordination further illustrates the usefulness of Bakhtin's ideas to educational practice and research.

Related Readings

Adams, M., Bell, L. A., & Griffin, P. (Eds.) (1997). *Teaching for diversity and social justice: A sourcebook*. New York: Routledge.

Apple, M. W. (1993). The politics of pedagogy and the building of community. In M. W. Apple (Ed.), *Official knowledge* (pp. 151–162). New York: Routledge.

Aune, B. (2002). Teaching action research via distance. *Journal of Technology and Teacher Education*, *10*(4), 461–480.

Baldwin, J. (1988). A talk to teachers. In R. Simonson (Ed.), *The Graywolf annual five: Multicultural literacy* (p. 4). St. Paul, MN: Graywolf.

Banks, J. A. (Ed.) (1996). *Multicultural education, transformative knowledge, and action: Historical and contemporary perspectives*. New York: Teachers College Press.

Freire, P. (1972). *Pedagogy of the oppressed*. Harmondsworth, Middlesex: Penguin.

hooks, b. (1994). *Teaching to transgress: Education as the practice of freedom*. New York: Routledge.

Luke, C., & Gore, J. (1992). *Feminisms and critical pedagogy*. New York: Routledge.

Maxcy, S. J. (1994). *Postmodern school leadership: Meeting the crisis in educational administration*. Westport, CT: Praeger.

Purpel, D. E. (1989). *The moral & spiritual crisis in education: A curriculum for justice and compassion in education*. New York: Bergin & Garvey.

Shapiro, J. P., & Stefkovich, J. A. (2001). *Ethical leadership and decision making in education: Applying theoretical perspectives to complex dilemmas*. Mahwah, NJ: Lawrence Erlbaum.

Starratt, R. J. (2003). *Centering educational administration: Cultivating meaning, community, responsibility*. Mahwah, NJ: Lawrence Erlbaum.

Villegas, M. M., & Lucas, T. (2002). Preparing culturally responsive teachers: Rethinking the curriculum. *Journal of Teacher Education, 53*(1), 20–32.
York-Barr, J., Sommers, W. A., Ghere, G. S., & Montie, J. (2001). *Reflective practice to improve schools: An action guide for educators*. Thousand Oaks, CA: Corwin Press.

References

Ahlquist, R. (1991). Position and imposition: Power relations in a multicultural foundations class. *Journal of Negro Education, 60*(2), 158–169.
Anderson, G. L. (1998). Toward authentic participation: Deconstructing the discourses of participatory reforms in education. *American Educational Research Journal, 35*(4), 571–603.
Bolman, L. G., & Deal, T. E. (2003). *Reframing organizations: Artistry, choice, and leadership* (3rd Ed.). Somerset, NJ: Jossey-Bass.
Bridges, A., & Hartman, H. (1975). Pedagogy by the oppressed. *Review of Radical Political Economics, 6*(4), 75–79.
Brunner, C. C. (2002). Professing educational administration: Conceptions of power (three parts). *Journal of School Leadership, 12*, 693–720.
Ellsworth, E. (1989). Why doesn't this feel empowering? Working through the repressive myths of critical pedagogy. *Harvard Educational Review, 59*(3), 297–324.
Ellsworth, E. (1994). Representation, self-representation, and the meanings of difference: Questions for educators. In R. M. Martusewicz and W. M. Reynolds (Eds.), *Inside out: Contemporary critical perspectives in education* (pp. 99–108). New York: St. Martin's Press.
English, F. W. (2003). *The postmodern challenge to the theory and practice of educational administration*. Springfield, IL: Charles C Thomas Publisher.
Gardiner, M. (1992). *The dialogics of critique: M. M. Bakhtin & the theory of ideology*. London: Routledge.
Holquist, M. (1981). (Ed.) *The dialogic imagination: Four essays by M. M. Bakhtin*. Austin: University of Texas Press.
Larson, C. L., & Ovando, C. J. (2001). *The color of bureaucracy: The politics of equity in multicultural school communities*. Australia: Wadsworth.
Marshall, C. (Ed.) (2004). Special issue: Social justice challenges to educational administration. *Educational Administration Quarterly, 40*(1), 3–163.
Marshall, C., & McCarthy, M. (2002). School leadership reforms: Filtering social justice through dominant discourses. *The Journal of School Leadership, 12*(5), 480–502.
Merryfield, M. M. (2001). The paradoxes of teaching a multicultural education course online. *Journal of Teacher Education, 52*(4), 283–299.
Oliva, M. (1997). *Zones of influence and discourses of preference in North American higher education cooperation*. Unpublished doctoral dissertation, The University of Texas at Austin.
Oliva, M. (2000). Shifting landscapes/Shifting langue: Qualitative research from the in-between. *Qualitative Inquiry, 6*(1), 33–57.
Prawat, R. S., & Peterson, P. L. (1999). Social constructivist views of learning. In J. Murphy & K. Seashore Louis (Eds.), *Handbook of research on educational administration: A project of the American Educational Research Association* (pp. 203–226). San Francisco: Jossey-Bass.
Schoorman, D. (2002). Increasing critical multicultural understanding via technology: "Teachable moments" in a university school partnership project. *Journal of Teacher Education, 53*(4), 356–370.
Slattery, P., & Rapp, D. (2003). *Ethics and the foundations of education: Teaching convictions in a postmodern world*. Boston: Allyn and Bacon.
Sullivan, P. (2002). "It's easier to be yourself when you are invisible": Female college participant learners discuss their online classroom experiences. *Journal of Innovative Higher Education, 27*(2), 129–144.
Valian, V. (1998). *Why so slow*. Cambridge, MA: MIT Press.

Warschauer, M. (1996). Comparing face to face and electronic communication in the second-language classroom. *CALICO Journal, 13*(2), 7–26.
Warschauer, M. (1999). *Electronic literacies.* Mahwah, NJ: Lawrence Erlbaum.

Endnotes

[1]All participant learners are assigned a letter or number that denotes their remarks in the chat room. A graduate student technician randomly assigns the letters/numbers; the professor does not know which letter/number represents which student. The professor is in the chat room with participant learners, but only contributes to time tasks and clarify instructions.

[2]A primary component of this "zone of influence" is an individual's socialization and experience, both of which unavoidably shape how messages are received and interpreted. In a sense, such zones seemingly surround an individual as they move through life and act as a filter through which interaction exchanges move. What this means, ultimately, is that there are no pure messages and communications—none that are not mutually constructed within and between the sender and the receiver. For a more extensive illustration of this in cross-cultural experience and interaction, see Oliva (1997).

[3]The ideas and processes of ES are protected by patent and copyright. Because of the costs, complexity, and labor-intensive nature of ES, the University of Minnesota (primary provider of funds for the project to this point) and Brunner are working to develop and produce it for sharing with interested universities in low-cost, user-friendly packages.

This project is one of several related projects partially funded by a grant from the Ford Foundation to Leaders for Social Justice (LSJ), a group, initiated and led by Catherine Marshall (University of North Carolina), of educational administration professors committed to educational equity and social justice within the field and U.S. public schools.

[4]The terms *monologic* and *dialogic* come from the work of early 20th century Russian literary scholar Mikhail Bakhtin (see Gardiner, 1992, for a longer discussion). In his work, he distinguishes two kinds of communicative discourse in literature: that of epic, which is one-way, all-knowing, and autocratic, and the more equitable and unconstrained discourse of the novel, in which authority over communication is decentered in the polyvocal and multifaceted communication of multiple characters. His term for the first discursive orientation is *monologic*, and *dialogic* for the second. Similarly, communication exchanges that privilege the epistemic authority of the "leader" can be understood to be monologic power-laden communicative exchanges.

[5]The following is a brief recap of the ES process:

- Class meets in a chat room for the first three sessions. Participant learners have not met. Each student is represented in the chat room by a letter or number. All participant learners are asked to retain this anonymity for the duration of the class's time in the chat room. Participant learners are asked to work together in the chat room to solve a problem or complete a task.
- Following the first chat room class session, participant learners are directed to a Web page where they can view photos of the class, including their own photo. (However, each student except the viewer is represented by someone else—an actor hired to "stand in" for a student on a class Web page. A unique Web page is prepared for each student.)
- Following the second chat room class session, participant learners are individually directed to return to that Web page, where now they can view video clips of their "classmates" saying, "Hi, my name is _____, and I'm excited to be taking this class."
- Just before the third chat class session, participant learners are individually directed to return to that Web page, where now the photo of someone who is not them appears where their photo was. (Participant learners are asked to maintain anonymity/identitylessness for all three chat sessions, which means that they cannot discuss these developments with their classmates.)

- An hour prior to the end of the third chat room class session, participant learners are collectively directed to visit a Web page where photos of the actual classmates appear (with rollover images to the photos which had been their "placeholders"). Finally, participant learners are allowed to identify themselves and compare notes.

[6]Contingency leadership theorists such as Bolman and Deal (2003) argue that it is important for leaders to know about the variety of leadership approaches that exist, their own default style, and the value of matching a leadership style to the problem that must be solved. At its base, it is, like ES, about defamiliarizing leadership from uncritical a priori assumptions, identifying a repertoire of tools for more effective practice, and (through the use of cases) about taking learning from cognitive to experiential understanding.

[7]Student answers in this chapter were taken from EdPA 5323: Women in Leadership class, University of Minnesota, Fall 2002.

12

Releasing Emotion: Artmaking and Leadership for Social Justice

Laura Shapiro

"Art is a way of knowing what it is we actually believe."
—*Pat Allen, Art Therapist*

"The special virtue of art is that it engages not only the minds but the feelings and the will of the individual. Drama . . . is truer than history because it makes it so clear that life itself is a process of unending choices, to be or not to be, to do or not to do."
—*Grace Lee Boggs, Activist and Writer*

Chapter Overview

The work of educational leadership for social justice requires hard work, imagination, and courage. It is work that engages the heart, mind, and body in ways that are exhilarating, yet highly stressful and physically exhausting. So much needs to be accomplished to transform schools into compassionate and just learning communities. However, any one educational leader cannot and should not do it all. If educational leaders continue to work in isolation, repress their emotions, explode with frustration, and work until they are exhausted, they will suffer, and their effectiveness as leaders will be decreased.

One tired principal shared her experience: "The other (administrators) stay 'til 6, but I stay 'til 10. My son asked me, 'How many sick days do you have?' I replied, '236.' My son came back, 'Great! So we can sell them on your death bed?' " Her son's biting questions made her think more deeply about the dilemmas she faced as a principal. Certainly, she thought her hard work was essential; she spent long days challenging the oppressive ideologies and structures that permeated her school. Each day she labored to remedy such inequities as the overrepresentation of African American boys in special education or the lack of responsiveness of the central office to her requests for the meager resources allocated to her overcrowded school.

However, she was exhausted. Her son's questions concerning her work made her pause. She asked, "How do I deal with the stress? How do I find the emotional release, balance, and support that I need to do social justice work in schools? How do I achieve balance in my life? What are sources from which I can draw the courage, joy, and imagination that I need to continue the struggle?"

This chapter examines artmaking as a potentially powerful means by which educational leaders can uncover injustice in their schools, release emotions, and gain important insights into their work. Poetry, movement, storytelling, collage, mask making, and Theatre of the Oppressed are explored as media for self and group expression, inquiry, reflection, and problem solving. The chapter presents a rationale for linking emotion, leadership for social justice, and artmaking. It offers three case examples of how educational leaders use artmaking in their social justice work and implications for practice. The chapter also offers a number of artmaking activities.

A Rationale for Linking Emotion, Leadership for Social Justice, and Artmaking

The work of educational leadership for social justice is a highly emotional endeavor. It evokes a range of emotions—hurt, fear, joy, anxiety, frustration, elation, shock, and others. As an educational leader, perhaps you experience anger when you challenge a teacher on the racist comment made during a faculty meeting. You may feel frustration, and then great satisfaction, after working late at night with a contentious site-based committee to develop a just school discipline policy. You may be thrilled as your students testify before the school board in favor of funding for an after-school program, and then suffer great disappointment when the program is cut from the budget. You may feel lonely if you are the only administrator on your team who supports an in-service program to address homophobia in the school. How might leaders deal with these varied and intense emotions?

Background

With some exceptions, research in educational administration offers little insight and guidance for educational leaders into the role of emotions in their work. Beatty (2000) argues that the emotions have been marginalized and treated, if they are mentioned at all, as "little more that pesky interlopers, distracting us from higher, rational purposes" (p. 334). The expression of emotion is generally considered unprofessional. Beatty (2000) states:

> The emotions are political. The hierarchical relationship between reason and emotion has particular implications for life in organizations in that it is often played out as one of mutual exclusions. Power positions in the hierarchy are ritually reasserted through strict emotional control and suppression—the maintenance of exclusively and dominatingly rational appearance. The notion that, optimally, saner heads prevail and that sane is synonymous with unemotional is reenacted continually. School cultures support the notion that the ideal "professional" demeanor is primarily rational and carefully controlled emotionally. (pp. 334–335).

Similarly, noted writer and teacher bell hooks addresses the pervasively repressive and distorted attitudes about emotion in the realm of education and intellectual life. She notes:

> The restrictive, repressive [school] ritual insists that emotional responses have no place. Whenever emotional response erupts, many of us believe our academic purpose has been diminished. To me this is really a distorted notion of intellectual practice since the underlying assumption is that to be truly intellectual we must be cut off from our emotions. (hooks, 1994, p. 155)

Many women in educational leadership have expressed the stress of having to repress and control their emotions. They may feel that they need to abandon emotional expression as a way of relating in order to fit into a predominantly male model of leadership in which emotions are undervalued or dismissed. Women administrators in Hackney and Runnestrand's (2003) study reported a sense of personal loss and of missing their authentic selves as a result of having to conform to the male structure and model of leadership and organization:

> For the sake of fulfilling the mission of the institution, these women had made huge personal sacrifices . . . And while many of these women would have been described as successful, many of these women were emotionally exhausted . . . and said that their souls had been damaged. (p. 9)

This is an enormous price to pay.

Negative views of emotion are reflected in the larger sociopolitical school culture. Just as educational leaders are often required to keep a lid on their own emotions, they also are pressured to keep things under control and not to open a can of worms. Conceptions and practices of leadership that idealize rationality, control, and harmony tend to favor dominant groups (White, male, middle and upper class) in schools. Voices of marginalized groups are often discounted as being angry and as the source of the school's problems rather than as an expression of discontent that needs to be heard. Disenfranchised groups are often accused of being disruptive, and their voices are systematically squelched via calls for strict discipline.

Education leadership scholars Larson and Ovando (2001) critique this "taming" role of administrators when they cite Sergiovanni's suggestion that effective educators often have to "domesticate the wild circles" in schools. They argue:

> The word *domesticate* means to tame, break or subdue. No doubt, there are "wild circles" of emotion in schools that need to be subdued; however when we assume that the system is right, without any examination . . . these "wild circles" are often the children and families who have historically benefited least in the educational systems that exist to serve them. (Larson and Ovando, 2001, p. 141)

Larson and Ovando suggest that closed patriarchal bureaucratic systems of control have the impact of shutting down intense emotion and critical inquiry into practices that privilege White middle-class populations. They argue that perhaps the "wild circles" of emotions could "potentially educate and improve a socially, culturally, and institutionally biased system" (p. 141). Emotion and conflict are inevitable parts of school life and the job of educational leadership and are essential to the process of opening up space for discussion and change in power relationships. Unjust power relations must be destabilized for genuine transformation to occur, and this will most likely involve strong expressions of emotion. hooks (1994) challenges repressive notions of harmony in schools when she argues that "exposing certain truths and biases . . . often creates chaos and confusion and challenges the idea that . . . [schools] should always be . . . harmonious place" (p. 30).

In summary, a dualistic and hierarchical view of emotion and reason denies important natural aspects of human experiences—dimensions that are needed if our schools are to be truly democratic and healthy places. Rather than being a "negative" in educational leadership, something to suppress and eliminate from leadership and school life, the emotions of leaders and all members of the school community are essential for creating just school communities. As hooks (1994) suggests, leaders need their "full body and soul" (p. 155).

Artmaking as a Tool

Artmaking is a powerful means by which educational leaders can express emotion and gain insight into their social justice work in schools. Artmaking can facilitate a personal, authentic engagement with social justice issues and provide opportunities for nonlinguistic meaning-making, which opens up emotions and ideas that cannot easily be accessed in other ways. Artmaking can provide expression of subjective experiences that are important in our lives as leaders.

But what is *artmaking*? Arts educator Booth (1997) reminds us that the word *art* is from the Greek and is a verb that means "to put things together." It is not a product but a process (Booth, 1997, p. 5). Booth articulates what he calls the "tools" of the art process as being "metaphor, improvisation, following impulses, making things that hold personal meaning" (Booth, 1997, p. 6). Artmaking can engage a sense of play, avoiding what Booth calls the binary thinking of right versus wrong, with its "focuses on what is more effective and less effective . . . and is a process of recognizing that the world is filled with paradox. . . . Paradox frustrates logic and catapults us into analogies, creating the possibility of new and deeper connections" (Booth, 1997, p. 123). Pat Allen (1995), an educator and art therapist, states, "Making images is a way of breaking boundaries, loosening outworn ideas, and making way for new. It is a form of practice through which, like any spiritual discipline, knowledge of ourselves can ripen into wisdom" (p. x).

Contrary to dominant cultural teachings, artmaking is not the exclusive domain of a talented elite of artists. Scholars suggest that artmaking has a biological origin and plays a significant role in other societies and is, in essence, our universal birthright. Art, according to ethnobiologist Dissanayake (1995), is "physically, sensually and emotionally satisfying and pleasurable to humans and a way that people can make their individual and collective lives more significant" (p. 225). Those who internalize the elitist and disenfranchising notions about artmaking may end up discounting the potential of its use in their development as educational leaders.

Greene (1995) suggests that artmaking can help educational leaders to recover "their imaginations and it may be the recovery of the imagination that lessens the social paralysis we see around us and restores the sense that something can be done in the name of what is decent and humane" (p. 35). She views engagement with the arts as potentially contributing to the creation of alternative structures and relationships in schools that challenge oppressive structuralist perspectives and practices. She proposes that the release of the imaginative capacity is a "prerequisite to being able to break with what is supposedly fixed and finished, objective and to see beyond what the imaginer has called normal or 'common sense' and to carve out new orders of experience" (p. 19).

Artmaking can bring forth the passions that are important to leadership for social justice. Spehler and Slattery (1999) suggest that the arts are vital in leadership for social justice work in schools because of their ability to "develop voice, sustain passion and evoke response" (p. 3). They argue, "It is this passion that gives us the energy to find expression for our vision" (p. 2). Educational leaders can take inspirations from curriculum theorist Barone's (2000) call to create communities of what he calls "strong poets" who

> . . . refuse to accept as useful the description of her life written by others. Instead, the strong poet is a strong storyteller, continuously revising her life story

in the light of her own experience and imagination. . . . She is necessarily a social being and a moral agent, a responsible citizen in a shared community. . . . (pp. 125–126)

The idea of building communities of strong poets can serve as a powerful vision of educational leadership for social justice. Artmaking can be a means by which educational leaders and all members of their school communities can emerge as strong poets.

Three Case Examples

The following are descriptions of how three educational leaders use artmaking as a means of expressing their emotions and gaining insight into their leadership for social justice practice. They participated in artmaking activities during retreats for women in educational leadership.[1]

From Rage to Empowerment

Artmaking can redirect rage. Susan is a dean of students in an urban high school and has held the position for three years. She is an African American woman in her early 30s and was a math teacher before she became dean. She takes an African dance class each Saturday and uses movement, "her comfort zone," to release her stress. In addition to movement, during the artmaking workshops she also ventured into art media that were relatively new for her: collage and Theatre of the Oppressed.

Through her artmaking, Susan was able to uncover her feelings about the racism and classism that she experienced and observed in her school. She was able to release her anger about the ways discussions about racism were systematically being avoided in her school. She pointed to the repressive and controlling culture in her school and its frantic pace as sources of her stress and exhaustion. She stated:

> Not everyone is ready to have those conversations (about race). Part of it is just the tone of the school . . . the school is always in crisis . . . so many demands from the parents and the superintendent . . . we don't always have time to talk about the issues that we need to talk about like issues of oppression. On some level it is not safe to have those conversations . . . I really think that the principal is very uncomfortable with these kinds of discussions and therefore it is just not something that is supported. . . . and it spreads out all the way through the school.

Susan began to get in touch with her exhaustion and anger around the repression in her school through an authentic movement exercise. According to Geissinger (2003), authentic movement is a "deceptively simple form of self-directed movement. It is usually done with eyes closed and in the presence of at least one witness. The mover follows inner impulses to move freely and the witness watches and tracks inner responses to the mover with the intention of not judging, but working on self-awareness" (p. 1). As Susan engaged in the authentic movement exercise, she began to breathe more slowly, sway, and relax. Then she began to cry. Later she said that the movement helped her realize how exhausted she was from overwork and emotional stress.

Following the authentic movement exercise, Susan created a collage to express her exhaustion and sense of oppression. She made an image of her daily subway ride to school and back. In her collage, she cut out a subway map and used sticky notes and memo pads, the tools of her daily work life, to list demands screaming to her at the end of her long ride to school. The notes read "PTA," "418 absences," "Where are all the lunch forms?" "Schedules," "50 copies," and "Regents." She was in tears as she told the group that there were many days she did not see daylight because she was leaving home early and returning home late at night (see moon sliver on upper-left corner of Figure 12.1).

Susan's artmaking helped her to realize how sexism and racism were contributing to her exhaustion. She expressed her rage about not only being asked to take on more work than the male administrators, but also more than the

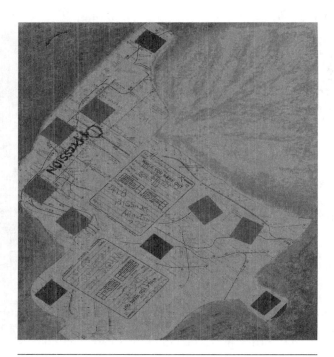

FIGURE 12.1 *Susan's Visual Journal Page Showing her Daily Subway Journey to School*

White women administrators. As someone concerned about social justice in her school, she was particularly vulnerable to taking on more than her share of work for the good of the kids. She decided to confront her supervisor with her feelings and the injustice that she felt.

Through the artmaking exercises, she realized how time was being used as a tool of oppression for her and some of the families in her school community. Susan examined how schools' use of rigid time schedules limits parents' access to the schools. She reflected:

> Time can be used as a power piece. How unfair it is ... the demands on students' time outside of school. What are we putting on families? What are we doing that is not pulling them up but pushing them down ... when we insist that they have to come to school at 8:30 in the morning when coming in may cause them to lose their jobs? ... I had a situation today where my student was suspended. He had served his (suspension) time but he was going to have extended time and days because his mother couldn't take time off until Monday. The child is going to lose out on two additional days of instruction because his mother doesn't have the time.... I spent time thinking about it during the retreats because it is something that was personally frustrating me and in this retreat I began to recognize it and label it and call it oppression.

The impact of artmaking for Susan was quite profound. She reflected,

> The artmaking really helping me express my own anger, frustration and rage. It allows me to just simply speak without being angry. But I can be passionate but not angry about it ... I can refer back to a healing experience, get out the rage and I can simply be an activist and advocate without shutting down people with my anger.

Susan seemed to experience what artist Smith Siegel describes as the transformative power of artmaking: "Not only do the arts provide a vehicle for validating human uniqueness and affirming life, but they offer an important opportunity for expressing and transforming a whole range of human feeling, including anger and aggression" (Siegel, quoted in Rogers, 1993, p. 237). Susan's transformation process was not linear but spiraling, moving from raw expression of feeling to analysis to feeling again to vision to strategy and back to feeling again.

Artmaking was a unique way for Susan to express her emotions and communicate with others about her leadership. She stated,

> With artmaking you can go deeper into yourself. It just means that I have something to say and I have something to do. Part of what I say and do is around ending, not even just ending, but bringing awareness of the ways oppression is played out in the school system. I didn't always feel like I had the words or the power or the ability ... to really do something about it.... I feel empowered ... I have the tools to confront oppression. It is just a blessing.

Inspired by her own artmaking experience, Susan created a space in her office for artmaking so that her students could use the materials to help them express their feelings and concerns.

Releasing Capacity and Courage

Can artmaking buttress one's courage? Lorraine, a Euro-American woman in her mid 50s, serves as a principal of an elementary regional magnet school and has served in that capacity for five years. Through her collage and Theatre of the Oppressed poetry work, she found more courage to stand up for her convictions.

In her collages and drawings, Lorraine depicted the forces impacting her school. She represented the children in her school with hands being pushed down by arrows that read, "lack of resources, testing, top down decisions, racism, accountability, mandates, and paper work" (Figure 12.2). In her collage (Figure 12.3), she expressed urgency about working toward social justice in her school by using the image of a clock running out of time. She exclaimed, "These children are only in third grade once!" Incorporated into her image is the question, "How much longer must we wait?"

Through artmaking, Lorraine's view of herself as an educational leader was reconfirmed. She reflected,

> I have always known that I have had the capacity to do this but it gave me more courage. It gave me energy to do it, more courage to do it and more impetus to do it. I have found a new energy and a new commitment around social justice issues; they weren't on the front burner. I made sure that they were on the front burner. . . .

FIGURE 12.2 *Lorraine's "Children's Hands" Drawing*

FIGURE 12.3 *Lorraine's "Time" Collage*

She used her renewed energy and vision to support a theater program in her school that addresses issues of homophobia:

> I had to have an entire conversation with a parent today because her child's third grade class is doing something called "Ode to Parents," which talks about two-mom families. I had to be very forthright with why it is very important to have these kinds of conversations and learning about this in school, I never would have had the courage to do that without this artmaking retreat.

In her leadership practice, Lorraine had been asking herself and members of her school community, "How can we build trust in a diverse community and become culturally responsive?" For Lorraine, the visual artmaking was a different and very powerful way for her to examine her leadership and build community. She reflected, "All we do is talk, talk, talk! It is time to use alternative methods to build community . . . to trust enough so that you can begin to approach these difficult issues."

She saw poetry as another way for staff, parents, and students to examine this question. One of the artmaking activities that was especially moving for Lorraine during the retreats was an "I Am From" poetry exercise, which is adapted from an exercise developed by the late actor Rebecca Rice. In the exercise, the author repeats the phrase, "I Am From," creating verbal images from her life from the perspective of oppression, pride, and privilege (see box on pp. 243–244).

Lorraine was moved by the process of writing and hearing the poems written by other school administrators and brought the exercise to her school:

> I used the "I Am From" poems as a way of opening the school year, and everybody sharing those poems in a small group was just a totally different way to get into the school year. Over the years, we have talked about how to confront social justice issues as a faculty in the past. What we realized was the place where we needed to start had to be personal experience stories. How do you get at the personal? The "I Am From" poems were amazing at being able to do that. I have begun to think of ways for my faculty to connect by collectively doing art together. . . . There are lots of walls and art is a way of redefining the power balance. At the faculty level there are walls between ethnicity and rungs of the hierarchy. . . . We wrote "I Am From" poems at a faculty meeting. The "I Am From" poem moved people to tears and moved people to do one on their own with students. The "I Am From" poems were then used in classrooms with children in the same way.

Theatre of the Oppressed, is a "system of physical exercises, aesthetic games, image techniques, and special improvisations whose goal is to safeguard, develop, and reshape this human vocation, by turning the practice of theatre into an effective tool for the comprehension of social and personal problems and the search for solutions" (Boal, 1995, p.184).

The following are excerpts from Lorraine, Susan, and Maria's "I Am From" poems.

Lorraine's "I Am From" Poem

I am from shul, on on bread and challah
   Foreign tongues not meant for my ears

I am from immigrants, guarded secrets
   Hushed in Yiddish

I am from long walks with grandpa
   Whose alias was Comrade Peters
   Who made French fries in the basements
   And set fire to his beliefs

I am from solitude and difference
   Watching sisters from a room down the hall
   Rushing through dinner, having nothing to say

I am from the 60s when delta's and sigma's
   Turned to S D's and S's, and the struggles turned outward

. . .

I am from struggle, to include all the voices
   To recognize children, their gifted and their talents
   To create safe harbors

I am from the fiber, the threads that I cherish
   Knitted together, winding the ball from
   My love's gentle notions
   Creating a rhythm that's been woven together

I am from a life, complex and compelling
   Where the values of childhood have returned full circle
   No longer a secret as the same battles rage.

Susan's "I Am From" Poem

I am From . . .
The backs of my ancestors
From Africa into Slavery
Enslaved on the plantation
Cotton picking
I am from freedom or so called freedom that is
Jim Crow, lynching, separate but not equal
White only
Water fountains, movie theaters,
Libraries, schools.

. . .

I am from equal but not quite equal,
Oppressed, working hard, yet making less
Affirmative Action

(continued)

Reparations and nothin less
I am from being Black.
I am from cornbread and collard greens
Fried chicken and string beans
Sundays after church
I am from a
House, car, 2.5 children and a dog
My parents achieved their dreams, they are not black, they are middle class
I am from
Looking perfect on the outside
Chaos and confusion on the inside
Nothing is really what it seems.

. . .

Finally
I am from He, who command light
His Son, the way, the truth, the Christ
I am from God.

Maria's "I Am From" Poem
I came from Gilberto Pando Polio
My father
He came from Mar de la lug
A tall slender woman with pale white skin and light blue eyes and
Jose the horse whisperer from Ojnagera al San Angelo and Lubbuck
and Rostia
They came from Texas
Before it was American, Mexican, a Spanish place.
I came from Maria Cisneros Cosia,
My mother
She came from Maria de los Angeles
A petite native woman with skin the color of cinnamon jet black eyes
and from Benito, a charro whose tall dark skinned ancestors rode
Arabian horses into Toledo (not Toledo).
I came from people who look for me
Who sing for me and dance for me
Who cry with joy or sorrow and scream with anger and pain and celebrate
And who still, still still come together
To celebrate that Luke and Mercedes and Desire and Joseph are from us all.

As a consequence of her Theatre of the Oppressed work, Lorraine also was inspired to bring theater into her school as a way to engage the school community in discussions of social justice:

> Theatre of the Oppressed helped me put a face not only on the oppression but the day-to-day occurrence of how power plays itself out. I look at my own leadership to see if I am an oppressor. I work hard at social justice. You know who I am and what I am about . . . People are still scared of me and often are silent because of my position. I work very hard to eradicate hierarchy, but everyone has been raised in that kind of paradigm and it is hard to make that shift.

. . . Once we entered the realm of theater, it became a safer place to deal, a venue to grapple with some of the things that we have been avoiding confronting.

For Lorraine, artmaking was a different and powerful way for her to examine her leadership.

Reaffirming Memories and Getting Personal

Storytelling can center one's values. Maria is the director of guidance for a large urban high school. She is a Mexican American woman, has a doctorate, and has worked as a counselor and administrator in a medical school. Maria found writing and sharing stories and mask making to be valuable tools for helping her to grapple with her relatively new position in a high school.

Writing about her own experiences in school as a child helped her deepen her insight into her work as director of guidance with many newly arrived immigrants. She wrote a short story about her memory of being told as a child in school that Spanish could not be spoken from the time she left the school bus to when she got on at the end of the day: "My mother thought that was ludicrous. She knew that speaking many languages could only enhance my knowledge and experience. So she insisted that we speak only Spanish from the time we got off the bus to when we got on in the morning." Maria's writing reconfirmed the importance of her advocacy work with immigrant students and their families.

Reflecting on her experience of writing and sharing stories with other administrators, she commented,

> We were telling our stories . . . about things that touched personal experiences in a way . . . that lecture or reading a book or talking about it, can't do. We listened to each others' stories. . . . So often in administration we stay very academic. We rarely get personal. Racism, sexism are personal . . . If I am dealing in art, if I am writing, if I am making poetry, if I am drumming, if my hands are dirty, hey, I think it is easier to be personal, both for leaders and for students if you are making art. . . . It has got to become personal.

Through her artmaking, Maria reaffirmed how important getting personal is to her practice of educational leadership for social justice. She wondered,

> One of my impressions when I first came to (my school district) was that the teachers match an increasingly smaller and smaller number . . . of students in the school I have one counselor who knows every student and every student's mother and grandmother, uncles, and the businesses they own (of the majority students). He happened to be very good. But, he doesn't know the names of any of the mothers of Vietnamese students. Think about that. Could he possibly be as effective when he doesn't know anyone's mother or brother or uncle or aunt?

Maria invited the counselors in the guidance department to write about a time they had made a difference in their students' lives: "I want to let staff and students know they can make art and tell their stories. It is important to dignify artmaking as a form of communication in school."

Mask making was also quite powerful for Maria. She described her mask as follows:

> I worked very hard to make (the eye) be only one sheet of paper. I wanted to make it very thin. I chose to leave a film over one eye. When you hold the mask up before your eyes, you see light, motion. The paper is brown, like me. I have not noticed mask making very much before. I have always been intrigued by it. I want to do it more. The idea of handling a face, of seeing faces, looking at faces, looking at masks. We do that every day; we wear masks every single day. I am noticing faces, what's in them more . . . .

A Different Kind of Professional Development

This type of development differs from other models of educational leadership development, which, as Mary, an elementary principal, stated, "tell you the way things should be," or as Beth, a middle school principal, commented, "are a snooze, haven't been relevant . . . and did not appeal to my values, much less my emotions." An arts-based professional development model embraces the "data" of the educational leaders' qualitative inquiry as important and valid in the process of leadership development.

Summary

Using various art media, these three educational leaders utilized artmaking to express their feelings, uncover social injustice, and gain insight into their practice. Artmaking can challenge notions of educational leadership that only hold quantitative descriptions of school life to be valuable. As arts-based educational researchers Diamond and Mullen (1999) argue, "retelling and expressing in our own words (and images) means learning to speak on our own behalf and no longer relying on authority and forms of others" (p. 58). Artmaking accelerated the intensity and pace of the participants' emotional connection with and intellectual understanding of the social justice issues that were being addressed. Through the artmaking, the women were able to integrate mind, body, and spirit in such a way that it seemed to help them develop their courage to act in the face of injustice. They were able to tap into their whole selves, "connecting the emotional heart, sensual body and ordering mind" (Heck, 1998, p. 23). Rather than their artistic selves continuing to be separate from their administrator selves, the women were beginning to see how they might become better integrated, and therefore empower themselves as leaders for social justice.

Implications for Practice

There are many ways to integrate artmaking into educational leadership practice for social justice. Leaders are urged to use the strategies described here, adapt them, and/or create their own.

Incorporating Artmaking into Leadership Development

Conference sessions at University Council for Educational Administration (UCEA), Association for Supervision and Curriculum Development (ASCD), and American Association of School Administrators (AASA); professional development sessions; and university courses should use artmaking as a tool to examine leadership for social justice. A variety of group compositions—for example, leadership groups for men and women, women of color, or gay and lesbian people—can provide different types of learning and support through artmaking. Artmaking needs to be validated as an important form of expression and inquiry in these venues.

Leaders can keep a visual journal, using collage, drawing, and newspaper images, as a way to document and process their social justice work in schools. These visual journals may be shared with others and used as a basis for dialogue.

Where can people working in the field of educational leadership find the time for artmaking? We need to critically examine the structure of the job of educational leaders so that it allows time for artmaking. Institutions that require leaders to produce more, work faster, and mass produce standardized outcomes need to be transformed in order to enable the potential of artmaking around social justice issues to be fully realized.

Conferences, journals, professional educational leadership organizations, and in-service and preservice educational leadership programs need more than intellectual experiences to engage participants in the work of social justice. Multiple forms of representation of the lives and visions of educational leaders that challenge patriarchal notions of leaderships and schooling are needed.

Making Art a Tool for Communitywide Engagement

Educational leaders can create spaces for all members of their school communities, including teachers, parents, and students, to tell their own stories. For example, artmaking activities, such as the ones described in this chapter, can be incorporated into faculty meetings, study groups, and professional development programs.

Using Art to Impact Policy

Sharing the many perspectives of members of school communities with policy makers can be very powerful. Parents, students, teachers, and administrators can present their experiences of social injustice through their own stories, poems, and images. In addition to the "numbers," artwork can present the human face of oppression and can be helpful in making a case for just policies.

Discussion Questions and Activities _____

1. Write your own "I Am From" poem. What connections do you see between the ideas in your poem and your leadership for social justice practice? How might

you use the "I Am From" poem in your school community? As you listen to others' "I Am From" poems, what insights do you have about the significance of the different "locations" that leaders bring to their schools?

2. The following is based on an activity created by the poet Janine Pommy Vega. Create a newspaper poem as a way to critically analyze and respond to an issue impacting education. Choose an article from a newspaper that relates to education that you feel strongly about. Write a poem that responds to the article, talks back to the article, or is written from the imagined perspective of a person in the article. Words and phrases in the poem can be either lifted directly from the news article or integrated with your own words. Submit the poem as an op-ed piece to your local newspaper.

   You may also consider the following variations on this activity:

   a. Rewrite want ads for teachers or educational administrators to reflect your vision of your leadership.
   b. Create a visual journal page using collage and writing as an emotional response to a newspaper article concerning an issue that you are passionate about.

3. Use found objects and objects from nature to create a "touchstone" (DeCiantis, 1996) for your desk that will remind you of the power and values you bring to your leadership for social justice.

4. Create a "Readers' Theater" and/or video that portrays your passions and frustrations over dilemma-laden social justice issues. Readers' Theater involves reading from a script during a performance. Unlike traditional theater, actors do not memorize their scripts and rely on oral expression to convey meaning. Readers' Theater is a theater of the imagination because it does not involve props, costumes, or sets. The audience is highly engaged because they need to imagine what is traditionally made more explicit in conventional theater.

   Create a script from your own experiences and from interviews from diverse members of your school community. Find funding to support a traveling show to use it to engage your expanded community in expressing these feelings and perspectives.

5. Imagine that you want to attend one of the professional development retreats or workshops listed in the endnotes. Write a mock or real memo to the appropriate person in your school district who is in charge of approving such requests. Develop a reasoned and passionate rationale as to why the district should grant your request. Make your case by drawing on one or more of the suggested readings, your professional development goals, and your district's goals.

Annotated Readings

Educational leaders can draw on research and writing from several fields to enhance their understanding of the concepts and methods discussed in this chapter. Highlighted here are works from the fields of arts-based qualitative educational research, philosophy, art education, art therapy, and popular theater.

   A number of researchers and educators have written about the value arts-based educational inquiry as a means of furthering social justice. Thomas Barone's (2000) essays, compiled in *Aesthetics, Politics, and Educational Inquiry: Essays and Examples*, present his ideas about how we might "break the mold" of American schooling in order to make schools more just and humane places. Barone argues for qualitative inquiry in the field of education that serves the "steady recovery of the human voice" (xii) through critical narrative storytelling. A related reading is Patrick Diamond and Carol Mullen's (1999) *The Postmodern Educator: Arts-based Inquiries and Teacher Development*, which provides a theoretical overview of arts-based inquiry. The book presents numerous examples of arts-based exercises that the authors use in college classrooms for preservice teachers. These activities can be adapted for educational leaders and all members of school communities.

In *Releasing the Imagination: Essays on Educations, the Arts, and Social Change*, noted philosopher Maxine Greene (1995) calls for approaches to education that involve the arts as a way to release the imagination. She argues that such imaginative thinking is essential to creation of a true democracy. She connects imagination to empathy and speaks openly about oppression: "Where people cannot name alternatives or imagine a better state of being they are likely to remain anchored or submerged" (p. 52). Her writing is quite eloquent and deserves to be quoted generously.

Several resources from the fields of art education and art therapy offer perspectives and strategies that can be adapted by educational leaders. Elliot Eisner (2002), a leading scholar in the field of art education, presents his rationale for arts education in our K–12 schools in *The Arts and the Creation of Mind*. He outlines the value of arts education, including its potential to transform consciousness, enlarge the imagination, expand perception, and develop problem-solving abilities. Another strong advocate for arts learning is Eric Booth. In his quite readable book, *The Everyday Work of Art* (1999), he explores ways in which all people can tap into their natural artistic skills and dispositions and apply them to their everyday lives. The book challenges elite notions of art, artists, and artmaking and offers further rationale for engagement with artmaking by educational leaders and members of school communities.

In *The Creative Connection: Expressive Arts as Healing*, Natalie Rogers (1993) writes from the perspective of an art therapist and artist. The beautifully illustrated book gives insights into the healing power of artmaking. Specific artmaking ideas are described, and she concludes the book with a chapter on artmaking as a path to cross-cultural understanding and social consciousness.

Another important resource is Augusto Boal's (1992) *Games for Actors and Non-Actors*. This comprehensive work details Boal's Theatre of the Oppressed games and exercises. Boal's work is philosophically aligned with his late colleague Paulo Freire's work in popular education and critical pedagogy. The games and exercises described by Boal can be adapted for class and workshops for educational leaders. Boal and his followers give training workshops throughout the world on this extraordinary methodology.

References

Allen, P. B. (1995). *Art as a way of knowing: A Guide to self-knowledge and spiritual fulfillment through creativity.* Boston: Shambhala.

Barone, T. (2000). *Aesthetics, politics, and educational inquiry: Essays and examples.* New York: Peter Lang.

Beatty, B. (2000). The emotions of educational leadership. *International Journal of Leadership in Education, 3*(4), 331–357.

Boal, A. (1995). *The rainbow of desire: The Boal method of theatre and therapy* (A. Jackson, Trans.). London: Routledge.

Boggs, G. L. (2003). These are times that try our souls. Plenary address at the National Exchange on Art and Civic Dialogue, October 9–12, Flint, MI, p. 3.

Booth, E. (1997). *The everyday work of art: How artistic experience can transform your life.* Sourcebooks.

Burnham, L. F., & Durland, S. (1998). *The citizen artist: Twenty years of art in the public arena* (First ed. Vol. 1). New York: Critical Press.

Coger, L., & White, M. (1982). *Readers' Theatre handbook: A dramatic approach to literature* (3rd ed.). Glenview, IL: Scott, Foresman Company.

DeCiantis, C. (1996). What does drawing my hand have to do with leadership? A look at the process of leaders becoming artists. *Journal of Aesthetic Education, 30*(4), 87–97.

Dissanayake, E. (1995). *Homo aestheticus: Where art comes from and why.* Seattle: University of Washington Press.

Eisner, E. (1981). On the difference between scientific and artistic approaches to qualitative research. *Educational Researcher, 10*(4), 5–9.

Geissinger, A., Webb, J., & Clements, P. S. (2003). *What is authentic movement?* Retrieved October 8, 2003, from www.movingjournal.org

Greene, M. (1995). *Releasing the imagination: Essays on educations, the arts, and social change.* San Francisco: Jossey-Bass.

Hackney, C., & Runnestrand, D. (2003). Struggling for authentic human synergy and a robust democratic culture: The wellspring community for women. Retrieved December 15, 2004 from *http://advancingwomen.com/awl/spring2003/HACKNE~1.HTML*

Heck, M. (1998). Artmaking and aesthetic inquiry: Critical connections among centering, social transformation, and pedagogy. *Journal of Critical Pedagogy, 2*, 1.

hooks, b. (1994). *Teaching to transgress.* New York: Routledge.

Larson, C., & Ovando, C. (2001). *The color of bureaucracy: The politics of equity in multicultural school communities.* New York: Wadsworth.

London, P. (1989). *No more second-hand art: Awakening the artist within.* Boston: Shambhala.

Rogers, N. (1993). *The creative connection: Expressive arts as healing.* Palo Alto: Science and Behavior Books.

Shapiro, L. (2004). *Disrupting what is going on: Women educational leaders make art together to transform themselves and their schools.* Unpublished Ph.D., Union Institute and University, Cincinnati, OH.

Shapiro, L. (2004). Women educational leaders transform themselves and their schools through artmaking. *Journal of Democracy and Education, 15*(3–4), 24–26.

Spehler, M. R., & Slattery, P. (1999). Voices of imagination: The artist as prophet in the process of social change. *International Journal of Leadership in Education, 2*(1), 1–12.

Endnotes

[1]Several organizations offer opportunities for educational leaders to release their emotions and examine social justice issues. For example, Artworks (http://artworksgroup.com) offers retreats and workshops that use artmaking as a tool for expressing emotion, for uncovering social injustice, and for action planning. Dr. Ysaye Barnwell (http://ymbarnwell.com), of Sweet Honey in the Rock, offers "Building a Vocal Community" workshops. Americans for the Arts (http://americansforthearts.org) has instituted the "Animating Democracy Initiative." The project is designed to develop civic dialogue through the arts and has inspired "convergences" of artists, educator and activists around the county. Community Arts Network (http://communityarts.net) often lists workshops and retreats that have a social justice focus. Augusto Boal, originator of Theatre of the Oppressed, comes regularly to the United States to offer workshops. For a listing of workshops and programs in the United States and internationally visit www.toplab.org.

13

Equity Audits: A Practical Leadership Tool for Developing Equitable and Excellent Schools

Linda Skrla

James Joseph Scheurich

Juanita Garcia

Glenn Nolly

Introduction

The No Child Left Behind Act of 2001 (NCLB) was signed into law on January 8, 2002, putting into motion what could be described as the most sweeping reform of U.S. federal education policy since the 1960s. At the center of this legislation is a *potentially* revolutionary premise—the explicit, direct commitment of the federal government to eliminating the achievement gaps that have long existed between the academic success of White and middle- and upper-income children and that of children of color and children from low income homes. However, given the terrible racial and class histories of this country and the deeply rooted inequality and injustice that continue to exist in the public educational system (e.g., see Ladson-Billings, 1997; Valenzuela, 1999), there is, not surprisingly, strong suspicion among many—scholars, policymakers, community activists, and practitioners alike—that this potential may be rhetorical at best or a sham at worst (Elmore, 2002;

Wilson & Segall, 2003). Nonetheless, this legislation has become law, and its implementation provisions will hold schools, districts, and states accountable for reducing the race and class differences in the academic success of their students.

Despite, then, the numerous critiques of this federal legislation,[1] thousands of schools and districts are already struggling, in many, many different ways, to implement its provisions and to reduce achievement gaps, as is evident from the content of the articles in each new issue of *Education Week*. Accordingly, as we have learned from studies of the implementation of earlier generations of accountability policy and from states, such as Texas, that have accountability systems similar to that required by NCLB, equally strong potential exists for both positive and negative effects of such policy on educational equity (Cohen & Hill, 2001; Keating, 2000). In fact, it would not be very speculative, given the complexity of the system and the number of individual sites, to predict that in virtually every state, district, and school, there will be *both* positive and negative equity effects associated with the implementation of NCLB.

Furthermore, we also know well that the key to positively appropriating the equity potential of such policy mandates often lies in the specific contextual responses of school leaders and the particular uses to which they put the achievement data derived from accountability systems (Donmoyer & Garcia Wagstaff, 1990; Hall, 2002; Nolly, 1997; Skrla & Scheurich, 2001). As Rorrer (2003) explained about the importance of leadership in shaping accountability implementation to facilitate improved equity:

> District leaders . . . can be characterized as "street-level bureaucrats" (Cohen & Hill, 2000; Lipsky, 1980) because of their significant role in filtering and implementing accountability policies. These local actors serve as a crucial link between policy intent and policy outcomes. (p. 256)

The work of school leaders, then, is vital in linking accountability policy intent to equity outcomes in local contexts, and these leaders need avenues of influence (Hallinger & Heck, 1998), strategies, and tools with which to successfully accomplish such work (see also Skrla, 2003). The purpose of this chapter, therefore, is to increase the likelihood of equity-positive leadership responses within the context of increasingly high-stakes accountability policy systems by proposing a new tool, a reconceptualized form of *equity audits*,[2] for school leaders to use in their equity-focused work. Thus, we begin with a brief discussion of the current accountability context in which this equity tool has been designed to operate. This is followed by a history of the broader concept of equity auditing from which our specific conception of equity audits is derived. We then outline the components of equity audits; discuss possible uses, including some we have implemented; and make some concluding comments.

Equity and Accountability

The mechanisms by which the framers of NCLB propose to accomplish the closing of historic achievement gaps rely heavily on increased accountability:

> The NCLB Act will strengthen Title I accountability by requiring States to implement statewide accountability systems covering all public schools and students. These systems must be based on challenging State standards in reading and mathematics, annual testing for all students in grades 3–8, and annual statewide progress objectives ensuring that all groups of students reach proficiency within 12 years. Assessment results and State progress objectives must be broken out by poverty, race, ethnicity, disability, and limited English proficiency to ensure that no group is left behind. School districts and schools that fail to make adequate yearly progress (AYP) toward statewide proficiency goals will, over time, be subject to improvement, corrective action, and restructuring measures aimed at getting them back on course to meet State standards. (U.S. Department of Education, 2002, ¶4)

As described in the NCLB executive summary, required development of state standards, annual testing, disaggregation of data, and adequate yearly progress (AYP in the new NCLB lingo) will force all states to follow the same path that states such as Texas, North Carolina, Virginia, and others have been following for the past 10 years. These are among the states most often cited as exemplars of progress in closing historic achievement gaps, though the very nature of this progress has been strongly contested by many respected scholars and educators (e.g., Anderson, 2001; Haney, 2001; Klein, 2001; Trueba, 2001; Valencia et al., 2001). Nonetheless, despite these serious and extensive critiques (see Elmore, 2002, for a useful summary of the issues), the U.S. Department of Education's requirement that states must use an accountability policy that is directly focused on the disaggregation of student scores by race, class, disability, and language and on a constant decrease over time in achievement gaps as a vehicle to increase educational equity is already being rapidly operationalized in every state.

Furthermore, as we have argued in other venues, the debate about the equity effects of accountability policies has tended to be reductively polarized into two camps, with each side simplistically claiming that the effects of accountability policy on educational equity are either primarily good or primarily bad (Scheurich et al., 2000; Skrla, 2001). In response to this reductive polarization and simplification, we have repeatedly argued that the relationships between accountability and equity are definitely not as simplistic as often portrayed, but are extremely complex, dynamic (changing constantly due to frequent changes in state policies in addition to local mediation through interpretation and implementation), and confusingly interactive with other policy initiatives. We have also pointed out that there is considerable empirical research documenting the whole range of positive to negative effects.

However, if the conversation on equity and accountability is actually going to be useful to the pursuit of real equity for children at the destructive end of the achievement gap, the dynamic complexity of these policy systems and their equally complex effects requires, even mandates, that researchers adopt an orientation to dialogue and debate that is careful, reflective, and respectful of different viewpoints, including a willingness to thoughtfully consider data supporting opposing viewpoints (see O'Day, 2002). Accordingly, participants in this conversation must be willing to set aside desires or needs to "win" the debates and must be willing to relax ideological stances sufficiently to see that these policy systems, their effects, and their multiple implementations at various sites and levels will inevitably yield contradictory and complex research results.

To promote this dialogue and move equity forward, over the past several years we have participated in several accountability debates in settings such as the annual conventions of the University Council of Educational Administration and the American Educational Research Association and in print in journals such as *Phi Delta Kappan*, *Education and Urban Society*, *International Journal of Leadership in Education*, and *Educational Researcher*. In all of these venues, we have explicitly and persistently called for a complex understanding of the systems, their effects, and their implementations, while, at the same time, we have been very clear about our support for some aspects of accountability policy because of the positive effects on equity we see in several areas, including:

- Providing a common set of explicit expectations for student achievement for all student groups that is not based on deficit assumptions
- Focusing strong public attention on achievement gaps
- Publicly providing accountability data for use by civic, community, and civil rights activists; parent groups; researchers; and the media (i.e., data transparency)[3]
- Focusing district and school leaders on their responsibility for educating equitably all students and holding them accountable for achieving equity and excellence

However, due to our efforts to maintain openness to criticisms of our work and to other opposing views (see Anderson, 2001; Haney, 2001; Klein, 2001; Sclafani, 2001; Trueba, 2001; and Valencia et al., 2001), we have ourselves gained a more nuanced understanding of and increased appreciation for the fact that accountability policy alone is not enough to support the broad-scale improvement of educational practices that will be required to close historic achievement gaps in every school in every district across the United States.

For example, as Walt Haney (2001) has compellingly argued, reducing school dropout rates is as critically important to achieving educational equity as is increasing student academic achievement. Additionally, as Valencia et al. (2001) pointed out, teacher quality is a highly significant factor that determines the equity of schooling that children receive. Also, Larry Parker (2001) has constructively argued that issues of overrepresentation of children of color in special education and the differential educational progress of African American boys and girls are critical issues that also influence the degree of equity in schooling. Indeed, both the content and focus of this chapter result partially from the effects of our critics on our views of accountability and equity.

Our view, then, of the relationship between accountability and educational equity has evolved, as we hope it has for all participants in this conversation. Although, to us accountability remains an extremely powerful and important force in the struggle for education equity, it is but one part of a larger system of schooling practices characterized by equity and inequity that is expressed in multiple dimensions of schooling. Thus, in order to close achievement gaps and to educate equitably all children, we suggest that a larger idea of equity, a *systemic equity*, will be required, which Scott (2001) has defined in the following way:

> Systemic equity is defined as the transformed ways in which systems and individuals habitually operate to ensure that every learner—in whatever learning environment that learner is found—has the greatest opportunity to learn enhanced by the resources and supports necessary to achieve competence, excellence, independence, responsibility, and self-sufficiency for school and for life. (¶6)

To accomplish this systemic equity, will require, in our view, the development of new, practical tools for educators to promote both equity and excellence throughout the entire public educational system.

Accordingly, school leaders and others will need to have access to practical tools to use in developing a more comprehensive, more insightful understanding of equity and inequity relationships in their current systems. These tools should be designed to be useful to professors in leadership preparation programs for the purpose of helping them develop leaders who have the knowledge and skills needed to create equitable and excellent schools. Consequently, we propose and describe here one such tool—*equity audits*—which has its roots in U.S. educational and civil rights history, but which we have redesigned, simplified, and streamlined to be of maximum utility in the current climate of high-stakes accountability and readily available data.

Historical Background of Equity Audits

Our idea for using equity audits as a tool to guide schools in working toward equity and excellence is based on an impressive history of the use of equity auditing in three areas: civil rights, curriculum auditing, and state accountability policy systems. The terminology *equity audit* (also known as a *representivity audit*) has a deep and significant history in civil rights enforcement in the United States and other nations (e.g., Scotland, Great Britain, and Australia) in a variety of arenas, including, but not limited to, education. For example, corporations and governmental entities commonly conduct (or are subject to) employment equity audits, health equity audits, pay equity audits, gender equity audits, and technology equity audits, among others.

In the U.S. educational arena, equity audits of school districts have been conducted by school districts (either voluntarily or under pressure by civic activists or ordered by the U.S. Department of Education Office of Civil Rights) as a way of determining the degree of compliance with a number of civil rights statutes that prohibit discrimination in educational programs and activities receiving federal funding. These statues include:

> Title VI of the Civil Rights Act of 1964 (prohibiting race, color, and national origin discrimination); Title IX of the Education Amendments of 1972 (prohibiting sex discrimination); Section 504 of the Rehabilitation Act of 1973 (prohibiting disability discrimination); Title II of the Americans with Disabilities Act of 1990 (prohibiting disability discrimination by public entities); and the Age Discrimination Act of 1975 (prohibiting age discrimination). (U.S. Department of Education, 1999, ¶1)

These applications of equity audits focused on compliance with federal civil rights acts have tended to be exhaustive, typically producing voluminous reports on a single district. Such civil-rights-based equity audits have been conducted in recent years by educational consultants, such as Harvard's Robert Peterkin, and in school districts around the country, including Urbana, Illinois; Ann Arbor, Michigan; Harrison, Colorado; and Albuquerque, New Mexico.

In addition to their use in the civil rights arena, equity audits have also been used, in a somewhat different way, in conjunction with curriculum audits. William Poston (1992) and Jacqueline Mitchell in collaboration with Poston (1992) described a design for school equity audits that was an adaptation of one standard area in a design for more comprehensive school curriculum audits developed by Fenwick English (1988). Drawing from and expanding on curriculum audit Standard 3: "A School System Demonstrates Internal Connectivity and Rational Equity in Its Program Development and Implementation," Poston proposed 15 areas of analysis for use in equity audits. These areas were: administrative and supervisory practices, course offerings and access, financial and funding resources, individual difference considerations, materials and facilities, special program and services delivery, student management practices, class size practices, demographic distribution, grouping practices and instruction, instructional time utilization, promotion and retention practices, staff development and training, support services provision, and teacher assignment and work load (p. 236). Mitchell and Poston published one report of the application of this equity audit to case studies in three school districts in 1992, but we were not able to find further published research on this method since that time.

A third area in which equity audits have been used is as part of state school reform and accountability efforts. Over the past decade, several state departments of education have developed instruments to evaluate equity levels in school districts in their state, though these instruments have varied widely in design. Some (e.g., Kentucky's) have been based in part on the logic of curriculum audits (Kentucky Department of Education, 1999; Steffy, 1993). In contrast, the State of Washington's Equity Self-Evaluation and Planning Documentation instrument was developed in 1993 by a task force and is mainly data based (Washington State Office of the Superintendent of Public Instruction, 1995). Also, since 1992, the State of Iowa has conducted on-site equity reviews of 13 to 14 school districts per year. These reviews are extensive and include interviews as well as reviews of 15 categories of documents, including such items as board policy books, master schedules for teachers and students, and school improvement plans (Iowa Department of Education, 2001).

These three significant streams in the history of equity audits can be used to create a potentially useful tool that can be applied to leverage educational equity in the present climate of federally mandated, high-stakes educational reform. In fact, as states, districts, and individual schools grapple with new NCLB requirements that they assess students, use disaggregated data, and demonstrate AYP in closing achievement gaps, there will be a great need for such tools for school leaders to use to make their schools both equitable and excellent and for leadership professors to use in training new school leaders who will need to be successful in the new high-stakes environment. The problem, though, with existing versions of equity audits (whether based on civil rights, curriculum auditing, or state accountability systems) is that they typically produce enormous amounts of data, which overwhelms decision-making efforts. Although such detailed examinations of macro- and micropractices of schools and districts are highly useful in some circumstances, such as documenting the violation of civil rights laws, it also limits the utility of this tool to be used more widely in thousands of contexts. Few people associated with a district or school will have time or motivation to read through a document 200 or 300 pages in length and then use the results well in planning school change.

In contrast, what we propose is a different, more focused, more limited descendant of equity audits. What is needed, in our view, is a way for school leaders and others to have data for their district displayed in a clear and understandable way that reveals the levels of equity and inequity in specific, delimited areas of schooling, which can subsequently be used for planning school change. In addition, with ever-increasing amounts of data being generated by state accountability systems, there is a major need for tools that will easily and simply reduce some of the complexity of the data without stripping it of its utility for increasing equity.

Our Reconception of Equity Audits

Teachers, administrators, school board members, community members, and policymakers may be aware of inequities in various aspects of their schools, but they rarely have systematically examined these areas and then devised ways to eliminate the inequities. Despite a decade or more of working within a context of increasingly high-stakes accountability, particularly in states such as Texas, that produces growing amounts of comprehensive data about schools and districts, the administrators and teachers we work with overwhelmingly do *not* have a clear, accurate, or useful understanding of the degree of inequity present in their own schools and school districts (for a longer discussion of this topic, see Scheurich & Skrla, 2003). Furthermore, some researchers (e.g., McKenzie, 2001, 2002; Pollock, 2001) have also found that in typical school settings teachers and administrators often routinely avoid overt discussions of race as a factor in inequitable school outcomes. In addition, it is also commonplace that when these educators are queried about why children of color and children from low income homes do not do well in their schools, they cite factors external to schooling as the cause, often blaming children's parents, their home lives, their communities, and even their genetics (McKenzie, 2001, 2002; Valencia, 1997), with the result that the educators can say that they have no responsibility for the inequitable achievement gaps.

For teachers and administrators to have a more productive orientation, one that is not deficit based or focused on issues external to schools, they need to be assisted in recognizing that there are substantial and persistent patterns of inequity *internal* to schools; that is, embedded within the many assumptions, beliefs, practices, procedures, and policies of schools themselves. However, we also recognize the complexities and difficulties of getting teachers and administrators to incorporate new perspectives when deficit assumptions about children of color are taken as the norm, as Sleeter (1996) has pointed out in the context of teaching teachers about multicultural education:

> Many educators conceptualize this task as helping [teachers] "unlearn" negative attitudes about race, develop positive attitudes and a knowledge base about race and various racial groups, and learn multicultural teaching strategies. . . . This task is more complex than that. . . . They integrate information about race provided in multicultural teacher education programs into the knowledge they already have [which is often highly biased or even racist], much more than they reconstruct that knowledge. (p. 65)

In response to these daunting challenges, practical tools that make intuitive sense to educators and that are easy to apply, while getting beyond old biases, can be highly useful. Thus, our reconception of equity audits is intended to facilitate ease of use and to promote insight into, discussion of, and a substantive response to systemic patterns of inequity in schools and school districts.

Accordingly, we suggest beginning with a manageable set of key indicators that together form a straightforward, delimited audit of equity. After careful consideration of the types of indicators available (from equity audits and from state accountability systems), we have come up with a set of 12 indicators grouped into three categories for our equity audits. We have labeled these three dimensions as *teacher quality equity, programmatic equity*, and *achievement equity*. These three dimensions can even be conceptualized as a simple formula, as shown in Figure 13.1.

Teacher Quality Equity

There is growing consensus among researchers and practitioners that high-quality teachers are key determinants of students' opportunities to be academically successful (Darling-Hammond, 1999; Ferguson, 1998). Determining what teacher quality is and how to measure it, of course, is a complicated issue (see Rowan, Correnti, & Miller, 2002). The state of Tennessee, for example, has chosen to define it as "value added"—the contribution each teacher makes to students' standardized test performance based on each student's prior achievement. The Tennessee model has attracted considerable attention due, in part, to research using this model that has shown startling and cumulative negative effects on children who have the least effective teachers for successive elementary grades (Prince, 2002; Sanders & Rivers, 1996). Students who had the least effective teachers for three years were shown by Sanders and Rivers (1996) to score 50 percentile points lower on achievement tests than did students who had three of the most effective teachers. However, the Tennessee model has also received considerable critique on methodological grounds (Bock & Wolfe, 1996) and on the basis of its extremely narrow definition of teacher quality (one based entirely on gain scores on standardized tests).[4] Consequently, other states have been slow to follow Tennessee's path.

Other indicators that serve as proxies for evidence of teacher quality, such as experience and training, are more commonly used (Rowan, Correnti, & Miller, 2002). Whatever the definition, though, there is ample evidence that access to quality teachers is not typically distributed on an equitable basis to all schools within a district, nor to all students within individual schools, particularly high schools. Students of color and students from low-income homes most often have less experienced teachers, teachers with less education and training, and more teachers teaching without certification and/or outside their areas of expertise (Ingersoll, 1999; Lankford, Loeb, & Wyckoff, 2002).

For a school district, then, evidence of teacher quality equity or inequity would result from an examination of the distribution throughout the schools

Teacher Quality Equity + Programmatic Equity = Achievement Equity

FIGURE 13.1 *A Simple Formula for Equity Auditing*

in the district of teacher quality or, for a single school, an examination of the distribution of teacher quality within the school. In other words, which students are getting the most teacher quality, however defined, and which are getting the least? If this quality is distributed inequitably, for example, children of color getting the lowest teacher quality and the White middle-class children getting the highest teacher quality, then we cannot expect equity in achievement outcomes. If the latter is true in a school or district, the result is a systemic distribution of teacher quality that will likely yield inequity in achievement.

To operationalize teacher quality, then, for examination for inequities such as those we have pointed out, we have chosen four variables for which data are commonly available from state and local sources and for which there is some research evidence (though mixed) of effects on student achievement (see Rowan, Correnti, & Miller, 2002): (1) teacher education (bachelors, master's, & doctoral degrees; number or percentage holding a particular degree); (2) teacher experience (number of years as a teacher); (3) teacher mobility (number or percentage of teachers leaving or not leaving a campus on an annual basis); and (4) teachers without certification or assigned outside of their area of teaching expertise (i.e., language arts teacher teaching a math course). Accordingly, at the district level, the central question would be what is the degree to which these indicators are distributed equitably or inequitably among the campuses within the district. In other words, do the schools serving primarily low-income students have the same percentage of teachers holding master's degrees or higher, the same percentage of experienced teachers, the same teacher mobility rate, and the same percent of uncertified teachers and teachers teaching outside their areas of expertise as do schools serving primarily children from middle- and upper-income homes?

We realize, of course, that the leadership in some districts or schools may argue that, because "senior" teachers (senior by experience, degree, or status) often choose the highest-level classes within a school or the "best" schools, it does not have any control over these four variables. However, we have seen too many schools and districts successfully change these "senior-

Auditing Teacher Quality

". . . access to quality teachers is not typically distributed on an equitable basis to all schools within a district, nor to all students within individual schools, particularly high schools. Students of color and students from low-income homes most often have less experienced teachers, teachers with less education and training, and more teachers teaching without certification and/or outside their areas of expertise (Ingersoll, 1999; Lankford, Loeb, & Wyckoff, 2002)."

ity" assumptions to accept that this kind of change is not possible for any school or district. Also, we understand that district leadership often argues that the district cannot do anything about the fact that the teaching staff of schools populated principally by White middle-class children are more highly educated, have more experience, are less mobile, and have more teachers who are certified or teaching within their area of expertise. Once again, though, there are simply too many districts that have successfully taken on this issue and rearranged their districtwide distribution of teacher quality to let this objection stand.

To apply, then, one conception of equity audits, Mitchell and Poston (1992) suggested that campuses that differed from district averages by more than 20% were indications of inequity. Alternately, we suggest, depending on the size of the school district, that a higher standard—perhaps 10% deviation from the district average—would ensure greater equity. However, it is certainly possible to think about this in a more complex fashion. For instance, a district might use a sliding scale that would for two years make a 20% inequity the standard, which would then be followed in the third year by a 10% standard. Whatever the decision, the point is to examine equity within the distribution of teacher quality in a district and then work with appropriate stakeholders to make the distribution of teacher quality equitable.

For example, let's take a district of 50,000 students (see Figure 13.2). A district this size will have numerous elementary schools, probably 50 to 60. Suppose we look at three of the schools serving families with the lowest incomes and three serving families from the middle class. If we examine the distribution of teachers by teacher education level, are the teachers at the higher socioeconomic status (SES) schools significantly more educated than those at the lower SES schools?

As Figure 13.2 shows, 50% of teachers in the middle-class schools hold a master's degree or higher, whereas only 20% do in the low-income schools. Also, is there more mobility of teachers in the low-income schools? In our example, there is 30% mobility at the lower SES schools, and 5% at the higher SES schools. Are there more teachers teaching outside their areas of expertise or without certification at the low-income schools? In this example, 10% are not certified in the lower SES schools, whereas at the middle-class schools only 2% are uncertified. Are the teachers at the high-income schools generally more experienced than those at the low-income schools? In this example, teachers at the middle-class schools have an average of 15 years of experience, whereas at the low-income schools the average is only 7 years. Though these particular figures were created for the purpose of illustration, they are based on our experience in working with schools and districts (large and small; rural, suburban, and urban) in which these kinds of differences are typical. Especially in larger districts, there is considerable teacher quality inequity that is taken for granted and thus never pointed out as a "cause" of the achievement gaps in a district (Lankford, Loeb, & Wyckoff, 2002; Prince, 2002; Rowan,

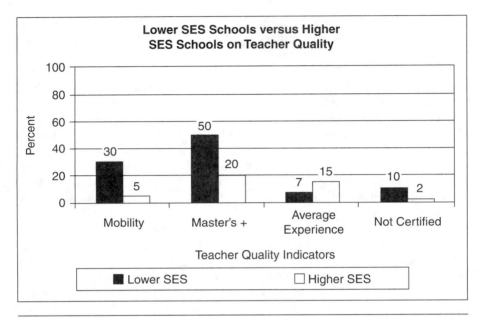

FIGURE 13.2 *Four Indicators of Teacher Quality Equity*

Correnti, & Miller, 2002). Our point, though, is that a district will have little hope of truly reducing its achievement gaps if it does not address the inequitable distribution of teacher quality.

It is not enough, however, to examine teacher quality across districts. These same kinds of patterns often exist within schools. For instance, are the Advanced Placement and the gifted and talented classes at the higher grades taught by the more educated, more experienced, more stable teachers, while the main classes or lower-track classes are taught by the least educated, least experienced, more mobile teachers? Or, is the highest teacher quality being used for high school seniors, but the lowest for high school freshmen? If this is occurring, this means that those struggling as they begin high school will get the weakest teachers, which may, in turn, drive up dropout rates for those students on the academic margins. Again, we have frequently found, especially in larger schools and in high schools, that such teacher quality assignments are taken for granted and that no one points them out as a possible cause of achievement gaps. Consequently, equity audits need to be done not only across districts but also within schools to determine whether there is an equitable distribution of teacher quality.

Programmatic Equity

Equally as important as teacher quality is the quality of the programs in which students are placed (or from which they are excluded). Though educators would often like to pretend otherwise, there are large variations of quality among different placements and programs within schools and school districts (e.g., see Schoenfeld, 2002, for an excellent discussion of differences in the quality of math programs). The potential indicators for an equity audit in this category are numerous, but we have identified four key areas that research has consistently shown to be significant sites of inequity: (1) special education, (2) gifted and talented education (G/T), (3) bilingual education, and (4) student discipline. Over-assignment of students of color and students from low-income homes to special education, especially the most severe categories of disability, has long been recognized as an area of gross inequity within our school systems (Artiles, 1998; Losen & Orfield, 2002; MacMillan & Reschly, 1998). Additionally, high-stakes accountability systems in the past have placed more pressure on educators to identify students for special education in order to exempt them from testing, though NCLB contains provisions to guard against this (Texas Center for Educational Research, 2000; Townsend, 2002). Special education is, therefore, an essential indicator in the programmatic equity category.

The problem of overrepresentation by race and SES in special education is mirrored in reverse in programs for the education of gifted and talented students (Ford & Harmon, 2001). Students of color and students from low-income homes are grossly underrepresented in the ranks of the students identified as gifted and talented, even though it is widely understood that intelligence and talent are distributed fairly equally by race, ethnicity, or SES. In addition, rates of gifted and talented identification vary greatly among school districts, with some serving less than 5% of children in a district and others serving upwards of 12%. Regardless of the rate, however, the indicator for the equity audit is whether all student groups are represented in reasonably proportionate percentages (i.e., if 15% of students in a district are African American students, then close to 15% of gifted and talented students should be African American).

A typical example is illustrated in Figure 13.3. These data are taken from an urban district with which we are familiar.

The district has about 50,000 students with 4,650 in gifted and talented courses districtwide, or 9.3% of the student population. About 73.0% of this district's entire student population, or 36,500, come from low-income families. However, only 734 students from these low-income families are in gifted and talented courses in this district. This means that although 73% of the district's students come from low-income families, only 15.8% of gifted and talented students come from low-income homes. As a result, students from low-income families are considerably underrepresented (about one-fifth of what would be proportional) in gifted and talented classes. This is an inequity pattern in this district and is a substantial hindrance to the removal of achievement gaps.

A third indicator for the programmatic equity category is the academic progress of students served through bilingual education. As growing numbers of culturally and linguistically diverse students enroll in our schools, it be-

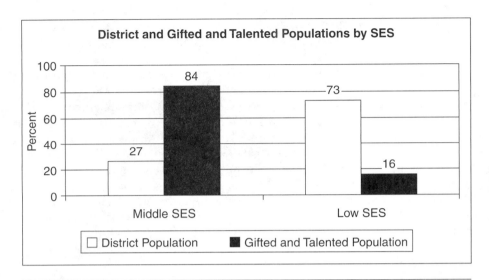

FIGURE 13.3   *Programmatic Equity in Gifted and Talented Programs*

comes ever more important to assess the quality of the bilingual instruction they receive. Unfortunately, in the past, bilingual programs all too often were language-oriented ghettos where students were segregated and neither became proficient in English nor progressed academically in their first language (Moll, 1992). The response in one state, Texas, was to begin including on its accountability reports for each school and district information about the progress of English-language learners on the state test of reading proficiency in English. This indicator (as well as other similar indicators that other states will likely develop in response to NCLB requirements that English-language learners be included in assessment and accountability) will monitor whether students in bilingual programs are being well served or simply warehoused.[5]

Though our fourth category, discipline, may seem an odd fit with the other three, students who are routinely and consistently caught up within a discipline system are commonly removed from their regular classes and thus denied equal access to learning. Indeed, for some students (particularly African American and Latino boys), the disciplinary system in their school or district becomes their de facto instructional program because it is where they spend the majority of their time.

The data in Figure 13.4 are drawn from actual percentages for the 2001–2002 school year of a small-town high school of 1,300 students.

African American males received discipline (all categories, from minor to severe, have been combined) at a rate that is nearly *three times* their proportional representation in the student population. For Latino males, the rate is *more than four times* their proportional representation. Clearly, this high school has an inequitable situation with respect to discipline, as is the case with many schools nationwide (Bowman, 2003; Gregory, 1995; Skiba, Michael, & Nardo, 2003). As a result, African American males and Latino males will spend much less time learning in the classroom, thus making it much more difficult to erase achievement gaps for these students.

In addressing each of these four programmatic equity areas, we are fully aware that many educators argue that the causes of inequities in each of these areas have little to nothing to do with schooling and are thus not under the control of educators. However, our point in all four areas is that the system of the school and the attitudes, assumptions, and practices of its educators are all largely in the control of the educators, which means that systems can be redesigned and attitudes, assumptions, and practices can be changed so as to create equitable and excellent schools. In addition, we have seen too many schools and districts that have developed systemic solutions that have substantially reduced or eliminated inequities in all these areas to be willing to settle for the judgment that programmatic inequities cannot be controlled by educators.

Achievement Equity

Unquestionably, achievement inequities or gaps have received the most attention from researchers, educators, policy analysts, and the public, with discus-

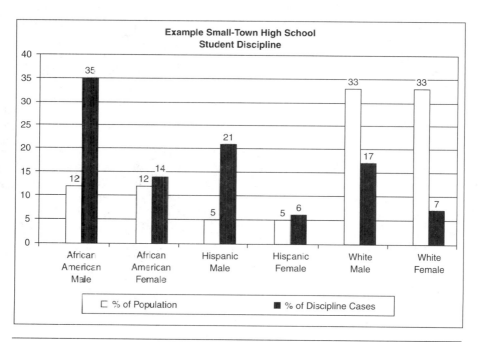

FIGURE 13.4 *Programmatic Equity in Discipline*

sions of test score gaps or achievement gaps becoming commonplace and debates about causes and solutions occurring in a wide variety of venues. Our
purpose, then, of including achievement equity as a category in equity audits
is to maintain this critical public focus on equity outcomes, but also to expand
the traditional attention on state achievement test results to include other evidence of student achievement and attainment, including high school completion, completion of college-prep curriculum, and higher level assessments such
as the SAT, ACT, and Advanced Placement (AP) exams. As we have learned
from our research with school districts that have made significant progress toward equity (Skrla & Scheurich, 2001; Skrla et al., 2000, 2001; Skrla,
Scheurich, Johnson, & Koschoreck, 2001a, 2001b), equitable achievement on
relatively low-level state assessments is generally not sufficient in indicating
"true" achievement equity when large gaps remain on other, more challenging indicators of student performance. In response to this need for a broader
definition of achievement equity, the four indicators we propose for this category include (1) state achievement test results, (2) dropout rates, (3) high
school graduation tracks, and (4) SAT/ACT/AP results.

All 50 states now have some form of state achievement test and soon
will be required by NCLB to disseminate performance results disaggregated
by family income level, student race, disability, and English proficiency, though
not by gender. Also, because results on these tests are now the primary evaluation measure of school performance, these test results need to be a basic
indicator included in equity audits. Beyond performance on these state tests,
however, are other areas that need significant scrutiny for evidence of levels
of equity within schools and districts. Dropout rates (or, alternatively, school
completion rates) are one key indicator that increasingly has come to the
forefront of discussions of educational equity and accountability (see Haney,
2001). Huge, unacceptably high percentages of students of color (particularly
males) and students from low-income homes drop out or are pushed out of
school before high school graduation, so this, too, needs to be a key indicator in equity audits.

A third area for consideration in the achievement category of equity
audits is high school graduation tracks. All students who graduate typically
do not pursue equally rigorous curricula, with most states having some form
of a tiered system that offers basic, advanced, and/or college preparatory curricula. Although the percentage of students completing high school under
each plan may vary widely from district to district, the central question addressed by this indicator is whether there is proportional representation of
student groups by race and SES in each graduation track within each district. For example, how can we expect to close the achievement gaps between children of color and White children if the percentage of children of
color in the college prep track is much, much lower than the same
percentage for White children (see Oakes, 1986; Sizer, 1997; Wheelock,
1993)?

The fourth indicator in the achievement equity category is performance on the SAT, the ACT, and/or AP examinations. As with other indicators we have discussed, students of color and students from low-income homes typically score much lower on these advanced measures than do White students and students from middle- and upper-income homes or do not even take SAT and ACT tests or AP classes (College Board, 1998). Additionally, even when students of color or those from low-income homes do enroll in AP classes, they may not actually take the examinations themselves or they may receive inflated grades in their classes but score poorly on the exams.

Figure 13.5, for example, shows data from an urban district of 78,000 students for student performance on Advanced Placement exams.

The demographics of this district's students are as follows: 16% African American, 48% Latino, and 34% White. It is clear in this example that much smaller percentages of students of color are taking these examinations and that students of color are scoring at or above the criterion for college credit (typically, a score of 3 or higher on a 1–5 scale) at lower rates than are White students. However, although leaving such AP percentages with these sizeable differences by race will limit the ability of this district to achieve equity and excellence, our studies (e.g., Skrla, Scheurich, & Johnson, 2000) of various districts have shown that districts can address these inequities and have success at significantly decreasing the gaps in this area, just as they have in other achievement areas.

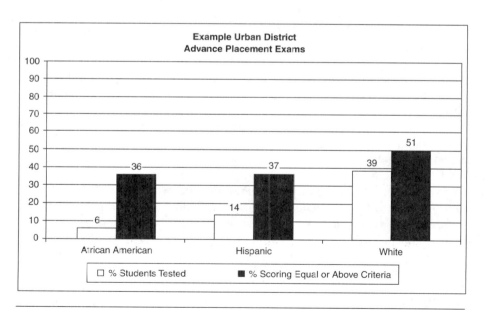

FIGURE 13.5 *Achievement Equity in Advanced Placement Exams*

Applications of Equity Audits

Thus far, we have discussed the broad array of different kinds of equity audits, and we have illustrated how they can be applied to three particular areas: teacher quality, programs, and achievement. Although we know there are many other areas of potential application that may have significant importance in particular contexts, we have tried to frame some specific variables, where data are widely available, to get anyone started in each of the three areas. In addition, we have shown some easily understood ways to communicate the inequities through charting some figures we had from our own work or created for illustration. Thus, we would expect at this point that virtually any researcher, professor, educator, college student, or layperson could take the equity audits that we have shown and discussed here and apply them to her or his own school or district.

In addition, we want to suggest a process for using equity audits and offer some brief examples of our use of equity audits with different stakeholder groups. The process that we describe for operationalizing equity audits is a simple one that has been used in many areas of organizational change and applications of action research. In fact, this method for using equity audits could easily be incorporated into existing campus and/or district planning and decision-making processes, such as the site-based processes required in many states.

The first step is to put together a committee of relevant stakeholders, such as a group of teachers or a group representative of both educators and parents. What is important here is to identify individual stakeholders who will collaborate in carrying out the process. It is important to identify individuals who are respected by the groups they represent and who are also people of good will who would be open to dialog and work focused on equity. Let's say, for instance, that what is at issue is the distribution of teacher quality in a district. Who, then, should be included? We would suggest influential teachers, especially representatives of teacher unions or other such groups; district and campus leaders; and representatives from parent and advocacy groups, such as the Parent Teacher Association (PTA), the Parent Teacher Organization (PTO), the National Association for the Advancement of Colored People (NAACP), the Mexican American Legal Defense and Education Fund (MALDEF), and so on.

Next, the numbers and percentages in a few areas, such as the distribution of teachers by experience, education, mobility, and certification, should be presented to this committee. Furthermore, we would suggest presenting these numbers so that each committee member actually takes colored pencils, crayons, or markers and lays out the numbers or percentages on graph paper that has been prepared for their use. For example, in Figure 13.2, 50% of the teachers at the middle-class schools had at least a master's degree, whereas only 20% at the low-income schools had the same. So, we are suggesting that the committee members be given these percentages and then that each member be asked to fill in a graph that illustrates these percentages. Our experience has been that though this takes a little time, actually charting the percentages on graphs gives people a much better sense of the differences that need to be addressed.

The third step we suggest is for the committee to have an open discussion of these teacher quality gaps. Experts could be brought in to offer analysis and advice. Educators from other districts that have had success in reducing teacher quality gaps could be brought in for this step. Whoever is brought in to add to the discussion for this step needs to be a good facilitator.[6] For example, issues of racism may be brought up at this point. Whatever comes up, though, needs to be addressed so that everyone perceives that they can say what they think and be heard by the other members of the committee; however, the process must not be allowed to get stuck at some negative, nonproductive point that would prevent moving on to positive change. Also, it is especially important at this step, or at any step, that the district leadership not become defensive or try to repress or derail discussion of difficult issues. A good facilitator will know how to provide support for discussion of difficult issues and also move the group forward in a positive way (see Sleeter, 1996, for an excellent discussion of how individuals and groups learn about racial and justice issues).

Our fourth step is that once there has been a good, open discussion of the problem, the group needs to move toward potential solutions. Again, experts or leadership from other districts may be helpful here; similarly, a good facilitator will be useful in this phase. The point is to come up with some positive solutions; to talk about the strengths, weaknesses, and costs of each; and then to commit to one or more of these solutions. The fifth step is the implementation of the solution or solutions by the district. The sixth is to monitor results and then report them to the committee. If the solutions are successful, celebrate; if the solutions are not successful, return to either step three or four and work forward again.

Here, then, are these same steps in a brief list:

Step 1: Create a committee of relevant stakeholders.

Step 2: Present the data to the committee and have everyone graph the data.

Step 3: Discuss the meaning of the data, possible use of experts, led by a facilitator.

Step 4: Discuss potential solutions, possible use of experts, led by a facilitator.

Step 5: Implement solution(s).

Step 6: Monitor and evaluate results.

Step 7: Celebrate if successful; if not successful, return to step 3 and repeat the process.

Our own experience with presenting our conception of equity audits and their use has occurred in three venues: presentations to school board members, presentations to school principals, and presentations to students in a principal-preparation program. In the first instance, presentations to school board members, we defined equity audits for 30 to 50 board members at a time, provided our three-category framework, and discussed some specific examples with actual data from schools or districts. In general, one of the strengths of equity audits, their simplicity, was easily evident, and the audience quickly understood the idea. However, although some school board members who already knew there were major inequities in their districts thought equity audits were an excellent way to get educators and the public to see the inequities and address them, a few board members expressed discomfort or even hostility at the very idea of examining such inequities.[7] This negative response was mentioned earlier; anyone using equity audits must be prepared to work with such responses.

We had a similar experience when we presented some equity audit data to the principals in a district that has long been struggling with persistent inequities. We used data from their own district that made the inequities within their schools very obvious. Some of the principals, like the board members, were significantly upset by the implications. For example, one principal who had significant overrepresentation of students of color in special education, though we did not present her school's data, became outspokenly defensive. Others just did not like the public presentation of the inequities in the district. In contrast, other principals said it was about time that the inequities were openly noted and discussed.

One important part of equity audits was highly successful with all the principals. Our way of presenting the data was easily understandable to everyone, which is one of our main goals—to make the inequities clearly visible and easily understandable so that it is possible to move forward to solutions that yield more equity. Nonetheless, that some in the audience did not like the results is an issue that must always be dealt with in doing equity audits. Many educators, parents, and others simply do not want to face or address the race and SES inequities within our public schools, but this must be done if achievement gaps are to be erased. It is important for people attempting to use equity audits and other equity-focused strategies with groups of stakeholders in their schools to understand that people start out in a variety of places with respect to their understanding of issues of inequity. Resistance is to be expected, but it is important to keep in mind that all views, even negative ones, should be treated with dignity, and every effort should be made to avoid defensiveness and to maintain open dialogue. This type of work is necessarily a process, and it is often a long one. Patience and persistence will be needed.

The third group we have used equity audits with was a group of students in a principal-preparation program. The concept of equity audits was presented along with examples to the students, and then the students were given actual data to chart and discuss in small groups of 7 to 10. This was done over three hours in one morning of an eight-week summer semester, the semester in which the students start the principal-training program. The students easily and quickly grasped the idea of equity audits and had no trouble applying it to their sample data. Throughout the rest of the summer, the students repeatedly used the concept and applied it to actual data on actual schools.

That they grasped the concept and ways to apply it was clearly evident in their capstone project. All the students were in teams, and each team had to take an actual school, study it, collect data on it, and then prepare both a written report and a presentation that included what they found and what recommendations they had for solving any problems they found. In all the reports and presentations, equity audits played a key role for the students to illustrate the inequities they found in their respective schools, even though the use of these audits was not required. Furthermore, they all used charts to present their data in the same way that equity audits were demonstrated to them. In other words, the concept of equity audits traveled well and easily with these students. It became a key way that they approached understanding their schools and the inequities in their schools. Indeed, in all three of the venues we have described here, the concept traveled well and easily. Even those uncomfortable with the results quickly grasped the idea of equity audits, even though they did not like focusing on the inequities or the implications of the inequities.

Conclusion

The pressure is finally on all schools and districts to produce year-to-year increases in equity in our public education system. In response, although many have blamed causes external to schooling for the achievement gaps, there unquestionably are inequities within our public schools, such as inequitable distributions of teacher quality or inequitable distributions of students in programs such as special education or AP courses, that must be addressed if the achievement gaps are to be eliminated. Given all of the readily available data on schools and districts, we are committed to designing practical, easy-to-understand tools for using these data to increase educational equity. Our goal in this chapter has been to describe and discuss equity auditing, which is one example of a simple, easy-to-understand tool for examining inequities within our schools and districts. We also presented applications of equity auditing to actual data and provided a simple process for understanding and addressing the resultant data in a school or district.

We view this tool both as a descendent of an important history of educational equity audits and as a focused instrument that has the potential to be highly useful in the U.S. educational climate of high-stakes accountability. We have identified a dozen key indicators grouped into three categories—teacher quality equity, programmatic equity, and achievement equity—that together can provide an initial audit of systemic equities or inequities within a school or district. We do not see our identified areas as the only ones; there are certainly many more areas to which equity audits can be applied. Still, in our effort to provide significant, useful, and easy starting points, we have chosen some areas to focus on for which the data are readily known and available and for which there is ample evidence of inequities in most schools and districts.

Implications for Practice

One of the major points we have emphasized in this chapter is that our reconceptualization of equity audits is designed to be applied by practitioners in schools and districts. Thus, we strongly encourage campus and district leaders and other educators to start using equity audits to increase equity within their systems. We also recommend that professors in leadership preparation programs teach their students about this tool and ways to use it. Finally, we even hope that consultants start using it in their own work. Our experience is that educators learn it quickly, even intuitively, and then easily make use of it. On the more general side, we advocate that educators, professors of educational leadership, and consultants start designing other practical tools that are easy to understand and use for increasing equity in schooling.

Discussion Questions and Activities

1. What do you think is the current level of awareness (among teachers, campus and district leadership, parents, community members) about inequities in teacher quality, program quality, and achievement in your school or district?

2. What issues might a campus leader and her or his leadership team need to consider prior to implementation of the types of changes that may result from an equity audit? For example, changes such as shifting teacher assignments from a seniority basis to a student-need basis or revising the process for nomination and selection of students for gifted and talented programs.

3. Compare and contrast the equity audit method described in this chapter with other campus and/or district improvement planning methods that you have experienced.

4. What indicators other than the 12 identified in this chapter do you think are critical for inclusion for your campus or district in any of the three main areas of the equity audit (teacher quality, programs, achievement)?

5. In small group discussion, generate and post on chart paper a list of all of the explanations for achievement gaps that are in circulation in conversations among

faculty and staff at your school or district. Group these explanations into categories and discuss them. Which explanations have to do with factors external to the school (e.g., homes, families, genetics, individual student characteristics)? Which explanations have to do with factors within the control of the school?

6. Identify (using available data and/or through knowledgeable people) examples on your own campus or in your own district of classrooms, programs, grade levels, or schools that have eliminated or have made substantial progress toward eliminating achievement gaps.

7. Choose one area from the 12 recommended in this chapter for an equity audit. Collect and format for display and dissemination the data in this area for your campus or district. Keep a journal in which you record all the steps necessary to obtain the information and reflect on your own thoughts about the process and what the data reveal about the equity and inequity in this area for your campus.

8. Conduct an Internet search on the concept of equity audits in general and equity audits for schools, specifically.

Annotated Readings

Ruth Johnson's (2002) recently revised 336-page book, *Using Data to Close the Achievement Gap: How to Measure Equity in Our Schools*, is filled with practical, clearly explained surveys, forms, and models to assist practitioners in the work of equity reform in their schools. The book is essentially a tool kit for educators, and many of the tools provided are ideal for use in equity audits.

Based on research conducted in highly successful schools along the Texas–Mexico border, *Lessons from High-Performing Hispanic Schools: Creating Learning Communities*, edited by Pedro Reyes, Jay D. Scribner, and Alicia Paredes Scribner (1999), contains chapters that explain in detail how the study schools focused efforts in a variety of areas (leadership, parental involvement, and so on) to improve achievement and equity.

Leadership for Equity and Excellence by James Joseph Scheurich and Linda Skrla (2003), two of the authors of this chapter, is written specifically for educators working in schools. It is focused on how to create schools that are both equitable and excellent, and it envisions educators as the new civil rights workers who must carry out within the public educational system the dreams of Martin Luther King, Wilma Mankiller (former chief of the Cherokee Nation), and César Chávez.

Dreamkeepers: Successful Teachers of African American Children, an American Educational Research Association award winner by Gloria Ladson-Billings (1997), is a beautifully written portrayal of the lives of eight teachers who have made the dream of academically rigorous and loving classrooms for African American learners into reality.

The Web site of the Public Education Network (PEN) (www.publiceducation .org) contains a wealth of information, publications, and links that are useful for anyone engaged in the work of improving schools that serve low-income children and children of color. According to its Web site, PEN "is a national association of local education funds (LEFs) and individuals working to advance public school reform in low-income communities across our country. PEN seeks to build public demand and mobilize resources for quality public education for *all* children through a theory of action that focuses on the importance of public engagement in school reform."

References

Anderson, G. L. (2001). Promoting educational equity in a period of growing social inequity: The silent contradictions of the Texas reform discourse. *Education and Urban Society, 33*(3), 321–332.

Artiles, A. J. (1998). The dilemma of difference: Enriching the disproportionality discourse with theory and context. *Journal of Special Education, 32*(1), 32–36.

Black, W. R., & Valenzuela, A. (2003). Educational accountability for English-language learners in Texas: A retreat from equity. In L. Skrla & J. J. Scheurich (Eds.), *Educational equity and accountability: Policies, paradigms, and politics* (pp. 215–234). New York: RoutledgeFalmer.

Bock, R. D., & Wolfe, R. (1996, March 15). *A review and analysis of the Tennessee Value-Added Assessment System. Part I: Audit and review of the Tennessee Value-Added Assessment System (TVAAS): Final report.* Nashville, TN: Comptroller of the Treasury.

Bowman, D. H. (2003). Report finds suspension disparities in KY. *Education Week, 22*(25), 6.

Cohen, D., & Hill, H. (2000). Instructional policy and classroom performance: The mathematics reform in California. *Teachers College Record, 102*(2), 294–343.

Cohen, D. K., & Hill, H. C. (2001). *Learning policy: When state education reform works.* New Haven, CT: Yale University Press.

College Board. (1998). College-bound students set records in racial and ethnic diversity, pre-college credit, and grades, but College Board sees growing disparities among subgroups. *News from the College Board.* Retrieved July 19, 2003, from *http://collegeboard.com/press/senior98/html/980901.html*

Darling-Hammond, L. (1999). *Teacher quality and student achievement: A review of state policy evidence.* Seattle: Center for the Study of Teaching and Learning.

Donmoyer, R., & Garcia Wagstaff, J. G. (1990). Principals can be effective managers and instructional leaders, too. *NASSP Bulletin, 74*(535), 20–25, 27–29.

Edmonds, R. R. (1979). Effective schools for the urban poor. *Educational Leadership, 37*(1), 15 18, 20–24.

Elmore, R. F. (2002). Testing trap. *Harvard Magazine, 105*(1), 35.

English, F. W. (1988). *Curriculum auditing.* Lancaster, PA: Technomic.

Ferguson, R. F. (1998). Teachers' perceptions and expectations and the Black–White test score gap. In C. Jencks & M. Phillips (Eds.), *The Black–White test score gap* (pp. 318–375). Washington, D.C.: Brookings Institution Press.

Ford, D. Y., & Harmon, D. A. (2001). Equity and excellence: Providing access to gifted education for culturally diverse students. *Journal of Secondary Gifted Education, 11*(3), 141–148.

Garcia Wagstaff, J. G. (2000). *Baskin Elementary School, hope for urban education: A study of nine high-performing, high poverty urban elementary schools.* Washington, D.C.: U.S. Department of Education.

Gregory, J. F. (1995). The crime of punishment: Racial and gender disparities in the use of corporal punishment in U.S. schools. *Journal of Negro Education, 64*(4), 454–463.

Hall, V. (2002). Reinterpreting entrepeneuralism. In C. Reynolds (Ed.), *Women and school leadership: International perspectives.* Albany, NY: SUNY Press.

Hallinger, P., & Heck, R. H. (1998). Exploring the principal's contribution to school effectiveness: 1980–1995. *School Effectiveness and School Improvement, 9*(2), 157–191.

Haney, W. (2001). Response to Skrla et al. The illusion of educational equity in Texas: A commentary on "accountability for equity." *International Journal of Leadership in Education, 4*(3), 267–275.

Ingersoll, R. M. (1999). The problem of underqualified teachers in American secondary schools. *Educational Researcher, 28*(2), 26–37.

Iowa Department of Education. (2001). *The Iowa educational equity review process.* Des Moines, IA: Author.

Johnson, R. (2002). *Using data to close the achievement gap: How to measure equity in our schools.* Thousand Oaks, CA: Corwin Press.

Keating, P. (2000, April). *Understanding standards.* Paper presented at the annual meeting of the American Educational Research Association, New Orleans, LA.

Kentucky Department of Education. (1999). *Equity analysis and data gathering instrument.* Retrieved December 18, 2002, from *http://kde.state ky.us/osle/equity/documents/inst99.asp*

Klein, S. (2001). Response to Skrla et al.: Is there a connection between educational equity and accountability? *International Journal of Leadership in Education, 4*(3), 261–266.

Ladson-Billings, G. (1997). *The dreamkeepers: Successful teachers of African American children.* San Francisco: Jossey-Bass.

Lankford, H., Loeb, S., & Wyckoff, J. (2002). Teacher sorting and the plight of urban schools: A descriptive analysis. *Educational Evaluation and Policy Analysis, 24,* 37–62.

Linn, R. L., Baker, L., & Betebenner, D. W. (2002). Accountability systems: Implications of requirements of the No Child Left Behind Act of 2001. *Educational Researcher, 31*(6), 3–16.

Lipsky, M. (1980) *Street-level bureaucracy: Dilemmas of the individual in public services.* New York: Russell Sage Foundation.

Losen, D., & Orfield, G. (2002). *Racial inequity in special education.* Cambridge, MA: Harvard Education Publishing Group.

MacMillan, D. L., & Reschly, D. J. (1998). Overrepresentation of minority students: The case for greater specificity or reconsideration of the variables examined. *Journal of Special Education, 32*(1), 15–24.

McKenzie, K. B. (2001). *White teachers' perceptions about their students of color and themselves as white educators.* Doctoral dissertation, University of Texas at Austin.

McKenzie, K. B. (2002, November). *Equity traps.* Paper presented at the annual convention of the University Council for Educational Administration, Pittsburgh, PA.

Mitchell, J. K. & Poston, W. K. (1992). The equity audit in school reform: Three case studies of educational disparity and incongruity. *International Journal of Educational Reform, 1*(3), 242–247.

Moll, L. C. (1992). Bilingual classroom studies and community analysis: Some recent trends. *Educational Researcher, 20*(2), 20–24.

Moses, R. J., & Cobb, Jr., C. E. (2002). *Radical equations: Math literacy and civil rights.* Boston: Beacon Press.

No Child Left Behind Act of 2001, Pub. L. No. 107-100. Retrieved May 13, 2003, from *http://ed.gov/legislation/ESEA02/*

Nolly, G. L. (1997). *Effective instructional strategies for teaching mathematics to African American children.* Doctoral dissertation, University of Texas at Austin.

Oakes, J. (1986). *Keeping track: How schools structure inequality.* New Haven, CT: Yale University Press.

O'Day, J. A. (2002). Complexity, accountability, and school improvement. *Harvard Educational Review, 72*(3), 293–329.

Parker, L. (2001). Statewide assessment triggers urban school reform: But how high the stakes for urban minorities? *Education and Urban Society, 33*(3), 313–320.

Pollock, M. (2001). How the questions we ask most about race in education is the very question we most suppress. *Educational Researcher, 30*(9), 2–12.

Poston, W. K. (1992). The equity audit in school reform: Building a theory for educational research. *International Journal of Educational Reform, 1*(3), 235–241.

Prince, C. D. (2002). *The challenge of attracting good teachers and principals to struggling schools.* Arlington, VA: American Association of School Administrators.

Reyes, P., Scribner, J. D., & Paredes Scribner, A. (Eds.). (1999). *Lessons from high-performing Hispanic schools: Creating learning communities.* New York: Teachers College Press.

Rorrer, A. K. (2003). Intersections in accountability reform: Complexity, local actors, legitimacy, and agendas. In L. Skrla & J. J. Scheurich (Eds.), *Educational equity and accountability: Policies, paradigms, and politics* (pp. 251–266). New York: Routledge Falmer.

Rowan, B., Correnti, R., & Miller, R. J. (2002). *What large-scale, survey research tells us about teacher effects on student achievement.* Consortium for Policy Research in Education, CPRE Research Report Series RR-051.

Sanders, W. L., & Rivers, J. C. (1996). *Cumulative and residual effects of teachers on future student academic achievement.* Knoxville, TN: University of Tennessee Value-Added Research and Assessment Center.

Scheurich, J. J., & Skrla, L. (2003). *Leadership for equity and excellence: Creating high-achievement classrooms, schools, and districts.* Thousand Oaks, CA: Corwin.

Scheurich, J. J., Skrla, L., & Johnson, J. F. (2000). Thinking carefully about equity and accountability. *Phi Delta Kappan, 82*(4), 293–299.

Schoenfeld, A. H. (2002). Making mathematics work for all children: Issues of standards, testing, and equity. *Educational Researcher, 3*(1), 13–25.

Sclafani, S. (2001). Using an aligned system to make real progress for Texas students. *Education and Urban Society, 33*(3), 305–312.

Scott, B. (2001, March). Coming of age. *IDRA Newsletter* [Online]. Retrieved May 13, 2003, from *http://idra.org/Newslttr/2001/Mar/Bradley.htm*

Sizer, T. (1997). *Horace's hope: What works for the American high school.* New York: Mariner Books.

Skiba, R. J., Michael, R. S., & Nardo, A. C. (2003). *The color of discipline: Sources of racial and gender disproportionality in school punishment.* Bloomington: Indiana Educational Policy Center.

Skrla, L. (2001). Accountability, equity, and complexity. *Educational Researcher, 30*(4), 15–21.

Skrla, L. (2003). Productive campus leadership responses to accountability: Principals as policy mediators. In W. Hoy & C. Miskel (Eds.), *Studies in leading and organizing schools: Theory and research in educational administration* (pp. 27–50). Greenwich, CT: Information Age Publishing.

Skrla, L., & Scheurich, J. J. (2001). Displacing deficit thinking in school district leadership. *Education and Urban Society, 33*(3), 235–259.

Skrla, L., Scheurich, J. J., & Johnson, J. F. (2000). *Equity-driven, achievement focused school districts: A report on systemic school success in four Texas school districts serving diverse student populations.* Austin, TX: The Charles A. Dana Center. Retrieved December 29, 2002, from *http://utdanacenter.org/research/reports/equitydistricts.pdf.*

Skrla, L., Scheurich, J. J., & Johnson, J. F. (2001). Toward a new consensus on high academic achievement for all children. *Education and Urban Society, 33*(3), 227–234.

Skrla, L., Scheurich, J. J., Johnson, J. F., & Koschoreck, J. W. (2001a). Accountability for equity: Can state policy leverage social justice? *International Journal of Leadership in Education, 4*(3), 237–260.

Skrla, L., Scheurich, J. J., Johnson, J. F., & Koschoreck, J. W. (2001b). Complex and contested constructions of accountability and educational equity. *International Journal of Leadership in Education, 4*(3), 277–283.

Sleeter, C. E. (1996). *Multicultural education as social activism.* Albany, NY: SUNY Press.

Steffy, B. (1993). *The Kentucky education reform.* Lanham, MD: Scarecrow Press.

Tennessee Department of Education. (2002). *Tennessee value-added assessment system.* Retrieved July 19, 2003, from *http://state.tn.us/education/tstvaas.htm*

Texas Center for Educational Research. (2000). *Strengthened assessment and accountability.* Retrieved July 19, 2003, from *http://tasb.org/tcer/publications/tx_policy/strengthened.doc*

Thompson, A. (1992). The ethics and politics of evaluation. *Issues in Educational Research, 2*(1), 35–44.

Townsend, B. L. (2002). "Testing while Black": Standards-based school reform and African American learners. *Remedial and Special Education, 23*(4), 222–231.

Trueba, H. (2001). Polar positions on the Texas Assessment of Academic Skills (TAAS): Pragmatism and the politics of neglect. *Education and Urban Society, 33*(3), 333–344.

U.S. Department of Education. (2002). *No child left behind act of 2001: Executive summary*. Washington, D.C.: Author. Retrieved December 18, 2002, from *http://ed.gov/offices/OESE/esea/exec-summ.html*

U.S. Department of Education Office of Civil Rights. (1999). *Impact of civil rights laws*. Washington, D.C.: Author. Retrieved May 13, 2003, from *http://ed.gov/offices/OCR/impact.html*

Valencia, R. R. (1997). *The evolution of deficit thinking*. London: Falmer.

Valencia, R. R., Valenzuela, A., Sloan, K., & Foley, D. E. (2001). Let's treat the cause, not the symptoms: Equity and accountability in Texas revisited. *Phi Delta Kappan, 83*(4), 318–321.

Valenzuela, A. (1999). *Subtractive schooling*. Albany, NY: SUNY.

Washington State Office of the Superintendent of Public Instruction. (1995). *Washington State equity self-evaluation and planning documentation*. Eisenhower National Clearinghouse. Retrieved October 27, 2002, from *http://enc.org/topics/equity/articles/document.shtm?input=ACQ-111584-1584*

Wheelock, A. (1993). *Crossing the tracks*. New York: John Muir Publications.

Wilson, A., & Segall, W. (2003, April). Glorification of accountability through federal legislation: Dislocating meanings with/in/through the *No Child Left Behind Act*. Paper presented at the annual meeting of the American Educational Research Association, Chicago, IL.

Endnotes

[1]Vigorous critiques of NCLB have arisen across numerous fronts and have included issues such as utility and comparability of test data across states; the wide range of preparedness to implement various provisions of the act among different schools, districts, and states; the lack of timeliness and clarity in implementation guidance from the U.S. Department of Education; disparate impact of the act's provisions on low-income, minority, English-language-learner, and disabled students; an almost certain backlash as large numbers of schools receive "failing" grades and inadequate funding for implementation; among many others (see Elmore, 2002; Linn, Baker, & Betebenner, 2002; Wilson & Segall, 2003).

[2]This project is one of several related projects funded by a grant from the Ford Foundation to Leaders for Social Justice (LSJ), a group of educational administration professors committed to advancing educational equity and social justice within our field and within U.S. public schools. Catherine Marshall, Professor of Educational Leadership at the University of North Carolina, is principal investigator of this grant and has taken the lead in organizing and maintaining LSJ. Without her commitment and efforts, none of this would have occurred.

[3]Despite the potential usefulness of data transparency, even this needs to be monitored for fairness and equity. Data as provided are not always sound, as demonstrated by recent scandals in several high-profile school districts. Schools and districts will be tempted to skew their data because of high stakes, particularly with NCLB. This means that stakeholders need to monitor and query the data, even as they use them to challenge inequities.

[4]The Tennessee Department of Education Web site provides the following explanation of their value-added system:

> Value-Added Analysis compares the gains each student makes from year to year to the gains made by a normative sample for that same subject between those same grades. Thus, if the normal gain from 4th to 5th grade in math was 15 points, a 5th grade teacher's students who averaged a 15 point gain for the year would score "100," or 100% of normal gains. A teacher whose students averaged an 18-point gain would score 120, and so forth. (Tennessee Department of Education, 2002, ¶3)

[5]Caution is in order in interpreting data for this indicator. As Black and Valenzuela (2003) point out, learning English should not be the only legitimate outcome of bilingual

programs. Equally important are program goals such as proficiency and literacy in students' home languages and valuing and preserving students' home cultures. Furthermore, bilingual programs themselves are not monolithic, but are differentiated by distinct philosophies and assumptions. For example, the transitional bilingual program (in which weaning students away from Spanish is the objective) is considerably different from a dual language program (in which English and Spanish speakers both get the opportunity to become expert language users). Districts and schools' program choices reflect assumptions about cultural justice, about respect versus cultural hegemony, and about the ability of diverse children to learn.

[6]Funds to support outside facilitation of the equity audit process that we have described and the availability of appropriate expertise are significant issues for many districts, especially small and/or rural districts. Principals and superintendents in these districts who are committed to addressing inequity may well be able to develop the expertise needed to lead the process in-house. Low-cost or free assistance may be available from state education agencies or intermediate agency arms, such as regional education service centers or boards of county education supervisors. A third possibility may be for pairs or teams of school or district leaders to engage as "critical friends" for one another by facilitating the equity audit process in each other's schools.

[7]Negativity and resistance to evaluation data and findings rooted in local politics is a common phenomenon and has been explored extensively in the evaluation literature. See Thompson (1992) for a useful summary of the issues in this area.

14

Dilemmas and Lessons: The Continuing Leadership Challenge for Social Justice

Maricela Oliva

Gary L. Anderson

Introduction

Although the term *social justice* has recently gained popularity in education, its meaning is often ambiguous. Rather than insist on a single definition in this book, the editors have encouraged a "big tent" approach that is inclusive of diverse notions of social justice. Nevertheless, we cannot ignore the meanings that philosophers and political scientists have given this term. In the minds of many, the term is associated more readily with issues of class, or what Fraser (1997) calls *distributive justice*, than with what she calls a justice of *recognition of difference*, which has more to do with ethnicity, race, gender, sexuality, and post-colonialism. According to Fraser, theories of social justice have traditionally addressed issues of economic injustice, whose solutions involve "redistributing income, reorganizing the division of labor, subjecting investment to democratic decision-making, or transforming other basic economic structures" (p. 15). Egalitarian theorists have long attempted to theorize the nature of socioeconomic injustices, from Marx's notion of capitalist exploitation as the appropriation of the surplus value of labor to John Rawls' (1971) account of justice as fairness in the choice of principles governing the distribution of a society's goods. Fraser (1997) argues that we are currently in a "post-socialist" period in which we must bring together struggles for recognition of diverse identities with struggles over the distribution of material goods and services.

Although Fraser sees social justice as moving toward a reconciliation of issues of distribution and identity, Starratt (1994) divides things differently. He describes the three-pronged approach of what he calls the "ethical school," which fosters ethics of care, critique, and justice. An ethic of *care* "focuses on the demands of relationships, not from a contractual or legalistic standpoint, but from a standpoint of absolute regard" (p. 52). An ethic of *critique* "provides a framework for enabling the school community to move from a kind of naiveté about 'the way things are' to an awareness that the social and political arena reflect arrangements of power and privilege, interest and influence, often legitimized by an assumed rationality and by law and custom" (p. 47). An ethic of *justice* splits along the lines just presented.

The more conservative view of justice flows from Thomas Hobbs to John Rawls and conceives of the individual as independent of social relations and prior to society. Much rational-choice theory that informs school choice reforms is premised on this view of justice. Individuals are governed by self-interest, and justice is conceived as "a social engineering to harmonize needs and wants of self-serving individuals in society" (Starratt, 1994, p. 50). Discourses of equal opportunity and compensatory education conform to this view of justice. A more radical view of justice flows from Aristotle to Hegel to Marx to Dewey, Vygotsky and critical theory, and views society as the prior reality within which the individual develops. Thus, an ethic of justice requires deep forms of direct democracy and an understanding of how constructions of reality and communication are distorted by power relations. Using Starratt's ethical dimensions, we can see that school leader preparation programs that are based on social justice would focus on the relational and affective domains of administration, on building the skills of social critique, and on creating conditions in schools that provide for justice in both its individual and social senses.

Chapters in this book make use of both Fraser's and Starratt's views of social justice. The school communities and individuals described can be underserved and marginalized by high dropout rates or by unproblematized centric views that position nonmainstream students in ways that make them objects of neglect and violence. Whether the former or the latter, authors in these chapters paint a clear picture of students and/or school personnel's unacceptably differential access to knowledge and self-actualization.

To remedy this continuing challenge, editors Marshall and Oliva have gathered into one accessible text the multifaceted insights of a wide-ranging group of social-justice-oriented scholars, researchers, and practitioners who are successfully addressing this problem. An equally important and interrelated objective was to better incorporate these authors' thinking and writings into school leader preparation. The latter objective has the potential to take the long-held idea and dream of inclusive, social-justice-conscious practice for all students from a theoretical, conceptual, and practice vanguard to that of more common practice in schools and university classrooms. The resulting text makes it possible to more closely attend to the varied, yet predictable, leadership and practice dilemmas faced both by school leaders and by university educators of school leaders. This can help make the vision of socially just practice real more quickly by conceptually revolutionizing practice through intentional leadership preparation that enhances not only the development of school leaders' critical capital (Morrell & Collatos, 2002), but also their experience and skill for addressing related dilemmas and problems.

In this chapter, we recap several recurrent social justice themes and leverage points for change that are identified and discussed throughout this book. If the content of the preceding chapters are, individually and in their entirety, dense with identified leadership problems and dilemmas and with recommendations or strategies for action, this chapter serves as a thematic overview. In turn, the overview allows us to illustrate the continuing challenges that many of us face, as exemplified by the experiences of students and professors at two public institutions in different parts of the country. Anderson's, a co-author's, experience with the California State University, Los Angeles school leader preparation program will be described at length. A curricular innovation in the leadership preparation of a Texas urban cohort at Texas A&M University also is briefly described. Both examples illustrate the need for faculty to not only make changes, such as those undertaken in California, but also to continue to challenge disciplinary assumptions as to the knowledge and partnerships that leaders require to better meet the needs of students that they serve.

Lest anyone become sanguine about the ability of leadership preparation programs to transform schools and society by themselves, the California State University, Los Angeles case study illustrates the need for sustained and multifaceted efforts to produce ethical schools that produce equitable school outcomes. In a similar vein, the Texas A&M University illustration reminds us of the need to think outside of the box with social justice as the objective. Rather than cookbook solutions for meeting diverse students' needs, leaders at all levels of public and postsecondary education must be engaged creatively and collaboratively in new, even more student-centered practices.

Recurrent Themes

Several ideas and themes are woven through the various chapters of this book. These include definitions and illustrations of socially just practice and why such practice matters in education and society; the negative effects of marginalization, underservice, and even *violence* that are the consequences of leaders not taking action; models and strategies that illustrate how readers can enact a social justice practice in leader preparation programs and in decision-making or policy arenas; explorations (explicitly or otherwise) of the role of

Two Universities' Experiences

> "Lest anyone become sanguine about the ability of leadership preparation programs to transform schools and society by themselves, the California State University, Los Angeles case study illustrates the need for sustained and multifaceted efforts to produce ethical schools that produce equitable school outcomes. In a similar vein, the Texas A&M University illustration reminds us of the need to think outside of the box with social justice as the objective."

experience and socialization in shaping a social justice disposition and how we might learn from and use them to help develop socially just leaders; repeated exhortations for educators to not only think about and reflect on the need for a social justice orientation, but to act from it in their teaching and leadership; and the challenges that arise as a result of thinking and working from within such a framework. Through the various chapters, the editors illustrate that while the work of achieving social justice in schools and in society is far from done, enough conceptual and practice groundwork has been developed upon which to confidently build for improved school leadership and school leader preparation.

School Leadership for Social Justice

The question of what social justice leadership is, what it encompasses, and why it matters in school leadership is answered in a myriad of ways by the authors of this edited volume. Dantley and Tillman (Chapter 2) get things started by connecting the concept of social justice to landmark legal cases, such as *Brown v. Board of Education* and *Lau v. Nichols*. They discuss the work of numerous scholars to establish exactly what they and others mean by *social justice* and *socially just school leadership*. In doing so, they help us to understand that social justice scholarship and socially just practice has emerged as a movement that is now activated and active not only in scholarship, but also in organizational structures, conference presentations, and teaching. They contend that socially just practice matters because it has moral foundations that connect school leadership not only to our civic and democratic national project, but also as individuals to our inner or spiritual core. Leadership of this nature is transformative in that it seeks not only to improve what we have in place, but if necessary, to change structures and practices whenever they impede or get in the way of children's educational needs.

Court cases and attendant policy shifts are discussed by others as examples of the ways in which social justice school leader preparation reflects and supports the changes outside of schools that are intended to mitigate bias and discrimination against various groups. Koschoreck and Slattery (Chapter 7) discuss *Romer v. Evans* [517 U.S. 620 (1996)] and *Lawrence and Garner v. Texas* [539 U.S. 558 (2003)] for their impact in combating heteronormative discrimination against GLBTIQ individuals. Policy and other shifts vis-à-vis GLBTIQ individuals are shown to be occurring with regard to other social institutions, such as with same-sex marriages, religious ordinations of openly gay ministers, political elections of GLBTIQ persons, and the emergence of organizations that fight against what the authors call the "societal permission to hurt and even kill" GLBTIQ persons. It becomes evident through these chapters that much of what is wrong in our current practice, regarding GLBTIQ and other underserved students, stems not from intentional exclusion, but from ignorance about the ways in which our tolerance of seemingly small things, such as antigay comments and school harassment, and larger things, such as stereotypic and intolerant views of certain groups, contributes to student underachievement and inequity. This chapter and others go a long way toward educating many about the negative effects of such practices and about the need for educational leaders to intervene with policy, outspokenness, and with their actions in the interest of students.

However, socially just practice is also seen as having to do with the reconceptualization of school leadership in ways that allow for leaders who are themselves different from the norm or who work in particularly unique geographies and social spaces. Two chapters in particular address this aspect of the social justice leadership—those by Sanders-Lawson, Smith-Campbell, and Benham on "Wholistic visioning" (Chapter 3) and by López, González, & Fierro on border leadership (Chapter 4). In both cases, the authors choose not to limit themselves to definitions of self, other, and leadership practice in ways that force them into singular rather than multiple identities and roles or that position them to serve educational but not other community needs. In different ways, the authors argue for and illustrate the need for leaders to be boundary crossers and integrators. In both cases, socially just leadership is shown to be about educating in ways that allow leaders and students to be who they are and about willingly cultivating boundary-crossing skills, because that is what it takes to provide effective school and community leadership. The leaders/scholars of these chapters do us a service by showing that socially just leadership preparation is as necessary for the diverse leader and diverse contexts as it is for diverse students. They document their own and others' particular paths to self-affirming and boundary-spanning school leadership to meet students' needs—sometimes at considerable cost to themselves. In doing so, they chart several possible paths to leadership and model the way for others.

The important role of policy is especially highlighted in Cambron-McCabe's (Chapter 6) meta-analysis and discussion of the current national standards for school leadership—the Interstate School Leader Licensure Consortium standards. A national policy such as ISLLC not only has the effect of setting expectations for school leaders, but of articulating a list of competencies that define exemplary ones. The question here is whether the standards, as defined in/by this policy, contribute to or ignore the question of socially conscious and socially just school leadership. Rephrased, the question is whether the standards are as much about the moral imperatives of the heart and spirit (Chapter 2) as they are about the technical and managerial competencies of the head. Investigations discussed in Chapter 6 revealed that state policymakers were often uneasy and evidenced a lack of comfort with an explicit social justice framework for thinking about and discussing school licensure. Although they tended not to believe that social justice was explicitly a part of their licensure standards, they contended that expectations for social justice could be "read into" their standards by critically conscious and justice-oriented leaders. Policymakers, therefore, seem to depend on the "right-thinking" of school leader policy interpreters and implementers if social justice is to be enacted in schools. However, this point needs to be addressed more openly and explicitly in leader preparation programs and with policymakers to "re/focus" preparation programs toward double-loop learning (Argyris & Schon, 1974) in which leaders do not uncritically accept current practice, but first ask whether existing practices are equitably meeting students' needs. We discover yet again that contexts for social justice action are numerous and extend beyond schools into higher education and policy domains involving politics, group interests, and power.

Negative Effects of Marginalization and Exclusion

The negative effect of marginalization and exclusion is the *raison d'être* for these scholars and practitioners' urgent calls for a different, justice-oriented practice. Whether the negative effect is physical and psychological harm (see also Lugg & Tabbaa-Rida, Chapter 7); inattentive and overly constraining models of leadership that limit a leader's effectiveness; or many students' truncated educational achievement, largely through no fault of their own, the evidence of harm is abundant. In each case, however, this evidence is used not as the end point of discussion, but as the starting point for authors' recommendations in favor of the justice-oriented practice that they present and model. A good example of this is the work of Skrla, Scheurich, Garcia, and Nolly (Chapter 13) on their adaptation of tools that were historically used to monitor and ensure nondiscrimination in education. They connect their reconceived and adapted "equity audit" process to the history of such policy instruments meant to monitor educational practices to ensure that they did not result in discrimination. Their equity audit process is a tool that can be used to identify group educational disenfranchisements in order to engage school and community stakeholders in making whatever changes are necessary to eliminate them. As these authors have themselves learned, undertaking a school equity audit can be a difficult process, because it forces school stakeholders to confront the reality of inequitable student achievement outcomes that have often been invisible but are made evident through the analysis of school data.

Nevertheless, when used well, the process can lead to evidence-based conclusions about where equity problems exist and to multiple stakeholder agreement about what to do collaboratively in order to remedy them.

Modeling Good Practice

The chapter on equity audits by Skrla et al. not only describes the equity audit process, but also models its use by providing step-by-step instructions and guidance for how to put equity audits to good use in schools and communities. Marshall and Parker's (Chapter 10) contribution in "Vignettes of Leaders' Social Justice Dilemmas" provides yet another example of how a social justice orientation can be used to excavate, deconstruct, and recast practice (Larson & Murtadha, 2002) in real-world situations that are typically encountered by school leaders. The authors present and then explore cases in order to illustrate potentially different outcomes and how one might arrive at explicitly socially just conclusions. Their discussion centers on two vignettes, one involving an English-language learner who is placed in special education and another on a homeless African American girl who is treated as though her home situation and her many other burdens do not impact her learning. Both school incidents are inherently problematic for the students and could be indicative of educators' lack of knowledge and narrow or stereotypic views. Because not all possible interventions to these dilemmas are informed by a social justice orientation, the use of these vignettes allows students to practice *applying and internalizing* the principles and theories of socially just practice that they encounter in other chapters.

In a similar way, Hafner (Chapter 9) discusses teaching strategies for social justice to model what this kind of teaching is like as both content and process. Her synthesis of the research and scholarship on this pedagogy is her launching pad for talking about how difficult issues are handled in her classes and with her students. For university professors and school teachers, curriculum leaders, and principals, Hafner models how a social justice orientation can fruitfully inform instruction and student learning. This helps readers to anticipate the dilemmas and contested terrain that can arise from this kind of instruction.

Shapiro (Chapter 12) further illustrates how leaders involved in this kind of work can maintain equilibrium and wholeness despite the emotional and other challenges of social justice work. Such work is presented as draining, disconcerting, laden with controversy, and likely to subject practitioners to burnout if care is not taken to nurture and renew the self. Yet, social justice leaders can nurture and renew themselves through *art-making* by connecting to their imagination, emotions, and courage. Because school leadership involves the positive, sometimes euphoric, emotions of success as well as the negative emotions that result from contention and controversy, Shapiro contends that leaders should connect to their feelings rather than partition them outside of their work. Through examples of school leaders who have used art to renew themselves and by discussing how art-making has impacted their school leadership, Shapiro models the purpose and process of a leader's emotional self-care.

The Role of Socialization and Experience

One of the questions that vex school leadership educators is whether social justice oriented school and community leaders are born or made. If it is the former, the impact of educational leader preparation can be expected to be limited in scope. If it is the latter, then there is much to be learned about how to affect more critical and socially conscious leadership. Merchant and Shoho (Chapter 5) focus on trying to understand the social justice orientation of community and education leaders in San Antonio, Texas. The individuals interviewed appear to share socializing experiences that include having discrimination events directed toward them, growing up in cohesive and loving families that nurtured their self-esteem and critical consciousness, and taking part in intentional acts of "confrontation" in which parents or older family members challenged inequitable social structures from within the relative safety of family and relational networks. Their study hints at what could well be necessary elements—those discussed previously and others—for producing socially conscious leaders. Likewise, Brunner, Opsal, and Oliva (Chapter 11) take this a step further when they describe Brunner's use of technology to temporarily disrupt student identities in an online course to produce interactions among students that deviate from the norm and position them in ways that are different from their real-world subject positions. This is done by keeping online students intentionally ignorant, for a time, of their peers' actual identities and subject positions. Students thus experience what it is like to be perceived as someone "other" than who they actually are and learn from that. For some students, this means experiencing membership in a marginalized gender or categorical group, whereas for others it is the experience, for the first time, of White or male privilege. Given that these experiences are orchestrated with technology, an instrument, and a process that can be replicated, it offers the potential of adding *experience* and *enhanced identity knowledge* to *curricular content* and *process* for developing social justice leaders through school preparation and licensure programs.

Need for Action

Like the editors' justification for this book, the exhortation to act for more equitable school outcomes is made repeatedly in the various chapters in order to more fully take leadership for social justice from theory to practice and from vanguard to routine implementation. Embraced uncritically, the optimism and passion with which this message is conveyed could result in school leaders becoming disenchanted if their individual and school efforts to effect change result in small, negligible, or exceedingly slow improvements. However, school leaders cannot be naïve in thinking that their efforts will not meet resistance, both from within the school and from the external environment. The interests of powerful segments of society are well served by the practices that currently prevail in schools, and they are likely to use the power of their privileged class, race, gender, and/or sexual orientation to maintain the status quo. Even without conscious and intentional resistance to school leader efforts, institutionalized organizational and social systems are difficult to transform and slow to change. There are so many layers to educational and social inequity that even an intentional and well-conceptualized school leader preparation program is unlikely to change them easily or alone.

The Challenge of Slow Change: A Cautionary Tale

This book documents the remarkable advances that scholars in the field of educational leadership have made into the complexities of social justice concerns. Keep in mind that as recently as five years ago, terms such as *social justice, equity, critical pedagogy, diversity, race, class, gender,* and *heteronormativity* rarely appeared in the formal documentation of university-based credential programs in educational administration; now they are increasingly common. However, this discourse is far from hegemonic in the field; a recent special edition of *Educational Evaluation and Policy Analysis* (Spillane, 2003) on educational leadership largely ignores such issues.[1] Nevertheless, significant spaces have opened up in the field to explore issues of social justice.

The same is occurring in school districts. Although far from a majority, many administrators and teachers have adopted a discourse of social justice and are attempting to integrate it into their schools and classrooms. Equity audits have become more common, and workshops on issues of poverty, culture, and race have proliferated (see Payne, 2001). However, much data continues to show that administrators and teachers are cautious about addressing social justice issues in the context of conservative local and national politics (e.g., see Chapter 6). Administrators work in a national context of increased corporate (Feuerstein, 2001; Mickelson, 1999) and military (Berlowitz & Long, 2003) influence and in either privileged communities that are empowered to defend a status quo that favors their children (Wells & Serna, 1996) or in disempowered communities that are often gutted of resources and hope (see Larson and Ovando, 2001; Ryan, 2003; and Chapters 3, 4, 5, and 7 of this book).

In this context, imagine an administrator credential program with a racially diverse faculty that reflects its diverse student body. Imagine also that the faculty members are all committed to placing social justice at the center of the curriculum, publish widely on social justice issues, and have succeeded in integrating social justice issues throughout the curriculum. Imagine that the program has a school finance course with a major equity project at its center, a technology course that emphasizes equity and social inclusion, a social foundations course that emphasizes class, race, and gender, and a required course in special education for leaders taught by special education faculty. Imagine a program design that includes ongoing cycles of critical reflection and inquiry linked to an evolving educational vision and integrated with coursework and fieldwork.

Imagine that standard course texts in this program include Anyon's (1997) *Ghetto Schooling*; Cuban's (2001) *Oversold and Underused: Computers in Education*; Johnson's (2002) *Using Data to Close the Achievement Gap: How to Measure Equity in Our Schools*; Larson and Ovando's (2001) *The Color of Bureaucracy: The Politics of Equity in Multicultural School Communities*; Lindsey, Robins, and Terrell's (1999) *Cultural Proficiency: A Manual for School Leaders*; Meier's (1995) *The Power of Their Ideas: Lessons from a Small School in Harlem*; Poplin and Weeres's (1992) *Voices from the Inside: A Report on Schooling from Inside the Classroom*; Shirley's (1997) *Community Organizing for Urban School Reform*; Spring's (2002) *American Education* (and previous editions), and Wasley, Hampel, and Clark's (1997) *Kids and School Reform*.[2]

This imagined program, in fact, describes the Educational Administration program at the California State University, Los Angeles (CSULA), where co-author Anderson taught for five years and documented the program for its unique demographics and its faculty's commitment to social justice (Anderson, 2002). CSULA is located in East Los Angeles and serves one of the most diverse regions of the United States. The program in Educational Administration is the primary educator of administrators for the Los Angeles Unified School District (LAUSD) and districts in the San Gabriel Valley. A typical cohort of credential students at CSULA is 50% Latino (mostly of Mexican ancestry), 23% White, 13% Asian American, and 10% African American, with the remaining 4% being Armenian or Iranian American. At the time of the study, the Educational Administration program consisted of three African American, two Latino, two White, and one Korean American full-time faculty members. A more diverse student body or faculty is hard to imagine. Although faculty differed somewhat as to what specific issues should be central to a social justice agenda, they were all committed to a program that places issues of social justice at its center—not at its periphery.

To study and analyze the impact of this integrated program, Anderson (2002) conducted a discourse analysis of texts produced by the program since 1995, when a discourse of social justice appeared. The following types of texts were analyzed: (1) program documents developed for public consumption as well as those prepared for external evaluation (e.g., National Council on Accreditation of Teacher Education, California Commission on Teacher Credentialing); (2) course syllabi developed by faculty and faculty publications that reflected their social justice concerns; and (3) student work (ongoing rewrites of vision statements and reflective fieldwork narratives). Student work was analyzed at various stages of the program to explore both how student's views had shifted and how, if at all, a social justice orientation had affected their administrative (or teaching) practices. An online student survey filled out by students and graduates of the credential/master's program was included in the analysis.

In 1995, the CSULA Educational Administration faculty developed guiding principles and learning outcomes that spoke to the professional characteristics and skills they believed every candidate should have upon completing their program:

1. Each candidate should be taught the skills of **critical pedagogy**.
2. Each candidate should develop an understanding of the power of **personal awareness and reflection**.
3. Each candidate should be taught the skills and values of being a **change agent**.
4. Each candidate should be taught how to **assess schools** in the **context of larger systems** utilizing a variety of proven strategies and **technological tools**.
5. Candidates should be able to assess students' needs in light of the realities of the **school and community** systems in which they function, serving the needs of students **in their community**.
6. Each candidate should have the **will** to put her or his **knowledge and passion** into practice.

Only three of the faculty members in place during 2003 were around when these guiding principles were drafted in 1998; however, most of the new faculty reaffirmed their support for them. Terms such as *critical pedagogy* and *change agents* and an emphasis on the students' community context could be viewed explicitly as social justice goals. This can also be said about terms such as *personal awareness, will, and knowledge and passion*. According to Kim (1996), the new program was designed "to produce highly qualified educational administrators who would be *bold* enough to make changes in their schools to meet the challenges." (p. 2). Affective language, such as *bold, will,* and *passion,* was infused throughout the original documents.

This more affective language was not part of the dominant discourse of school reform. It indexes an affective realm that is unique among guiding principles for administrator preparation programs. This more affective emphasis is particularly evident in recent work by African American scholars (Ladson-Billings, 1994; see also Chapters 3 and 12 of this volume) who have made connections between school leadership and the civil rights movement in which church-based spirituality and social change are central themes. Faculty felt that more academic conceptions of social justice that were more theoretical needed to be supplemented in urban educational administration programs by the pas-

CSULA 1995 Guiding Principles

1. Each candidate should be taught the skills of **critical pedagogy**.
2. Each candidate should develop an understanding of the power of **personal awareness and reflection**.
3. Each candidate should be taught the skills and values of being a **change agent**.
4. Each candidate should be taught how to **assess schools** in the **context of larger systems** utilizing a variety of proven strategies and **technological tools**.
5. Candidates should be able to assess students' needs in light of the realities of the **school and community** systems in which they function, serving the needs of students **in their community**.
6. Each candidate should have the **will** to put her or his **knowledge and passion** into practice.

sion, will, and self-awareness that is required to carry out social projects in urban schools.

Students' Beliefs and Practices

Students' beliefs and practices as they moved through the program were tracked through an analysis of reflective essays written as part of their culminating portfolio evaluation and an online survey. The essays consisted of multiple iterations of students' initial vision statements and essays in which students described their fieldwork in light of the 10 California Standards. Neither of these assignments required students to address social justice issues. In fact, the requirement that they use the California Standards to evaluate their fieldwork activities, if anything, would discourage a discussion of social justice issues, because such issues are largely missing from the current California Standards.[3] Because they were not solicited, the appearance of social justice issues in these student texts has perhaps even greater significance. Despite the extensive thought and intentional planning that went into designing the program, the results were disappointing. Although some of the changes in student vision statements reflected a greater sensitivity to social justice issues, given the design of the program and the espoused commitments of the faculty, one might have expected more.

Educational Vision Statements

Students enter the program with a wide variety of political and philosophical stances with regard to education and society. For this reason, Anderson focused on shifts in language as students rewrote the statement periodically throughout their program. All students were asked to do at least one final revision of their initial statement, and many included other revisions in their portfolio that they had made along the way. Generally, changes over time in vision statements reflected new course content. For example, after students took the technology for administrators course, their vision statements often would include calls for greater access to technology. In fact, technology was the one area that was generally missing in the initial vision statement and included in the final one. Students' references to technology often focused on access/equity issues, suggesting that the orientation of the technology course had some impact on their belief system in this area. The same was true following their taking school law or school finance. Many students associated school law and finance with equity, resulting in statements such as, "Knowledge about legal and fiscal issues is necessary for administrators, so that every student receives an adequate and equitable education." Their finance course included an equity project assignment, and the school law course, although strictly following a mainstream text, also integrated equity issues. Students also showed an increased awareness of the need for community and parent support in their revisions, although this was often limited to parent education and limited forms of parent involvement. It should be noted here that no coursework focused specifically on school–community relations.

Although critical pedagogy is a central value of the program, there was little evidence of it in vision statements other than the view that *all* students should be successful. Typical of initial visions was one student's statement: "I envision a school culture that not only nurtures the learning paths of all students regardless of their socioeconomic status or language levels, but also one that challenges learners to ask critical questions." This student's only addition to his vision statement upon completion of the program was the following: "I see a teaching community that embraces content standards, supports students in the process of owning the standards, and assesses in an ongoing fashion the progress towards mastering the standards." Although standards were emphasized in the instructional leadership course, students were also exposed to culturally relevant pedagogy and equity indicators, such as the survey from Johnson (2002) on "the equitable school classroom," which conforms closely to a critical pedagogy approach. Little reference to this more critical literature was systematically addressed in the final vision statements.

Aside from the survey on an equitable school classroom, there is little clarity among program faculty as to what constitutes a "critical pedagogy." Some faculty who teach the course that focuses on instructional leadership place more of an emphasis on standards and testing than others. Second, students are under pressure from their school districts—particularly LAUSD—to espouse a vision that promotes a language of standards, performance indicators, and testing. Because these vision statements are shared with professionals at their school sites, the inclusion of a language more compatible with district mandates could have been a pragmatic move on the students' part.

In both the vision statements and the reflective essays, discourses and practices promoted by students' school districts tended to be more powerful than those of the program. As with the above case, it was often difficult to identify the source of the discourse. For instance, the language of professional learning communities for teachers tended to appear in initial vision statements as well as in final versions. However, in final versions these learning communities were more likely to include parents and community, rather then merely school professionals. This suggests that students enter the program with a set of discourses, beliefs, and values inherited from their school districts and perhaps from social constructions of schooling and its purposes, to which the CSULA program makes minor modifications.

Student teachers enter the teaching workforce already having some idea of what teaching is like, because they spent so many years as a student in schools. This often makes it difficult to change student teachers' image of what a classroom should look like. Administrative interns have spent years as both students and teachers in schools, and their image of what a school should be like is even more ingrained. Given the level of professional socialization that our students bring into the program, transmission modes of teaching appear to have limited impact on students in administrator preparation programs. Although student reflections often mentioned class readings and course concepts, they seemed most impacted by inquiry-oriented projects that required a more active, constructivist approach to learning. In the CSULA program, this included such activities as action research or equity projects, producing a school budget, analysis of case studies, role-plays, and so on.

The notion of seeing schools as cultures was introduced in later revisions, and this often included concepts that were clearly drawn from coursework. One student stated, "I envision a community that focuses on the goal of keeping the lifeworlds of the school at the center of all action thus keeping the systemworld in perspective." This language is borrowed from a Sergiovanni (1999) book used in their instructional leadership course. Many references to organizational learning and inquiry also appeared, referencing their reading of the Argyris and Schon (1974) text listed earlier. However, although there were many testimonials to the fact that students saw themselves as reflective practitioners who struggled to make their espoused theories congruent with their theories-in-use, they were unable to provide very many concrete examples. Their descriptions of fieldwork tended to reflect a business as usual, step-by-step, albeit detailed, description of program implementation.

Lessons of the Integrated Program

We have to ask what this limited evidence of progress from a discourse analysis of documents from the CSULA leader preparation program—despite the program's coherent and integrated focus on social justice—means for other efforts to make social justice more significant and prevalent in preparation programs. Professors of educational administration have much to learn from previous work by advocates of multicultural education. Sleeter and Grant (1993) describe how multicultural education must be comprehensive to be effective. In other words, it cannot simply be an add-on to curriculum; it must address changes in a school's curriculum, instruction, evaluation methods, home/community relations, staffing, and extracurricular activities. A social justice focus in the preparation of educational administrators must be approached in the same way, although I would add to the list the recruitment of a diverse, activist, and talented pool of applicants to educational administration programs. This, in effect, is what the CSULA program faculty attempted to do with the program (see Figure 14.1). The following discussion of this educational leadership preparation program using Sleeter and Grants' (1993) approach may help to point out why putting this into practice presents its own challenges.

Curriculum

If the definition of curriculum is limited to the mere identification of courses and the content of those courses, then many educational administration programs, like the program at CSULA, are succeeding in shifting the curriculum to a social justice focus. However, if we use a deeper definition of curriculum that includes fieldwork and long-term program effects, then the social justice aims of programs may be viewed as less than successful. In the first sense of curriculum, fewer and fewer programs are using traditional texts in educational administration, organizational theory, finance, and supervision that portray a rational, functionalist world with white males at the helm. Not only are these traditional texts no longer used, recent editions of these texts are increasingly becoming more inclusive and aware of competing leadership paradigms. Shifts in thinking among scholars committed to social justice have impacted UCEA recommendations for a knowledge base and have critiqued the ISLLC national standards and a national examination developed by ETS (Anderson, 2001; Cambron-McCabe, Chapter 6 of this volume).

Although the curriculum in the CSULA program has increasingly focused on social justice and modes of critical reflection, most students' descriptions of their fieldwork did not reflect this curriculum. Robinson (1994) has argued that critical theory and research has failed to deliver on its promise because it lacks effectiveness. According to Robinson, the effectiveness of a theory is enhanced to the extent that it generates explanations that point the way to a problem's resolution, that it fosters the identification and motivation of agents whose energy and commitment can drive the change process. In other words, much critical theory with a goal of social justice lacks a theory of change. This may be why the students espouse many of the beliefs the program attempts to instill, but in everyday field practice they find it difficult to see how these beliefs inform their actions.

Integration of coursework with inquiry, equity and vision development

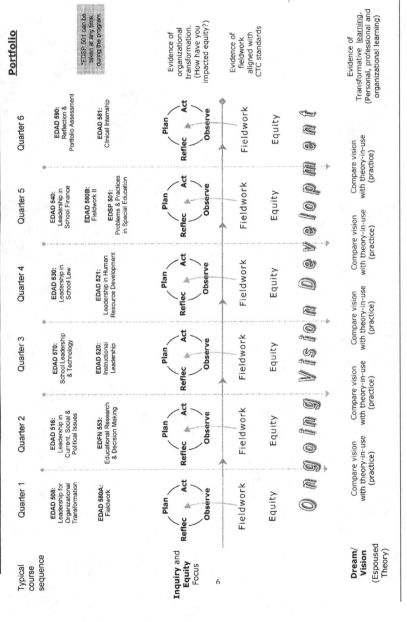

FIGURE 14.1 *Integration of Coursework with Inquiry, Equity, and Vision Development*

Instruction

The Sleeter and Grant model illustrates the idea that courses in educational administration programs must be the focal point for ongoing inquiry, field-work, vision development, and equity/social justice concerns. Although instructors in the CSULA program engage in these types of activities in individual courses, the habits of inquiry, equity, and ongoing vision development are not yet reinforced *across* courses. Given the intense socialization students receive in their school sites, where critical thought and inquiry are seldom rewarded, administrator preparation programs have to constantly model and reinforce new ways of thinking and acting.

Evaluation

Programs that use comprehensive examinations as culminating experiences assume a transmission or banking model of education (Freire, 1970). Such examinations have largely been replaced by portfolio assessments in recent years. However, there is nothing inherently dynamic or superior about portfolio assessment. Portfolios can turn out to be static scrapbooks that represent little more than the documentation of activities that represent business as usual—even when they are electronic portfolios with clip art. It is crucial that portfolios be structured to represent dynamic instruction. Although potentially superior to comprehensive exams, unless students are required to conceptualize their practice using research and social theory, portfolio creation can become an anti-intellectual exercise that returns us to an apprenticeship model of administrative learning.

University–School District–Social Agency Relationships

Sleeter and Grant's (1993) model is designed for schools and calls for home–community–school relationships. Similarly, university-based administrator preparation programs with a social justice focus must maintain close relationships with school districts and social agencies that provide services for low-income children. Educational administration programs need to attract faculty who have both a strong commitment to social justice and who also either have strong links to school districts or extensive administrative experience. This is a difficult combination for programs to achieve. Most programs do not pay salaries that are competitive with school and district administrators and often hire faculty with Ph.D.'s but little or no administrative experience and sometimes with little teaching experience. These new scholars may have a strong commitment and research record on social justice issues, but little understanding of the constraints and opportunities that provide the daily context for practitioners.

Extracurricular Activities

While the notion of *extracurricular activities* may seem irrelevant for an educational administration program, many professional development activities can and should be required of students and integrated into their portfolio evaluations. For example, CSULA students are encouraged to attend conferences, join professional associations, and subscribe to professional journals. This is also a way to introduce students to conferences and organizations that center on social justice issues.

The CSULA program had recruited a diverse faculty committed to a rigorous and equitable education for all children and a society that provides equity for all its citizens. This faculty had designed and delivered a curriculum with a strong social justice orientation, balancing the theoretical with the practical. In Starratt's (1994) terms, the faculty espoused a strong ethic of care through the affective and relational discourse infused in its documents. They developed an ethic of critique through their use of social-justice-oriented readings and class discussions and activities. And they created an ethic of justice through camaraderie and democratic decision-making as well as through the program's emphasis on practical ways to create just schools through inquiry and data analysis. All of the pieces appeared to be in place for the program to have a significant impact on the administrators and schools that it touched. Nevertheless, the program did not immediately show evidence of producing synergism among its components and in the broader social environment that would create the powerful impact on students that would be observable in more explicitly social justice educational practices at their school sites.

Conclusion

Although our description of the limited impact of the CSULA program is meant as a cautionary tale, we should not be too hard on the faculty who struggled to create and sustain it, nor underestimate its impact. First of all, it is very difficult to evaluate a program in the short term, and the long-term data on graduates of the program was very thin. As we know anecdotally, outstanding teachers and administrators when asked about influences on their practice will often refer to a professor who inspired them or an activity they did in class that opened their eyes. After all, university-based programs are not hands-on workshops. Good ones work within the tensions that exist in the spaces between theory and practice. As Morgan (1997) states, "The ability to read and understand what is happening in one's organization is a key managerial competency" (p. 355). Preparing teachers and administrators may be as much about encouraging an attentively thoughtful and critical attitude as about imparting specific content or skill knowledge.

The dilemma of developing these critical habits of mind in teachers and administrators is that we are sending them into settings in which such critique is seldom rewarded. In the case of CSULA, many graduates were entering LAUSD, the second largest school district in the country and one that mandated a highly scripted reading program (Open Court) for all teachers—even those teaching English-language learners, for whom the program made no accommodation.

The process of professional socialization in the workplace is so powerful that even the most critical among us often find ourselves engaging in practices in direct contradiction to our espoused theories. We rationalize that we must pick our battles or that we don't have tenure yet or that we won't be promoted or the boss will retaliate. Before long, we find ourselves comfortable in a system that, in theory, we find indefensible.

Even in administrator preparation programs with a social justice focus, we may be preparing teachers and administrators as double-loop learners for single-loop learning systems (Argyris & Schon, 1974) and expecting them to figure out on their own how to successfully function there. In the battle between espoused theories and theories-in-use that are reinforced by habit, custom, and professional self-interest, guess which one is likely to win? No wonder Cambron-McCabe says in Chapter 6 that working for social justice is not for the faint of heart.

It is increasingly important to prepare a generation of school administrators who see themselves as advocates for low-income communities rather than paternalistic leaders with a deficit model of urban children and their parents. In our current de-industrialized society that fails to provide a living wage for millions of Americans, low-income parents see fewer options for their children. Two options that loom large in poor communities are incarceration and the military. Zero-tolerance policies in schools and society are viewed as getting tough without having to do the difficult work of building relations and trust with local communities.

One solution to this dilemma that both provides some political leverage for administrative risk-taking in schools and empowers low-income communities and communities of color is to move the preparation of teachers and administrators into these communities. Even more democratic approaches, such as distributed leadership and school-community collaboration, tend to be timid about shifting the locus of control very far from the principal or school professionals. Crowson and Boyd (1999) are eloquent on this point:

> The need to preserve strong norms of professional discretion against private-regarding parents and narrow-minded communities was a theme as early as 1932, in the work of Willard Waller. Generations of school administrators in the U.S. have been trained around the dangers of losing managerial control to the "politics of their communities." (p. 11)

Nevertheless, recent scholarship is documenting a potential alliance between school administrators and community organizing groups, such as the

Association of Community Organization for Reform Now (ACORN), the In-
dustrial Areas Foundation (IAF), and other groups, such as Pacific Institute
for Community Organization (PICO) (Gold, Simon, and Brown, 2004; López,
González, & Fierro, Chapter 4 of this volume. Shirley, 1997). Such alliances
provide political leverage both for administrators and communities.

Organized communities that are linked to schools have helped schools
get the attention of local political leaders to get access to additional resources
and infrastructure improvements such as bond initiatives, after-school programs, more crossing guards, and improved traffic patterns in school areas.
Once social-justice-oriented administrators, like Phil Jones of Chapter 4, realize that local communities have concerns that overlap with theirs, they are
more willing to take the necessary risks—such as the risk of increased conflict
and some loss of power—that democratic participation always entails. Schools
with intimate connections to local communities are also in a better position
to build on a community's "funds of knowledge" (Moll, Amanti, Neff, &
González, 1992) to improve educational outcomes.

In their study of 19 community organizing groups supporting school reform, Gold, Simon, and Brown (2004) found that authentic community involvement in the leadership of the school helped to sustain positive changes
in the face of administrative turnover:

> In several of the sites we studied, teachers who were working with community
> organizing groups became principals in other schools and were instrumental in
> developing the next generation of reform educators. Even when they remained
> as teachers in the school setting, they would often play an important role in
> keeping up strong school/community connections by "socializing" incoming prin-
> cipals and teachers. In both cases, the assumptions and practice of these teach-
> ers and administrators changed as they began to value the community/school
> connection. In one instance, professionals who considered themselves part of the
> community organizing effort moved up to central office positions, bringing a
> community-oriented perspective to the district level. (p. 28)

Alliances with community organizations cannot only bring benefits to a
school or district, but it also brings a form of public accountability lacking in
reforms efforts directed by distant politicians and business leaders. In the absence of real influence on their local schools, poor communities logically turn
to the kinds of quick fixes, such as vouchers, that seem to promise a short-
term escape from nonresponsive urban schools.

What we are suggesting here is that although we need more administrator preparation programs like CSULA's that have faculty diversity and an
integrated, social justice curriculum that teaches the skills of critical reflection
and dialogue and that link field experiences with coursework, this is not
enough. If our social justice goals are aimed at empowering disenfranchised
students, then we can only do this in alliance with disenfranchised communities and by thinking creatively and outside of the box about how to work to-

ward social justice. A brief anecdote involving Oliva is illustrative of such out-of-box thinking.

In their work at Texas A&M University, Jean Madsen and Linda Skrla organized and obtained funding for a cohort of high-level K–12 urban administrators who were ready to pursue doctoral study in school leadership and administration. All of the identified doctoral students in school leadership and administration were from the Houston Independent School District, a district whose approximately 212,000 students are 57.1% Hispanic, 30.5% African American, 9.3% White, 3% Asian, and 0.1% Native American (Stockwell, 2004). Both Madsen and Skrla were looking for elective-type courses to put into the curriculum for this cohort, and Skrla sought out Oliva, one of this chapter's co-authors, to design a course on postsecondary issues. Madsen confided later that she was not sure that the postsecondary content would be beneficial for the principals, district administrators, directors, area superintendents, and chief academic officers for the district. Nevertheless, both decided to put this on the students' schedules.

Not only did the K–12 administrators value the postsecondary focus and content of the course titled "The College Student: Issues and Influencers on School to University Transition," but several indicated that it dramatically expanded how they think about their administrative work for children. To paraphrase what several students subsequently said, they knew they wanted to help their kids succeed in college, but they did not have concrete information from the postsecondary research about (a) things to do to help students, particularly under-represented minority students, get into and succeed in college; (b) what the college experience was like for students, particularly for diverse students; (c) the kinds of strategies and activities that they might begin to incorporate into school practice for students' eventual postsecondary success; or (d) how state policy mandates were already requiring and compelling them to act more concretely and creatively in school–university partnerships for children's benefit. As a result of the postsecondary information acquired in class,

Bridging School and University for Students

"As a result of the postsecondary information acquired in class, one administrator decided to look at the outcomes for K–16 alignment teams that are already in place for her high school, feeder schools, and local universities. Another decided to recommend districtwide changes to the school counseling program . . . to make sure that important postsecondary information would be provided to all students, not just to the top students in each school. District staff development directors also are considering whether new and additional professional development training with a K–16, postsecondary orientation should be developed."

one administrator decided to look at the outcomes for K–16 alignment teams that are already in place for her high school, feeder schools, and local universities. Another decided to recommend districtwide changes to the school counseling program of high schools to make sure that important postsecondary information would be provided to all students, not just to the top students in each school. District staff development directors also are considering whether new and additional professional development training with a K–16, postsecondary orientation should be developed.

It is easy to forget, but caring for children with the objective of working toward social justice for them and for their communities means caring about them in their whole lives. Oliva, among others, has for this reason argued that college and university faculty cannot just worry about and attend to the needs of the students in college. There is value, from a postsecondary and social justice perspective, to thinking about students and how they are doing *before* college. Particularly with students from groups that are underrepresented in college, it is fundamentally important to consider and address why they are not adequately prepared to attend college or are systematically disenfranchised from that possibility by limited access to information, low levels of legitimated social and cultural capital, and inadequate family and adult school guidance about how to successfully navigate the school-to-university pathway.

Children should neither drop out of school administrators' lives after high school nor be invisible to college faculty and administrators before they walk through their ivy-covered college gate. As the California and Texas examples illustrate, we must stop "expertly" developing programs and curricula to empower local communities and begin developing traditional as well as community-based programs *with* them. Whether such community-based and boundary-spanning administrator preparation programs are feasible or not is an open question. The point is that we need to go deeper and wider in our understanding of how to leverage change in large systems that are kept in place not just because of what mainstream change literature calls "dynamic conservatism" (Argyris & Schon, 1974), but also because some privileged groups benefit from it. Nor should we abandon the system and run off to find better cheese (Johnson, 1998) as business-inspired rational choice and voucher models suggest. This book provides some guideposts along the path of widening and deepening our understanding of the meaning of social justice, gives us a sense of how to build programs with a social justice orientation, and— here's the really hard part—suggests how to effect enduring change in schools, students, communities, and within ourselves to eradicate the policies and practices that currently serve to marginalize students.

Discussion Questions and Activities

Chapter 1 ended with "When confronted by the need to act in real life social justice challenges, . . . educational leaders will have the will, the words, the facts, and the guts to make a difference." What do you still need, now, at the end of this book, to make a difference?

Several exercises and activities are suggested here that can be used in conjunction with this chapter or can serve as capstone activities for the book as a whole. Suggested readings are listed after each activity.

Documenting Experience to Excavate and Transform Inequity

1. Locate childhood friends from your home community, particularly those from a different racial, ethnic, gender, sexual orientation, religious, socioeconomic class, or other background than your own. Have them describe their K–16 (kindergarten through college) educational histories to you and listen particularly for how those histories were subjectively experienced by them. For example, did they attend the same elementary, middle, and high schools that you attended? Did they go to college? If so, where did they attend? If they did not attend the same educational institutions as you, what shaped their educational trajectory? Why did they attend certain institutions or none at all?

   As you listen to these histories, compare whether and how your childhood friends' educational histories mirror your own. Where those educational histories are different, how did the broader community's social and political history and its taken-for-granted educational practices influence those different experiences? Reflect on and describe the extent to which differences in categorical membership for you and for your friends explain these varied educational experiences.

2. Consider how today's high school students from your current community are experiencing their education. Do their categorical memberships shape their experiences in the same way as they shaped your and your friends' experience in the previous activity? What still needs to be changed about the ways that schools interact with students who have racial, ethnic, gender, sexual orientation, religious, socioeconomic class, or other backgrounds that are different from the norm?

3. With the reflections on your childhood community or your community of current practice from the previous two activities in mind, design an action plan to effect the changes that are required to make school practices and educational systems more socially just and equitable. This action plan should include identified domain areas for social justice interventions (i.e., personnel, policies, curriculum, etc.), goals and objectives, strategies for action, time lines, as well as a rationale for the proposed actions. Include a description of community supports for proposed actions, steps that might need to be taken to galvanize multiple community stakeholder collaboration for the proposed action, forces of resistance for your proposals, as well as a description of how that resistance might be overcome or mitigated to achieve your social justice objectives. Whenever possible, use the tools provided in this text—such as equity audits, policy levers, border crossing, boundary bridging, etc.—to conceptualize the rationale, justification, and proposed actions. For 1–3, see also Linde's (1993) *Life Stories: The Creation of Coherence.*

Building Powerful Alliances between Schools and Communities

4. Answer the following preliminary questions about your school and community:

   • To what extent does the person with position authority speak for your school?
   • To what extend does some form of representative group speak for your school?
   • To what extent are there organized groups in your community that genuinely represent community interests?

- If your school is located in a middle- or high-income community, to what extent is the community supportive of social justice initiatives?
- What might such initiatives look like in your community?
- What might they look like in a low- or mixed-income community?

In order for reciprocity between schools and communities to occur, schools must be restructured along democratic lines, and low-income communities must be sufficiently organized to build alliances with local schools. With your school community of practice in mind, create a list of groups and individuals in the larger community and in your region that could become part of an advocacy coalition for the powerful assertion of social justice issues. List the resources each would bring and the motivations each would have to join and be active in such a coalition. Consider presenting this list to the most powerful person on your list as your beginning contribution to developing the momentum for action.

5. Issues of reciprocity between schools and local communities are very complex. Cornwall (1996) has adapted a continuum of purposes for participatory action research, which we have adapted in Table 14.1 for school–community relations. Identify your own school's relations with its community from among these positions. What would it take to move your school in the direction of co-learning and collective action? For more on community participation, see Anderson (1999); Gold, Simon, and Brown (2004); Goodman, Baron, and Myers (2004); and Shirley (1997).

6. Patricia Hill-Collins (1990) writes of the "outsider-within," the person who is an insider in a group by virtue of appointed position, but who is never totally accepted in the group because of something about him or her, such as religion, skin color, ethnicity, gender, social class, sexual orientation, disability, political ideology, etc. If you have ever been in that position as an educator, write a paragraph expressing not only the negative feelings, but also the revelations, freedom, and power that might come from standing outside and looking in at a group. Discuss this as related to the border (Chapter 4) and/or to wholistic visioning (Chapter 3) leadership or to the experiential simulation (Chapter 11). Also see Adams, Bell, and Griffin (1997); Adams et al. (2000); and Anzaldúa, G. (1987).

Annotated Readings

Many institutions work hard to place social justice at their center, but as with the CSULA program, the real test is the extent to which faculty have truly internalized the values and are able to act on them. In the *Power of Their Ideas* (1995), Deborah Meier describes how one of the values her school attempted to instill in students was a sense of political agency and citizenship. She describes how the students and her faculty were tested during the week of the Rodney King verdict and the high school walk outs that occurred in high schools across the country. The struggle of the Central Park East faculty to trust and empower their students during this difficult time is documented by Frederick Wiseman, who happened to be producing a documentary at the school during that week. The result, *High School II* is a powerful documentation of a school struggling to implement its social justice values.

In *The Color of Bureaucracy* (2001), Colleen Larson and Carlos Ovando provide a case study of white administrators responding to a racial incident at the school. While

TABLE 14.1. *School–Community Interaction*

Mode of Participation	Involvement of Local People	Relationship of School and Action to Local Community
Co-option	Token: Community representatives are hand-picked but have no real input or power. Mere appearance of participation.	Action *on* community.
Compliance	Community representatives are elected. Tasks are assigned, but school controls agenda.	Action *for* community.
Consultation	Community opinions are solicited. School analyzes feedback and decides on a course of action.	Action *for/with* community.
Cooperation	School works together with community to determine priorities; school is responsible for directing the process.	Action *with* community.
Co-learning	Community and outsiders share their knowledge to create new understandings and work together to form action plans, with facilitation by school personnel.	Action *with/by* community.
Collective action	Local community members set their own agenda and mobilize to carry it out. They seek school support for community agendas.	Action *by* community.

implementing a policy that they felt was fair, but that offended the African American community, they learn that being aloof from the surrounding community leads to devastating misunderstandings. These administrators did not have racist intentions, but their policies were viewed as racist by a sector of the community. Likewise, the social-justice-oriented rhetoric of the No Child Left Behind legislation and its associated policies of high-stakes testing and disaggregation of test scores by race can also have unintended consequences. These consequences are documented by Linda McNeil (2000) in *Contradictions of School Reform* and by Angela Valenzuela (2004) in her edited book, *Leaving Children Behind: How Texas-Style Accountability Fails Latino Youth*.

A young person's ultimate success in life is greatly influenced by whether he or she transitions to and graduates from college. Nonetheless, the pressures of high-stakes testing and the myriad of issues that are addressed in schools result in school leaders' rarely having time to do little more than hope that students' postsecondary lives will largely take care of themselves if they successfully graduate from high school. In *Choosing Schools: How Social Class and Schools Structure Opportunity*, Patricia McDonough (1997) illustrates how the administrative practices of four different high schools actively construct the likelihood that a student will go to college as well as the ultimate college choice of students from different racial, ethnic, and socioeconomic groups. Used in conjunction with primary and secondary texts on social and cultural capital and with recent studies such as the Tomas Rivera Policy Institute's *College Knowledge: What Latino Parents Need to Know and Why They Don't Know It* by Tornatzky, Cutler, and Lee (2002), the social justice value of school leaders attending to their students' post-high school life comes into high relief. Additional dialogue is needed about how school and college administrators, faculty, and policymakers can work more closely together for the benefit of students, particularly those who are currently underrepresented in college.

References

Anderson, G. (1999). Toward authentic participation: Deconstructing the discourse of participatory reforms. *American Educational Research Journal, 35*(4), 571–606.

Anderson, G. (2001). Disciplining leaders: A critical discourse analysis of the ISLLC National Examination and Performance Standards in educational administration. *International Journal of Leadership in Education, 4*(3), 199–216.

Anderson, G. (2002). Can we effectively build credential programs for educational administrators on principles of social justice? Retrieved October 15, 2004, from *http://leadershipforsocialjustice.org*

Anyon, J. (1997). *Ghetto schooling: A political economy of urban educational reform.* New York: Teachers College Press.

Argyris, C., & Schon, D. (1974). *Theory in practice: Increasing professional effectiveness.* San Francisco: Jossey-Bass.

Berlowitz, M., & Long, N. (2003). The proliferation of JROTC: Educational reform or militarization. In K. Saltman and D. Gabbard (Eds.), *Education as enforcement: The militarization and corporatization of schools* (pp. 163–176). New York: Routlege Falmer.

Collins, P. H. (1990). *Black feminist thought: Knowledge, consciousness and the politics of empowerment.* New York: Routledge.

Cornwall, A. (1996). Towards participatory practice: Participatory rural appraisal (PRA) and the participatory process. In K. De Koning and M. Martin (Eds.), *Participatory research in health: Issues and experience* (pp. 94–107). London: Zed Books.

Crowson, R., & Boyd, W. L. (1999). Coordinated services for children: Designing arks for storms and seas unknown. *American Educational Research Journal, 101*(2), 140–179.

Cuban, L. (2001). *Oversold and underused: Computers in education.* Cambridge, MA: Harvard University Press.

Feuerstein, A. (2001). Selling our schools? Principle's views on schoolhouse commercialism and school–business interactions. *Educational Administration Quarterly, 37*(3), 322–371.

Fraser, N. (1997). *Justice interrupturs: Critical reflections on the "postsocialist" condition.* New York: Routledge, 1997.

Freire, P. (1970). *The pedagogy of the oppressed.* New York: Seabury.

Fusarelli, L. (2001). Administrator preparation programs: Reforming again, again, and again. *UCEA Review, 17*(1), 10–12.

Gold, E., Simon, E., & Brown, C. (2004). A new conception of parent engagement: Community organizing for school reform. In F. English (Ed.), *Handbook of educational leadership.* Newbury Park, CA: Sage.

Goodman, J., Baron, D., & Myers, C. (2004). Constructing a democratic foundation for school-based reform: The local politics of school autonomy and internal governance. In F. English (Ed.), *The handbook of educational leadership*. Newbury Park, CA: Sage.

Johnson, R. (2002). *Using data to close the achievement gap: How to measure equity in our schools*. Thousand Oaks, CA: Corwin Press.

Johnson, S. (1998). *Who moved my cheese?* New York: G. P. Putnam's Sons.

Kim, L. (1996). CSULA's effort to walk the talk for beginning administrators. *The Journal of CAPEA, 8,* 21–28.

Ladson-Billings, G. (1994). *The dream keepers*. San Francisco: Jossey-Bass Publishers.

Larson, C. L., & Murtadha, K. (2002). Leadership for social justice. In Joseph Murphy (Ed.), *The educational leadership challenge: Redefining leadership for the 21st century* (pp. 134–161). Chicago, IL: The University of Chicago Press.

Larson, C. L., & Ovando, C. (2001). *The color of bureaucracy: The politics of equity in multicultural school communities*. Belmont, CA: Wadsworth.

Linde, C. (1993). *Life stories: The creation of coherence*. New York: Oxford University Press.

Lindsey, R., Robins, K., & Terrell, R. (1999). *Cultural proficiency: A manual for school leaders*. Thousand Oaks, CA: Corwin Press.

McDonough, P. (1997). *Choosing colleges: How social class and schools structure opportunity*. Albany, NY: SUNY Press.

McNeil, L. M. (2000). *Contradictions of school reform: Educational costs of standardized testing*. New York: Routledge.

Meier, D. (1995). *The power of their ideas: Lessons from a small school in Harlem*. Boston: Beacon Press.

Mickelson, R. (1999). International business machinations: A case study of corporate involvement in local educational reform. *Teachers College Record, 100*(3), 476–506.

Moll, L. C., Amanti, C., Neff, D., & González, N. (1992). Funds of knowledge for teaching: Using a qualitative approach to connect homes and classrooms. *Theory into Practice, 31*(2), 132–141.

Morgan, G. (1997). *Images of organization*. Thousand Oaks, CA: Sage.

Morrell, E., & Collatos, A. (2002). Toward a critical teacher education: High school student sociologists as teacher educators. *Social Justice, 29*(4), 60–70.

Payne, R. (2001). *Framework for understanding poverty*. Highlands, TX: Aha Process, Inc.

Poplin, M., and Weeres, J. (1992). *Voices from the inside: A report on schooling from inside the classroom*. Claremont, CA: The Institute for Education in Transformation at the Claremont Graduate School.

Rawls, J. (1971). *A theory of justice*. Cambridge: Belknap Press of Harvard University Press.

Robinson, V. (1994). The practical promise of critical research in educational administration. *Educational Administration Quarterly, 30*(1), 56–76.

Ryan, J. (2003). *Leading diverse schools*. Boston: Kluwer.

Sergiovanni, T. J. (1999). *The lifeworld of leadership*. San Francisco: Jossey-Bass.

Shirley, D. (1997). *Community organizing for urban school reform*. Austin: University of Texas Press.

Sleeter, C., & Grant, C. (1993). *Making choices for multicultural education: Five approaches to race, class, and gender*. New York: Macmillan.

Spillane, J. P. (2003). Special Issue on Educational Leadership, *Educational Evaluation and Policy Analysis, 25*(4), 343–488.

Spring, J. (2002). *American education* (10th ed.). New York: McGraw-Hill.

Starratt, R. J. (1994). *Building an ethical school: A practical response to the moral crisis in schools*. London: Falmer Press.

Stockwell, R. (2004). College access data profile for the Houston Independent School District. Unpublished manuscript.

Tornatzky, L. G., Cutler, R., & Lee, J. (2002). *College knowledge: What Latino parents need to know and why they don't know it*. Claremont, CA: Tomás Rivera Policy Institute.

Valenzuela, A. (Ed.). (2004). *Leaving children behind: How Texas-style accountability fails Latino youth*. Albany: SUNY Press.

Wasley, P., Hampel, R., & Clark, R. (1997). *Kids and school reform*. San Francisco: Jossey-Bass.

Wells, A. S., & Serna, I. (1996). The politics of culture: Understanding local political resistance to detracking in racially mixed schools. *Harvard Educational Review, 62*(1), 93–118.

*Endnotes*_____

[1]Some scholars, such as Fusarelli (2001), have argued that social justice issues should be implicit in all scholarship on school improvement. However, if this were the case, one would have expected greater improvement in these areas than we have experienced under the hegemony of a school improvement paradigm.

[2]More traditional texts were used because many social-justice-oriented books engage in a strong ethic of critique but may not provide an ethic of "applied" justice for future administrators (Starratt, 1994). Some of these more traditional texts are by authors well known to professors of educational administration (i.e., Barth, Glatthorn, Glickman, Imber & van Geel, LaMorte, Sergiovanni, etc.)

[3]California is about to adopt a modified version of the ISSLC Standards that are somewhat more focused on social justice issues. Franklin Campbell Jones, a faculty member of the CSULA educational administration program, was a member of the committee that attempted to infuse social justice concerns into the new standards.

15

The Wider Societal Challenge: An Afterword

Catherine Marshall
Michelle Young

Although the education and welfare of school children has been the primary concern of educational leaders and those who prepare them for many years, it is clear that this concern has been strengthened and focused over the past decade. Moreover, within the context of higher education a movement is growing—a movement to prepare educational leaders to support social justice within our nation's schools.

The chapters that make up this book bear witness to both the field's commitment to high quality and equitable education and the movement to prepare leaders for social justice. Throughout the book, authors have shared stories, statistics, and helpful ideas. They have focused on educational leaders, communities, leadership faculty, policymakers, and organizations. Their work, taken as a whole, sends a clear message: Social justice leadership is a critical building block in the educational equity project.

In this "afterword," we discuss the wider societal context and the role that social justice leadership plays within a larger equity project. Some have questioned whether it is possible to prepare leaders to work for social justice, noting that not only have we had little success in this area in the past, but that success would depend on much more than leadership preparation (e.g., Lytle, 2004). In response to these concerns, we make several bold assertions; delineate continuing challenges, as well as examples of people who do "walk the talk"; and chart several societal and political maneuvers toward revolutionary change in educational leadership.

A Bold Assertion: Those Who Can't or Won't Shouldn't

Chapter 1 introduced this book with an idealistic assertion, that "educational leaders will have the will, the words, the facts, and the guts to make a difference." Making a difference for kids is important. Closing the achievement gap is important. Ensuring student safety is important. Hiring and developing quality teachers for all classrooms is important. Moreover, all of these activities (and others) can support the development of social justice in schools, but they will not automatically move a school as a whole in this direction. Social justice leadership is needed. We would argue that social justice leadership is leadership with one's eyes wide open; it is purposeful, it is resourceful, it is systemic, and it is informed. We would also argue that at times it is neither easy nor comfortable to lead for social justice. Thus, the first bold assertion that we will make is that individuals who are unable or unwilling to purposefully, knowledgeably, and courageously work for social justice in education should not be given the privilege of working as a school or district leader.

Leadership matters. Leaders can both positively and negatively influence the education and educational experiences of the children in their schools. Currently, far too many students are negatively impacted. Indeed, schools across our nation, regardless of district size, resources, and student populations, are failing to educate, develop, protect, and include all students (Capper & Young, in press). Moreover, the students who are most negatively affected by this failure are students from marginalized groups (e.g., students of color, students with disabilities, low-income students, girls, and gay/lesbian students). Educational leaders occupy key leverage positions within a system that simply must change if we are to ensure that all children receive an equitable and high-quality education. The will, facts, skills, and guts to prevent schools from failing children and instead to support social justice in our school systems must prevail among present and future educational leaders. However, for most individuals, developing into a leader who works for social justice is not an easy process. Many of those dedicated to social justice have benefited from concrete experiences, training, and reflection. For most school and district leaders, formal training in social justice content and experiences will be an important part of an inclusive and well-rounded leadership development experience (Young & Laible, 2000).

This brings us to our second assertion: Educational administration professors and practitioners who provide initial preparation and continuing professional development for educational leaders must actively engage in the development of social justice leadership. Although there are many areas of knowledge and skill that must be developed, social justice must be placed at the core of faculty work.

> If educational administration programs, in particular, and the field, as a whole, claim to be interested in broad-based reforms in the preparation of school ad-

minis:rators ... then knowledge about the historical and current conflicts between the school system and groups outside the mainstream of society (e.g., minorities, differently able) should be a part of the new curriculum. (Parker & Shapiro, 1992, pp. 8–9)

Even if the curriculum debates encounter roadblocks over academic freedom, professors must engage in collegial debates over ways to envision social justice through education.

Talking and Walking Social Justice

Some of our readers may not find our assertions to be that bold, and some may strongly disagree. However, as Marshall and Ward (2004) found in their study of National Policy and Professional Association leaders, widespread agreement that social justice is an essential part of effective leadership is not the same as believing that leaders can work for and achieve social justice in their schools; nor is it the same as committing oneself to ensuring that this is done. The "yes, but" responses of the policy leaders in the Marshall and Ward study remind us of the all too common response of educators, leaders, and other organizational participants to essential but difficult change. Although members of these groups express support for social justice, including preparing leaders to support social justice in schools, few are willing to argue that social justice is integral to quality and equitable education. This leaves social justice easily displaced by other "priorities." Instead of viewing social justice as integral to decreasing the achievement gap or as a foundational value in school improvement, there is a tendency to see social justice as something you do when all of the "important things" are done, that it is an elective practice rather than an essential one.

We now draw your attention to another equally dangerous tendency. It is not uncommon for individuals to become paralyzed by the despair they feel about organizational barriers to achieving social justice. In his book *The Courage to Teach*, Parker Palmer (1998) poses the question, "Is it possible to embody our best insights about teaching and learning in a social movement that might revitalize education?" In almost all of his conversations on this topic, he found that, in the end, educators would make their way to a disheartening conclusion:

> "These are wonderful ideas, but every last one of them will be defeated by the conditions in my school." That claim is followed by a litany of institutional impediments to reform: a president or dean who understands business better than education; course loads so heavy or classes so large that quality cannot be maintained; an institutional reward system that claims to value teaching but promotes only professors who publish. (Palmer, 1998, pp. 163–164)

Although such institutional barriers can be daunting when an individual or program is working for change, organizational change occurs in spite of such barriers and in spite of resistance to change. Moreover, "only in the face of opposition [to such barriers] has significant social change been achieved" (Palmer, 1998, p. 164).

We caution the readers of this book to be wary of and avoid these traps, because they have costly consequences for millions of children, adults, and communities. What we need is an ever-growing group of courageous and committed individuals who believe that social justice can be achieved and who will work to see that it is done. Luckily, there is compelling evidence that both leading for social justice and preparing leaders for social justice are possible and important.

We Know It Can Be Done Because It Is Being Done

The chapters included in this book include descriptions of and references to schools and leaders that operate from a foundation of social justice. Moreover, a growing number of scholars are publishing case studies of socially just leaders and their schools (e.g., Capper & Young, in press; Garza, Reyes, & Trueba, 2004; Reyes, Scribner, & Paredes-Scribner, 1999; Scheurich, 1998). Similarly, the National Association of Secondary School Principals (NASSP) has released findings from its national study of high schools, Breaking Ranks II, which identifies how leaders and their staff have reached equity and social justice in their schools. Schools cited in the NASSP study include Manual High School in Denver, Colorado; Noble High School in North Berwick, Maine; Fenway High School in Boston; Souhegan High School in Amherst, New Hampshire, and Feinstein High School in Providence, Rhode Island (DiMartino & Miles, 2005). We can learn much from these success stories, but the message we want readers to take from them today is that "it can be done." Leaders can support social justice in their schools, and when they do, the results can be phenomenal.

This book also provides glimpses into the changes individual higher education faculty members and entire educational leadership preparation programs have made. Hafner's chapter, for example, described some of the work higher education faculty have undertaken in their programs, and Chapter 2 shared how social justice has been not only infused within faculty teaching, but also within research, service, and broader organizational changes. The University Council for Educational Administration has created the Barbara Jackson Scholars Network to provide mentoring, ensuring that students of color in educational administration can succeed and expand their participation in the educational administration professoriate. These are real stories. Social justice has taken hold, and it is spreading in meaningful ways. This is very good news.

Essential Characteristics

For many, it is comforting and inspiring to know that there are places where social justice has taken hold. Not only are these cases proof positive that social justice is possible, but it also points to a network of information and support. Even so, just as working for social justice can be exciting, meaningful, and inspiring, it can also be difficult, uncomfortable, and draining. Those who have worked for equity and social justice, particularly as social justice educators, have identified characteristics important in social justice work. Derman-Sparks and Phillips (1997) offer three: (1) an individual must believe that oppression undermines the quality of human life and work; (2) an individual must have a desire to oppose oppression and be willing to engage in actions that resist oppression; and (3) the individual must be willing to be self-reflective, to take risks, and to be a learner. Capper and Young (in press) offer an additional three specifically for educational leadership faculty: (1) one needs to acquire background knowledge in both leadership and social justice; (2) one must become familiar with pedagogies that support effective social justice education; and (3) one must be able to plan, implement, and value a curriculum that supports leadership for social justice.

Being a social justice leader begins, for many individuals, with a deep reexamination of their personal and career capacities. As the movement for social justice in education grows, opportunities must be provided for both professors and practitioners to facilitate this process. For example, preparation programs could develop retreats for faculty members and leadership candidates to support reflection, gain knowledge, and develop and/or maintain determination. Additionally, higher education faculty and professional organization leaders should work together to ensure that leaders have ample opportunities to network with social justice leaders to share information and enhance their sense of possibilities.

The Wider Context: Politics and Strategy for the Revolution

The work of social justice leaders and leadership professors has the potential to contribute in positive ways to the improvement of schools, society, and the education of our children. However, even those with strong wills, facts, courage, and opportunities for renewal cannot single-handedly ensure that our schools and society support our nation's children: "Leaders cannot fix the problems of society by leading better, nor can leaders alone, transform the lives of the children in their schools, particularly if larger societal and institutional issues of oppression and inequity are not addressed" (Pounder, Reitzug, & Young, 2002). Lytle, a superintendent with years of experience in urban schools administration writes of his guide, William Julius Wilson (Wilson, 1987, 1996), saying,

> Wilson's research has brought him to a straightforward conclusion: unless employment opportunities are dramatically increased for men in ghetto communities, the probability is slim of significant changes in their children's life chances. (Lytle, 2004, p. 574)

Indeed, the border leaders in Chapter 4, such as Phil Jones, show how one must attend to children's lives outside in the community, not just in schools.

Many scholars have written about the importance of societal change in the effort to improve education. For example, Bowles and Gintis' (1976) ground-breaking book, *Schooling in Capitalist America*, is an analysis not only of the inequities of public education, but also of the inequities of the social order of which education is a part. They wrote, "the mixed record of schooling in capitalist America is a capsule history of the successes, failures, and contradictions of capitalism itself" (p. vii). Moreover, the inequities embedded in the economy and larger society (e.g., the growing gap between the rich and poor, homelessness, prejudice based on sex, race, language, ability, etc.) help to perpetuate dominance for dominant groups and oppression for oppressed groups: "Power, privilege, and economic advantage and/or disadvantage play major roles in the school and home lives of students, whether they are part of language, cultural, or gender majority groups or minority groups in our society" (Cochran-Smith, 1999, p. 117).

Coalitions and Collaborations

Scholarship on educational politics and policy is instructive, both for reconceptualizing and for strategizing. In the 1990s, when there was growing attention and resources dedicated to linking schools and social services, this was one way of addressing the press of societal problems on education and our nation's school children. Adler's (1993) model for systemic thinking about the arenas that impact children also provides a potential map of stakeholders with whom educational leaders and leadership professors might collaborate for the benefit of children.

Adler's model is fairly simple (see Figure 15.1). She places the child in the center of several nested boxes. The two boxes closest to the child include the family, primary caregivers, and direct service providers. This includes all school and district employees, school board members, social service providers, healthcare providers, and recreation services. The adjacent box includes individuals and agencies at the state or regional level that indirectly impact children, such as funding sources, regulating agencies, and organizations, such as universities or professional associations that provide training. Surrounding them are the political influences, such as unions, special interest groups, politicians, business, and professional associations, which are influenced by societal level norms and values.

Coalitions can include members of stakeholder groups from each of these arenas, coalitions that have as their ultimate goal supporting equitable and high-quality education for all children. Part of this responsibility would be supporting school leaders in their efforts to promote social justice in their schools. For example, communities need to elect school board members who

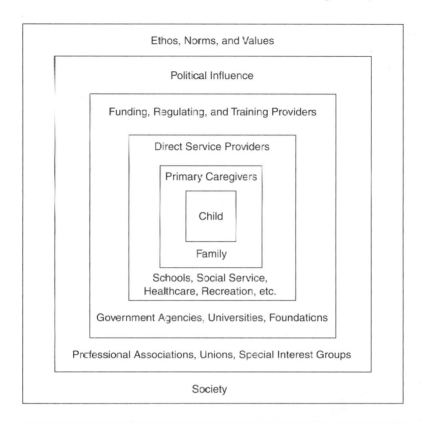

FIGURE 15.1 *Centering a Child Within Multiple Contexts*

Source: From L. Adler and S. Gardner, eds. *The politics of linking schools and social services.* © 1994 by Taylor and Francis Publisher. Reprinted with permission.

would hire school and school district leaders who were strong social justice leaders. Professors and district staff development directors must find social justice interventions. National and state professional associations and their conferences must demand programs and standards that address social justice issues in substantive ways. Policymakers must set standards for licensure and certification that require leaders to demonstrate competencies and willingness for addressing social justice, not just the ability to manage such issues or sweep them under the rug.

Gutsy and Passionate Leadership

Effective political coalition leadership, however, requires a great deal of work, both in designing and implementing a plan of social justice action. The plan would need to include continuous work on goals consensus, steps for individuals and organizations within each arena, time lines and benchmarks, and a strategy for evaluation and learning along the way. Here, again, politics of education scholars provide insights. Leaders must know how to act politically, how to anticipate resistance, and how to form policy advocacy coalitions, even among strange bedfellows.

Along the way, coalitions must have leaders in education, other professions, grassroots social movements, and in political positions who will take tough stands and persevere against resistant powerful forces. The picture of Mary Berry (Figure 15.2) illustrates such a person. Berry held on to her high position in the Office of Civil Rights through multiple presidencies so that she could be an advocate, and sometimes a thorn in the side, ready to jump when rights were threatened.

FIGURE 15.2 *Mary Berry Maintains Power* and
Passion for Civil Rights
Phyllis Graber Jensen, Bates College

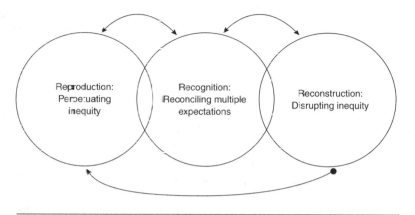

FIGURE 15.3 *Leadership for Equity Framework*

Source: Rorrer, A. (2002). Educational leadership and institutional capacity for equity. *The UCEA Review*, 43(3), 1–5. Reprinted with permission.

Educators, however passionate, however well prepared, and however politically attuned, must be prepared for backlash (Marshall & Gerstl-Pepin, 2005; Rorrer, 2002). Their missions may upset people. Some parents would be upset over a school philosophy promoting an inclusive, diverse, respectful, democratic collaborative school where children learn cooperation rather than competition. Some professors and superintendents will resist demands that leadership preparation and licensure be overhauled for social justice, preferring instead to just add on an ethics and social justice course. Rorrer's framework for school leaders' change processes is useful. As shown in Figure 15.3, it depicts slow and developmental, yet revolutionary change.

In this model, the upsetting and radical proposals are promoted, creating disequilibrium. But then the system (whether societal or school based) is given time and resources to adjust, to learn, and to create new equilibrium. Thus, the power of the resistance from anticipated backlash is diminished, and the social justice agendas can move ahead.

The Wider and Deeper Revolution

The school leader must know how to propose alliances with the epidemiologists, the Muslim mothers, and organizations like the Council of Great City Mayors. Most important, they must understand that social justice is not merely an education issue. As the superintendent of Trenton, New Jersey schools, James Lytle, said, we are merely speaking in tongues with the social justice graduate courses and licensure changes, "unless we and our students and colleagues are ready to lobby for more equitable tax policies, provide employment for released prisoners in our custodial and food service divisions, advocate for Section 8 housing in our own neighborhoods, insist on health care and nutrition programs for poor children, and support two-directional, interdistrict busing in our communities" (Lytle, 2004, p. 576). Preparing social justice leaders is a large task. But the truly huge task is that of creating wider political will among powerful elites, for, even among those who assert a willingness to eliminate school-based inequities, they often see no incentive or see it as an unattainable goal, a dream (Lopez, 2004).

Thus, we can now see the revolutionary nature of social justice leadership in education. Such leadership must move outside the school building and the ordinary central office routines. Such leadership must prevail even though it upsets comfortable assumptions and privileges embedded in the global context. Social justice in education is about schooling (e.g., reasons for dropouts, for high minority placement in special education), but it is also about sweatshops, prisons, and the economic policies that create structures of opportunity for some but not others. It is about street violence and guns and about the domestic violence that affects too many children's families. It is, more subtly, too often unnoticeably, about quiet children in nice suburban schools who are placed at the margins of schools' adolescent cultures because their Nikes came from Goodwill. It is about advertising's denigrating depictions of women that can distort girls' developing identities. Without the self-critique and self-understanding, as depicted, for example, in Chapters 9 through 13, well-intended administrators may never experience "otherness" enough to know social justice challenges.

With recognition that social justice in education entails such wide, deep, and entangling contexts, clearly, educators cannot take on such challenges without wider and powerful societal support. Clearly, too, this is not management science; it is more about the values, missions, and leadership for transforming society. Social justice leadership for schools is values based. It is ethical, moral, and transformative. It is more akin to the proselytizing, the spiritual leadership, and the accompanying pastoral care of the ministry. The assertions in these three simple sentences are the grounding for revolution in educational leadership.

References _____

Bowles, S., & Gintis, H. (1976). *Schooling in capitalist America: Educational reform and the contradictions of economic life.* New York: Basic Books.

Capper, C., & Young, M. D. (in press). *Educational leaders for social justice.* New York: Teachers College Press.

Cochran-Smith, M. (1999). Learning to teach for social justice. In G. Griffin (Ed.), *The education of teachers* (pp. 114–144). Chicago: University of Chicago Press.

Derman-Sparks, L., & Phillips, C. (1997). *Teaching/learning anti-racism: A developmental approach.* New York: Teachers College Press.

DiMartino, J., & Miles, S. (2005). Reaching real equity in schools. *Education Digest, 70*(5), 9–13.

Garza, E., Reyes, P., & Trueba, H. (2004). *Resiliency and success: Migrant children in the United States.* Herndon, VA: Paradigm.

Laible, J., & Harrington, S. (1998). Leaders with alternative values. *International Journal of Leadership in Education, 1*(4), 19–43.

Lytle, J. H. (2004). A superintendent's reaction. *Journal of School Leadership, 14*(5), 573–577.

Marshall, C., & Gerstl-Pepin, C. (2005). *Reframing educational politics for social justice.* Boston: Allyn and Bacon.

Marshall, C., & Ward, M. (2004). "Yes, but . . .": Education leaders discuss social justice. *Journal of School Leadership, 14*(5), 530–563.

Palmer, P. (1998). *The courage to teach: Exploring the inner landscape of a teacher's life.* San Francisco: Jossey-Bass.

Pounder, D. G., Reitzug, U. C., & Young, M. D. (2002). Restructuring the preparation of school leaders. In J. Murphy (Ed.), *National Society for the Study of Education 2002 Yearbook: Educational Administration.* Chicago: National Society for the Study of Education.

Reyes, P., Scribner, J., & Paredes-Scribner, A. (1999). *Creating learning communities: Lessons from high performing minority schools.* New York: Teachers College Press.

Rorrer, A. (2002) Educational leadership and instructional capacity for equity. *UCEA Review, 43*(3), 1–5.

Scheurich, J. J. (1999). Highly successful and loving public elementary schools populated mainly by children of color: Core beliefs and cultural characteristics. *Urban Education, 33*(4), 451–592.

Wilson, J. (1987). *The truly disadvantaged.* Chicago: University of Chicago Press.

Wilson, J. (1996). *When work disappears: The world of the new urban poor.* New York: Knopf.

Young, M. D., & Laible, J. (2000). White racism, anti-racism, and school leadership preparation. *Journal of School Leadership, 10*(5), 374–415.

Index